the World on your PLATE

the World on your PLATE

MARTHA ROSE SHULMAN

CARROLL & BROWN PUBLISHERS LIMITED

First published in the UK in 2002 by
Carroll & Brown Publishers
20 Lonsdale Road
Queen's Park
London NW6 6RD

Managing Editor Becky Alexander
Project Editor Kirsten Chapman
Designer Justina Leitão
Design Assistant Justin Ford
Editorial Assistants Tom Broder and Kelly Thompson

Text copyright © Martha Rose Shulman 2002
Illustrations and compilation copyright © Carroll & Brown Publishers
Limited 2002
A CIP catalogue record for this book is available from
the British Library

ISBN 1-903258-24-3

Reproduced by Colourscan, Singapore
Printed in Singapore by Tien Wah Press

CONTENTS

Introduction 6

EUROPE

Britain and Ireland *10*, Scandinavia *16*, Russia and Eastern Europe *26*
Central Europe *34*, Austria *39*, Germany *42*, Switzerland *46*
The Low Countries *48*, France *54*, Spain *74*, Portugal *82*, Italy *86*
Greece *98*, The Balkan Peninsula *104*, Turkey *110*

AFRICA AND THE MIDDLE EAST

The Middle East *118*, North Africa *126*, Africa *134*

ASIA AND AUSTRALASIA

India *144*, Central Asia and the Caucasus *156*, China *164*, Indonesia *176*
Malaysia *179*, Cambodia *182*, Laos *184*, Myanmar *187*, The Philippines *190*
Singapore *192*, Thailand *194*, Vietnam *198*, Korea *202*, Japan *206*
Australia *212*, New Zealand *216*

THE AMERICAS

The United States *220*, Canada *230*, Central America and Mexico *232*
The Caribbean *238*, South America *241*

Recipes 252
Further reading 283
Index 284
Acknowledgments 288

INTRODUCTION

This is a book about the flavours of the countries of today's world. And being that, it is a geography and history, a story of migrations, religions, commerce, farming, ethnology and culture. For one cannot consider the food of, say, Central Asia, without talking about the influences of the Persian Empire and the impact of the windswept, inhospitable nature of its environment; or that of the Balkan Peninsula without understanding the reach of the Ottoman Empire. We cannot look at the cooking of China and South-east Asia without taking note of the chilli pepper, which arrived with European traders during the Age of Discovery and became so linked with local cooking that it is almost impossible to imagine these cuisines without that fiery ingredient. The cuisines of the Mediterranean owe much to the Arab expansion of the Middle Ages, and what would they be without the foods that came from the Americas, particularly the tomato?

Foodways migrate with peoples, whether that migration is the result of emigration (Chinese into South-east Asia; Europeans to the Americas, Australia and New Zealand), imperial expansion (Romans, Persians, Arabs, Turks, Mongols and Europeans) or commerce (the medieval and colonial spice trade and the New World sugar boom). Even forced emigration – such as the African slave trade – contributes to the evolution of the cuisines of a place, and the influences work in both directions. In parts of Brazil, the Caribbean and the American South, signature dishes mirror their African counterparts.

Religion, too, has a profound effect on diet. Throughout the orthodox Christian world, for example, a wide range of vegetable dishes became a necessity because of the stringent fasting requirements of the Church. The vegetarian traditions of India, China and much of South-east Asia evolved because of similar requirements imposed by Hinduism and Buddhism. In countries where Islam and Judaism have dominated, pork is not part of the repertoire. And, of course, every place in the world has its special dishes associated with particular religious holidays and festivals.

Weather and geography are the great determining factors when it comes to the traditional staples of a place. If a land is not conducive to farming, societies may depend on grazing animals for their sustenance, and the foodways that result accommodate the nomadic lifestyle of a herder. Staples might consist of unleavened flat breads, which can be quickly made, fermented dairy products and grilled and wind-dried meats. Maritime countries and regions depend on fish, both fresh and preserved. The richer the agriculture of a place, the more possibilities there are for a varied cuisine.

Often geography, climate and the course of history have worked hand in hand. New staples were introduced into many countries from the outside and took hold because they thrived. Olives, for example, were planted throughout the Mediterranean by the Phoenicians and the Romans; the Romans cultivated wheat throughout their Empire; and the Arabs brought rice to Spain. While it sometimes took time for these new foods to catch on, eventually they became defining ingredients. This type of evolution is still happening today – perhaps now more than ever because of the huge and rapid migrations of large numbers of people. Today, one would be hard pressed to find a country whose food did not reflect outside influences of one kind or another.

With this in mind, I set out to write this book about food in its geographical context. It asks the question: what do places taste like, and why? What are their key ingredients, their signature dishes, and how and why did these evolve? It is a formidable project, one that could take a lifetime, and obviously I have barely scratched the surface here. Yet my own learning curve has been tremendous; understanding authentic flavours entailed a crash course in world history and ethnographics. And because I've included a smattering of recipes to illustrate the text, I've eaten very well along the way.

A WORD ABOUT GASTRONOMIC BORDERS

I could have drawn *The World on your Plate* in different ways. Gastronomic regions are not always easily defined by political borders, which are often drawn and then redrawn by statesmen at the end of a conflict. I would have found it difficult, before the break-up of the Soviet Union, for example, to include the Middle Eastern influenced Caucasian cuisines in a chapter on Russia. For this reason, countries are grouped according to their influences rather than their locations and, where further links exist, these are referred to in the text.

Regionalism within a country illustrates another way in which the map of the world doesn't always define the map of its cuisines. One cannot, for example, talk about the cuisine of China, Italy, France and the United States, without looking closely at the cooking of particular regions. Italy was not even a unified country until quite recently, and the food varies considerably from one area to another. These countries are subdivided into areas of culinary similarity.

EUROPE

BRITAIN AND IRELAND

Agricultural countries with distinct cultures and histories, England, Wales, Scotland and Ireland are rooted in farming traditions. They share many signature dishes, but each has its own variations.

KEY INGREDIENTS

BUTTER

SUET

PORK

BEEF

LAMB

GAME

EGGS

POTATOES

ONIONS

PARSNIPS

CABBAGE

BERRIES

The British fry-up (*opposite*)
Fried bacon, eggs, sausage, black pudding, mushrooms and bread, as well as grilled tomatoes, are all typical in a traditional cooked breakfast.

Beer appreciation
There is a great beer-drinking tradition in the British Isles. Pubs serve light ales and lagers and dark ales and stouts by the pint and half-pint.

These large islands have landscapes that vary from marshland to lush pastureland, and from cliff-lined coasts to windswept moors and rocky mountains. Rainfall is plentiful and the soil rich, providing good conditions for farming, which dominates much of the countryside.

England, Scotland and Wales

The island of Great Britain – bounded by the English Channel to the south, the North Sea to the east, the Irish Sea to the west and the North Atlantic to the north – is an island of many rivers, lakes and lochs, as well as highlands, moors and pastureland. Eighty-five per cent of the land here is used for farming, although today, most of the population lives in cities and much of Britain's food is imported.

A taste of history
Though originally inhabited by local tribes, such as the Celts, England, Scotland and Wales were colonized by the Romans in the 1st century AD, and prospered until the 5th century, when they were overrun by Germanic tribes. There were Scandinavian invasions in the 9th and 10th centuries, and, in 1066, the island was conquered by the Normans. An important world power from the 16th century to the middle of the 20th, Britain colonized countries as far-flung as North America, India, Hong Kong and parts of Africa. All of these factors have helped to shape British cuisine.

Britain's love of sugar took hold during the colonial period, when vast amounts were suddenly available from the West Indies.

Formerly an expensive commodity, reserved for the well-off, sugar quickly became affordable for the middle and working classes. From the beginning of the 19th century to its end, sugar consumption grew by five times. Using sugar as a preservative, canning also became possible. Even more importantly, sugar was associated with three other imports, coffee, chocolate and tea, all of which became fashionable among the middle and upper classes. Of the three, tea was by far the most popular (see box, page 12).

For a long time, Scottish cuisine was greatly influenced by France. These two countries maintained a special relationship for hundreds of years; they were allies during many conflicts with the English. During the 16th century, this 'Auld Alliance' brought about a change in culinary fashions among the upper classes. It soon became fashionable in court circles to have a French chef, and French wines and brandy were adopted. The taste for the lavish became so out of hand that a

Llangloffan cheese
Made in a farm near a small village in Wales, this hard, full-fat cheese is typical of the farmhouse cheeses that are once again becoming popular.

food shortage occurred, and, in 1581, a law that limited certain dishes to the very rich was passed. During this period, many French-derived Scottish food terms came into being, like 'jiggot' from *gigot*, meaning a leg of mutton, and 'ashet' from *assiette*, meaning a meat dish. The Scottish refer to a flavourless dish as one with no 'gout', from the word *goût*, the French for 'taste'.

During the 20th century, there were two major influences on British gastronomy as a whole. The first was the Second World War, during which time there was severe food rationing. This probably led to the plainness that is often associated with British food. The second and contrasting factor has been the growing influence over the last 50 years of the many immigrants from Britain's former colonies, particularly from the Indian subcontinent and

the West Indies. Indian food is widespread in Britain, although its authenticity is often questionable. Recently voted as Britain's most popular dish, the curry-house dish, chicken tikka massala, was actually invented in Britain rather than India. Balti cooking, so-called after the wok-like pan in which the food is cooked, is better known in England, particularly Birmingham, than in Pakistan its home country.

European immigration has also made its mark, particularly in London, where there are many Italian and Greek Cypriot restaurants.

Over the past couple of decades, British restaurant cooking has enjoyed a renaissance, as people travelled more and tastes broadened. The food journalist R.W. Apple laments the loss of British tradition, describing modern British cooking as 'about 40 per cent French bourgeois, 30 per cent Italian, and – after factoring in bits of Thai, Japanese and American south-western – only about 20 per cent British.'

Staple foods

Meat has for many centuries been at the centre of British gastronomy. With the country's lush pastureland, it has always been abundant. Beef is widely eaten, with Scottish Aberdeen Angus being particularly prized. A roast joint of beef, served with Yorkshire pudding (made from batter and the meat drippings), is a signature dish throughout the United Kingdom. Lamb is another favourite, particularly in Wales and other sheep-herding regions. Again, roasting is the preferred cooking method, and a sweet mint jelly is the usual accompaniment. Pork is another widely eaten meat.

No matter what the animal – bull, sheep or pig – it was the custom until recently to use every part of it – head, tail, feet, offal, ears and even the blood. Some of Britain's traditional dishes, including black pudding, Scottish haggis and Lancashire hotpot (a lamb and kidney stew), grew out of this practice.

Meat is also used to fill pies, which are made often with a pastry shortened with suet. In the past, these were easy for workers to carry down into the mines or out into the fields. Sometimes

---

■ **TEA: THE DRINK OF ALL CLASSES**
BRITAIN IS KNOWN AS A NATION OF TEA DRINKERS, AND THIS TRADITION TOOK HOLD IN THE 16TH TO 18TH CENTURIES, WHEN COLONIAL EXPANSION MADE TEA AND SUGAR - ONCE LUXURY GOODS - MORE AVAILABLE TO ALL CLASSES. SWEETENED TEA SOON BECAME A CHEAP SOURCE OF ENERGY FOR THE WORKERS OF THE GROWING INDUSTRIES, AND IT WAS SOON REGULARLY DRUNK WITH THE EVENING MEAL OF THE LESS WELL-OFF; IN SOME HOUSEHOLDS THE WORD 'TEA' HAS BECOME SYNONYMOUS WITH DINNER, THE MEAL EATEN IN THE EVENINGS AFTER WORK.

the pastry would be filled with meat at one end and something sweet at the other, making an entire meal in a package. The best-known of the British meat pies is the Cornish pasty, a miner's meal usually filled with beef and potatoes. Pork pies, fish pies, vegetable pies and steak and kidney pies are also traditional.

Great Britain, particularly the north of England and Scotland, is rich with game. Roast venison, guinea fowl, hare and various game birds are part of the gastronomic landscape. Hunting is a traditional sport among the upper classes, but people of all classes have always appreciated what the countryside has to offer.

It is worth noting that until relatively recently, country people and the poor subsisted largely on grain porridges and dairy products. Animals were only used for meat when they had outlived their usefulness for producing wool, milk and eggs.

With Britain's many rivers and long coastlines, fish has always been an important element in the national diet. Battered fish with chips is Britain's original fast food, but there are many finer dishes based on fish, like salmon, turbot, sole and the abundant shellfish found in the cold seas.

Scotland is particularly rich in seafood. The deep seas around it provide a wide variety, and freshwater fish, such as carp, tench and trout, thrive in Scottish rivers. The salmon that go up these rivers to spawn are world famous. In Celtic times the sea was sacred, and the eating of fish was forbidden. However, by the 11th century, fish became important because the Roman Catholic Church forbade meat on Fridays. Fishing has since been a major source of income.

Other specialities

Britain produces some renowned farmhouse cheeses, such as Cheshire, Wensleydale, Cheddar, Double Gloucester and Stilton. Cheese is enjoyed on its own as a course, and it is an ingredient in many dishes, such as Welsh rarebit (eggs and melted cheese on toast).

England, Scotland and Wales also have strong baking traditions. A variety of goods are made – yeasted breads and tea cakes, griddle breads and

SMOKED FISH: REGIONAL SPECIALITIES

Because Scotland's fish supplies are seasonal, preserving methods were developed hundreds of years ago, probably introduced by Viking raiders from Scandinavia. These evolved into regional specialities. Kippering (salting, drying and cold-smoking) is a west coast tradition, as this is where the best herring is found. Finnan haddock are cured in Findon, a village south of Aberdeen. To the north, whitings are wind-dried and moistened during curing to produce speldings. Arbroath smokies are smoked haddock, tied in pairs and smoked over halved whisky barrels sunk into pits.

There are two main types of smoking: hot smoking leaves fish ready for the table, as with smoked salmon; cold smoking preserves the fish, which then must be cooked. When home curing became illegal in the 19th century, factories in Aberdeen came into being, and were the basis of much of the town's prosperity.

scones. Oatcakes and griddle-baked breads called bannocks are specialities of Scotland. England is also known for its rich desserts, which are commonly referred to as 'puddings', probably because so many of the traditional desserts are just that: baked or steamed puddings made with generous amounts of butter, eggs and cream. Summer pudding, made with berries and bread, spotted Dick, trifle (a custard and cake dessert) and jam roly poly (a jam-filled sponge cake) are regular favourites.

Traditional fruits
Seasonal produce forms the basis of many English foods and drinks. Strawberries are picked for jams or eaten with cream. Apples are cooked into pies or made into cider.

Festive

~~~ FOOD ~~~

In Ireland, a deeply Roman Catholic country, many eating customs evolved because of the Church. Fish is traditionally eaten on Fridays, caught from local waters and streams. Cakes, to which spices or dried fruits are added, are made for occasions like weddings, baptisms, Christmas and Easter. Pancakes derive from the Shrove Tuesday tradition, when all the milk, butter and eggs, which were not be permitted during Lent, were mixed into a batter and fried. According to village lore, a woman's marriageability was determined by how well she tossed pancakes.

Ireland

At the western edge of Europe, this is a land of rich, green farmland and bounteous coastal waters. The climate is relatively mild and quite wet. A microclimate produced by the Gulf Stream allows yucca and palms to grow in some areas.

A farming country with strong Celtic traditions, many Irish originally came from Scotland – the two countries are only 80 km apart at the island's north-eastern edge. Late in the 12th century, the Normans invaded from England, and many years of English control ensued. The English controlled only the eastern part of the island until Elizabethan times, but then the whole of Ireland was subjugated. It was not until 1922 that Ireland was declared a free state, independent from Britain. Northern Ireland remains part of the United Kingdom.

Before the arrival of the potato in the 18th century, the Irish staples were dairy products and cereals – oats, barley, rye and wheat – foods that remain important in the diet today. Cereals were used to make coarse flat breads and porridges, and butter was required to moisten these abrasive foods. Ale, consumed throughout the day, was brewed from barley. Milk was soured, made into curds and into soft and hard cheeses – Ireland has a fine farmhouse cheese tradition. The affluent ate meat – mutton and fresh and salted pork, beef and venison – which was roasted on spits or boiled in cauldrons. For most people, though, meat was restricted to salted bacon. Fresh meat was a treat for holy days or festivals.

After the English conquests of the 16th and 17th centuries, more foods were introduced and Irish cooking evolved again. The cooks in the

SIGNATURE DISHES

Cullen skink *A Scottish chowder made with Finnan haddock, onions, potatoes and milk.*

Roast beef *Traditionally served with horseradish sauce and Yorkshire puddings.*

Fish and chips *Deep-fried, battered fish served with chips and mushy peas, traditionally served wrapped in newspaper.*

Haggis *This Scottish sausage-like dish is made from a sheep's stomach lining, stuffed with offal, oatmeal and suet.*

Colcannon *Mashed potatoes with cabbage, kale or parsnips, popular in Ireland.*

Bacon and cabbage *Sometimes considered Ireland's national dish.*

Bread and butter pudding *A baked dessert made with buttered bread.*

Bara brith *Spicy Welsh fruit bread.*

households of the Anglo-Irish gentry drew upon French cookery and adapted recipes brought back from the European 'grand tours'. The most important food brought into Ireland during this period was the potato. By the 19th century it was the staple food of a third of the population. It was probably introduced into Ireland from plundered ships of the Spanish Armada, which were wrecked on the west coast. Over-dependence on the potato led to the Potato Famine of the 1840s, when successive harvests failed. At this time, Ireland lost much of its population; those who did not die of starvation emigrated.

The Potato Famine affected for subsequent generations the way people thought about food. Nettles, wild greens, herbs, game and oatcakes, which had been eaten out of necessity during the Famine, were later eschewed because of their associations with the 'great hunger'. The Irish diet became bland and conservative; plain food symbolized economic comfort. Until the 1960s the average dinner consisted of meat, potatoes and a vegetable, eaten with buttered bread and strong black tea. Tea, along with processed foods like sugar, jam and white bread, had become available to the general Irish populace during the latter half of the 19th century. As in Great Britain, tea grew to be an important part of the diet, considered as both a food and a beverage.

In recent decades Ireland has prospered, and more of its people have travelled abroad and been exposed to ethnic foods. The nation's palate has broadened, and many cooks are now committed to developing indigenous Irish foods and products – farmhouse cheeses, fish and shellfish, seaweeds, baked goods, farm-raised produce and meats. There is also a great revival of home baking using domestic wheat. Soda-raised bread, made with delicious wholemeal flour and soured milk, is an Irish speciality. Many Irish baked goods come from the North and have ties with Scottish breads and pastries.

One of the riches of Ireland is its fish, and particularly its salmon. The salmon is revered in Irish folklore, as there is said to be a connection between this fish and the soul. A salmon is even pictured on one of the country's coins.

The country Irish have a tradition of hospitality, which dates from Celtic times. People were long taught to leave their doors open, inviting passers-by to partake of whatever food was on the table.

Food through the day

There are strong breakfast customs in the British Isles, and large, fried breakfasts have long been much-loved, though light breakfasts are now more the norm. In Ireland and Scotland porridge is commonly eaten. Though traditionally a country dish, Scottish students off to college would take porridge bags with them. During holidays the bags would be brought home for refilling. This student holiday is still celebrated as Mealy Monday at Scottish universities.

Lunch can be a light meal, as simple as a sandwich or a soup, and this tends to be the case in cities. It could also be a more filling meal, though, today, dinner is usually the main meal of the day, often consisting of a stew or meat or fish, with a vegetable and a starch, like potatoes.

Time for tea
Whether it's half-time or between the hours of 3 to 5 pm, tea and cakes are a welcome treat. A cream tea consists of tea drunk with dainty cakes and scones. Tea may also be a more substantial meal with sandwiches or sausages and beans.

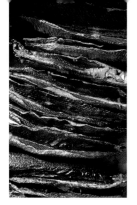

SCANDINAVIA

At various times in history one Scandinavian country has held sway over another, as they each struggled for control. Cuisines, as well as histories, overlap, but each country retains its national dishes.

KEY INGREDIENTS

PICKLES

VINEGAR

FISH AND SHELLFISH

PRESERVED COD

REINDEER

GAME SAUSAGE

RYE BREAD

POTATOES

BEETROOT

TURNIPS

SEA VEGETABLES

BERRIES

Cloudberries
A member of the rose family, these delicious, soft, orange berries are abundant in northern climes. They are served often on sugared bread, or with whipped cream in a bowl.

The northern European countries of Denmark, Sweden, Norway and Finland are 'officially' considered Scandinavia, but Iceland, which is close in climate, has much in common with these countries, including its eating traditions. Winters in this area are very long; in the northern reaches the sun never rises at the height of winter, and it never sets in mid-summer. Consequently, growing seasons are short, and the Scandinavian people have long had to rely on preserved foods for sustenance. Dried, smoked, cured and pickled fish, meats, fruit and vegetables are an outstanding feature of the gastronomy. Finland, with its Russian border and history, has many Russian elements to its cooking also, and Denmark has affinities with Germany.

All of the Scandinavian countries have long coastlines and have been seafaring nations from the time of the Vikings. The Baltic and North Atlantic, as well as the thousands of lakes and rivers gouged into these countries by glaciers, provide Scandinavia with abundant fish, which has been important both as sustenance and as trading commodities. Fish is all the more important to the diet, because, with the exception of Denmark, only a small proportion of the land is suitable for farming.

Two foods, however, did come to Scandinavia from abroad, and today they are gastronomic fixtures: potatoes are eaten daily, and coffee is a much-loved drink. Scandinavians consume more coffee than any other Europeans. Coffee shops abound, selling pastries as well. The pastry tradition is also well developed and highly regarded, particularly in Denmark.

Scandinavians are great breadmakers, too. Their breads are made principally with grains that do well in northern climates, particularly rye. Flat, unleavened breads and twice-baked breads evolved, because, with the short growing season, the grains did not have long enough to ripen in the fields. They were harvested before they could rot, and the green grains were immediately ground and baked into breads, which were hung from rafters or stored in chests. These hard but long-lasting loaves sustained people through the long winters.

The Sami
The earliest inhabitants of Scandinavia were the Sami, also known as the Lapps. The Sami probably arrived as long ago as the last ice age, retreating northwards as European and Balkan tribes pushed into Scandinavia. They ended up north of the Arctic Circle, which is where they live today, in an icy region of Norway, Sweden and Finland known as Lapland. A nomadic people with their own language and culture, the Samis rely on reindeer, game and fish as their main sources of nutrition. They have domesticated the reindeer, and many make their living as herders.

Food through the day

Eating patterns are fairly consistent throughout the Scandinavian countries. Breakfast may include milk, a boiled egg, cured fish, cheese, bread, butter, jam, coffee and oatmeal. In Finland *viili* (fermented milk curds) and *piima* (buttermilk) are typical breakfast foods, as well as open sandwiches and a porridge called *puuro*, made from rice, oatmeal or farina. On farms and in rural communities, breakfast might be supplemented by hot, cooked meat, fish or potato dishes. Icelanders usually have bread of some kind with a mild cheese called *braudost* (bread cheese) and/or fruit preserves. Everywhere, coffee is the morning beverage. Icelandic children drink milk or cocoa.

In Iceland there is a mid-morning coffee break and another one in the afternoon. Workplaces all have coffee rooms for these breaks, which are an important part of the day.

Lunch is light, usually an open sandwich and coffee or beer. In Denmark the *smorrebrod* (open sandwich) is a national food; Danes often take these sandwiches to work in a flat, metal sandwich box. Another popular Danish lunch is sausage, bought from one of the many sausage stands that line city streets. Finnish lunches might be a bit more substantial, beginning with the cold selection of a *voleipapoyta*, the Finnish *smorgasbord* (see page 20), followed by a hot fish or meat dish served with potatoes and milk. Open sandwiches, *voileivat*, are popular lunch dishes also. Nourishing soups are common at both lunch and dinner.

Dinner, eaten early, is the main meal of the day. It is likely to include a hot soup, a casserole, or meat or fish served with boiled potatoes, and possibly a dessert. Hot open sandwiches are common Finnish dinner foods. Berries, rice pudding, sweet soups and hot or cold fruit soups are popular desserts. Later in the evening, people may have a coffee with a snack, followed by a piece of cake.

Dinner in Iceland is a little later than in other Scandinavian countries, normally around 7 pm. This is the main meal of the day, usually based on seafood or lamb, with winter vegetables, like potatoes, carrots, broccoli or cauliflower. Vegetables might include hothouse produce like tomatoes and cucumbers. Coffee is generally taken after dinner. Most people drink water or fruit juices with meals and wine on special occasions. Children drink milk or fruit juice.

Helsinki market
Finland's capital city is built around its harbour, and the lively fish market is at its heart, selling everything from fish to fruit to local craft goods.

Norway

Occupying the western portion of the Scandinavian peninsula, Norway is a long, narrow country of spectacular landscapes. Most of the country is sparsely populated, with the majority of people living in cities. Long inlets of sea, called fjords, cut into Norway's coast, forming natural harbours and sheltering farmers and fishermen. Most of the farmland here is situated at the head of these fjords, but very little of Norway's land is suitable for agriculture, leading to a reliance on fish and imported foods.

Despite the country's northern location, its climate is tempered by the Gulf Stream, which keeps the coastline free of ice and allows fishing to be a year-round occupation. In addition to ocean fish, Norway's many rivers and lakes – there are over 160,000 – keep the country well stocked with salmon, trout and other freshwater fish. Salmon and cod are among Norway's most important exports, and salmon is widely eaten in the home. *Stokkfisk* (dried cod) has been an important Norwegian product since the Middle Ages, and trade in it has, in turn, exposed Norwegians to foods and flavours from afar; almonds, rice, sauerkraut and wheat were all traded for *stokkfisk*, and the potato is now on the table at most meals.

Staple foods

In general, the diet here is simple, nourishing and plain. Fish, particularly salmon, cod and trout, are widely eaten. Cured Norwegian salmon, called *gravad lax* or *gravlax*, is a well-known dish, which is often accompanied by boiled potatoes. Norwegians excel at making forcemeat and fish balls using high-quality fish. The flaked fish they require is sold at special shops, *fiskemattbutikks*, either as forcemeat to be taken home and used in other dishes, or already made up into balls and puddings. Another speciality is fermented salmon trout, *rakorret*, a strong-tasting food, which is usually washed down with aquavit.

Although reindeer has always been an important staple for the Sami, most Norwegians consumed little meat in the past, relying on fish as a protein. There are however, a few traditional meat dishes, such as the peasant dish *far i kal*, which consists of lamb simmered with cabbage and peppercorns. It made use of the cheaper cuts of lamb available to the general populace, as the finer cuts went to the rich. With modern transportation and food storage, however, more meat is eaten here today than ever before.

The need to preserve food means that milk is soured and made into several types of cheeses. *Romme* (soured milk or cream) is a key ingredient in many dishes, the most traditional being *rommergrot*, a sweetened, sour-cream porridge served at breakfasts, at weddings and childbirths, and at summer picnics, accompanied by flat bread and dried cured meat. Norway's most well-known cheese is Jarlsberg, named after a Viking

A fishing culture
Norway is mountainous and peppered with offshore islands, like the Lofoten Islands, shown opposite. Fishing is a mainstay here, and the catch may be preserved by being dried on racks.

SMORGASBORD: LITERALLY THE 'BUTTERED BREAD TABLE'

Originating in Sweden, the *smorgasbord* evolved from an 18th-century tradition called the *brannvinsbord*, in which a barrel of aquavit was served surrounded by food. Many toasts were made with a loud '*Skal*', and songs were part of the celebration. The number of dishes grew with time, and evolved into the current buffet, of which there are versions in Norway, Denmark and Finland.

A *smorgasbord* might appear like an endless feast, but there is a definite order to it. A meal in four courses, it begins with a herring table. At a large *smorgasbord* there might be as many as 20 herring dishes on offer, as well as breads, cucumber salad and garnishes. The anchovy and potato casserole, *Janssons frestelse* (Jansson's temptation), is a traditional herring table dish.

The cold buffet consists of a fish dish followed by a meat dish. Smoked salmon, *gravlax* and smoked eel all feature, as well as sausages, cold cuts, pâté, smoked veal, ham and roast beef.

The next section is the *smavarmt* – literally 'small warm'. This includes meatballs, emphatically served without gravy. Omelettes, croquettes and *lokdolmar* (stuffed onion rolls) are also typical.

Finally, there is dessert, which might include fruit compotes, berries with cream, cakes and cheeses, all served with coffee.

settlement near Oslo and only invented in 1959. Other cheeses include: Geitost, a caramelized goat's cheese; Gammelost, a pungent cow's cheese, in which the mould on the developing rind is pressed into the cheese; Mysost, a popular breakfast cheese; and Gudbrandsdalsost, made from a combination of cow and goat whey.

Wild berries are abundant in Norway. In the past, they were dried for out-of-season consumption, but are now as often preserved with sugar. Blueberries, cranberries and cloudberries are favourites. Raspberries and strawberries, both cultivated and wild, show up in many desserts. Apples, cherries and rhubarb are also widely eaten and are the main ingredients in many typical Norwegian desserts.

Although both wine and beer are drunk with meals in Norway, the national spirit is aquavit. It is made from potatoes or rice and flavoured with caraway. Usually served chilled in small glasses, the tradition is to drink it in one go. One special kind of aquavit, unique to Norway, is shipped across the equator in oak containers to 'finish' it. It is thought that the change of temperature mellows the flavour, and each label is dated with the day the ship crossed the equator.

The Norwegians have several ways of preserving cod, and each type is cooked differently. *Stokkfisk* is soaked and then poached. *Persetorsk* is pressed cod, which has been lightly salted and weighted for two days; to cook, it is poached. *Rokerumpe* (smoked tail end of cod) is preserved by light salting and smoking, then baked slowly with butter, sour cream and carrots. *Klippfisk* is salted and dried rock cod, which is cooked like *stokkfisk*. *Lutefisk* is *stokkfisk* that has been soaked in water and a solution of lye. It is a traditional Christmas food. In recent years, Norwegians have started to cook their *stokkfisk* in the Mediterranean manner, with garlic, olive oil and tomatoes.

Sweden

The fourth largest country in Europe and one of the least densely populated, Sweden has existed as an independent state for over 1000 years and is one of the world's longest-standing democracies. Bounded by Norway to the west and Finland to the east, Sweden has a long coastline on the Baltic Sea, and is separated from Denmark by a narrow channel. Much of the country is forested, with many rivers and thousands of lakes and small offshore islands.

The economy here was once dependent on subsistence farming, but in the last 100 years Sweden has evolved into one of the world's most prosperous and technologically advanced nations. When the country embraced industrialization at the end of the 19th century, large farms were created to increase agricultural production, resulting in the break-up of small farms and villages. Close to a million disenfranchized farmers left at this time and emigrated to America. Now, only three per cent of the Swedish population works in agriculture, fishery and forestry. The country's most important agricultural products are grains, sugar beets, potatoes, meat and milk. Potatoes are eaten at just about every meal.

Staple foods

As with its Scandinavian neighbours, fish – particularly herrings, salmon, prawns and freshwater fish – are major elements in the Swedish diet. The variety of fish on the west coast of Sweden, on the side of the North Atlantic, is large and is greater than that available in the Baltic cities. Cod, mackerel, plaice, char, halibut, salmon, trout, sprat, pike and perch are widely eaten. Gothenburg, on the west coast, is the country's main fishing port; its fish market is known as the *Feskkekorka*, meaning 'fish church' in local dialect.

The Swedes cure and pickle their herring in many ways. They ferment it also, resulting in a strong-tasting, canned speciality called *surstromming*, which is served with chopped onions, potatoes and bread and butter. *Sotare* are grilled herrings, served with dill butter and potatoes. It is thought that *gravlax*, the cured salmon with dill preparation, which is available throughout Scandinavia, originated in Sweden.

Meat is important here also, and is eaten more frequently than it is in some of the other Scandinavian countries. Most often, the Swedes grind their meat for meatballs or sausages. Typically, meats are served with thick cream gravies. Reindeer are domesticated in the north, and game thrives in the woods and forests. Elk, roe deer and hare are hunted for their meat. The Sami in the north eat a staple diet of reindeer meat, liver and marrowbone, as well as reindeer milk and cheese.

Because Sweden is such a wealthy country, foods from all over the world can be imported. Much of the produce sold in markets comes from elsewhere – artichokes from Spain, oranges from Israel and beef from America. International dishes are enjoyed in restaurants and extolled in cookbooks. Yet the everyday Swedish diet remains fairly plain. A typical dish is yellow-pea soup, a thick, porridge-like meal, which makes a regular Thursday night supper. It may be followed by crisp pancakes and lingonberry preserves for dessert.

Swedes eat *knackebrod* (crispbreads), as do the Norwegians, but also rye breads and sweet rich breads. *Vetelgand*, a somewhat sweet, braided loaf, often glazed or sprinkled with almonds, is served with coffee. And coffee here is important: Swedes rank second in the world for coffee consumption and first in Europe. They drink it for breakfast, after lunch, during work breaks and at special parties called *kafferaps*, where coffee is served with cakes, biscuits and buns.

■ BEER: THE VIKING DRINK

BACK IN THE MIDDLE AGES, DRINKING ALCOHOL WAS A MAJOR PART OF VIKING LIFE. BEER AND ALE WERE BREWED FROM BARLEY, AND LATER HOPS WERE USED. TRADITIONALLY, IT WAS A DRINK OF THEIR WINTER SOLSTICE, AND HOME-BREWED BEER LATER EVOLVED INTO A CHRISTMAS DRINK.

IN SCANDINAVIA TODAY, THERE ARE MANY DIFFERENT SHADES AND STRENGTHS OF BEER BREWED. ONE OF THE MOST POPULAR IS LIGHT, PILSNER-STYLE BEER, OFTEN SERVED WITH MEALS. PER CAPITA, FINLAND AND SWEDEN NOW RANK IN THE TOP 20 CONSUMERS OF BEER IN THE WORLD, WHILE THE DANES ARE NUMBER TWO AFTER THE GERMANS.

As in Norway, aquavit, distilled from potatoes and grain and flavoured with herbs, spices or fruit, is the national drink of Sweden. The Swedes also drink *punsch*, made from fermented fruit, herbs and spices. Beer and imported wine are drunk with meals. At the end of a party, guests are sometimes offered beer and a snack of a rich dish like *Janssons frestelse* (see box, opposite) before leaving.

Denmark

The southernmost of the Scandinavian countries, Denmark has an extremely flat landscape and a variable climate. Although less than one in ten of Denmark's population works in agriculture, almost three-quarters of the country is cultivated. Barley and root vegetables are the most important crops, grown mainly as fodder. Animal products represent 90 per cent of the country's agricultural income; cattle and pigs outnumber people by almost three to one. Danish pork, in the form of roasts, sausages and bacon, is world renowned. Dairy products, particularly cheese and butter, are also highly esteemed.

Staple foods

Food in Denmark is much like the food in the other Scandinavian countries: it is plain and nutritious, with much emphasis on preserved foods. There are also German influences, which are most obviously reflected in the Danish love of pork and pork products, and of thick, rich gravies. In contrast, in the upmarket restaurants of the capital, Copenhagen, the food has French overtones. French chefs have been coming to work in aristocratic Danish kitchens since the 18th century. The Danes have always been a seafaring people and the country had an important trade link with Asia in the 16th and 17th centuries; a culinary legacy of this is the use of curry powder in some dishes.

Despite the exceptionally long coastline around its many islands, and its important fishing industry – the annual catch is over 1.5 million tonnes – Denmark is a country of meat-eaters. Per capita, Danes eat about 75 kg of pork yearly, in the form of loins, hams, bacon and sausages. Meat has always been expensive because so much is exported, so the Danes have developed many stews and casseroles to make it go further. Ground veal and pork are extended with breadcrumbs, eggs and milk or soda water to make meatballs. Chopped beef, *hakkebof*, is made into patties and served with brown sauce and sautéed onions. Chicken, once a luxury item, is now mass-produced. Roast chicken with cream sauce is a popular Sunday meal.

Their love of meat notwithstanding, the Danes, like other Scandinavians, do enjoy their fish. According to Alan Davidson, in his book *North Atlantic Seafood*, 'the Danes rank second to Norwegians, among the peoples of Europe, in consumption of fish per capita'. Baltic herring is a mainstay, served in myriad ways. Smoked herring, *roget sild*, is the basis for many dishes, as are pickled, salted and fresh herring. Fish is often seasoned with a special coarse-ground mustard called *fiskesennep*. Oysters and mussels from Limfjord are highly regarded, as are Tivoli prawns, named after the Tivoli Gardens. The Danes, like other Scandinavians, also flake fish and make it into forcemeat for fish balls.

Eel, most often eaten smoked or jellied, is also considered a great delicacy. *Alesuppe* (eel soup) from South Jutland is very popular, and is much like the eel soup served in nearby Hamburg in Germany. Eels hold an important place in Danish mythology, as they were once thought to eat drowned sailors.

Bread is a staple food, and the foundation of the common Danish lunch and light supper, the open sandwich called *smorrebrod*, which literally

DANISH PASTRY: AN ADAPTED DELICACY

The filled, puff pastry, known elsewhere as Danish pastry, is called *wienerbrod* (Vienna bread) in Denmark, because this layered dough originally came from Austria. It happened in the mid-19th century when Danish bakery guilds dissolved leading to a strike. Austrian bakers were recruited, and they brought with them a new puff pastry, which quickly caught on. The Danes made the pastry their own by adding more butter and fillings, such as jams, creamed butter and sugar, chopped nuts, dried fruits and *ganache* (chocolate icing). The pastries come in various shapes, too, with names like *hanekam* (cockscomb) and *skrubbe* (scrubbing brush).

means 'buttered bread'. These sandwiches are made on thickly buttered slices of dark, sour rye bread or white bread, topped with any number of foods, including meats, fish, cheese and sausage. Typical toppings include: liver paste with bacon and lettuce; roast beef and gherkins; prawns with lettuce; and smoked salmon with scrambled eggs. The last two are traditionally served on white bread. *Smorrebrod* shops are as popular in Danish towns as cafés are in France.

Finland

Lying between Sweden and Russia, Finland has been part of both at various points in its history. When the country broke away from Russia in 1917, one province, Karelia, remained within the Soviet Union. About 400,000 Karelians left their province and settled in other parts of Finland, bringing Russian foods with them. *Piirakka*, from the Russian word *pirog*, are pies or pasties. *Kalakukko*, a fish pasty or pie, is related to Russian *kulibyaka* (see page 28).

Finland shares many gastronomic features with Sweden. The cold or hot buffet, *voileipapoyta*, is a big part of the culture. The Finnish version features more freshwater fish dishes than other Scandinavian *smorgasbords*, as well as Karelian pastries and cold meats, called *leikkeleita*. As in Sweden, meatballs are eaten regularly. A popular fish pudding, *kalamureke*, probably originated in Norway and Sweden.

A heavily forested country, with over 55,000 lakes, many rivers and extensive marshland, much of the agriculture is based in the coastal regions. Dairy farming accounts for about two thirds of the agricultural output. Consequently, the Finns are great milk drinkers, and they consume a lot of *viili* (soured milk) and *piima* (buttermilk). *Viili* is a common breakfast dish or snack, and often it is served with fresh berries, sugar and cinnamon, or mixed with a powder of milled oats, barley and peas, called *talkunna*.

The forest that covers so much of this country provides many of its most popular foods. Berries of all kinds – cranberries, cloudberries, raspberries, blueberries, strawberries,

lingonberries (the most abundant of the berries) and honeyberries (the rarest) – are all very important to the Finnish diet. They provide a rare source of vitamin C in a country with such a short growing season. During the berry season, from early summer to autumn, they are gathered and made into jams, syrups, juices, liqueurs and

conserves. Strawberries and raspberries are transformed into 'snows' (desserts with beaten egg white and whipped cream) and into puddings called *kiisseli*; blueberries and other berries are made into tarts; and lingonberries are used for baked or whipped puddings.

Mushrooms and game are other important products of the forests. Mushroom gathering is a national pastime. Every spring the Finns gather the first fresh morels of the year, which must be blanched several times before they can be eaten, because of a poison they contain. Over 50 other varieties of wild mushroom are available to be used in soups, pies and stews. In addition to deer, elk, reindeer, moose and game birds, the Finns hunt and eat bear. Game is often seasoned with juniper and eaten with lingonberries.

Finland, like the other Scandinavian countries, is a great fish-eating nation, but here the status of freshwater fish from the country's

Dried reindeer meat
The Sami of Lapland rely on reindeer for milk and meat. When dried, the meat will last for months, and is a potent source of energy in winter.

Available produce
With the spread of greenhouse farming, consumption of vegetables has grown in recent years in Finland, but potatoes have long been a staple.

many lakes and streams is higher than that of salt-water fish. This is partly because the Baltic Sea, which touches Finland's shores, is low in salinity, and few species of salt-water fish can survive there. Crayfish, though increasingly rare, are a delicacy. Summer crayfish parties, where crayfish by the dozen are washed down with vodka, aquavit, beer or white wine, used to be common. Salmon is widely eaten, both fresh and cured. A unique Finnish salmon preparation is called *ristiinnaulittu lohi* (crucified salmon), in which the fillet is attached with wooden nails to a board and placed vertically next to a fire so that the fat runs off. The Finns make caviar from several kinds of fish, including sturgeon, forel (a kind of trout) and whitefish.

Meat used to be reserved for Sundays because of its high cost, and many of the traditional Finnish meat dishes are casseroles or stews, where the meat is made to go further by combining it with other ingredients. Casseroles were important also as a slow-cooking dish, which could be left over fires lit for other tasks. As the standard of living has gone up in recent years, meat has become easier to buy. Pork is the most widespread meat. Reindeer, raised by Sami

reindeer breeders in the north, is a favourite meat, particularly when smoked. Beef is growing in popularity, and game is widely eaten.

In Finland, bread is the real staple – a legacy of the Russians. Crisp, rye flat breads, which often have a sour taste, are eaten as much as yeasted breads. In eastern Finland, rye breads are soft and round, whereas in the west, they are like those of Sweden, baked twice and left to dry out, with holes in the middle for hanging and storing. A popular breakfast food and snack, served with coffee, is *pulla*, a sweet bun or ring made from wheat flour. Thick grain porridges and soups are traditional foods of the countryside, eaten for breakfast, lunch and dinner.

The Finns are probably most famous for their invention of the sauna, the dry-heat steam bath. The original saunas were heated up with a wood fire, which would produce quite a bit of smoke. The smoke was cleared out before people entered, but while the sauna was heating, hams and other meats or fish could be smoked. Sauna-smoked ham is called *savukinkku*; sauna-cooked sausage is *lenkkimakkara*. These meats are traditionally downed with beer.

Iceland

Though only 800 km north-west of Scotland, Iceland is nonetheless considered part of Scandinavia. Originally inhabited by Celts, it was colonized by Vikings from Norway in 874 AD, and remained Norwegian for the next four and a half centuries. After that, it was ruled by the Danes. Iceland became a sovereign state of Denmark in 1918, and declared its independence after the Second World War.

SIGNATURE DISHES

Gravlax *A dish of salmon cured with salt and sugar, seasoned with abundant dill.*

Hokarepanna *'Coachman's pan': a meat casserole baked in beer and beef stock.*

Sol over Gudhjem *'Sun over Gudhjem': this Danish smoked herring dish, with raw egg yolk, is prized by herring connoisseurs.*

Kalakeitto *A Finnish fish soup, with onions, allspice, new potatoes, chives and dill.*

Hakarl *This strong sharkmeat from Iceland is buried to leach out deadly cyanic acid. It is sliced thin and washed down with aquavit.*

Fruktsoppa *Sweet Scandinavian fruit soup that can be served hot or cold.*

Tilslorte bondepiker *In this Norwegian dish, apples are layered with cream and crumbled butter biscuits or breadcrumbs.*

The island is actively volcanic, with many solfataras (volcanic vents) and frequent earthquakes. About 90 per cent of Icelandic homes are heated by hot springs. A country of abundant rainfall, which lies at the crossroads of the tropical Gulf Stream and the cold Polar Current, Iceland has many rivers and lakes. Parts of the coast are rocky and irregular, with inlets and fjords, while other areas are smooth and sandy. The inlets form natural harbours, and fishing is big business.

The long, dark winters, and the fact that little of this volcanic island can be cultivated, have had a limiting effect on agriculture here. Sheep feed on lichen and tundra, and there is some pastureland for cattle, but much of it has been overgrazed. However, the country's hot springs mean that greenhouse farming is possible, and Icelanders grow many vegetables and fruits – including bananas – under glass.

Staple foods

The Icelandic diet is simple and, like the rest of Scandinavia, based mainly on fish or meat, dairy products and potatoes. In contrast to other Scandinavian countries, lamb and mutton are mainstays here. A traditional Icelandic Christmas and New Year's Eve dish is called *hangikjot* (hanging meat). This is grass and lichen-fed mutton, hung and smoked in a special dung-fuelled smokehouse for two days or more. To cook, it is boiled for three hours and served with boiled potatoes in a sauce made from peas and cream. *Hangikjot* is traditionally followed by a dessert of crêpes with boysenberries and cream, known as *ponnukokur*.

Iceland owns some of the richest cod fishing grounds in the world, though haddock is the favourite fish here. Salmon and trout, from Iceland's many rivers and lakes, are popular fish, too. There are several Icelandic herring preparations, and lumpfish are plentiful. Female lumpfish, called *grasleppa* and male lumpfish, called *raudmagi*, are prepared in different ways. Female lumpfish, which is less tasty but important for its roe, is cured or hung, then poached to make *sigin grasleppa*. Male lumpfish is poached with bay leaves and vinegar, then served with more vinegar, melted butter and boiled potatoes. This is *sodinn raudmagi*.

Skyr, a yogurt-like product made from fermented skimmed milk, is a unique Icelandic dairy product. It is eaten as a dessert, sweetened with sugar and enriched with cream. It is used in some fish soups and herring dishes. When *skyr* is made, by curdling milk with rennin and bacteria, the whey is poured off and used in preserving other foods.

Festive

~~~ FOOD ~~~

Pagan and Christian seasonal rituals have come together in Scandinavia as they have throughout Europe. In Sweden, the last night of April is celebrated with bonfires and the eating of buns stuffed with almond paste and whipped cream, known as semlor. In Finland there is a large May Day carnival, at which people drink a lemon-scented mead called sima *and eat fried pastries called* tippaleipa. *Traditional Christmas meals vary from country to country. The Danish Christmas table is likely to feature roast pork or goose stuffed with apples and prunes. A popular dessert is rice pudding, which contains a hidden almond. Finland's Christmas foods include the hot, spiced wine, glogg, as well as salt cod, caviar and herring salad.*

RUSSIA AND EASTERN EUROPE

The climate in much of this area is harsh and the farming season short. People have survived for hundreds of years on a hearty, grain-based diet, which incorporates as much fat as conditions and the Orthodox Church permit.

KEY INGREDIENTS

GARLIC

HORSERADISH

DILL

PICKLES

SAUERKRAUT

SMETANA (SOUR CREAM)

TVOROG (CURD CHEESE)

POTATOES

ONION

CABBAGE

MUSHROOMS

BEETROOT

In-store ice cream
Russians' love of this treat is legendary. It is even, on occasion, available in the Moscow department store, TsUM.

This region is a vast one, stretching from the Baltic Sea in the north to the Black Sea in the south, from Poland and the Balkan peninsula in the west and south-west to the outer reaches of Siberia in the east. Vast forests cover large areas, providing a seemingly endless supply of strong-tasting honey and mushrooms, widely used ingredients in these countries' cuisines.

A taste of history

The early Slav inhabitants of the area had ways of surviving: they stored root vegetables; preserved foods; and cultivated grains suited to the harsh climate. When Vikings arrived in the 9th century, they introduced the art of salting and drying fish. Later, pastoral, nomadic Tatars brought a penchant for rice, tea, dried fruit and nuts and the drink *airan* (yogurt and mineral water). They taught the Slavs how to ferment vegetables, and brought spices, herbs, and honey pastries – all tastes and methods that remain today.

As the Russian Empire expanded in the 17th and 18th centuries, new foods and cooking techniques arrived. Peter the Great introduced many foods from Holland, Germany and Poland, such as white bread, honey cakes, cheeses and sausages. French cuisine became the rage among the upper classes, mostly because of Catherine the Great's fondness for all things French. Russian dishes acquired a distinct French style; for example, pies were made with flaky wheat-based dough, rather than the heavier rye-based products. Russian tastes, in turn, became more widespread, such as the style of cooking and serving whole animals, like suckling pigs or sturgeons, or one animal stuffed with another stuffed with another.

In the courts of the tsars and the homes of the nobility, the culinary heyday was the late 19th century. Russians often spent the social season in Paris, so their chefs created French-style dishes to please their masters – dishes such as beef *stroganoff* and veal *orloff* were essentially French dishes that included ingredients beloved by the Russians, particularly sour cream. After the Bolshevik Revolution of 1917, however, the domestic arts were regarded as bourgeois and women became part of the workforce, so the role of cooking was de-emphasized.

Throughout the often troubled history of this region, peasant cookery has remained fairly constant. Bread has always been important; and offering bread and salt is a symbol of hospitality. Salt, once in short supply and very costly, is always added at the end of cooking. Certain characteristics are found throughout the region,

including: a taste for sour foods; the use of dough to enclose fillings; the widespread use of salted vegetables and sweetened fruits to accompany meat and fish; and a general love of pancakes, grain porridges, preserved vegetables and soups.

The influence of religion

One of the most unifying factors in the cooking of these lands has been the Russian Orthodox Church. The Church has more or less shaped and regulated eating habits, with its strict calendar of fasting and feasting days. On *postnyi* (fasting days), which make up more than half the days of the year, all meat, eggs and milk products are proscribed. An outcome of these rigorous demands was the evolution of inventive dishes: fish and mushrooms take the place of meats; vegetable oils, made from hemp, mustard seeds, poppy seeds or nuts, are used instead of butter; and rose water or almond milk are used instead of milk in pastries and breads.

Staple foods

Nutritious soups and pies are mainstays in these cold countries. Soups are almost always soured, often by adding sauerkraut juice or *kvas*, a fermented mix of vegetable juice. Dumplings and pies accompany soups and are always served at banquets. In cities, pies are everywhere, sold on street-corners and in cafés. The pastry may be shortcrust or yeasted; fillings are both sweet and savoury. Large pies are called *pirogi*, and oval, pocket-sized pies are called *pirozhki*.

Potatoes tend to be present at every meal. They were introduced into Russia in the 18th century, but were not readily accepted by the peasantry, even after the government tried to force people to grow them. The peasants rebelled time and again, culminating in the Potato Mutiny of 1842, the largest Russian uprising of the 19th century. Tsar Nicholas I issued an edict enforcing their cultivation, and by the mid-19th century potatoes were accepted and cultivated with pride.

Food markets
There are around 50 local markets in Moscow, where many people still buy their daily foods, such as garlic and pickled vegetables.

In Russia, the food eaten at Easter is part of a week-long celebration after the Lenten fast. The table is always set with decorated eggs, the pyramid-shaped cheesecake, paskha, and the Easter bread, kulich, *decorated with a crown. A lamb moulded out of butter may be at the centre, holding a sprig of greenery in its mouth. There is much visiting between households.*

Frozen milk
In the colds of Siberia, sour-milk products are sometimes frozen in blocks for storage.

Kasha (cooked grains) is the other major staple throughout these countries. It is served in some form, either sweet or savoury, pretty much daily, sometimes taking the place of potatoes. It might be mixed with such ingredients as mushrooms, onions, *tvorog* (curd cheese), sour cream, nuts, herbs and fruit.

Russians and their neighbours are passionate mushroom gatherers. The wooded countryside provides many varieties, and gathering expeditions are a favourite pastime. Wild mushrooms are dried, pickled and salted, or eaten fresh, fried with spring onion and garnished with sour cream. Marinated mushrooms are a standard *zakouski* table dish.

Meat has always been in short supply here. This, along with the exigencies of the Russian Orthodox Church, has meant that meat is not of primary importance. With the exception of the aristocratic recipes of the 19th century, most meat dishes are stretched with other ingredients. *Kotletki* and *bitki* (cutlets) can be made with vegetables, and meat mixed with vegetables or grain is used to fill cabbage rolls and dumplings.

Salt-water fish are more widely eaten in the Baltic countries than in Russia, Ukraine, Belarus and Moldova, where freshwater fish like sturgeon and carp are more popular. Herring is the exception; it is eaten, usually pickled or salted, everywhere. Salmon is also common. It is the filling for the Russian signature dish, *kulibyaka* (salmon in pastry with mushrooms, eggs and rice). One of the most popular Russian soups is *ukha*, a fisherman's broth made with freshwater or salt-water fish – but never the two together.

■ VODKA: FROM THE RUSSIAN FOR 'WATER'

THOUGHT TO HAVE BEEN PRODUCED AS FAR BACK AS THE 9TH CENTURY, VODKA IS THE DAILY DRINK OF RUSSIANS, CONSUMED IN LARGE QUANTITIES WITH MEALS AND *ZAKOUSKI*. IT HAS BEEN ESTIMATED THAT THE AVERAGE RUSSIAN DRINKS OVER A LITRE OF VODKA EACH WEEK.

ANY NUMBER OF FLAVOURS ARE ADDED TO VODKA. ORIGINALLY THIS MAY HAVE BEEN TO MASK IMPURITIES, BUT VODKA IS STILL AVAILABLE IN CHILLI, LEMON OR BISON GRASS FLAVOURS, AMONG OTHERS.

Food through the day

Breakfasts in Eastern Europe are similar to those eaten in Scandinavia and Germany, with bread and butter, cold meats and vegetables or grain porridges. Pancakes, filled with meat or cheese, are eaten also.

The main meal of the day is at lunchtime. Elaborate meals begin with *zakouski* (see box, page 32) and vodka, followed by soup and perhaps filled pies or pancakes. Meat, poultry or fish and potatoes follow, and then there is a fruit-based dessert or ice cream. Alternatively, the main meal might be a one-dish stew. At dinner the leftovers from lunch are polished off.

Russians drink tea throughout the day and, in the Baltic states, afternoon coffee with pastries is a ritual. In the south, vines are grown and wine is drunk with meals.

Russia

Spanning two continents, this is the largest country in the world. Two-thirds of Russia's population live in European Russia, mostly in the big cities, Moscow and St Petersburg, and along the mighty Volga River. There is much industry here and a great deal of intensive farming. Cold-weather grains and potatoes are grown in the north, whereas vegetables, citrus and tobacco are cultivated in the south. Russia is the world's largest producer of rye, barley, oats and potatoes, and the third biggest wheat producer.

Cooking is varied in the Volga regions, but the chief influences are Russian and Tatar. The upper, forested section of the Volga region is the source of much of Russia's honey; bee-keeping is practised by the Mari people, a Finnish-Ugric race. The central and lower Volga regions, known as Tatarstan, are home to over 4 million Tatars, Islamic descendants of the original tribes. The cooking of the Tatars has much in common with that of their Central Asian neighbours, but there are Russian influences as well. Yogurt, cream cheeses and milky soups characterize the cuisine, as does the widespread use of mushrooms, honey, wild berries and wild greens. Sourdough bread is a speciality.

Because Russia was at the centre of a huge empire for centuries, many foreign dishes have entered its repertoire. Dishes such as Georgian chicken, Central Asian pilafs, Ukrainian *borshch* and Baltic pastries are routinely found on Russian menus. The European influences from the days of the tsars are still evident in formal dining.

The main flavourings used in Russian cooking are onion, garlic, horseradish, dill and parsley. Thick, stew-like soups are an important feature of Russian food. The cabbage soup, *shchi*, is the classic Russian soup. Originally this was a winter soup made with fermented cabbage, known as *kislye shchi*, but eventually people began to make a summer version with fresh cabbage, which is called *lenivye shchi*, meaning 'lazy cabbage soup'. The Tatars introduced *lapsha* and *pel-meni*, soups with noodles and dumplings, after Russia annexed Astrakhan, Kazan, Bashkiria and Siberia in the 17th century. Sweet dishes were also introduced at this time.

Georgian kebabs
Specialities from areas formerly under Russian control can still be found on the streets of Moscow.

SIGNATURE DISHES

Chornyi khleb *A sticky, Russian black bread containing rye and molasses.*

Borshch *This Ukrainian beetroot soup is now ubiquitous in the region.*

Blini *Small, yeasted pancakes.*

Ikra *Once a food of the tsars, caviar (the roe of a sturgeon) is a Russian symbol of luxury.*

Gribnaya ikra *A Russian vegetable 'caviar' made with mushrooms.*

Selyodka *Herrings may be pickled and served with sour cream, dill or mustard sauce, or served in salads.*

Golubtsy *In the Baltics these stuffed cabbage rolls are layered with bacon; the Jewish versions are sweet and sour.*

Okroshka *Russia's most popular cold soup, made of cold meats and vegetables.*

Ukraine

With a long agricultural and horticultural tradition, this densely populated country, of vast, fertile plains, was the breadbasket of the Soviet Union, supplying it with over 20 per cent of its grains. The 'black earth belt', which produces huge quantities of wheat, maize, barley, oats, buckwheat and rye, runs through the country south of Kiev, through wooded steppeland – famous for its honey – and steppe to beyond the Urals and Siberia. The Dnieper is its most important river and supplies many fish.

Food here is quite Russian in character, but the country has some speciality dishes. Ukraine has been invaded many times, and these invaders have all influenced the cuisine; Lithuanian, Hungarian, Polish and Romanian, as well as Turkish and Tatar cooking legacies can be detected. In much earlier times, there were Scandinavian influences; Ukraine was settled in the 8th and 9th centuries by the Varangian people, ancestors of the Swedes.

Staple foods

Abundance – of fresh vegetables, pies, breads, rich pastries made with dark, Ukrainian honey and a variety of sausages and charcuterie – is the defining feature of Ukrainian cooking. Foods borrowed from the Russian kitchen include *shchi*, *solianka* (preserved cabbage soup) and *kulibyaka*. In return, Ukraine has given Russia the beetroot soup, *borshch*, *varenyky* (soft dough dumplings), cheese pastries, larded meats, stuffed fish and many pork sausages. In western Ukraine there are Austro-Hungarian influences, particularly in the local torte tradition.

Ukrainian food is tart and textured. The fermented drink, *kvas*, made with beetroot, is used as a base for soups, gravies and stews. Fermented cabbage is another souring agent, used in many dishes. *Smetana* (lightly soured cream) is a popular condiment and flavouring for soups, sauces, marinades, dressings and desserts.

Vegetables are highly regarded, and often eaten as main dishes. They are usually stewed in oil in the Greek and Turkish fashion and served hot or cold. Puréed vegetables are used to thicken soups. Beetroot is by far the most popular vegetable, and each region has its *borshch*, of which there are over 100 variations: Kiev-style *borshch* is made with lamb and mushrooms; Poltava *borshch* is made with poultry and dumplings; Galician-style contains potatoes; and Chernigov contains yellow squash. Ukrainians often eat *borshch* with small ear-shaped dumplings called *ushki*, whereas Muscovites accompany theirs with *vatruschki* (dumplings) or *pirozhki* (small pies). The meat used to make the stock for *borshch* is often eaten as a second course or cold the next day.

Ukrainians are renowned for their baking, and a great variety of breads are made here. White bread is favoured in the south and west, and oat bread in the mountainous regions. The many festival breads on offer through the year are made with rich doughs and shaped in different ways, depending on the festival. At Christmas, elaborate plaited breads called *kolach* are made, which are often decorated with candles.

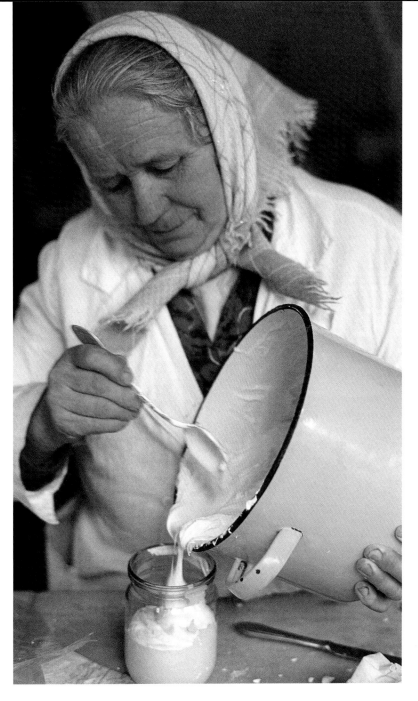

Belarus

Much of this sparsely populated country is agricultural. However, the land is low-lying and a large part is covered by the Pripet Marshes – the largest expanse of marshland in Europe. People here have long had to make do on the few products that grow in the poor soil and climate conditions, and most grains are imported.

Belarus has been marched over by many invading armies, and there are Polish, Lithuanian and Russian influences in the cuisine, with a mixture of peasant and more refined dishes.

Local milk products
Nomadic Tatars introduced the regional taste for curd cheeses and fermented milk goods, such as sour cream and yogurt.

Staple foods

Potatoes are the main Belarussian staple, eaten at every meal including breakfast. They were accepted earlier in Belarus than they were in other parts of the Russian Empire. Excess potatoes are fed to pigs, an important animal here. As in the rest of this region, mushrooms are widely gathered. They are dried and pickled, and cooked with sour cream. Though grains are limited, Minsk is known for its sourdough rye and oat breads. When harvests are bad and grains are in short supply, people rely on pancakes, called *drachoni.*

Belarus has always been known for the quality of its meat and charcuterie, and particularly for its butchers. Before the Second

ZAKOUSKI: SNACKS THAT SPAN BORDERS

These little Russian dishes are the equivalent of Turkish *meze. Zakouski* can be hot or cold, elaborate or simple. They are served to guests at any time of day, usually with an ice-cold glass of vodka. Formal dinners will always begin with a small selection. Classic dishes include: pies, dumplings, salads, pickled vegetables, *blini* and caviar, and, most important of all, herrings, in a sour cream sauce or a salad with potatoes.

World War, the Jewish population here was quite large. Butchers were required for preparing kosher cuts of meat, and they had far-flung reputations. People would travel long distances to Minsk just to obtain meat. Many dishes require minced meat, evidence of the Polish influence on Belarussian cooking.

As is so common in this part of the world, the Belarussians like thick soups and slow-simmered stews. Outside of the Jewish communities, pork fat has long been the traditional medium for frying, but today, people use more sunflower oil.

The Baltic States: Estonia, Latvia and Lithuania

The cold, wet climate of these countries bordering the Baltic Sea allows for a limited range of crops – rye, oats, barley, potatoes and sugar beets are the most important. Rye is used for breads and porridges, mixed with oats, barley or peas. It is used also for pie doughs, which can be on the heavy side. Some of the food here has Germanic overtones, such as dark breads sweetened with honey and malt. Baltic pumpernickel (black rye bread) is popular.

Farmers raise pigs and dairy cattle, which graze on the wet, green pastures of these lands. As in Germany, smoked bacon or pork fat is often used for flavouring. Cream and butter are used liberally in the cuisines. Many of the soups here are milk-based.

Fishing is extremely important, particularly for the small, delicate and sweet-tasting Baltic herring, which is eaten throughout Central and Eastern Europe. Fish is eaten fresh, but also preserved, dried or smoked, as it is in the Scandinavian countries.

Estonia actually belonged to Sweden in the 17th and 18th centuries, so its foods have Swedish and Finnish influences. It then became part of the Russian Empire, achieved independence following the Bolshevik Revolution and again fell under the sway of the Soviet Union in 1940. It had been a farming nation until this time, but the Russians transformed it into an industrialized, urban nation. Food processing was, and still is, one of the country's main industries.

Latvia has concentrated on farming, fishing and timber since it became independent from the Soviet Union in 1991. Its climate is good for dairy farming and meat production. Cooking here is mainly influenced by the other two Baltic republics. Latvia does have one speciality, an ancient dish called *putry*, which is a vegetable and grain porridge with smoked meat and mushrooms or suet and pork fat, enriched with sour-milk products.

During the Middle Ages, Lithuania was a powerful country with important trade links to Germany, Poland and, later, with the khanates of Crimea, the Turkish Ottoman Empire and the Mongol-ruled, western Russia. Unlike the other two Baltic States, which still have sizeable Russian groups, the population here is ethnic Lithuanian, and there are strong folk traditions. This is a more fertile country than Estonia and Latvia, and farming is more important to the economy than fishing. The food here has strong Polish and German overtones, and in the eastern part of the country there are Tatar influences. Eastern influences can be seen in stuffed vegetable recipes and the pomegranate juice used in old recipes. Lithuanian forests are abundant with wild game and fowl, which were traditionally smoked and preserved for sale to Germany and Western Europe. This is still done today on a limited scale. The woods are known, too, for producing high-quality honey, which is used in many Lithuanian dishes.

Moldova

Linguistically and culturally, Moldova is closer to Romania than it is to Russia, and indeed the country was once part of Romania. One of the warmest regions of the former Soviet Union, the southern parts of Moldova are dry and treeless and require irrigation, but most of the country is quite fertile and productive. Vines and fruit grow in the valley of the Dniester. Farmers raise wheat, barley, maize, sunflowers, sugar beets and many vegetables. Common flavours include fresh coriander, tarragon, tomato juice and wine vinegar. Being a wine growing region, wine vinegar is used as a souring agent here.

Although many typical Russian and Ukrainian dishes are made here, such as marinated vegetables with sour cream, and fermented and salted foods, the foods of Moldova have more widespread influences. The country used to trade with Greek, Black Sea settlements and Byzantium, so the cuisine here has much in common with that of Greece and the countries of the Balkan Peninsula. Specialities include: *givech*

(vegetable ragout), moussaka (here made with goat's cheese) and filo pastries. There is also a Mediterranean culinary style, including olive oil and wine. Maize is an important staple, as it is in neighbouring Romania; *mamalyga* (polenta) is widely eaten and the basis for many savoury and sweet dishes.

There are many vegetarian dishes in the Moldovan repertoire, some made simply by combining sauces with vegetables. Bean and lentil purées are widely eaten, as they are in the Mediterranean. Here they are served with a garlic sauce called *muzhdei*.

Omul: a unique fish
Lake Baikal in Siberia is the only place where this delicacy can be found. They are often grilled and eaten on the shore.

CENTRAL EUROPE

A landscape of fertile plains, mountains and forests has given Poland, the Czech Republic, Slovakia and Hungary a rich culinary heritage, which has been further enhanced under the influence of the great empires of Europe.

KEY INGREDIENTS

LARD

PAPRIKA

VINEGAR

PORK

BACON

SOUR CREAM

MUSHROOMS

BEETROOT

CABBAGE

ONION

TURNIPS

TREE FRUITS

About a quarter of Central Europe is covered in forests, which have long played a key role in providing much of the region's food. The other major influence is agriculture. A quarter of the Polish workforce, for example, is employed in farming, growing mainly potatoes, sugar beets and cereals, and raising livestock on small, privately owned farms. In the Czech Republic and much of Slovakia, farmers work on large state-owned farms or cooperatives that specialize in cereal crops for livestock. In Slovakia a rural, mountainous country, there are also many small family farms, but a much greater proportion of the population is employed in industry.

Paprika and garlic
A distinguishing feature of Hungarian food is the widespread use of paprika. Together with onion and garlic, paprika is the basic seasoning for many dishes.

A taste of history

The Slavs were the early inhabitants of this area. The custom of souring food with lemon juice, sour cream or vinegar is a Slavic legacy, as, too, is the local reliance on breads, grains and cereals. Through the centuries, various invaders have swept across these flat lands, and borders have been redrawn many times.

Four empires surrounded, threatened and, at times, held sway over the region: Russia, Austro-Hungary, Prussia and the Ottoman Turks. After the Second World War, the countries of Central Europe came under the influence of the Soviet Union, and have only been independent since the end of the 1980s. All of these empires left culinary legacies: strudels and many of the cakes and pastries of the region, *Wiener Schnitzel* and *gulyas* came from the Austro-Hungarian empire; soups, pancakes and many dumpling, noodle and grain dishes were contributed by German, Russian and Lithuanian invaders.

Staple foods

Although each of the Central European countries has its specialities, many of the foods and tastes overlap. Winters here are long and cold and the food is accordingly filling and nourishing. Staples throughout the region include root vegetables, potatoes, rich meat stews, warming soups, sausages, grains and dense wheat and rye breads. Lard and butter are the fats of choice. Cabbage is eaten in many forms: stuffed; in stews; in layered dishes; and pickled and made into sauerkraut. There is a wide selection of dumplings, made from wheat flour, rye, barley, buckwheat and potatoes, and these are served as main dishes, desserts, side dishes and soup garnishes. Noodles, too, are common; they are stuffed and baked, served plain with butter, added to soups and stews, and made into sweet noodle dishes. Bread is called 'life' by many country people.

The important products of the forests are game and wild mushrooms, and hunting for both has been popular for centuries. In Poland, 31 varieties of edible mushrooms are recognized. They are used not only as a food, but also as an aromatic for soups, stews, roasts, game, poultry and even fish. A great variety of game is eaten everywhere, seasoned with juniper berries and accompanied by cabbage, beetroot, cranberries and grains or potatoes.

Although the Central European countries are meat-eating, long periods of poverty have taught people to stretch meat in stews and soups, in which the bulk of the calories come from vegetables and grains and meat is present more as a flavouring. Of the meat that is eaten, pork is the most popular, followed by beef and veal. There are also meat specialities here: Hungarian geese are prized; Polish and Czech sausages are world renowned; and Prague ham is highly regarded.

Soups are probably the most widely eaten dish in Central Europe. Many are soured with beetroot juice, grain juice or sour cream. They are invariably thickened, usually with a roux made using butter, lard, cream or sour cream. As in Germany, soups are almost always garnished with plain or stuffed dumplings or noodles, further completing the meal. Fruit soups – served hot in the winter and cold in summer – are popular throughout the region.

In Poland, despite the prominence of the potato, *kashas* (grains) are important. Buckwheat groats and barley, flavoured with ingredients such as pork fat, cheese, mushrooms or plums, are made into soups, baked in the oven, served with meats or made into thick porridges with milk.

Cakes and pastries are very important too. There are rich, bread-like cakes, yeasted cakes, honey cakes, gingerbreads and the rich, fancier cakes like *Sachertorte* and *Dobosch Torte*, which are a legacy of the Austro-Hungarian Empire.

Food through the day

Mornings are cold in Central Europe, so breakfast has always been a filling meal; thick, bean soups and grain porridges are served at breakfast, as well as at lunch and dinner. Dense breads, cold meats and cheeses are also eaten at breakfast, and in addition to coffee and tea, some people wash down the morning meal with schnapps or beer.

The main meal of the day is traditionally lunch, but that is changing. Whether the midday meal is the main meal of the day or not, lunch always begins with a soup. This may be a sustaining one-dish meal, or it may be a lighter vegetable or fruit soup. To follow there may be a meat, noodle or main-dish vegetable course, such as a savoury strudel filled with cottage cheese, or stuffed cabbage leaves. Meat is usually accompanied by grains, potatoes or noodles, and sometimes by cabbage or root vegetables. Dessert is all-important, usually consisting of the region's highly regarded pastry or, particularly in Hungary, a sweet, noodle dish. In summer, dessert could be fruit. If lunch is the main meal of the day, then dinner might consist of leftovers from lunch, cold meats or a noodle or egg dish.

Meals in this area often begin and end with a fruit brandy. Wine is drunk with meals in Hungary, while beer is more common in Slovakia, the Czech Republic and Poland where brewing traditions go back to the Middle Ages. Vodka is also widely drunk in Poland.

Hungary

The cooking of Hungary is distinct from that of the rest of Central Europe. The Turkish influence is stronger here, and, as it is warmer in Hungary than in the rest of this area, it has a wider range of produce. Hungarians are known for their passion for food and wine, their *joie de vivre* and for their wonderful hospitality, rooted in a dining tradition that goes back many centuries. A combination of paprika, onion and lard lies at the base of many Hungarian dishes.

A taste of history

Hungarian cuisine has been influenced by all the peoples who have passed through it over the last 1000 years. The original Hungarians were nomadic Magyars, who appear to have come from the Ural Mountains, on the borders between Asia and Europe, and settled in this area in the 5th century. Many Magyar foods still exist in Hungary today; soups, for example, have a sour or semi-sour taste and are thickened with flour, milk and egg yolk, or with a browned flour and fat mixture. These nomads used many techniques for preserving meat, which allowed them to make instant meals and put them at an advantage against their foes. The Magyars also re-established vineyards that the Romans had planted in the 3rd century.

Hungarian cuisine reached a very high standard under King Matthias, who married Princess Beatrice of Italy in 1475. Along with Italian chefs and pastry makers, foods such as pastas, ice creams, chestnuts, garlic, figs, aniseed, dill and capers were imported. Onion became the most important vegetable in the cuisine. The Hungarian technique of cooking meats and fish in their own juices was also established, and domestic fowl were introduced to Hungary from France and Italy. Hungarian geese, ducks, hens and other birds soon became well-known throughout Europe.

During the 16th and 17th centuries, the Ottoman Turks attacked and divided the nation. Part of it was Habsburg ruled, and the cuisine that evolved here was tempered by sophisticated French court chefs. In the other areas, Turkish

STEWS: IN FOUR FORMS

These nourishing dishes were probably introduced by the Magyars, who cooked in *bogracs* (kettles) over an open fire. *Gulyas* (goulash), the best-known Hungarian stew, is either liquid and called *gulyasleves* (*gulyas* soup), or has a drier form, *gulyashus* (*gulyas* meat). It is usually a beef-based dish flavoured with onions and caraway.

Porkolt, on the other hand, can be made with fish, game or many types of meat and is seasoned with paprika, lard, bacon and onion. *Paprikas* is much like *porkolt*, but finished with sweet or sour cream just before serving. *Paprikas csrike* (with chicken) is the best-known *paprikas*, but the dish is also made with veal and carp. *Tokany* is a sort of ragout in which strips of meat are cooked in their own juices and seasoned with pepper, marjoram and summer savory. Beef, lamb, veal, chicken and game are used for this dish.

flavours and techniques became commonplace. Paprika, cherries, maize, coffee and stuffed meats and vegetables were all introduced by the Turks.

The Habsburgs prevailed again in 1686 and Hungarian aristocrats' kitchens remained French-oriented by imitating those of the Viennese court. The Habsburgs, in turn, used Hungary as a food basket for their empire, with positive consequences on the gastronomy: vineyards were replanted and the quality and variety of wines were augmented. Ice cream, lemonade and other refreshments were sold along the Danube. Later, in the late 19th and early 20th centuries, luxurious restaurants, tea rooms, coffee houses and patisseries came into their own in the cities.

Polish vodka
Flavoured vodkas such as *zubrowka*, made by adding bison-grass to the vodka, are a popular Polish speciality.

A regional flavour

Transdanubia – a name meaning 'beyond the Danube' – is the mild, western part of Hungary. Lake Balaton is at its centre, and it supplies Hungary with many of its freshwater fish, the most highly regarded being the *fogas*, a pike perch. Thousands of acres of vineyards grow along the shore, producing some of the best wines in Hungary. They are white wines, mostly made from Riesling and Pinot Gris grapes, the most highly regarded being Badcsonyi Kéknyelu.

The southern part of Transdanubia has a mild, Mediterranean climate and produces fruits, grapes, vegetables and chestnuts in abundance. Many early folk customs are still practised here; gingerbread and cakes, for example, are made into particular symbolic figures. Milk is drunk every day, and often accompanies bread at lunch instead of soup. The region's many spas produce a range of mineral waters.

The rolling countryside of northern Hungary is dotted with forests, castle ruins and valleys with ancient villages and towns. Some of the best hunting preserves in Europe are in this part of Hungary. In the valleys of the Matra hills, village life is lived the way it has been for hundreds of years, with much outdoor cookery and the preparation of traditional foods, such as flat breads baked in ashes, called *pogacsa*; smoked, dried and salted fish; and smoked farmer's cheese wrapped in paper. This is home to Hungary's most famous wine, Tokaj.

The Great Plains east of the Danube are the wheat and fruit basket of Hungary. Rice, barley, maize and grapes are grown, and ranching is important. The region is known for its marvellous fruit brandies – the most popular are made with apricot and plum. The region's main city, Szeged, is the centre of the Hungarian salami and paprika industries. The city also has many elegant restaurants and pastry shops, and is known for its fish cuisine based on the local catch from the Tisza river.

The flat, vast Hortobagy Puszta region is a country of herdsmen who raise cattle, oxen and sheep. Noodles are eaten at every meal, in soups, main dishes and desserts. Meats are barbecued or stewed and all parts of the animals are used. Game birds, wild ducks and geese are plentiful.

AUSTRIA

Now in the middle of Europe, Austria was once at the centre of a vast empire ruled by a powerful royal family. Traces of the country's imperial wealth remain in its cuisine, with its thick soups, stews and rich buttery pastries.

Modern Austria is just a small part of an empire that once stretched south to Turkey and into Italy, north and west into Germany, France and Switzerland, and east through Hungary to the edge of Russia. Vienna was its dazzling capital and one of the great cities of Europe. The Habsburg influence went as far afield as Spain, Mexico and America, and ingredients like chocolate and red peppers – New World foods – are still important in Austria's cuisine.

A regional flavour

Austria's ethnically mixed population reflects the reaches of its former power. Signature dishes, such as *Wiener Schnitzel* (breaded, sautéed veal cutlets), *Strudel*, paprika-spiced goulashes and *Linzertorte*, all have their counterparts in Italy, Hungary and Germany. *Strudel* made with paper-thin dough are direct descendants of Turkish filo-wrapped pastries. In eastern Austria there are dishes with names like 'Balkan soup', 'Hungarian goulash' and 'Westphalian bean soup'. Throughout southern Austria, particularly in Tyrol, Mediterranean influences are strong: parmesan cheese is widely used, as are tomatoes and Mediterranean herbs.

Viennese cooking is the cuisine of the former royal court, and here the influences are mainly French and German, with many roux-based sauces and rich, buttery, formal dishes, as well as magnificent pastries (see box, page 40). Pastries made the Viennese *Konditoreien* (coffee houses) famous. Coffee was introduced to the French court of Louis XIV by an ambassador of the Ottomans in 1669, and its popularity quickly spread throughout Europe. By 1730, there were already 30 coffee houses in Vienna. Modern urban Austrians still pay regular visits to coffee houses, where they might meet with friends or relax with a newspaper. Viennese favour strong blends of coffee – mocha is particularly popular – and brew it the Italian way, in espresso machines or through filters. Thick, strong Turkish coffee is also available.

SIGNATURE DISHES

Liptauer *This cheese spread is flavoured with paprika and other condiments.*

Wienersaft Gulyas *This paprika-spiced beef stew derives from Hungary.*

Wiener Schnitzel *The quintessential Austrian dish of breaded veal cutlets.*

Kalbsrücken Metternich *Saddle of veal with paprika sauce.*

Knödel *Dumplings, usually made from flour or potatoes.*

Sachertorte *This classic chocolate cake was created in 1832 by the Viennese hotelier, Franz Sacher.*

Linzertorte *Almonds, lemon rind and spices flavour this rich, latticed jam tart.*

Dobosch Torte *A rich cake with thin layers of sponge spread with chocolate buttercream.*

Dairy farming is a major occupation in the mountainous western regions of Austria, and cheese an important product. The cheeses made here are mainly Emmenthal-type or resemble German Limburger. Liptauer, which comes from and is named after a region in Hungary, is also a favourite; it is a herbed or spiced, soft cheese, and

KEY INGREDIENTS

LARD

SUGAR

JUNIPER

DILL

HORSERADISH

SPECK (CURED HAM)

VEAL

PORK

TOPFEN (COTTAGE CHEESE)

NOODLES

POTATOES

CHOCOLATE

each cook has his or her individual way of seasoning it, the most usual condiments being caraway, paprika, chopped chives and various mustards. *Gervais* (cream cheese) and *Topfen* (cottage cheese) are made by every farming family in the region and are widely used, particularly in cooking and baking. Some types of *Strudel*, which also came to Austria by way of Hungary, are filled with cottage cheese beaten with egg yolks, sugar and raisins.

CAKES AND PASTRIES: RICH BUT DELICATE

Austria, and Vienna in particular, is probably most famous for its baked goods, especially its cakes and pastries. During the 19th century, chefs competed to produce elaborate creations, laden with sugar, eggs, cream and butter, and hundreds of individual confections were created. These are still on offer today, along with sturdier yeast-based pastries, and served up in Viennese *Konditoreien* with tea, chocolate or strong Viennese coffee.

The rich pastry that originated here soon spread throughout Europe. What many people know as 'Danish pastry' is called 'Viennese bread' by the Danes, and the French refer to their brioches, egg breads and puff pastries collectively as *viennoiserie*.

Staple foods

Noodles, dumplings and potatoes are the essentials of the Austrian diet. Traditionally, egg noodles were the first thing mothers taught daughters how to make. *Knödel* (dumplings) are made with either flour or potatoes, and they come in many sizes. They garnish soups and meats. Some dumplings are traditionally matched with particular meats: potato-based ones are served with game, and flour dumplings with veal. Sometimes dumplings are filled with cheese, spinach, parsley, toasted bread cubes or bits of ham or liver to serve as a main dish – or, in the case of dessert dumplings, with jam or fruit. Noodles are tossed with butter, or with vegetable or meat sauces, or are made into casseroles or puddings for an evening meal. Potatoes, too, are served in many ways. They are cooked into pancakes and casseroles, sliced and fried, or used as a gratin with seasonings or cheese. Rice is also popular, particularly in Vienna. Several rice dishes are inspired by Italian risottos; others by Turkish rice pilafs.

Meat is at the centre of the Austrian plate. Beef is popular, and veal the most widely eaten meat. Beef is most often simmered or braised in liquid to make *Sauerbraten*, or cut up and used for Hungarian-style goulashes. Veal is roasted, served as cutlets, or used for goulash. There are a number of cutlet dishes besides *Wiener Schnitzel*, such as *Paprikaschnitzel*, which has a rich, sour cream-based sauce. Game – hare, venison, partridge, quail and pheasant – is also important. It is often marinated in red wine, seasoned with juniper berries and served with lingonberries, flour dumplings and red cabbage.

Austria has been a landlocked country since it lost its little bit of the Adriatic coast at the end of the First World War. Although ocean fish and shellfish are offered on restaurant menus, freshwater fish, like trout and carp from the country's many streams and lakes, are much more common. The most well-known Austrian fish preparation is 'blue trout'. This is trout that is cooked soon after being caught and while still alive. A chemical reaction in the simmering stock causes the fish to turn blue.

Although meat takes pride of place in Austrian cuisine, vegetables are also important and are often served as a course on their own. When vegetables are at their freshest and most tender they will be prepared simply, often as a garnish for meat. Otherwise, vegetables are transformed into soufflés, puddings, tarts, purées, ragouts and stuffed vegetable preparations. Some vegetable dishes contain a little bit of meat to add taste. Certain salads traditionally accompany specific meat dishes: cucumber salad is served with breaded meat and fish; beetroot salad with boiled beef; and green salad with *Wiener Schnitzel*. Potato salads are much loved, as are cabbage salads. Other, more substantial salads are served as a separate course.

Food through the day

Breakfast in Austria is typically light, consisting of coffee and a roll or Viennese-style pastry, such as an almond croissant. At mid-morning, as in Germany, there is a second breakfast, which might consist of a vegetable dish and a pastry, or sausage and bread.

The midday meal, lighter than the evening meal, might consist of two or three courses – a vegetable tart and salad, a soup and a soufflé, or cold meats and a salad.

Dinner is the main meal of the day. It can range from two to seven courses, depending on how formal a meal it is to be. A typical multicourse meal begins with an appetizer, followed by a soup, a main course, a vegetable course, perhaps a salad and a dessert.

An Austrian meal without a dessert is unthinkable; in fact the menu is often planned around it. Desserts are divided into three categories: *Mehlspeisen*, made with flour, include soufflés, pancakes, puddings and *Strudel*; *Süssespeisen* contain no flour, and they include creams, ice cream, bombes, mousses and puddings; and *Bäckerei* are the pastries, cakes and tarts. At formal dinner parties, two types of dessert might be served. Some flour-containing desserts, such as pancakes with apple sauce, often serve as a meal in themselves.

Vienna coffee house
A mid-afternoon break with a mocha or hot chocolate and a rich pastry or cake is a wonderful way to socialize.

GERMANY

Beer, sausages and cabbage dishes, while well-known, are just a few examples of German food. A country of many landscapes, dialects and regions, it is one of the world's wealthiest nations, and this is reflected in its meat-based cuisine.

KEY INGREDIENTS

LARD

BACON FAT

CHICKEN AND GOOSE FAT

CARAWAY SEEDS

DILL

JUNIPER

HORSERADISH

VINEGAR

PORK

SAUSAGE

POTATOES

ROOT VEGETABLES

The north of Germany is flat and fertile, the Baltic and North Sea climate damp and chilly. This is a landscape of dairy farms and windmills, fishing villages and moors. To the south-west, the Rhineland is mild by comparison, a wine-growing region with green landscapes and romantic castles. The Black Forest and Swabian Alps dominate the south-eastern state of Baden-Württemberg; this is the land of luxury hotels and spas, game forests and fruit orchards. However, the archetypal German setting is Bavaria in the south-west, its largest state, and its best-known tourist area, with many medieval villages, ski resorts, lakes and woodlands dotting the Alps. The best-known German food – dumplings and *Würste* (sausages), beer, pork and cabbage dishes – are Bavarian.

A regional flavour

Germany became a republic only as recently as 1871, when the various independent states were united into a federal system of government. After the Second World War, the country was divided into the communist state of East Germany and the democracy of West Germany. Re-unification came in 1989, with the fall of the Berlin Wall. However, the original, pre-republic states have retained some degree of political and cultural autonomy – the latter is reflected in the individual regional cuisines, which are influenced by local customs and neighbouring countries. The food of eastern Germany, for example, has much in common with that of Austria, the Czech Republic, Slovakia and Poland, with widespread use of ingredients like caraway, paprika, sour cream, dried mushrooms, large dumplings, sauerkraut and pork. In Swabia, just across the Rhine from France, tarts

SIGNATURE DISHES

Sauerkraut *Shredded cabbage fermented with salt and sometimes spices, a traditional accompaniment to sausages.*

Sauerbraten *Marinated pot roast cooked by slow simmering to produce a tender dish.*

Pichelsteiner *A Bavarian stew made with beef, pork, fish or vegetables.*

Badischer Hecht *Pike baked in sour cream, with onion and bacon.*

Wiener Schnitzel *Breaded veal cutlets, which originated in Vienna.*

Bratkartoffeln *A side dish of potatoes fried in butter, lard or bacon fat.*

Stollen *Christmas fruit bread.*

Schwarzwälderkirschtorte *This Black Forest cherry cake is a speciality of Swabia.*

resembling quiche Lorraine are made with creamy cheese, bacon and onions, and wine and fruit brandies are drunk as commonly as beer.

There are differences, too, in the names of dishes and the way in which food is served. In Berlin *halbes Hähnchen*, meaning 'half a chicken', is just that. But in Cologne *halber Hahn* (also 'half a chicken') refers to a small round roll with cheese, which looks like a chicken breast. In the north, a potato is called a *Kartoffel*; in the south, a potato is an *Erdapfel* – literally 'earth apple', a direct translation of the French *pomme de terre*. People from Schleswig-Holstein serve carp with whipped cream, whereas in the south it is served with a sauce made from beer and ginger biscuits.

Staple foods

Despite these specialities, the basic diet throughout Germany is one of meat and potatoes. Germans of all regions love pork, beef, veal and lamb, and they serve it up in huge portions. Pork – called *Schwein* when fresh, and *Schinken* or *Speck* when smoked or cured – is the most widely eaten meat. Every part of an animal is used: liver, kidneys, brain, sweetbreads, heart, feet, tail, ears, cheeks and tongue. The fats used for cooking are animal fats – butter, lard and bacon fat. Germans love thick gravies, too, enriched with flour, egg yolks or cream.

With Germany's Baltic and North Sea coastlines and its many rivers, mountain lakes and streams, there is, nonetheless, quite a bit of freshwater and salt-water fish and shellfish in the German diet, predominantly in ports like Hamburg and Bremen. The small island of Helgoland, off the Hamburg coast, is famous for its lobster served up with mayonnaise. In Hamburg, oysters are much loved. They are served in restaurants called *Austernstuben*, along with slices of English Cheshire cheese and a glass of dry red wine. Herring is widely eaten, particularly in the state of Schleswig-Holstein. Smoked fish is also popular, as is simply prepared shellfish. Carp is traditionally served on Christmas Eve and Silvester (New Year's Eve).

The Germans have long been traders and travellers, and they have adopted many flavours from other countries. Spices, like cinnamon, cardamom, pepper and allspice, are used in baking and in sweet and sour combinations. Curries are popular, and, because many Turkish immigrants, were invited to work in factories in West Germany after the Second World War, Turkish food is widely eaten.

Potatoes are another common food. They are prepared in many ways, and sometimes two types of potato dish will be served at the same meal. Potatoes are used in soups and stews, in marvellous salads and entrées, and as side dishes. Potato flour is sometimes used as a thickener. Boiled potatoes are a favourite; a rule of German etiquette is that they should be broken up with a fork, and not a knife.

WÜRSTE: THE GERMAN SAUSAGE

The quintessential German food is the sausage. Every part of the country has local *Würste*, and there are about 300 varieties in the German repertoire. A typical *Wurstladen* (sausage shop) will have about 100 types on its price list and 50 to 60 on hand at any given time. Munich is particularly renowned for the choice in its shops. Sausages are served with black bread and butter, with pretzels, radishes and pickled gherkins. They are eaten at all times of the day: as a mid-morning breakfast, a light lunch, an afternoon snack, at dinner or as a late supper.

Würste are named for their ingredients and the way in which they are cooked. *Bratwurst* for example, literally means 'fried sausage'. It is made mostly of coarsely ground pork, sometimes a little veal, and is seasoned with nutmeg, caraway, marjoram, pepper and salt. The *Weisswurst* gets its name from the whiteness of its meat; generally made of veal, it is steamed and eaten hot. A *Blutwurst* is a sausage made with pig's blood; this is sometimes studded with bits of pork or veal tongue and other meat and called *Zungenwurst* (tongue sausage). However, sausages may also be named for their consistency – the *Dauerwurst* (meaning 'hard' or 'lasting' sausage) is smoked, cooked and dried, and can keep for months – or are named after their place of origin – the well-known *Frankfurter* may be coloured with paprika to make a *Debreziner*, named after the Hungarian town Debrecen.

Like potatoes, dumplings, called *Knödel* and *Klösse* interchangeably, are a signature German food. Boiled or steamed, they can constitute a main course or be served as a side dish with meat, fish and vegetables. They come in various sizes and shapes and there are even some dessert dumplings, served with sweet sauces or fruit, particularly in Swabia. When dumplings are cut up into little pieces they are called *Spätzle*.

Soups are eaten by most people once a day in Germany. Usually made with chicken or beef broth, they also contain garnishes, such as dumplings and *Spätzle*. *Teigwaren* are noodle and noodle-derived garnishes, and include the ravioli-like *Maultaschen* and *Riebele* (flecks of noodle dough). Cold fruit soups are refreshing in the summer; in winter, they are made with juices bottled the previous year. A creamy soup made with greens, called 'spring soup', is traditionally eaten on Holy Thursday before Easter.

Game is also widely eaten in Germany. Much of it comes from the Black Forest, in the form of venison, wild boar, hare, pheasant, partridge and grouse. As in neighbouring Alsace, juniper berries are a favourite seasoning. Game is usually accompanied by sweet sauces, such as *Johannisbeergellee* (redcurrant jelly) or cranberry compote, or by cooked fruit, such as pears, pineapples or apples. *Spätzle* are often served with it, as are aromatic wild mushrooms called *Pfifferlinge*. Otherwise, potatoes or noodles will accompany the dish, flavoured with melted butter or bacon fat and paprika, poppy seeds, dill, parsley, diced ham or onion.

Germany is well-known for its baking traditions. Christmas biscuits and the sweet bread, *Stollen*, are appreciated all over the world, but cakes, tortes, pastries, coffee cakes, *Strudels* and dark rye and pumpernickel breads are also made. As in Austria, there is a tradition of having afternoon *Kaffee und Kuchen* (coffee and cake) in *Konditoreien* (coffee houses). In addition to cakes and tarts, Germans love many other rich desserts, like apple pancakes and puddings. Many desserts contain fruit, such as apples, cherries and lemon rind, as well as whipped cream and rum. Rice desserts are popular, as are gelatin puddings.

Food through the day

No matter what the meal is, portions in Germany are large. *Frühstück* (breakfast) is the only exception, usually consisting of bread and coffee with milk. Sometimes a soft-boiled egg is served; schoolchildren might have hot cereal with milk.

A larger meal, *Brotzeit* – literally 'bread time' – is served mid-morning. The contents of this meal vary from region to region: in Munich it is often *Weisswurst* (white sausage) and beer; in Cologne the cheese sandwich, *halber Hahn*, might be served; in Swabia it could be *Vesper* (raw bacon on rye bread) and a glass of kirsch; in other parts of Germany people eat cured ham or *Würste*.

Lunch, served at noon, used to be the big meat-and-potatoes meal of the day and still is in rural areas and places where workers go home for lunch. Nowadays, workers in large cities bring lunch to the office or eat in restaurants, and the main meal is at night. Another snack may be eaten at about 4.30 pm, which could be hot dogs and beer or coffee and cake at a *Konditorei*.

Dinner is usually eaten at about 7 pm. If lunch was big, dinner is light, consisting of a cold cheese-and-meat platter and a rich dessert, or a thick soup and dessert or fruit. Anyone who is awake late at night may eat another snack around 11 pm or later, of sausage and cheese, open sandwiches, goulash soup or coffee and cake.

The Oktoberfest (opposite)
The huge tents at Munich's beer festival can hold up to 10,000 people. This popular event started in 1810 with the marriage of Ludwig of Bavaria to Princess Therese.

SWITZERLAND

Three-fifths of this small country are covered with high Alpine ranges, so it is not surprising that the landscape has shaped almost every aspect of Swiss culture, including its gastronomy.

KEY INGREDIENTS

BACON FAT

FRESHWATER FISH

SAUSAGE

AIR-DRIED BEEF

CHEESE

MILK

POTATOES

PEARS

PLUMS

BERRIES

CHESTNUTS

CHOCOLATE

There are three geographical regions to Switzerland: the Alps, stretching diagonally across the south; the Jura Mountains, along the north-western borders; and, between the two, the midland region – an area of hills, plateaus and valleys cut by rivers and filled with beautiful lakes. Most of the major cities are located here.

Tucked between Germany, France, Austria and Italy, Switzerland has gained much from its location. It has four official languages – Italian, French, German and Romansch – and its position has helped the country to grow into an important economic and technological centre, with one of the highest per capita incomes in the world. The cuisine, too, is suffused with imported flavours.

Like nearby Germany, Switzerland produces many sausages – *Schübling*, *Bratwurst*, *Wienerli*, *Emmentaler*, *Chalberwürst* (a veal sausage) and the French-style *saucisson*. In German-speaking Switzerland, a popular light meal is *Wurstsalat*, a selection of sausage and cheese. Delicate, air-dried beef, called *Bünderfleisch* or *Walliserteller*, is an important product of the mountain regions.

In the Italian-speaking part of Switzerland, the Ticino, signature dishes include many northern Italian specialities: polenta, risottos, pastas and Italian soups are all part of the gastronomic landscape. Rabbit and kid are also popular in this part of the country.

Staple foods

Although much of the food has outside influences, there are many specialities particular to Switzerland. Apart from chocolate (see box, left), the most well-known of these is probably cheese. The country's mountain ranges do not make good farmland, but the fertile midland valleys are used extensively for agriculture. Dairy farming is the main occupation here. The milk of cows, goats and sheep is used to produce world-renowned cheeses, such as Gruyère, Emmenthal and Vacherin. Dishes based on cheese are popular, and the most famous of these is fondue: a dish in which Swiss cheeses are gently melted in wine. Another cheese-based speciality, from the Valais region, is *raclette*, in which mountain cheeses are melted and served with potatoes and pickles. Other cheese specialities include *croûte au fromage* (cheese on toasted bread), *Malakoffs* (cheese fritters) and *chäs-chüechli* (cheese tarts).

As in France and Germany, bread is a staple. In addition to French-style baguettes, there are many crusty, country breads and rich, egg breads,

CHOCOLATE: AND SWISS INNOVATION

Some of the biggest names in chocolate – Suchard, Lindt, Tobler, Nestlé – are Swiss, and the Swiss are great consumers of the confection, each person, on average, eating five times as much as the average American.

The importance of manufacturing here is largely a result of technology. In 1826, Philippe Suchard was the first to use a mixing machine, called a *mélangeur*, in his factory. Another major innovation was that of Henri Nestlé and Daniel Peter who combined evaporated milk with chocolate to make milk chocolate. Rudolphe Lindt invented 'conching', a method of breaking down molecules for a smooth texture.

Muesli *This common breakfast cereal was designed as a health food in the 19th century.*

Fondue *Variations on the cheese fondue include beef dipped in savoury sauces, or bits of fruit or cake dipped in a chocolate fondue.*

Raclette *For this dish, Raclette cheese is traditionally melted over a fire and served with potatoes, bread and pickled vegetables.*

Rösti *Swiss-German potato cakes, which are flattened while browning.*

Bünderfleisch *This Romansch dish consists of air-dried meat, sliced paper thin.*

Papet vaudois *Swiss-French dish of smoked sausage on a bed of leeks and potatoes.*

Busecca *A Swiss-Italian tripe soup.*

Engadiner Nußtorte *A walnut torte from the Romansch regions.*

as well as rich breakfast pastries, like croissants and brioches. The Swiss also have a great dessert pastry tradition.

Switzerland's many lakes and streams provide abundant freshwater fish. Perch is particularly prized; it is poached, steamed, baked, pan-fried or made into dumplings, called *quenelles*. The fish is served simply or with French-style sauces. Little fish from Lake Geneva are deep-fried, and salmon is widely eaten.

The woods and forests on the lower Alpine slopes offer up a wide selection of mushrooms and game. Mushrooms are served on toast, cooked into fragrant risottos and baked into tarts, another popular Swiss dish. Pies and tarts are filled with meat, cheese, vegetables, potatoes and bacon; they are often served on Fridays.

The Swiss also invented muesli, a breakfast cereal consisting of grains – usually finely cut oatmeal – nuts and dried fruit. Muesli is a typical Swiss breakfast; but, depending on the region, breakfasts also mirror their French, German or Italian counterparts.

Food through the day

Swiss dining customs are similar to those of their neighbours. Breakfast can be light and continental-style – with just bread or pastry and coffee, chocolate or tea – or it can be more substantial, particularly in the mountains and in German-speaking Switzerland, where muesli and savoury foods – cheeses and cold meats – are served. Lunch is generally the main meal of the day and is usually a three-course meal with a starter, main dish and dessert. Dinner may be light – soup and/or a savoury tart, or sausage and bread – or it may also be as substantial as the midday meal.

Dairy-based dishes
Many Swiss specialities are based on cheese. Fondue is a dish of melted cheese and wine, which is kept at a slow bubble so that squares of bread can be dipped into the communal pot.

THE LOW COUNTRIES

The eating habits of Belgium, the Netherlands and Luxembourg, which are known for flat and low-lying landscapes, have been shaped principally by their key activities of farming, fishing and trade.

KEY INGREDIENTS

GARLIC

FISH AND SHELLFISH

EEL

BACON

CHICKEN

BEEF

BUTTER

CHEESE

CREAM

ONION

ENDIVE

PLUMS

Seafood bounty
Oysters and mussels from the North Sea join freshwater fish and eels from the rivers and canals.

Located between Germany and France, these countries are collectively named Benelux, after the economic union that Belgium, the Netherlands and Luxembourg formed in 1948. The foods of Belgium and Luxembourg have Germanic and French overtones, while that of Holland is plainer, with Scandinavian influences. The North Sea borders the north-western part of this region, providing abundant fish and seafood.

Belgium

A small, but densely populated country, Belgium has been overrun by many peoples over the centuries, including the Vikings, French, Spanish, Austrians, Dutch, English and Germans. The towns and cities of the north, including Bruges and Ghent, were centres of a thriving textile industry in the Middle Ages, and, through trade with neighbouring countries and the Arabs, foods such as almonds and spices entered the Belgian repertoire. Other legacies of the Middle Ages include a widespread use of mustards, vinegars and dried fruit, and a taste for sweet and sour, and sweet and salty dishes. The Spanish dominated the country for 200 years and left behind a love of saffron.

Belgians boast that their cooking is done with French finesse, but served with German largesse. This describes the food well; it draws upon many French techniques and uses the same ingredients – like butter and cream – but is, by and large, richer than French food. Other ingredients used in Belgian cooking, such as beer, honey and spices, give the food its unique character.

Staple foods

Although only 5 per cent of Belgium is devoted to agriculture, the country is known for its garden vegetables, many of which are exported. One speciality is the Belgian endive, which was accidentally developed by a farmer named Jan Lammers in the 19th century, when his chicory, left in a barn while he went off to war, sprouted white leaves. When he returned he tried some of these leaves and found them to be very tasty. It took some time for endives to catch on, but when they were introduced in Paris in 1872 they were hailed as 'white gold'.

Dairy cattle graze over much of the flat, fertile land, contributing milk, cream and butter to the rich national cuisine. Cheese is another important food – there are over 165 different types produced here.

Cakes, pastries and tortes are found throughout Belgium, as are *gaufres* (waffles), which are made from batter poured onto specially shaped waffle irons. Often beer is added to the batter, resulting in a very light, crisp waffle. Other sweet foods are found in various forms throughout the country, from gingerbread shapes in Dinant to nougat cakes in Bruges. In the Borinage province of south-west Belgium, there is a festival called the Goûter Matrimonial, at which marriageable men and women participate in a feast of fruit pies and rice tortes.

Two other foods that Belgium is known for are chocolate and beer. Local chocolate-makers are renowned for their skill, and their products are delicately and beautifully shaped, containing luxurious fillings, such as ganache, chocolate truffles and nuts. Belgian beers are national treasures. Hundreds of different types are brewed by small artisanal brewers, as well as by the larger national concerns. They range in style, from dark, heavy, malty beers to lighter lagers. Belgians consume more beer than wine and use it in much of their cooking, such as the Flemish beef stew, *carbonnade à la flamande*.

A regional flavour

Even though the country is quite small, there is some regional variation in the cuisine. In Flanders, mussels are farmed up and down the coast. They are served fresh and in copious portions with french fries, in eateries that range from pavement stands to three-star palaces. A key agricultural occupation in Flanders is dairy farming, which has led to a gastronomy that is rich with cream sauces.

In Antwerp, food is cosmopolitan and served with French style, but in the nearby countryside of Kempen, the food is simple, based on speciality garden vegetables such as baby carrots, cauliflowers, beans and peas.

At the edge of the Ardennes is the country's coal country, an area famous for its strawberries, which grow at the foot of slagheaps, and for its *cûtes peüres* (baked bergamot pears). Local plums are used for *quetsch*, a much-loved plum brandy.

The rugged region of the Ardennes has been known since medieval times for being a rich hunting ground. The forests are filled with wild mushrooms and the rivers teem with trout. The

region is known also for raising a special breed of pig, fed on acorns and mountain grass; the pork is smoked over juniper wood to produce the dark, dry *jambon d'ardennes*.

Brussels, the country's capital, is an international food centre, but even here the cuisine is unique with high-quality chocolate, excellent street food, pastries that are richer than their French counterparts, and a strong beer-drinking culture.

Food through the day

Breakfast can include cold meats and cheeses, coffee and bread, or it can be more like the French-style breakfast of coffee and bread or pastry. In the country, people often stop mid-morning for a 'second breakfast', which can be a simple coffee and pastry – raisin bread or honey cake – or something more substantial like *saucisson*. Lunch is the main meal of the day, served around noon; it can consist of three or four courses. Supper is early, usually around 6 pm, and features simple fare like eggs, bread, cheeses, pâtés, sausage or perhaps a soup.

Rue des Bouchers
Brussels is a haven for food lovers. In this 'street of butchers', every building houses a restaurant.

Festive

~~~ FOOD ~~~

Belgium is a devout country, with many religious festivals. People congregate in Furnes and Bruges, for example, for medieval processions, which are legacies of the Spanish. Feasts include generous amounts of black sausage, saffron-hued rice pudding, creamy coffee, hot chocolate and beer.

The Netherlands

Physically the lowest of the Low Countries, the Netherlands is also called Holland, the name of two of its provinces. Located between Germany to the east, Belgium to the south and the North Sea, about one-third of this densely populated country lies below sea level. With a drainage system dating from the Middle Ages, another quarter of the land requires dunes, dykes and regular pumping to prevent flooding.

CHEESE: A CENTURIES-OLD TRADE

Gouda, Edam and Quark are just a few of the Dutch cheeses known throughout the world. The cheese trade here dates back to the Middle Ages, when official weigh-houses and dairy markets were introduced. Though largely a tourist attraction, there is still bidding or haggling at cheese markets, which continue age-old practices.

Haggling, called 'cheese bashing', is highly ritualized. First, the buyer bangs his hand against the cheese to determine the size of the holes. With each subsequent slap of the hand, the offer increases or the farmer's price decreases. When a price is agreed, the cheese is sampled for flavour and age. Then the cheese is weighed and carried off by cheese bearers.

The cheese market
Though largely for the benefit of tourists, bearers still use stretchers to carry the large cheeses and are dressed in the colours of their firms.

Intensive farming on this precious reclaimed land is very important to the Dutch economy. Potatoes are a staple, barley is widely grown, but even more widespread is the production of salad vegetables, like lettuce, tomatoes, cucumbers and peppers, grown in hothouses. These are mainly for export, though they are also consumed locally. Meats and dairy products, mainly butter and cheese, are also major commodities.

With the Netherlands' long coastline on the North Sea, fishing is an important occupation, and herring in particular is a Dutch signature food. The opening of the herring season, on a Saturday in late May, is celebrated with much fanfare. A festival called Vlaggetjesdag ('Flag Day') takes place at Scheveningen, a resort and seaport near The Hague. Ships of all sizes, decked out with flags, parade along the coast, while hundreds of people, dressed in traditional costumes, watch from the dunes. That night the herring fleet has a race to see which ship can net, process (gut, debone and lightly salt) and bring back the first catch of the year. The skipper who wins gets to present the first herrings of the season to the Queen. The nation then delights in the young, delicate, juicy herrings called *groene* or *nieuwe haringen* ('green' or 'new' herring). The fresh, lightly salted herrings are served on ice, with toast and butter. During the season, *nieuwe haringen* are sold from special street carts, decorated with the national tricolour.

For the rest of the year, herring is eaten in various forms, sometimes pickled in brine, which varies in strength and composition: *schmaltz* are herring, pickled with spices and sugars; *Bismarck haringen*, named for the German chancellor, who loved them, are marinated in vinegar, with onions and salt; and *panharingen* have been fried, then pickled in vinegar.

The Dutch are great beer drinkers, and famous for their breweries, such as Heineken, Amstel, Grolsch, Skol and Oranjeboom. The country began importing hops from Germany in the 9th century, and, by the 15th century, they were growing hops and brewing beer. By the 17th century there were 700 breweries in Holland, mostly in the Amsterdam area. In addition to the large companies, there are now many small boutique breweries producing fruitier, more complex beers than the traditional, lighter lagers.

The other national drink of the Netherlands is *jenever*, a spirit made from juniper. Though sometimes referred to as 'Dutch gin', *jenever* is not mixed with water or tonic, but drunk straight. There are two types, *oude* (old) and *jonge* (young). *Oude* has a higher malt content than *jonge*, and consequently a yellowish colour and mellow, aromatic taste. *Jonge* is clear and blander than *oude*. Both are drunk as aperitifs, and sipped at special tasting houses known as *proeflokaalen*, which were established by distilleries to introduce their products to the public and merchants. Bols, founded in 1575, and Heineken are the main distillers of *jenever*.

A taste of history

The 17th century was a golden age for Holland. The success of Dutch spice merchants and sailors led to the creation of an empire that stretched from South-east Asia to the Caribbean. The Netherlands eventually lost control of the sea to England, but retained some of its colonies. Indonesia, for example, only attained its independence from Holland in 1949. Indonesian food is one of the highlights of eating in the Netherlands. Dutch colonials created the *rijsttafel*, meaning 'rice table', an Indonesian buffet, which was meant to show off their wealth. The colonials would serve up banquets with tremendous platters of rice surrounded by up to 60 or 70 different dishes. Indonesia abandoned the *rijsttafels* when it achieved independence, but the term remains in use in the Netherlands.

Food through the day

The Dutch palate is, by and large, a conservative one, and there is not a great deal of variation in the cooking. Meat or fish and potatoes are central to the diet, cooked simply and often served with thick gravies and dairy-based sauces. Smoked and pickled fish, various sausages, cheeses and light and dark breads, are the staple foods.

The Dutch breakfast is a large one, consisting of tea or coffee, bread with lots of butter, cheeses and cold meats. Children sometimes eat porridge. At mid-morning, work stops and coffee is served with a biscuit or pastry. Lunch is a light meal. A typical Dutch lunch is a *Hollandse koffietafel*, at which various breads, cheese, sausages and perhaps one hot dish are served, with many cups of coffee. The meal might be polished off with a piece of fresh fruit. In the afternoon, people might take another break for tea, served with biscuits or cakes.

Dinner is the main meal of the day. Sometimes beginning with an aperitif, it usually consists of soup, followed by fish or meat, accompanied by potatoes and abundant gravy. Dessert can be a sweet bread or noodle pudding, thin pancakes called a *flensje*, or fruit. People drink beer or water with meals, though wine is drunk on special occasions.

Dutch apple cake
A delicious dessert, made with large chunks of apple topped with crumbs and sugar.

Luxembourg

The Grand Duchy of Luxembourg is a tiny country with arguably the highest standard of living in Europe. Bordered by Belgium to the west and north, Germany to the east, and France to the south, there are several different landscapes here despite its small size. The north-western part of the country is part of the densely forested Ardennes region, and is dotted with medieval hilltop castles. Game, mushrooms and honey are abundant here. The countryside to the north-east of the city of Luxembourg, the Müllerthal, is a region of sand-rock formations and woods, and is often called Luxembourg's 'little Switzerland'. Rolling farmland and woods cover the central Gutland, and, in the east, bordered by the Moselle River, is the scenic, wine-producing Moselle River Valley.

Luxembourg's strategic position has meant that the country has been criss-crossed and occupied by many foreign armies. Prussia, Germany, Austria, Holland, Burgundy and Spain have all left their mark. The international element is still reflected in today's population, a third of which holds foreign passports. Workers were initially brought in from other countries to man the iron-ore mines and the steel industry. These industries were superseded by financial companies, but the workers have remained.

Luxembourg's cuisine is most influenced by the cuisines of France and Germany. As with Belgian food, Luxembourgeois cooking combines French finesse with German largesse. However, despite similar ingredients, such as smoke-cured ham, French pastry, pâtés and German sausages, Luxembourg has its own specialities. Its recent immigrants, mainly from Italy and Portugal, have also had an impact on the cooking.

Because of the high standard of living and large international community, there are many fine restaurants in Luxembourg – the country has more Michelin stars per capita than any other country in the world. Most of the starred restaurants feature French food, though some serve traditional Luxembourgeois cuisine. A number of foreign restaurants – Japanese, Italian, Portuguese, Thai, Indian, American and Russian – cater to the international population.

Food through the day

Breakfast here is light and continental style. Coffee, tea or chocolate are drunk with bread or croissants. The main meal is often at midday, unless there is an important dinner to attend or the evening meal is to be in a restaurant. Dinner is light, perhaps an omelette, soup and salad, or sausage and bread.

Mouth-watering waffles
A favourite snack throughout the region, waffles can be small and biscuit-like or large and spongy. Both are often served topped with whipped or sour cream and sugar or strawberries.

FRANCE

Here, there are really two cuisines: haute cuisine, the foundation of fine cooking everywhere; and cuisine bourgeoise, regional home cooking that has evolved from peasant lifestyles. The real flavours of France have their roots in the latter.

KEY INGREDIENTS

BUTTER

STOCK

GARLIC

MUSTARD

BEEF

CHICKEN

GAME

CREAM

CHEESE

ONIONS

LEEKS

WINE

The rural way of life is important in France. Despite widespread difficulties, one in sixteen Frenchmen still works in agriculture. The cuisine revolves around their labours and that of artisans who craft farmers' goods, such as crusty breads, pastries, charcuterie and cheeses. Even people who have migrated to cities retain ties with their regions of origin and, though they may now do their shopping at the *hypermarché* (supermarket), they usually buy seasonal produce at markets and cook the dishes they grew up eating.

Bread has always been the staple here; it is so important that its price is regulated. But the quality of French bread has deteriorated over the years, and only a handful of artisanal bakeries are still devoted to turning out excellent loaves. Meat and fish are widely eaten, as are vegetables, which play a much more important role in home cooking than they do in haute cuisine.

France is one of the biggest and wealthiest countries in Europe. Sometimes referred to as *l'Hexagone* because of its shape, France shares borders with Spain, Italy, Switzerland, Luxembourg, Belgium and Germany. A fertile country with long rivers and a variety of landscapes, there are 22 official regions, each with its own identity. Some have their own dialects, such as Alsatian, Flemish and Provençal; all have a distinctive cuisine.

Despite these differences, however, all French cuisine is connected by its deep flavours and its ability to satisfy the senses – a result of refined cooking techniques and impeccable ingredients. The ingredients are often simple; the French do not rely on pungent spices and aromatics to achieve strong tastes. It is their techniques that bring out the essence of food. Sauces are the glory of French cooking; they enrich, enhance and complement dishes, and transform ordinary economical meals into memorable ones. Stocks made from meat, bones and aromatics are literally the foundation – though many great French dishes don't require them.

Although French cuisine has a very strong identity, there have been some outside influences exerted on the cooking. Workers have come from Italy, Spain, Portugal and, most recently, from North Africa and the former French colonies. This has not greatly altered French culinary habits; however, North African food is quite easy to find in cities like Paris and Lyons, and throughout the south. Southern French cooking is Mediterranean and there are Arab inflections in the southwest.

Food through the day

Eating and mealtimes are fairly consistent throughout the north, west and centre. Breakfast is a light meal, usually eaten between 7 and 9 am. Strong coffee with milk, hot chocolate or tea are

the habitual beverages, taken with buttered bread and jam, or a pastry such as a croissant, brioche, or *pain au chocolat* (chocolate-filled pastry). In cities many people have their breakfast in cafés.

Until quite recently the midday meal was the main meal of the day, and this is still true in some rural areas. Even in cities, where eating on the run has caught on with alacrity in recent years, many people still sit down to a three-course meal in a café or a restaurant. A typical French meal begins with a salad, charcuterie, soup, a vegetable tart or quiche; the main course is meat or fish with a vegetable garnish. Cheese and/or dessert follows. The French like their desserts, and they have a large repertoire to choose from. Wine and water are the usual beverages, and a demitasse or a herbal tea invariably ends the meal. Bread is always present at the French table.

If lunch was a light one, dinner will be the main meal of the day and will be like the meal described above. Just as often, however, dinner is light: a soup with bread or charcuterie and a salad, followed by cheese and perhaps dessert; or it could be meat or fish.

The north and west

These regions of France stretch from the borders with Germany, in the east, and Belgium, in the north, all the way to the Atlantic coast. The foods of each region often reflect these neighbours and their surroundings and all are unique. This part of France also includes Paris, with its concentration of some of the best regional specialities from all over France.

Champagne, Le Nord and Picardy

The region of Champagne extends from Chablis in the north of Burgundy to the Belgian border. Although primarily known for its great sparkling wines, it is actually more of a wheat and cereal growing region, with only 5 per cent of the land devoted to viticulture.

The cuisine here is hearty and simple; specialities include *andouillettes* (small tripe sausages) and ham from the Ardennes, which is the same dried ham that is enjoyed across the border in Belgium. Boiled dinners with lots of cabbage and other vegetables, called *potée champenoise*, are common. The lakes and streams from the southern part of the region provide cooks with trout and other freshwater fish.

To the north and west of Champagne, Le Nord, which includes Picardy and Flanders, is a region of unstable weather influenced by the windy English Channel; the food is accordingly rich and warming. Belgian Flanders extends into France here, and the foods of the two countries have much in common. Beer is widely drunk, and it is used in cooking the same dishes that are cooked in Belgium, like *carbonnade* and *coq à la bière*. Shellfish from the English Channel and North Sea – particularly mussels and oysters – is a mainstay. As in Belgium, *moules-frites* (mussels and chips) is a local dish. Endives, which originated in Belgium, are a speciality and are known by their Belgian name, *witloof*, meaning 'white leaf'.

Fresh salmon
Fish, such as this delicate salmon, are used in many classic French dishes, often poached and served with *beurre blanc* – a style for which both Angers and Nantes claim credit.

Cakes and pastries (opposite)
Specialized *patisseries* throughout France sell marvellous pastries, tarts, gateaux and other sweet baked goods.

Artichoke harvest
The farmland around Brittany is known for its tasty globe artichokes, called *gros camus de Léon*.

Sugar beets are the main crop of Picardy. Napoleon experimented with extracting sugar from beets to get around the English embargo on sugar in the 19th century. His success established French 'sugar independence', and most of the country's sugar still comes from the fields of Picardy. Locals have consequently developed a love of sweet foods. Hard sweets are popular, particularly the mint-flavoured *bêtises* from Cambrai. Sugar is widely used in cooking, even in beef stews and with vegetables like cabbage.

Potatoes are another staple of Le Nord. Antoine-Auguste Parmentier, who led a campaign in the late 18th century to get the French to adopt the potato instead of bread as their staple, came from Picardy. He didn't fully succeed with his mission, but the potato did become established as the most popular vegetable in France.

Alsace-Lorraine

A narrow region bounded on the west by the Vosges Mountains and on the east by the Rhine, Alsace was for centuries part of Germany, until the Treaty of Münster in 1648. For the next 300

years the region was passed back and forth between the two countries. It has been French since the end of the Second World War.

Linguistically and culturally, Alsace shares much with Germany. The Alsatian dialect is a German one, the architecture is Bavarian, with half-timbered houses adorned with geranium-filled window boxes, and the food, such as its vast array of charcuterie, has much in common with that of its neighbour. Sauerkraut with all the pork trimmings is the region's signature dish. Dining in Alsace is informal and convivial; where there are wine bars in the rest of France, there are *winstubs* here. As in other areas with a combined German and French influence, Alsatian cooking exhibits both the robustness of German food and the subtle refinements of French cuisine.

The soil in Alsace is rich, and the agricultural output abundant. The region's products are celebrated with village festivals throughout the year – there are grape and harvest festivals; a cheese and folklore festival; a cheesecake festival; a sauerkraut festival; a redcurrant festival; an onion festival; and fairs that honour turnips, frogs, herrings, pâtés and snails.

Alsace is known for its foie gras and its pâté de foie gras. Foie gras is eaten plain, but also used by local chefs as an ingredient in other dishes. The tradition of force-feeding geese and ducks to fatten their livers has always been a speciality of Jewish farmers. Today, though, about a third of the livers processed in Alsace are imported from Hungary, Bulgaria, Poland and Israel.

Lorraine, to the west of Alsace on the other side of the Vosges, is a country of rolling pastures and farms. The region has been important since the Middle Ages as a source of salt, a valuable commodity in the past due to its preserving characteristics. Much of the area's wealth was derived from its trade in salt, and today there are still more than 20 working *salines*.

Game is important in both Lorraine and Alsace. The forests around Ribeauvillé and Riquewihr supply game not only to local cooks but to top chefs throughout France. Freshwater fish from the River Ill include pike, perch, eel and roach. Carp, from ponds of Sundgau in the south, is also popular. A freshwater fish stew, called *matelote alsacienne*, is the best-known fish dish in the region. Snails, crayfish and frogs' legs are also widely eaten, though now much of the supply is imported.

Alsace has a home-baking tradition that is unique in France. Local breads include rye breads with caraway seeds, a dense, dried pear and fruit bread called *berawecka* or *bierwecke*, and a fluted, yeasted cake called *kugelhopf*. Alsatians also bake wonderful thin-crusted main-dish and dessert tarts.

The famous cheese from this region is Münster, a strong cow's milk cheese, made in the Vosges mountains in the summer and early autumn. It is aged to varying degrees, and goes perfectly with the wines of the region, particularly Gewürztraminer.

Normandy

Settled in the 9th century by Vikings – Norsemen who gave the Normans their name – Normandy is a rainy region of beaches and chalky cliffs, of lush green, rolling pastures, apple orchards and farms. It is a land of farmers and sailors, with a cuisine that is a mix of delicate dishes based on cream and butter, and nutritious peasant fare based on earthy ingredients like tripe, charcuterie and *graisse à la normande* (pork and beef fat simmered with vegetables and herbs).

Norman fishermen supply the region and much of the rest of France with many kinds of fish and shellfish. Sole is prized here, and other popular fish include plaice, lemon sole, mussels, prawns, crabs and oysters. Norman towns lend their names to various fish preparations, such as *sole à la dieppoise*, a preparation that includes shrimp, mussels, mushrooms and cider or white wine, and *les demoiselles de Cherbourg*, baby lobsters served with bouillon flavoured with calvados brandy.

The northernmost department in Normandy is the Manche, a name that refers to the English Channel which surrounds it on three sides. Some of the food here overlaps with that of neighbouring Brittany, such as *présalé* lamb, delicate-tasting lamb that has fed on the salt marshes around Le Mont-Saint-Michel, and *morue à la cherbourgeoise*, salt cod with potatoes and onions. This part of Normandy is known for earthy dishes, such as *andouillette* and *andouille*, sausages made with pig stomach and intestines.

The eastern Norman department of the Calvados is dairy and apple country. Black-and-white cows are prized for their meat and their high milk yield. The local butter is wonderful. The top of the line is Isigny butter, which is sold in wooden containers; a sweet butter with a low whey content, it is ideal for puff pastry. Other dairy products include some of France's most highly regarded cheeses: Camembert, Livarot, Pont-l'Evêque and Brillat-Savarin.

Brittany

France's westernmost region, Britanny juts out into the Atlantic, with the English Channel to the north and the Bay of Biscay to the south. The

CAFÉS AND BRASSERIES: EVERYDAY TREATS

The Paris café was created by people from the Massif Central during the 19th century. At this time, many poverty-stricken peasants were forced to leave the region and seek work in the city. They made a living selling firewood and coal from small shops that doubled as wine shops, and these eventually grew into cafés. Much of the Paris catering trade is still owned by Auvergnats and their descendants.

The brasserie, on the other hand, is a creation from Alsace. This is a region of beer drinkers as well as wine drinkers, so these large, informal restaurants specialize in both drinks, as well as simple French dishes. Brasseries are a fixture throughout France, and many still have Alsatian connections.

CRÊPES: FROM BRITTANY

Well-known throughout France, crêpes here benefit from the region's high-quality eggs, butter and milk. Savoury crêpes, called *galettes,* are made with buckwheat flour; sweet crêpes, are made with wheat flour. *Galettes* are topped or filled with various foods, including Gruyère cheese, ham, spinach and seafood. Jam, honey, apple purée and chocolate are the most common toppings for sweet crêpes. In crêperies, these light pancakes are usually served with regional cider. However, locals traditionally dip their warm crêpes into *lait ribot* (buttermilk).

westernmost administrative department is called Finistère, meaning the 'end of the earth'. Between the two coasts is fertile farmland and the forest of Paimpont, a reputed home of King Arthur and his knights. The Gauls gave this land the name of Amor, which means 'the country by the sea'; this name echoes in the names of dishes such as *homard à l'armoricaine* (lobster in a tomato and shallot-based sauce). The people here were called Bretons because they had originally come from Britain after Anglo-Saxon invasions.

Along the north and south coasts of Brittany there are many bays and inlets, which provide perfect environments for oysters, scallops and mussels. Farther out in the shoals, lobsters thrive – both the big Atlantic *homards* and the smaller, clawless *langoustes.* Bretons have always been a seafaring people; for hundreds of years Breton fleets have fished for cod as far away as Greenland and the Newfoundland banks. Local fishermen go out daily in small, colourful boats. When they return in the afternoon, the wholesale fish markets begin. Throughout the restaurants of this region, fish and seafood are served incredibly fresh and unadulterated: raw oysters and other *fruits de mer* (shellfish) are presented on huge platters lined with seaweed; and mussels are steamed, gratinéed or made into soup. Scallops

from the bay of Saint-Brieuc on the north coast are considered the best in France.

Brittany's ports were important until Napoleonic times, and there was much trading with Mediterranean, Indian and, later, with New World merchants. Salt was the region's most valuable commodity (sea salt from the Guérande Peninsula is still an important product of Brittany), providing Europe with most of its supply during the Middle Ages. It was traded for oranges and dried fruits, wines and spices. Spices were made up into curry mixtures by apothecaries, and the seasoning became part of the traditional cuisine. This is why today dishes like *homard au cari* (lobster with curry sauce) are seen on many Breton menus. Mediterranean ingredients like tomatoes, garlic, olive oil and saffron were also incorporated into some local dishes. *Bouillabaisse des kermokos* is one such dish, which takes its name from the word *kermokos,* used to describe the children of Breton sailors and Provençal women.

For the most part, the cooking here is the simple food of poor country people, adorned with only the best local butter and cream. The region is well known for its produce, particularly its huge globe artichokes and its strawberries. Over 20 different kinds of strawberries are grown in the Plougastel region, near Brest, and every village has a strawberry tart recipe. Country people make porridges and polenta-like *fars,* which use oats, wheat flour, barley or buckwheat flour. The batter for one type of *far* is poured into a linen bag, which is tied and simmered for several hours in a *pot-au-feu,* with which it is served. The best known *far* is the *far breton,* a rich prune flan that is found all over Brittany.

Paris and the Ile de France
Paris and its suburbs – the Ile de France is the area within a 50-km radius of Notre Dame – have sprawled over the years, overtaking land that, until recently, was all agricultural. *Maraichers* (market gardens) used to supply Paris with much of the city's fruit and vegetables, and many French dishes are named for the once-famous produce of specific towns – Montmorency for its

cherries, Clamart for its peas and Chantilly for its cream. Cultivated mushrooms, *champignons de Paris*, now grown in the Loire Valley, were once grown in caves outside of the city.

Although much of this production is now gone due to urban sprawl, there are still many farms just outside of Paris. No matter how many supermarkets spring up in and around the city, each neighbourhood still has its weekly or bi-weekly market, where local farmers sell their fruit and vegetables.

In Paris you can find all of the best regional foods of France: cheeses, wines, breads, pastry and cold meat products. Charcuteries sell not only pork products but also classic prepared dishes such as quiches, pizza, terrines, *pâtés en croûtes* and *galantines* (stuffed meat rolls) This is take-away food at its best; many of the

The *boulangerie*
Parisian bakers sell many different regional breads. This one specializes in dense, sourdough, country bread, *pain de campagne*.

SIGNATURE DISHES

Tarte flambée *A cream, bacon and onion tart from Alsace-Lorraine.*

Pot-au-feu *The name of this boiled meat and vegetable dish is literally 'pot on fire'.*

Plateau de fruits de mer *This shellfish platter is a speciality of brasseries.*

Moules marinières *This dish of steamed mussels originates in Brittany.*

Steak frites *The quintessential Paris meal of strip steak with chips.*

Andouillettes à la lyonnaise *The Lyonnais-style tripe sausage is stuffed with veal and served with fried onions.*

Ravioles au chèvre *Ravioli filled with goat's cheese from Val d'Isère.*

Clafoutis *This baked fruit custard is usually made with cherries.*

---

charcuteries specialize in food of a particular area, and along with the prepared meats and salads, they sell local dishes like *choucroute garnie* – an Alsatian speciality.

A city of cafés and tea salons, bakeries and *patisseries*, wine bars, bistros, brasseries and fine restaurants, Paris is home to some of France's greatest chefs, many with two or three Michelin stars. Chefs from all over the world come to train here, in restaurants and at cooking schools.

The Loire Valley and the Sologne

A country of chateaux and refinement, the Loire Valley is one of France's most fertile regions, providing the country with much of its fruit, vegetables, grains and some highly regarded red and white wines. Vast grain fields spread through the north-eastern part of the region, giving way to rolling, soft countryside. It is often said that the purest French is spoken in the Loire, and the same can be said of the cuisine: it is pure, classic French – for example, poached salmon and other Loire river fish with *beurre blanc*, local white asparagus, fresh goat's cheese and game from the forests of the Sologne.

Outside the main cities of Orléans, Tours and Angers, much of the Loire and Sologne is agricultural. Crops include wheat, millet and beetroot, and melons, pears and raspberries. Mushrooms are cultivated in caves near Saumur, where there are many troglodyte dwellings, which were built into the volcanic rock along the

HERBS AND SPICES

CHERVIL this delicate herb brings a sweet, aniseed-like flavour to dishes

CHIVES a mild, oniony herb, one of the *fines herbes* added to omelettes and salads

PARSLEY an essential element of the chopped, mixed *fines herbes* added at the end of recipes or in quickly cooked dishes

TARRAGON combines with classic chicken dishes. This is the key ingredient in *sauce béarnaise*

Loire. During the Renaissance, huge rocks were cut out of the stone to build the great chateaux and cathedrals, and the resulting caves were perfect places for cellaring wine.

The Renaissance nobility were attracted to the region because of the hunting in the game-rich forests of the Sologne, south of Orléans. They filled the moats of their chateaux with carp and their chefs came up with some of France's more elaborate haute cuisine dishes like *carpe à la Chambord*, stuffed carp garnished with *quenelles* (light dumplings), truffles, fluted mushrooms and fried caviar. Hunting is still an important pastime here between the first of October and the end of February; this is the season for duck, pheasant, partridge, deer and quail.

Freshwater fish from the Loire is one of the great delicacies of the region. Perch, sandre, pike, lamprey, eel, herring and salmon are plentiful. Eel is stewed in local wine to make the dish *fricassée d'anguille*, and *civelles* (baby eels) are commonly cooked in oil and butter. Between spring and autumn *friture de la Loire* (small deep-fried fish) are a speciality.

Orléans, in the easternmost part of the region, is France's vinegar capital. This evolved because wine produced in the region, before rapid transport, had often soured by the time it reached this important city. Businessmen turned the spoiled wine to profit by making it into vinegar. Another product of Orléans and its environs is *pain d'épices* (spiced honey bread).

The Loire is wine and goat's cheese country. Regional goat's cheeses include: Selles-sur-Cher, a soft, fresh goat's cheese, sometimes sprinkled with powdered charcoal; the pyramid-shaped Pouligny-Saint-Piere; Sainte-Maure Fermier, which has a straw running through it; and the cheese disks called Crottin de Chavignol, which can be aged or fresh. Vineyards in the Loire extend from its Brittany frontier, the Pays Nantais on the Atlantic, to Sancerre and Pouilly-sur-Loire in Burgundy. The wines are fresh and uncomplicated, both white and red. They can be drunk early and many age well.

The day's catch
These fish, caught in Lake Haute-Saôn in the Franche Comté, will be on the local market stalls by afternoon.

Atlantic Coast and Bordeaux

From the Vendée and Poitou-Charentes regions south of Brittany to the town of Arcachon, south of Bordeaux, the land is flat and fertile, ripe for the grapes that make the great Bordeaux wines. The Atlantic offers an abundance of oysters and mussels, raised in large beds along the coast. Eels and snails are also specialities here. Farmers grow highly esteemed garlic, used in many local dishes, particularly roast goat. They also grow special white beans called *mojettes*, which are served, both dried and fresh, with ham. Over 50 varieties of goat's cheese are produced here.

Earth and sea come together in the cooking of the Atlantic region. This is embodied in one of the area's signature dishes, *huîtres à la charentaise*, made from local oysters with spicy sausage. The Vendée and Poitou produce excellent beef and dairy cattle, goat, lamb, poultry and vegetables. South of the Vendée and Poitou is the province of Charentes, which, alongside cognac, produces some of the best butter in France.

The *fromagerie* (*opposite*)
Over 300 varieties of cheese are produced in France. The goat's cheeses sold at this market in the Loire are a regional speciality.

Burgundy vineyards
The vintners of this region make fine wines according to traditions that date back to the Middle Ages.

The prosperous city of Bordeaux sits on the Garonne River, where it converges with the Dordogne river in the Gironde estuary. From the 12th to the 15th centuries this was a disputed area, violently fought over by England and France. Although France eventually resumed control, there has always been an important trade relationship with England, particularly in the wine business. Bordeaux became wealthy through wine, a legacy of the Romans who originally planted the vineyards south of Bordeaux, and the English, who, when they held sway in the area, encouraged viticulture.

Dordogne

The cooking of the Dordogne is much like that of south-western France. Also known by its ancient name of Périgord, this is a rich, green country, where agriculture is key. The Dordogne river winds through a valley of sheer cliffs and caves decorated with prehistoric paintings. Perched on the cliffs are dramatic chateaux built in the

Middle Ages, vestiges of the French–English wars. It is a country of unchanged medieval villages and a rural way of life.

The Périgord has long been a region of small farms, where people raise geese, ducks, pigs, chickens, maize and tobacco. This is the largest walnut-producing region in France, and the oil from the nut is used in everyday cooking. The walnuts are pressed in the mills dotting the region's many streams. Walnut oil is particularly noticeable in salads and local cakes.

Historically, many of the farmers were sharecroppers who passed small parcels of land down the generations. Recently, the government has encouraged the consolidation of holdings and the farming of cash crops like tobacco.

Food here is rich and rustic, but even simple dishes can be adorned with the region's luxurious specialities, foie gras and truffles. The term *à la périgourdine* refers to a peasant recipe that has been refined by the addition of truffles and/or foie gras: eggs stuffed with foie gras are *oeufs à la périgourdine*; *cou d'oie farci à la périgourdine* is goose neck, with the skin filled with minced pork, goose, foie gras and chopped truffles; and *poulet à la périgourdine* is chicken stuffed with foie gras and truffles, flavoured with cognac.

The Dordogne is also a land of goose fat, which is used for cooking and for *confit d'oie* (meat and gizzards in rendered fat). Goose rind flavours soups and is eaten as an aperitif. Duck foie gras is also produced here, and duck *confit* is a regional mainstay. The breasts of both goose and duck are widely eaten, cooked rare like beef.

The 'black diamond' of Périgord and nearby Quercy is the black truffle. The region supplies about 70 per cent of French truffles. Cèpes and other wild mushrooms are also treasures. They are cooked in omelettes and ragouts, and used as a garnish for meat and poultry.

Central France

The regions of Central France have widely varied landscapes of lush vineyards, rolling hills and snow-capped mountains. This area includes Burgundy, Lyons and its environs, which are considered by many to be the gastronomic heart of France.

Burgundy and the Lyonnais

A country of flat land in the north, limestone hills around Chablis, rugged forest towards the centre, and lush vineyards in the south and east, the Duchy of Burgundy was once more powerful than the Kingdom of France. During the 14th and 15th centuries, under the rule of the Dukes of Valois, its territory stretched as far as Belgium and the Netherlands.

Dijon, once the seat of the Dukes of Burgundy, is the administrative seat of the region. Every year, during the first two weeks of November, it hosts an international food fair, where Burgundian specialities, like *jambon persillé* and *coq au vin*, are judged. Dijon's specialities include mustard and crème de cassis (a blackcurrant syrup). Kir, the aperitif made with white wine and cassis, evolved here as a way to use up inferior white wines.

Lyons, south of Mâcon, is thought by some to be the gastronomic capital of France. The surrounding regions supply fine raw ingredients, such as Dauphiné cream, Bresse poultry, and Auvergne lamb. Beaujolais is the wine of the Lyonnais, and a characteristic snack is called *le mâchon*, an assortment of cooked pork meats and sometimes pan-fried tripe, washed down with a pitcher of Beaujolais. The area is known for its sausage, and produces an impressive assortment of charcuterie, including the long *rosette de Lyon*

■ BRANDIES AND LIQUEURS: A REGIONAL TASTE

JUST AS THE FOOD VARIES FROM REGION TO REGION IN FRANCE, SO TOO DO THE FLAVOURS OF SOPHISTICATED BRANDIES AND LIQUEURS. ALSACE, RICH IN ORCHARDS, PRODUCES *EAUX DE VIE*, CLEAR, FRUIT BRANDIES, WHICH ARE AMONG THE BEST IN FRANCE. IN NORMANDY OVER 100 VARIETIES OF APPLE ARE GROWN. THOSE THAT ARE UNFIT FOR CONSUMPTION ARE OFTEN DISTILLED FOR CALVADOS. FURTHER SOUTH, THE FLAT, FERTILE LAND OF THE ATLANTIC COAST IS PERFECT FOR THE GRAPES THAT MAKE THE FINE COGNAC FROM CHARENTE AND BRANDY FROM ARMAGNACS. IN THE DORDOGNE, THE LARGEST WALNUT-PRODUCING REGION IN FRANCE, LOCALS MAKE A STRONG, DARK LIQUEUR BY MACERATING THE NUTS IN BRANDY. THE FRANCHE-COMTÉ, ON THE SWISS BORDER, IS THE HOME OF KIRSCH, MADE FROM WILD CHERRIES. OTHER *EAUX DE VIE* AND LIQUEURS ARE ALSO MADE HERE; NEAR GRENOBLE, FOR EXAMPLE, CARTHUSIAN MONKS STILL MAKE THE CENTURIES-OLD LIQUEUR, CHARTREUSE.

and *sabodets* made from pork, beef, pig's head and skin. Earthy food like pig's trotters, crackling and sow's ears are popular in bars and bistros. Lyons is also a city of rotisseries, restaurants specializing in roast meats.

Bresse, south of Dijon and east of Lyons, has always been famous for its chicken. Bresse chickens are free-range, maize-fed chickens that live in a special finishing room drinking milk and eating maize during the last 15 days of their lives. They are sold with special bands on their legs to denote their place of origin. A mature chicken from Bresse is a *poularde de Bresse*; a younger chicken is a *poulet de Bresse*. When cooked with truffles or morels (a type of mushroom) inserted under the skin, it is called *poularde* (or *poulet*) *demi-deuil*; when cooked in a pig's bladder it is *poularde en vessie*.

Jura, Franche Comté and the Alps

This is rugged mountain terrain and, as in nearby Switzerland and Italy, it is dairy country. Some of France's noblest cheeses, like Beaufort, Comté, Morbier, Vacherin and Saint Marcellin, are made here. The cows go to pasture between mid-June and the end of September, and the best cheese is made during this period.

Villages still have working bread ovens here, where huge, dense loaves are made. In some villages breads are only made a few times a year. The bread is dried, and moistened in soups and stews before serving.

The mountains are also sausage country. There are many kinds of local sausage, much of it smoked. Twice a year, on 11 November (St Martin's Day) and the week preceding Ash Wednesday, farmers slaughter pigs and make smoked hams, bacon and sausages. The best known is *saucisse de Morteau*. *Saucisse aux choux*, (sausage with cabbage) is eaten on New Year's Eve. *Bresi*, which is smoked and salted beef served in paper-thin slices with bread and butter, is another regional delicacy.

The French Alps contain lakes filled with freshwater fish. Its forests abound with wild strawberries, raspberries, cranberries and mushrooms. Orchards fill the valleys. There are Italian and Swiss influences in the cooking here, with rich pastas and cheese dishes like fondue and *raclette*.

Some rare and fine wines are produced in the Jura around Arbois. The most famous is a sherry-like wine is called *vin jaune*. The fruity white wines made in Savoie go well with the area's rich, creamy foods.

The centre

This part of France encompasses several regions: flat Berry in the north-west; the more rolling countryside of Bourbonnais; hilly Limousin to the west, which has much in common gastronomically with south-west France; and, at its heart, Auvergne in the Massif Central.

The sparsely populated Auvergne is remote and mountainous, rugged and poor, and the cuisine appropriately nourishing, based on foods like mountain hams and sausages, country cheeses and rustic rye breads. Streams and rivers are rich in salmon trout and a related species, *omble chevalier*. Forests supply game and wild blueberries, morels and cocherelle mushrooms. This is charcuterie country. Every family has a pig or two, and each year the pig is slaughtered so that every part of its body can be used; blood is used for blood sausage, the organs are frozen, and the rest of the meat is used for fresh and dried sausages, salt pork, hams and pâtés.

Le Puy is famous for its lentils – a small green variety, which are cooked with regional sausages and salt pork. Laguiole, in the Aubrac plateau, gives its name to a cheese, and the town also makes wooden-handled, folding knives that are sold all over France. To the west of the Aubrac plateau is an area known as the Châtaigneraie, or chestnut grove. Chestnuts are used extensively in meat and poultry dishes. Here stockfish (dried cod) is traditional, a legacy from the times when this was the only fish to be had on Fridays. It is cooked with eggs, cream, potatoes, and garlic for *estofinado*, a dish normally associated with the Mediterranean.

The Auvergne produces some marvellous cheeses, including Salers, Saint-Nectaire, Bleu d'Auvergne and Cantal. The last of these comes

Camargue rice
A chewy, slightly nutty flavoured rice is grown in the Camargue region, where the salt marshes and flat, wide plains are well suited to its cultivation.

from the Monts du Cantal, a group of extinct volcanoes, with grassy slopes that make perfect grazing pastures. Every spring the cowherders take their cows up the mountains to graze at altitude. The best Cantal is Salers, made from the milk of Salers cows. One of the Auvergne's signature dishes is *aligot*, a garlic-rich mix of potatoes and the whey of Cantal cheese.

Some of the oldest vineyards in France are around Saint-Pourçain-sur-Sioule. The robust wine goes well with the hearty local food. A third of the bottled water drunk in France comes from the Bourbonnais and the Auvergne. Vichy is the best-known and largest spa.

The Berry is a land of plains, woods and marshland. Wild produce, such as fish, frogs, mushrooms and berries, have always supplemented the cuisine here. Sheep and goats are raised for meat and cheese. Berrichon lamb is highly regarded, and the area's well-known goat's cheeses include Valençay.

The Limousin, to the west of the Auvergne, is a stock-breeding and chestnut-growing region. *Boudin aux châtaignes* (black pudding with chestnuts) is a speciality of the Limousin. The region gives its name to a chestnut-eating breed of pig, a sheep breed and a small reddish cow highly regarded for its meat. It is the home of one of France's classic desserts, the *clafoutis*, which is called *milliard* in the Auvergne.

Provence

The eastern end of this French region juts up from the Mediterranean into the Alpes-Maritimes, continuing into the rugged Alpes-de-Haute-Provence. As you move west, the terrain moves gently away from the sea into hills, where fruit trees, vineyards and lavender commingle; then it climbs into the mountains that inspired Cézanne. The Rhône delta spreads into the flat plains of the Camargue, an area that produces cattle and, more recently, rice. This is cowboy country where bull-meat is a great delicacy.

The gastronomic constants of Provence stretch from the coast to its northern limit. They include: olive oil, garlic, salt cod, anchovies and

SIGNATURE DISHES

Tapenade *An olive paste, made with capers, anchovies, garlic and herbs.*

Anchoiade *A seasoned anchovy paste, usually spread on garlic-rubbed croutons.*

Aioli *The* aioli monstre *is a feast in which a variety of vegetable, egg and cod dishes are served with this garlic mayonnaise.*

Soupe au pistou *A thick vegetable and bean soup, enriched with a pesto-like basil paste, called* pistou.

Pissaladière *The onions for this pizza are cooked with the* pissalat *(capers) until soft, then spread over the crust.*

Artichauts à la Barigoule *This fragrant artichoke stew can be eaten hot or cold.*

Nougat *This chewy confection is made with almonds, honey and egg whites.*

goat's cheese. Seasonal fruits used are figs, cherries, peaches, apricots, sweet melons, strawberries and quinces. Popular vegetables of the region include tomatoes, aubergines, onions, summer and winter squash, artichokes and leafy greens. Local aromatic herbs, used as seasonings, are thyme, rosemary, sage, bay laurel, basil, fennel and parsley.

On the coast, fish dishes are plentiful and are made from the morning's catch, sold daily on the pier of practically every seaside village. The most famous of these is the nourishing fish stew called bouillabaisse. As you get closer to Italy, particularly in Nice and its environs, dishes begin to resemble those of adjacent Liguria, with an abundance of pasta, pizza, gnocchi and basil-scented sauces. During the first half of the 19th century, Nice bounced back and forth between France and the Italian house of Savoy. In 1860, it voted to become part of France, but its cuisine retained elements that we associate with Italy. An Italian ravioli, however, could never be confused with the ravioli of Nice. This is filled with *daube*

Festive

~~~ FOOD ~~~

Le gros souper *is the traditional Christmas Eve dinner of Provence. A repas maigre – meaning it doesn't contain meat – it is a feast nonetheless. Every dish is traditional, and each detail filled with symbolism. The meal always ends with the '13 desserts'. These desserts are innately Provençal; they are simple and unadorned. The number probably symbolizes the number of Christ and his apostles. Pompe à l'huile, an olive oil and orange-flower-scented bread, is always present, as are dried fruit and nuts, and oranges or tangerines. Dates, pâte de coings (quince jelly) and candied fruits are big treats at the Christmas table.*

(beef stew), with ricotta cheese, known as *brousse*, or with pork and Swiss chard. Nor is the distinctly Provençal onion pizza called *pissaladière* typical of its neighbour to the east. Many other dishes in the Comté de Nice are rarely seen in other parts of Provence: the chickpea-flour pancake called *socca*, double-crusted vegetable and rice tortes, batter-fried vegetables and squash blossoms, named *beignets*, stuffed vegetables known as *farcis Niçois*, and polenta-like *panisses* made with chickpea flour.

As you move north into the thyme and rosemary-covered mountains of the interior, fish gives way to lamb, rabbit and hearty meat stews.

Harvest in Provence
All of the fresh vegetables required to make ratatouille, a popular Provençal dish, are for sale on this open air market stall.

Although today's economy has brought an abundance of meat into Provençal supermarkets, it used to be scarce and of a sinewy quality but ideally suited to long stewing. As the country climbs into a more severe Alpine, landlocked region, olive oil gives way to walnut oil, butter and lard. Grains, and potatoes, cooked into filling, cheese-topped gratins, are important staple in the mountains of Provence.

A taste of history
Provence, like the rest of southern Europe, has absorbed elements of the cuisines of its neighbours, its trading partners and its immigrants. Saffron and hot peppers arrived long ago from the eastern Mediterranean, through the ever-important western Mediterranean port of Marseilles. Tomatoes came from the Americas via Italy, and Nice's taste for sweet and savoury combinations is informed by the cuisines of the eastern Mediterranean and North Africa. During the first half of the 20th century, the largest wave of immigration came from southern Italy; so, in addition to the pizzas and pastas of Nice we find Neapolitan-style pizza and pasta throughout the region. In the last 35 years, the cuisine has been most influenced by North African immigrants, and by the colonials who returned to France after the Algerian war and brought their beloved dishes like couscous with them.

The gastronomic traditions of Provence have also been influenced by the Christian calendar. As in Greece and Italy, cycles of fasting follow cycles of feasting. On the fasting days – Fridays and during Lent – fish is eaten instead of meat or, in the interior, salt cod and legumes (beans, lentils or peas) replace fresh fish. Villages all over Provence celebrate their patron saints, from spring through to the autumn equinox, with huge feasts, where tables groan with great platters of salt cod and vegetables served with aioli (garlic mayonnaise), *daube* and vegetable gratins.

Food through the day
Breakfast in Provence is light, as it is throughout the rest of France. *Café au lait* or tea is drunk with bread or croissants. Locally made fruit jams and the many honeys produced throughout the region make luxurious condiments.

In the past, workers took bread to the fields or to the olive oil mills for their mid-morning meal, which they would eat with anchovy paste, *tapenade* (olive paste), aioli or tomatoes. Agricultural workers would take portable lunches, like flat omelettes filled with Swiss chard, vegetable tortes, or *pan bagnats* (Niçoise salad-filled sandwiches), and they would then come home to a fragrant stew, which had simmered slowly as they worked. Today, many workers drive home or to a village for their lunch. However, the traditional dishes have not completely disappeared with the lifestyle.

Reading the
MENU

PROVENÇAL MENUS ARE GREAT FOR LOVERS OF FISH, OLIVES AND GARLIC. THERE ARE ALSO SOME WONDERFUL, WARMING VEGETABLE DISHES.

aperitif

If you like fish, then anchoïade *is good, or you can try the olive paste,* tapenade, *which sometimes has tuna added.*

first course

The entrées in this region are delicious. For example, there is pissaladière, mesclun *salad or* salade niçoise.

main course

Light dishes include fish, chicken or meat served with a vegetable gratin such as tian de courgettes. *For a warm dish on a winter's day try a nourishing* soupe au pistou *or* bouillabaisse.

dessert

Fruit is available fresh or baked into tarts.

drinks

Choose a local red, rosé or white wine from the Rhône Valley, Bandol or Coteaux d'Aix. For dessert, you could pick Muscat de Beaumes de Venise, a sweet wine that tastes just like muscat grapes.

Lunch, which is eaten between noon and 2 pm, can either be light or substantial. In the past this was the main meal of the day, and in many households this is still the case, particularly during a harvest like the *vendanges* (grape harvest). The main dish might be roast leg of lamb with *tapenade*, a beef or rabbit stew, or grilled fish served with tomato and caper sauce, or with an intense onion and wine sauce, called *raito*. This might follow a first course of salad,

▪ PASTIS: THE PROVENÇAL APERITIF

THIS CLEAR, ANISEED-SCENTED LIQUEUR IS A REGIONAL FAVOURITE. CAFÉS SERVE MEASURES OF PASTIS IN GLASSES CONTAINING A COUPLE OF ICE CUBES AND ACCOMPANIED BY A PITCHER OF WATER. THE JUGS ARE USUALLY ADORNED WITH THE NAMES OF RICARD OR PERNOD – THE LARGEST PRODUCERS OF THE LIQUEUR. WHEN THE WATER IS ADDED, IT TURNS THE LIQUEUR WHITISH AND CLOUDY. A SLOW DRINK, YOU CAN SIT FOR HOURS ON A SUMMER DAY, TOPPING UP YOUR PASTIS TO MAKE IT LAST. IN NICE, A BIT OF ALMOND SYRUP, ORGEAT, IS ADDED TO THE MIXTURE TO PRODUCE A COCKTAIL CALLED THE MAURESQUE.

---

most typically *salade niçoise* or *mesclun* (mixed baby greens), or of a Provençal speciality like *pissaladière*, *anchoïade*, or a chard omelette. The main dish might be accompanied by a delicious vegetable gratin. Dessert is light, usually seasonal fruit, such as sweet Cavaillon melon, cherries, apricots, peaches, fresh figs or stewed quince. All of this is washed down with local wine, which may be a light, dry rosé or red from the southern part of Provence, or a bigger, more elegant wine from the Rhône valley. To finish the meal a herbal tea, made from local plants, like verbena, linden, mint or chamomile, might be offered, as well as small cups of strong black coffee.

If lunch was the main meal, then dinner is most often soup. When summer vegetables are at their height, this would be a tomato soup with vermicelli or a thick vegetable soup enriched with a basil paste called *pistou* (pesto). One typical light supper in Provence is a simple garlic soup made by simmering garlic and a few sprigs of herbs in water, with a little olive oil and an egg beaten in at the last minute. Bread is important, not only as an accompaniment to meals, but as an ingredient in many dishes. Soup is poured over thick slices of stale or toasted bread rubbed with garlic. Stale bread is rubbed with garlic and added to salads, and breadcrumbs top gratins and fill vegetables. *Fougasse*, a ladder-shaped bread often seasoned with olives, anchovies or bacon, is the classic bread of Provence.

HERBS AND SPICES

BASIL as in nearby Italy, basil is a widely used herb, in dishes like *soupe au pistou* and *salade niçoise*

MINT a link to the cuisine of North Africa, mint is often drunk in herbal tea after a meal

ROSEMARY this native herb goes well with the meat stews of the interior

SAFFRON this echo of the eastern Mediterranean is found in bouillabaisse

THYME this herb's pungent flavour is a theme running through much of Provençal cooking

South-west France

Known as the Midi-Pyrénées, south-west France is a very large area, which stretches from the Mediterranean to the Atlantic and from the Pyrénées to the dramatic mountains of the Massif Central. The region is home to Provençal people and Catalans in the east, Gascons and Basques in the west. However, the ancient language of the troubadours – *langue d'oc,* or 'language of the West' – unites this ancient land of Occitania. Throughout this vast area you can taste links with Spain, and particularly Hispano-Arab influences, a legacy of the 800-year Arab occupation of Spain and their frequent forays into France.

Languedoc Méditerranéen

At its eastern limit, and right down the coast, the Languedoc Méditerranéen shares the flavours, culture and history of Provence. The same Greeks and Romans who founded Marseilles and Nice also founded – and brought vines and olives to – Narbonne, Montpellier, Arles and Nîmes.

Although the flat plains of the Camargue cover part of Provence, it is really the Languedoc that is known for its cowboy culture. There are still bullfights in Nîmes and in Arles, and one of the region's most beloved dishes is the *gardiane*, a bull-meat stew containing black olives, which is served with the chewy rice of the Camargue.

The long coastline that stretches down to Spain provides France with abundant oysters and other seafood – *cigales de mer*, clams, *langoustines* and strong iodine-tasting violets, a delicacy of the Mediterranean – as well as one-third of the country's annual mussel production, from the Bassin de Thau, a large salt-water lagoon near Sète. One of France's most beloved fish soups, *bourride*, comes from the area around Nîmes.

Pays Catalan

The Spanish region of Catalonia extends, culturally speaking, north into France, all the way to Salses, about 16 km north of Perpignan. Perpignan is the proud capital of the French Pays Catalan – officially, the Roussillon – and second

MENU

*MENUS WILL VARY FROM EAST TO WEST IN THE VAST
SOUTH-WESTERN REGION OF FRANCE.*

aperitif

*In the Languedoc-Roussillon this might be a pastis
or a glass of dry rosé. Otherwise a restaurant might
offer a sparkling Blanquette de Limoux, a sweet
Muscat de Rivesaltes, or a Banyuls. In the central
and western south-west an aperitif might be a dry
white wine from Gaillac, or a sparkling Blanquette
de Limoux or Gaillac Mousseux.*

first course

*In the Languedoc-Roussillon you may encounter
several fish options for a starter, such as roasted
peppers with anchovies or mussels from Thau.
Central and western menus are likely to include
foie gras, pâté, terrines and Bayonne ham. Salads
often contain meat in the form of foie gras or duck
gizzards and walnuts.*

main course

*Along the Mediterranean, fish dishes, such as
bourride, civet de langoustine and grilled fish,
predominate. Alternatively, you could choose a meat
dish of the region: for example, in the Languedoc it
could be the stew called gardiane; in the Pays
Catalan, boles de picolat (meatballs in green olive
sauce), or agneau à la pistache (lamb with garlic)
will be present; farther inland, duck dishes such as
magret de canard (duck breast) are available, as is
the ever-popular cassoulet.*

dessert

*Restaurants may offer fresh fruit; prunes in red
wine; or, in the central and western areas,
tourtières, and ice creams containing prunes and/or
Armagnac. In the Pays Basque you may prefer to
save some room for a gateau.*

city of Catalonia. The gastronomic landscape of
the Roussillon reflects, in part, a cuisine much
like the Provençal-inflected cooking of the
Languedoc Méditerranéen, but the food here is
much like the food found in Spanish Catalonia
(see page 78). Dishes include unusual
combinations of olive oil and lard, meat and fruit,
meat and fish, or meat and snails. The lay of the
land is similar to that on the Spanish side of the
Pyrénées – an impressive coastline that climbs
quickly to jagged mountain peaks, bringing meat
and fish abruptly together. The Arab influences of
Spain are also felt here: pulverized nuts are used
to thicken sauces; spices are used in savoury
dishes as well as sweet; and pastries are
essentially Moorish. Most of the gastronomic
feast days enjoyed in Spanish Catalonia – the
Cargolada and the Calçotada (barbecued snail
festival and barbecued green onion festival,
respectively) – are also celebrated in the French
Pays Catalan.

Because the Catalan culture in the Roussillon
is so strong, the description *à la Catalane* is

Market stall
Local markets are an
excellent place to find
seasonal produce and
local delicacies at
affordable prices.

France **69**

applied to many of the region's best-known signature dishes. *Salade à la catalane* is a delicious combination of slightly green tomatoes, young onions, sometimes olives, hard-cooked eggs, anchovies and other tender vegetables in season. *Pain catalan* in the rest of France is what the Catalans call *pa amb olli* (pieces of bread rubbed with garlic and tomato). A tomato sauce seasoned with bitter (Seville) oranges, which is a speciality from the Perpignan area, is known as *sauce catalane*, and a popular fried egg dish topped with sautéed aubergine slices and tomatoes is called *oeufs à la catalane*.

ANCHOVIES: FRESHLY CAUGHT

The village of Collioure, near the Spanish border, is known for its anchovies, which are fished nightly from nearby Port Vendres and cured in cellars in Collioure. On a good night, the Mediterranean will yield up to 50 tonnes of the delicate fish to a determined fisherman; but if the weather is bad, a boat can return from its four-hour journey with nothing. The anchovies, packed in salt and olive oil, are shipped all over France, but many remain in the Pays Catalan where they are used as a garnish in salads, or baked with red peppers, *pain catalan* and pizzas.

In the Pyrénées the same cured pork products popular in Spain are widely eaten: namely white *botifarra* sausage and hams, spicy sausage and complex pâtés. A hearty pork, bean and vegetable stew called *ouillade* is considered to be the national dish of the Pays Catalan. *Crème catalan*, Catalan custard, is as popular here as it is across the border, as are other Moorish-inflected sweets.

The Languedoc Toulousain and the central south-west

As you travel west from Montpellier, you leave the Mediterranean inflections inherent in the southern cuisines of France. Olive oil gives way to goose fat, cured pork products to foie gras and to *confits* – preserved duck, goose or pork that has been salted to draw out moisture, slowly cooked in rendered fat, then stored in the fat. Confit and foie gras are the defining flavours of this part of France. The *ouillade* (pork stew) of the Pays Catalan becomes *cassoulet*, a rich, thick stew of beans, pork and *confit*. People here are passionate about *cassoulet*: those from Castlenaudry maintain that the Toulousain sausage has no place in a *cassoulet*, whereas cooks in Carcassonne insist on mutton. The dish has variations, but it always contains beans and preserved meat, and it is probably descended, like other bean and meat stews of the region, from an Arab (or Hispano-Arab) bean and mutton stew.

Cool limestone caves near Montpellier provide the perfect aging grounds for pungent, blue-veined, Roquefort cheese, made from the milk of sheep that graze in the nearby Pyrénées – and also, today, in Corsica.

Between the mountains of the Massif Central and the Pyrénées the land is gentle and rolling, fertile farm country dotted with medieval fortified villages and feudal villages, called *bastides*. The rich land yields up: maize for fattening the livers of its many geese and ducks; prunes and other fruit trees; vines that produce robust red and white wines; wild mushrooms, particularly cèpes; and black truffles. Arab influences are evident everywhere in the cuisine; *confit* is preserved in exactly the same way as the red-meat based *khelea* of Morocco; aniseed is used to flavour breads; cinnamon, nutmeg and saffron season poultry and tripe dishes; prunes and quince are used in rich meat stews; and fish are cooked with onions, spices and raisins. The region's pastries, particularly, have Arab inflections. A beloved traditional tart called a *tourtière* is made with paper-thin, filo-like pastry and filled with fruit, such as apples and prunes. Crêpes are flavoured with orange-flower water, anisette (anise liqueur), lemon and almonds; cakes are perfumed with orange-flower water and biscuits are made from almonds.

Eating outside (*opposite*)
Many people take at least one meal a day in a café. These are often outdoors, and can be found on just about every street of every town.

Plum *tourtière*
The renowned plums from the area around Agen make a delicious filling for the strudel-like fruit pastries called *tourtières*.

SIGNATURE DISHES

Salade landaise *Duck breast and wild mushroom salad.*

Ttoro *Basque-style fish soup, containing sweet and hot Espelette peppers.*

Omelette au Roquefort *Roquefort omelette, cooked in lard.*

Civet de langoustine *A spiny lobster stew which contains ham or salt pork.*

Gardiane *A beef or bull meat stew containing black olives, served with rice.*

Poulet basquaise *Chicken with peppers, ham and tomatoes.*

Piperade *A stewed pepper and tomato sauce from the Basque region.*

Croustades, pastis and tourtières *Filled, double-crusted fruit pastries made with thin, filo-like dough.*

Basque country

As in the Pays Catalan, the Spanish border means little when it comes to the culture, gastronomy and language in the Basque country – the Pays Basque – of south-western France. Here, as in Spain, people speak a language that is unrelated to French or Spanish, and are fiercely proud of their culture.

The long coast along the Bay of Biscay and the high mountains of the Pyrénées have produced fishermen who make wonderful fish dishes, especially with tuna, and shepherds who make good sheeps' milk cheeses, known as *brebis*. France's most highly esteemed salt-cured ham, *jambon de Bayonne*, has been made here since the Middle Ages. The secret to its special taste, it is said, lies in the salt used to preserve the pork, from Salies-de-Béarn, and the salt used to cure it, from Bayonne. The ham lends its distinctive flavour to many Basque dishes.

The other ingredient that distinguishes Basque cooking came from the New World, perhaps as far back as the 15th century. This is the chilli pepper, grown around the tiny village of Espelette and called by that name. The *piments d'Espelette* are harvested either green, when sweet and only slightly picante, or mature, when they are red and hotter. They are stewed with tomatoes, onions and garlic to produce *piperade* (a rich-tasting sauce, which can top grilled tuna or meat), to flavour scrambled eggs (also called *piperade*) or to fill an omelette. Add Bayonne ham to this mixture and it becomes the sauce for the region's most beloved chicken dish, *poulet basquaise*. Green *piments d'Espelette*, white onions and tomatoes complete the triumvirate of Basque colours, and they have a particularly regional flavour when they are used on top of white-fleshed monkfish, another popular regional dish.

Food through the day

Breakfast in south-western France is light, as it is throughout the rest of the country. An agricultural worker, who might begin working in the fields at 4 am, also might have a bowl of garlic soup at 8 am, made with the renowned, pink-skinned garlic from Albi. *Café au lait* or tea is drunk with bread or croissants, accompanied by locally made fruit jams and honeys.

Lunch, eaten between noon and 2 pm, is traditionally the main meal of the day. A three-course lunch might begin with foie gras, a salad or a seafood entrée, then continue with a main dish, of fish or meat, and finish with a local dessert or fresh fruit. In the cities this is changing, as businesses are now less likely to shut down at midday; lunch might be as light as a sandwich. In the Languedoc Méditerranéen, the Roussillon, and in the Basque country, main dishes are often fish dishes, simply grilled, topped with *piperade* or aioli (garlic mayonnaise), or rich fish soups. If the main dish is meat, it could be lamb, Catalan meatballs with a green olive sauce, or, in the Camargue, a rich beef or bull-meat stew. Moving west from the Mediterranean, main dish choices are bound to include *confit*, sausage and duck breast. Dessert could be simple fresh fruit in season, but this part of France also produces marvellous pastry and other desserts: rich *gateaux basques*, strudel-like *tourtières* and *croustades*, and prunes in red wine and Catalan custard.

Dinner, eaten between 8 and 10 pm, can be a multicourse meal like those described above, or it can be simpler. Soup is the most widely eaten dinner in the south-west, whether garlic soup, fish soup, a light soup called a *tourain*, or heartier *garbure* and *ouillade*. They can be accompanied by pâté or terrine, salad and fruit. Omelettes and egg dishes, such as roquefort omelettes, truffle omelettes, *piperade* and *oeufs à la catalane*, also make delicious light dinners.

▪ WINE: RECENT IMPROVEMENTS

THE LANGUEDOC-ROUSSILLON PRODUCES 40 PER CENT OF FRANCE'S WINE. FOR YEARS, MANY OF THE REGION'S WINES WERE NOTORIOUSLY BAD, CONTRIBUTING TO FRANCE'S INDUSTRIAL 'WINE LAKE'. BUT IN RECENT YEARS THE SERIOUS WINEMAKERS HERE HAVE BEGUN TO BE RECOGNIZED.

THE LANGUEDOC-ROUSSILLON IS BEST KNOWN FOR PRODUCING LIGHT, SPICY REDS AND FRUITY ROSÉS, AS WELL AS FORTIFIED WINES, WHICH CAN BE TAKEN EITHER AS APERITIFS OR AS DIGESTIFS; REDOLENT MUSCATS ORIGINATE IN RIVESALTES AND FRONTIGNAC, AND RICH, PORT-LIKE WINE COMES FROM BANYULS. THE RED WINES OF THE SOUTH-WEST ARE ROBUST AND TANNIC, AND ARE DESIGNED TO ACCOMPANY THE STRONG-TASTING MEATS OF THE REGION. ARMAGNAC IS ALSO MADE HERE, AND IS THE AFTER-DINNER DRINK OF CHOICE.

Bread is all-important. Thick, brown country loaves are sliced and added to soups to soak up the broth, and in the Basque country people might eat yeasted corn bread called *méture*.

SPAIN

A varied landscape makes this a country of regional cuisines, each unique, yet all informed by the same historical influences. The Spanish are united, too, by their love of food – eating is an important social affair.

KEY INGREDIENTS

OLIVE OIL

SAFFRON

RICE

SEAFOOD

ANCHOVIES

SALT COD

CHORIZO

MANCHEGO CHEESE

PEPPERS

ONION

GROUND ALMONDS

SHERRY

Restaurant culture (opposite)
Specializing in Castilian roasts, fish and snails, Los Caracoles is just one of many restaurants in Barcelona popular with tourists and locals alike.

A Roman tradition
This stall in Barcelona sells cured hams and chorizo sausage as a delicacy. Meats were originally smoked and salted by Roman invaders for preservation purposes.

The food eaten along Spain's coasts – the longest in Europe – differs greatly from the meat-oriented diet of its vast inland areas. The dishes of the lush, damp, mountainous north-west are not the same as those you will eat in the hot, arid south, nor in the flat, rice and vegetable-producing Levante. Yet there is a national character to this country's food, and this is defined perhaps more by the spirit in which the Spanish eat than by the dishes they cook: good food is a tremendous source of pride here and the Spanish devote many hours of the day to eating.

A taste of history

It was the Romans who brought vines, wheat, garlic and olives to Spain. Later, the Moors brought rice, citrus fruits, spinach and aubergines, and popularized almonds, hazelnuts, sweets and Eastern flavours, such as saffron and aniseed. Then, during the late 15th-century Age of Discovery, came the foods brought back from the New World; the tomato, the potato, and sweet and hot chilli peppers have become Spain's favourite vegetables.

The influence of religion

The presence of the Roman Catholic Church has had a great influence on the cuisine of Spain. The fasting requirements of the Church have made fish an important element in Spanish cuisine, even in landlocked regions. Towns and villages celebrate local patron saints' days with feasting. Also, convents and monasteries were the places where many of the Moorish food traditions, such as sweet-making, were kept alive after the Moors were expelled from Spain in 1482.

Catholicism plays an indirect role in Spain's enthusiasm for pork. After the Moors and the Jews were expelled from Spain in the 15th century, the Roman Catholic kings and the population, in their effort to erase all traces of 'foreign' cultures, embraced pork, which is forbidden by Judaism and Islam. Eating pork was a way for converted Jews and Muslims to prove their Christianity and avoid persecution.

A regional flavour

There are at least seven culinary regions in Spain, and within certain geographical areas you will find more than one style of cooking. Spain is the second-most mountainous country in Europe after Switzerland, and its mountain ranges isolate one region from another. Yet there are some dishes – like the nutritious meat and bean stews, *cocidos* – that have evolved in their own regional versions. The paellas that originated in the rice country of the Mediterranean plains are also popular in the northern Atlantic provinces. Dishes that can be found everywhere include chicken in garlic sauce, shrimp cooked with garlic, and almond-based sweets. Due to the general Spanish love of eggs, the flat potato omelette called *tortilla española* is ubiquitous.

■ SHERRY: THE DRINK OF HOT SUMMERS

THIS WINE, PRODUCED IN ANDALUSIA, WAS NAMED 'SHERRY' BY THE ENGLISH – A CORRUPTION OF JEREZ DE LA FRONTERA, THE TOWN WHERE IT IS MADE. OUTSIDE SPAIN, SHERRY IS ALWAYS CONSIDERED TO BE AN APERITIF, BUT IN SPAIN, IT HAS AN ENTIRELY DIFFERENT REPUTATION. IN AN ANDALUSIAN SUMMER, IT IS OFTEN TOO HOT TO SIT DOWN TO A MEAL. PEOPLE PREFER TO GRAZE THROUGHOUT THE DAY ON TAPAS, TO WHICH SHERRY IS THE PERFECT ACCOMPANIMENT. A DRY *FINO* IS PARTICULARLY GOOD WITH FISH OR SPANISH CURED HAM.

Fresh Atlantic fish
There is an abundance of seafood off the shores of the northern coast. This area, and Galicia in particular, is famous for the quality and variety of its seafood.

The northern coast

Galicia, Asturias, Cantabria and the Basque country make up the cool, green, north coast of Spain. They share a love of fine food, and, in particular, seafood. Shellfish is the speciality of Galicia. This was the last outpost of the Celts as they spread across Spain on their way to the British Isles, and the Celtic heritage remains here. Galicia is a land of blond, blue-eyed people, where bagpipes are played at traditional festivals and where *empanadas* – double crusted meat or fish pies reminiscent of savoury pastries eaten in England and Scotland – are a much-loved food. Another Celtic gastronomic tradition is the *queimada*. This drink, served at the end of the meal, is made with a grappa-like spirit called *orujo*, which is mixed with sugar and apple in a large earthenware bowl and lit to the sound of Celtic chants. After the flames die down the *queimada* is drunk from demitasses.

The misty coastline of Galicia is spectacular, accented by fjord-like estuaries called *rias*. Inland, the gentle mountains provide lush grazing country. Beef and veal are plentiful. There are similarities here with the cuisine of northern Portugal, Galicia's neighbour to the south: breads are dense, country loaves made with maize and rye, like the rustic Portuguese *broas*; greens are highly esteemed and an essential ingredient in Galicia's favourite meal-in-a-bowl, *caldo gallego*, a beef, greens and beans soup; and egg and almond desserts, based on monastery recipes, are much like the egg sweets of Portugal.

Asturias, to the east of Galicia, has a more rugged terrain, with the high mountains of the Picos de Europa. This is cider country, and the drink is poured into glasses from high overhead. In addition to seafood, Asturias is renowned for its blue cheese, Cabrales, which is aged in mountain caves, and for its large, pale fava beans. Asturian chorizo and black sausages are also distinctive, and not surprisingly, the signature dish of Asturias is a bean and sausage stew, called *fabada*.

Along with that of Catalonia, the cuisine of the Basque country is considered to be one of the two great cuisines of Spain, particularly when it comes to fish dishes. The Basques, who speak a language that is in no way related to Spanish, are very serious about their cooking, as evidenced by the formal, men-only cooking and eating societies where men prepare huge banquets to eat at long wooden tables. They know when each fish is at its best and what part of the coast the most succulent specimens come from. One of their specialities is *kokotxas*, a delicate part of the head of a hake, cut from just under the chin, which is simmered slowly with garlic, parsley and peas. Dishes cooked by slow simmering in olive oil, called *pil pils*, are typical of Basque cooking. Sauces are restrained, and are either red, made with tomatoes and red peppers, or green, made with parsley, and sometimes peas and asparagus tips. Salt cod is popular, a legacy of the Basque sailing prowess. Because so much of the area is devoted to grazing, you often find cream used in Basque savoury dishes.

The northern interior

In the inland regions of Navarre, Aragon, La Rioja and Alava, traditional cooking is simple and unpretentious. Often it relies on local sweet red peppers called *pimientos del piquillo*. The red pepper is usually present in Spanish dishes with the words *a la riojana* in the title. These regions, which are desolate in some of the mountainous areas, and lush where traversed by rivers, are rich in other vegetables, such as white asparagus, baby artichokes, peas, beans and local potatoes. Bread is not only an accompaniment to meals,

SIGNATURE DISHES

Tortilla española *This potato omelette is usually served as a tapas or a light supper.*

Bacalao en samfaina *Salt cod with aubergines, peppers and onions.*

Gazpacho andaluz *Cold and uncooked tomato soup, usually eaten in summer.*

Fabada asturiana *A warming bean and pork stew from the damp north-west.*

Albóndigas *Meatballs, usually pork but sometimes beef or mixed meats.*

Paella valenciana *A rice dish cooked in a wide, flat pan, with snails, rabbit or chicken, usually coloured with saffron.*

Arroz negro *A squid paella, coloured with squid ink and garnished with* allioli.

Cocido *A boiled beef and chickpea dinner with regional variations.*

but it is also torn into *migas* (pieces) and sautéed, then cooked with meats, vegetables or eggs. The streams of northern Navarre are famous for their trout, and Ernest Hemingway loved to fish here when he wasn't running with the bulls in Pamplona. Trout is often cooked with mountain ham, a speciality of Aragon, or preserved *en escabeche* (in wine and vinegar).

Spain's most famous red wines – Riojas – come from the Rioja and the Alava regions, but the Navarre and the Aragon are great wine-producing areas as well.

Ubiquitous olives
Many of the fresh olives eaten in Spain are served with tapas, while olive oil is a key cooking medium.

*A deeply religious
country, Spain has
many feast days.
Specific sweets are
associated with each
holiday: in Catalonia
little marzipan biscuits
called* panellets *are
always served on All
Saints' Day; marzipan,
shaped as fruit and
vegetables, is
associated with Twelfth
Night; and fish-shaped,
cream pastries are the
choice at Easter.
Food itself is the focus
of other celebrations:
the Catalonian
Cargolada is a
barbecued* cargol
(snail) *festival; the
Calçotada is a
celebration of* calçots
*– leek-sized green
onions; and in
Vilanova i la Geltrú
there is the Xatonada
Popular, a festival for
the* xato *salad, of salt
cod, endives, lettuce
and* romesco *sauce.*

Catalonia

The cuisine of this area, which encompasses that of the Balearic Islands in the Mediterranean, exhibits many influences: Roman, Visigoth, Moorish, French and Italian. It is also influenced by restaurateurs from other parts of Spain and abroad. The region became a great European power in the early Middle Ages, when Catalonia and Aragon were joined together by marriage. During the 13th, 14th and 15th centuries much of the European Mediterranean was ruled by these two kingdoms and Catalan cuisine became widely known.

Colman Andrews, in his book *Catalan Cuisine*, writes that this complex and distinctive food probably remains closer to its medieval roots than any other European cuisine. In Catalonia, as in the French Pays Catalan (see page 68), many cooks use unconventional combinations, reflecting the area's varied landscape of rugged mountains and lush coastline. Menus might include: squid stuffed with pork; rabbit cooked with snails; or salt cod with raisins. Pulverized nuts are used to thicken sauces, and cinnamon and chocolate appear in savoury dishes as well as sweet.

Four basic preparations define Catalan cooking. Most dishes begin with the *sofregit* – like the Spanish *sofrito* – of chopped onions, or onions and tomatoes, cooked in oil until melted to a purée. Many recipes end with the addition of the *picada*, a paste of garlic, almonds, fried bread and olive oil, which acts as a thickening agent and final flavouring. *Allioli*, a garlic and olive oil emulsion much like the Provencal aioli, but without eggs, is served with snails, fish, meats or salt cod, and is sometimes part of a more complex dish. Finally, *samfaina* is a ratatouille of sorts, made with onions, aubergines, peppers and tomato, and eaten as a side dish or a sauce.

The central plains

Castile, La Mancha and Estremadura comprise the huge, windswept central plains of Spain. This is wheat country, and is a land where sheep-herding has been important for centuries. These sheep produce excellent cheese; the production

of Manchego cheese has grown in importance over the centuries. A compact, brown-rinded cheese, it is sold at several stages of maturity and is at its best when well-cured.

The central plains are known for roast meat, particularly roast suckling pig and roast baby lamb, which is sometimes only a few days old. Stews made with beans, vegetables and meat products are much loved. The Castilian *cocido*, made with vegetables, chickpeas, sausage products and sometimes with meatballs, is Spain's answer to the French *pot-au-feu*.

Madrid sits in the middle of this region. Being the capital of Spain, and an international city, all the regional cuisines can be found here. Landlocked Madrid may be, but it has some of the best seafood in Spain, with a greater variety

than in cities along the coast: shellfish from Galicia, white anchovies and squid from the Mediterranean, and, from the Basque country, baby eels, hake and sea bream – Madrid's fish of choice, often served with an almond sauce.

The south-eastern coast

The Levante, the flat, coastal region that begins south of Catalonia and extends to Andalusia, is known as the 'region of the rices'. The Moors introduced rice to Spain, enabling its growth by creating an intricate irrigation system for this flat, fertile delta area. The region was transformed into the 'garden of Spain', and to this day, a rich variety of vegetables is grown on small family plots called *huertas*. This is a region of vast citrus groves, and is the home of the Valencia orange.

TAPAS: A DISTINCTLY SPANISH TRADITION

The origin of these little dishes, served at bars and cafés, probably lies in Andalusia, where sherries require food to accompany them, because of their high alcohol content. The name 'tapas' derives from the word *tapar*, 'to cover', as the earliest versions consisted simply of slices of chorizo sausage or cured ham, which were placed over the sherry glass.

Since the 19th century, when the custom of eating tapas began, their repertoire has expanded to literally hundreds of dishes, from simple dishes of slices of sausage and ham or plain olives or almonds, to thick potato omelettes and complex, hot, sauced dishes. It is not unusual to make an evening of eating tapas, either staying in one bar or visiting several.

It is the rice dishes of this region that really make the cuisine stand out. Named after the wide, flat pan in which it's cooked, paella originated in the Levante. Though paella elsewhere in Spain may incorporate seafood, it started as an inland dish, made with chicken, rabbit, snails and vegetables, all cooked with Spanish short-grain rice over an open fire. Saffron, another gift from the Moors, is used in paella more often than not, but some variations, such as *arroz negro*, a heady mixture of rice, squid and prawns, coloured with squid ink, do not require it.

Beyond paella, you can find many other rice dishes in the Levante, such as rice cooked with saffron and pine nuts, rice cooked with duck, sausage and chickpeas, and rice baked with pork ribs and vegetables. A favourite peasant dish from this region is a thick, stew-like rice soup with beans and turnips.

Andalusia

Spain's southernmost province is a land of olive trees, with a long coastline lapped by both the Atlantic and the Mediterranean. As Andalusia is Spain's largest olive oil-producing region, it isn't surprising that frying is the cooking medium of choice. Seafood is abundant and varied, and fish are usually lightly floured and fried quickly in very hot oil, a few at a time.

Churros
Deep-fried spirals of dough make a delicious morning snack, particularly when dipped in hot chocolate.

Reading the
MENU

SPANISH RESTAURANTS GENERALLY SERVE LOCAL SPECIALITIES. HOWEVER, THE STRUCTURE OF A MEAL IS MUCH THE SAME THROUGHOUT THE COUNTRY.

aperitif

Sherry – a dry fino *or sweeter* amontillado – *makes a natural choice for an aperitif. In Catalonia you might try the sparkling wine,* cava. *Drinks are normally accompanied by tapas.*

first course

Starters are light and fresh. Gazpacho *makes a good choice for the summer. For a vegetable dish try* escalivada *(grilled aubergines and peppers) or* bolets *(grilled or pan-fried wild mushrooms). If you prefer seafood try* almejas marineras *(mussels or clams with garlic) or* sardines en escabeche *(cooked and marinated in vinegar).*

main course

Fish and meat dishes will both be on offer, such as calamares en su tinta *(squid in ink sauce),* merluza a la vasca *(hake in green sauce),* pollo al ajillo *(garlic chicken) or grilled quail. For a rice-based dish try a* paella.

dessert

If you can manage it, try a creamy dessert such as crema catalana *(Catalan custard), Asturian-style rice pudding or almond cake. Otherwise stick to fruit and Manchego cheese.*

drinks

Dry Spanish wines will go well with most of these dishes. Choose reds from the regions of Rioja, Penedes, Valladolid or Ribeira del Duero, or whites from Galicia and Tarragona. For a rosé, try wines from Penedes.

Andalusia is also the home of gazpacho. The summers here are long and hot, and gazpacho is the perfect nourishment in this weather. Cooling, thirst-quenching and nourishing, it is often the only food that labourers eat throughout the summer days. Originally, before the tomato took hold in Europe, the dish was a mixture of bread, garlic, oil and vinegar. Today, red gazpacho, including vine-ripened tomatoes and regional sherry vinegar, is the most popular. There are also chopped vegetable gazpachos, hot gazpachos, green gazpachos, and white gazpachos made with blanched almonds or pine nuts and garlic.

The Moors occupied Andalusia for 800 years, and their legacy is everywhere, particularly in the exotic architecture of the region, but also in the cuisine, in dishes like lamb with apricots, lamb with honey, and chicken in pomegranate sauce. Sauces are seasoned with cumin, coriander and saffron, while honey and sesame sweets are scented with aniseed.

Canary Islands

Though these islands belong to Spain, the cooking here has its roots in Africa, the coast of which lies just to the east. Coriander, a vestige of the Moors, is a common ingredient in Canary Island cookery, and sweet potatoes show up in classic Spanish dishes like chickpea stew and black sausage. When Spain took control of the Canary Islands in the 15th century, it introduced wheat, bananas and sugar cane. The Spanish also brought goats, pigs and chickens, and planted grapevines, which produced acclaimed *malvasía* wine. The islands provided a perfect environment for New World fruits and vegetables, and the cuisine soon included tomatoes, maize, avocados, papaya and pineapple.

The signature sauces of Canary Island cookery, called *mojos*, are also evocative of Moorish and African tastes. They are uncooked dipping sauces, also used as marinades and cooking sauces, made in a mortar and pestle with olive oil, vinegar, abundant garlic, peppers, and spices like cumin or paprika. Green *mojos* contain a generous amount of coriander or parsley; red *mojos* contain sweet and spicy dried red peppers.

Food through the day

Spain devotes more time to eating, and keeps later hours, than any other European country. Breakfast, served anytime between 8 and 10 am, is light – coffee, tea or chocolate and bread or croissants. At mid-morning, around 11 am, there might be a snack of tapas, or coffee and pastry. Then, at about 2 pm, the country grinds to a halt for the two- to three-hour *comida*, a lunch that usually consists of at least three courses. Work resumes at 4 or 5 pm, but not without the possibility of a mid-afternoon *merienda* (snack) of tea or coffee and pastries. From 8 to 10 pm, bars and cafés are bustling with the evening tapas hour (see box, page 79); sherry, wine, cider or beer is sipped, while tapas are served on platters. Often served on toothpicks, the tab is tallied according to the number of toothpicks on your plate. Finally, dinner, *la cena*, is served at about 10 pm. Restaurant dinners can be as elaborate as the midday meals, but at home, dinner is usually light, most often an omelette or a soup.

The paella debate

Cooks in the Levante consider paellas combining meat and fish as inauthentic. Catalan cooks disagree, and include chicken, sausage and seafood in their paellas.

PORTUGAL

Portugal has western Europe's most under-appreciated cuisine, and also one of its most interesting. It shares elements with other Mediterranean cooking styles, but remains unique, particularly in its love of fish, soups and sweets.

KEY INGREDIENTS

OLIVE OIL

SUGAR

CORIANDER

GARLIC

MINT

PIRI-PIRI (HOT PEPPER)

SEAFOOD

SALT COD

CHOURIÇO (SAUSAGE)

DRY-CURED HAM

ONION

WINE AND VINEGAR

Contrary to many preconceived notions, the cooking of Portugal is very different from that of Spain. It was influenced by the same invading cultures prior to the 15th century – the Romans, who brought vines and olive trees, and the Moors, who left a legacy of citrus fruits, vegetables, almonds and a love of sweets – but Portugal, at the western edge of the Iberian Peninsula, was, until quite recently, isolated from the rest of Europe and the Mediterranean, which led to its cuisine developing an individual style. Many of the key Portuguese flavours were introduced during the country's most brilliant period, the 16th and 17th centuries, when it set its sights abroad, away from the Mediterranean and out across the Atlantic, which borders its southern and western coasts.

A taste of history

Portugal launched the European Age of Discovery at the end of the 15th century. The caravel – a ship that could sail into the wind as well as with it – was a Portuguese innovation, and in it, Portuguese sailors discovered the maritime routes to India, Asia and the Americas. They came back with pepper from Indonesia and tea, rice, cinnamon, nutmeg and cloves from China, India and Ceylon (now called Sri Lanka). From Africa they brought back coffee and broad beans; and from the New World they brought back tomatoes, potatoes, hot and sweet peppers, maize and pineapples, which are still an important crop in the islands of the Azores. *Bacalhau* (salted, dried cod) fished from the Grand Banks off Newfoundland, was the sailors' staple on long sea voyages, and remains the cornerstone of the country's cuisine.

The Portuguese also introduced foods to their colonies. Madeira and Brazil were ideally suited to the production of sugar cane, and this became a great source of Portuguese wealth. The abundance of sugar perpetuated the Portuguese sweet tooth, which the Moors had instilled by the end of their 500-year occupation. Confectionery and cakes, puddings and pastries are still served widely today, in tea shops, bakeries and homes.

■ FORTIFIED WINES: PORT AND MADEIRA

PRODUCED AROUND THE RIVER DUORO IN NORTHERN PORTUGAL, PORT DERIVES ITS NAME FROM THE CITY OF OPORTO, WHICH IS WHERE IT WAS EXPORTED FROM ORIGINALLY. VINTAGE PORT, THE FINEST TYPE OF FORTIFIED WINE, NEEDS TO BE AGED FOR AT LEAST 15 TO 40 YEARS OR MORE TO DEVELOP ITS FULL FLAVOURS.

THE OTHER WELL-KNOWN FORTIFIED WINE OF PORTUGAL IS MADEIRA, FROM THE ISLAND OF THE SAME NAME. MADEIRA WAS POPULAR IN ENGLAND AND THE AMERICAN COLONIES IN THE 18TH AND 19TH CENTURIES, BUT LOST FAVOUR WHEN A LOUSE DEVASTATED THE VINEYARDS. HOWEVER, THERE ARE STILL VINTAGE VARIETIES AVAILABLE DATING BACK TO 1795.

During the great period of colonization and commercial expansion, there was little or no investment in the country itself. As the nobility ran up debts, they lost interest in local agriculture. Much of the population emigrated, a trend that continued into the 20th century. Gradually, Portugal went from being a great power to one of the poorest countries in Europe.

Portugal's cuisine has been as influenced by this poverty as it has been by its relatively short-lived wealth. A paucity of food called for ingenuity in everyday cooking, and so you can now find a large range of full-flavoured dishes based on simple ingredients, like greens and cabbage, or on a combination of fish and small amounts of meat. This resourcefulness can also be seen in the widespread love of tripe and offal, in the use of preserved-pork products and sausages in cooking, and in the creative use of stale bread for thickening soups.

A regional flavour

Portugal can be roughly divided into two main gastronomic regions, one north of the Tagus river, the other south. The north has a more Atlantic climate; the country is mountainous and receives plenty of rain. Here is where you will find rustic, mountain recipes; pig and kid are eaten widely, and dark, heavy breads, made with maize, wheat and rye, accompany soups and stews. Potatoes and rice are often eaten at the same meal, and pork fat is used in conjunction with olive oil.

In the fertile, gently rolling, wheat-producing southern provinces, bread is all-important. The breads here are hard-crusted white breads, sometimes containing maize and sometimes containing wholemeal flour. Bread is not only eaten on its own, but is used as the basis for pap-like soups, called *açordas,* and for the mixed bread, meat, fish and vegetable dish, *migas*, the name of which translates as 'crumbs'.

The daily catch
The popular tourist area of the Algarve retains many traditional seafood dishes, including Lagos-style octopus, dried on the grill, clams cooked in a *cataplana* and grilled calamari and cuttlefish.

Salt cod

Known locally as *bacalhau*, salt cod may be eaten several times a week, but taste different each time. It is said that there are as many ways to cook it as there are days in the year.

The south is a land where the cuisine speaks of the sun. Olive trees grow widely, and their oil flavours many dishes, and, in the Alentejo region, cork oak groves produce acorns to feed the pigs that provide much of the local meat. *Carne de porco a alentejana* is a local dish of diced, marinated pork with red peppers and clams.

Throughout the country, however, regional dishes have evolved into national ones. If you had to name one Portuguese dish, it would be *caldo verde*, literally 'green soup', which is made with potatoes, finely shredded cabbage, turnip greens or kale, and the seasoned sausage *chouriço*. Unsurprisingly, for a maritime nation with a very long coastline, nearly half of the Portuguese diet is derived from seafood; besides the more well-known *bacalhau* and sardines, the Portuguese enjoy red mullet, stuffed crabs, clams, mussels, swordfish, sole and conger eel, and this seafood is all cooked in a vast array of ways: grilled, stewed, fried, baked or steamed in a covered, metal pan, called a *cataplana*.

Reading the MENU

RESTAURANT MEALS CAN BE SPREAD PLEASANTLY OVER AN EVENING BY HAVING MANY SMALL COURSES.

aperitif

To accompany your Madeira or white wine aperitif you might find assorted olives, cod fish cakes and presunto (smoke-cured ham) with figs or melon.

first course

Starters will often consist of soups, such as fresh coriander soup or the well-known caldo verde. Açordas are bread-thickened soups which may include salt cod or other seafood.

fish course

Though traditionally served separately, this could also be a main course. Salt cod will feature heavily, in dishes such as bacalhau a bras (scrambled with eggs, potatoes and onions) or bacalhau à Gomes de Sa (with potatoes, boiled eggs, milk and olives). Other seafood might include sardines and clams.

meat course

The choice for this course is wide, with meats ranging from roast kid to bean and sausage stew or tripe. Salad is served with the main dish. With the exception of potatoes, vegetables are more often included in a soup or stew than served on the side.

dessert

Desserts are very sweet. You might choose, for example, arroz doce (rice pudding) or a type of pao de lo (light sponge cake).

drinks

With fish, try a vinho verde or a white wine from Douro, while meat or game go with a red from Colares or Dao. With cheese, try a port or Malmsey.

The influence of religion

Roman Catholicism has played an important part in the cuisine of Portugal, too. The tradition of confectionery, cake and pastry making started in monasteries, and the egg sweets that are so beloved throughout the country were originally developed in convents, beginning in the Middle Ages. It is said that the monks, who were also involved in wine production, used the egg whites to clarify the wine, while the nuns at nearby convents used the yolks for their sweets. Some of the most delicious of today's cakes and pastries include *queijadas de Sintra* (cheesecakes from Sintra) or marzipan cakes from the Algarve. The names of sweets sometimes reflect their religious heritage: the evocatively titled *barriga de freiras*, for example, translates as 'nun's belly'.

Religion is also at the root of one of Portugal's favourite sausages, the *alheira*. This sausage originally contained no pork at all, but was based on chicken, partridge, rabbit and bread, seasoned with garlic, hot peppers and paprika. Marranos (Jews who claimed to have converted to Christianity to avoid persecution) developed it to prove their conversion, fooling the Inquisition into thinking they were eating pork. Today, however, the *alheira* often does contain pork, as well as other meats, such as turkey or beef. It is eaten boiled or grilled and is usually accompanied by potatoes.

Food through the day

Breakfast in Portugal, normally eaten between 7 and 10 am, is light, usually consisting of tea or coffee drunk with bread. The Portuguese take their coffee seriously, and drink it throughout the day. It is served in various ways: many people breakfast on a large glass of milky coffee called a *galao*; a smaller milky coffee is a *garoto*, or a *garoto escuro* if less milk is preferred. A strong, espresso-type coffee is called a *bica* or simply a *cafe*, and a watered-down *bica* is called a *carioca*.

Mid-morning and mid-afternoon snacks are widespread in Portugal. They usually consist of coffee or tea, accompanied by a sweet pastry or a savoury bun filled with cheese, ham or omelette.

Both lunch and dinner are substantial meals, although it is possible to eat lightly – a sandwich or a soup – at one or the other. Lunch is usually eaten between 12.30 and 2.30 pm, and dinner is served around 8 pm. These meals consist of several courses, invariably beginning with one of Portugal's many soups, followed by a main dish – meat or fish accompanied by potatoes and/or rice. Cheese is often served, and at more formal meals there will be both a fish course and a meat course. Formal meals generally include hors d'oeuvres, which might consist of a choice of cod cakes, Portuguese sausage or *presunto* (a dried ham that is much like the prosciutto or Parma ham of Italy).

Dessert usually involves very sweet puddings or pastries, or a selection of fresh fruit, which may include oranges from the Algarve, bananas from Madeira or pineapple from the Azores.

Christmas is the most important family gathering of the year. In the early hours of Christmas Day, families sit down to the consoada, *a feast at which extra places are set for* alminhas al penar *(the souls of the dead).*

SIGNATURE DISHES

Bolinhos de bacalhau *Fried codfish balls or cakes. Portugal's favourite hors d'oeuvre.*

Caldo verde *Literally 'green soup', this is a thick potato and greens soup made with kale, cabbage or turnip tops and sausage.*

Açorda de bacalhau *A bread-thickened salt-cod soup with tomatoes, garlic and egg.*

Caldeirada *A bouillabaisse-like dish, made with between one and seven types of fish.*

Ameijoas na cataplana *This dish, cooked in a sealed metal* cataplana, *combines clams with smoked ham and* chouriço.

Cozido a portuguesa *A boiled meat and vegetable dinner, served with thick bread.*

Toucinho de ceu *A cinnamon and almond confection called 'bacon from heaven'.*

Grilled sardines
Cheap and delicious, sardines cooked over charcoal are good for everyday meals or outdoor celebrations.

ITALY

Modern Italy has only been a unified country since 1870. It is a country of many regions, each unique in their histories, cultures and flavours. Yet the food is always recognizably Italian.

KEY INGREDIENTS

OLIVE OIL

GARLIC

PASTA

CURED PORK

ONION

HOT RED PEPPER

BEANS

GREENS

SPINACH

ARTICHOKES

SQUASH

TOMATOES

The boot-shaped peninsula, with its long and rugged Mediterranean coastline, has the highest mountains in Europe at its northern end, flanked by the fertile Po Valley to the south, with more mountains running down the centre. Its various cuisines have been informed by Greeks and Etruscans, Romans and Arabs, French and Germans, and by the countries it borders. Italy has experienced great wealth in its powerful kingdoms, as well as tremendous poverty. Some of its dishes have roots in the laws of the Roman Catholic Church, others in Celtic rituals. But diverse as it is, wherever you are in Italy, the food in undeniably 'Italian'. A reverence for quality foods, pasta, fresh ingredients and for eating itself can be seen everywhere, from the top down to the tip of the boot and the island of Sicily.

A taste of history

All of the countries of Europe eventually adopted New World foods that arrived from Mexico and South America in the 16th century. It may have taken the Italians about 100 years longer than the Spanish to accept the tomato, but when they did, nothing could stop them. Maize found a special place in Italian cuisine in the form of polenta, the maize mash that is much beloved in the north of Italy. Fish, too, is important throughout Italy.

Poverty has shaped Italian cuisine, as it has that of so many other Mediterranean countries. Up until the beginning of the 20th century, peasants did not own their land and suffered famines regularly, brought on by agricultural disasters, population pressures, war and plague. But Italians have been ingenious in their creation of a *cocina povera*, a 'poor cuisine', which draws on humble, seasonal ingredients to evoke full and memorable flavours and lasting satisfaction.

Food through the day

Breakfast in Italy, often taken at bars and cafés, is light: a brioche or *cornetto* (croissant) and a cappuccino or *caffèllatte*. *Caffè* (espresso) is usually saved for after mid-morning.

The midday meal is served between noon and 2.30 pm, and is generally earlier in the north than in the south. This was traditionally the main meal in Italy, eaten at home. However, as Italy has grown more prosperous, work days in cities have grown longer, and the lunch break seems to have shrunk proportionately. Now most Italians eat near the office, perhaps having a light meal of pasta or soup and fruit. Dinner has increasingly become the important meal of the day. When Italians eat a light dinner, particularly in the south, it is often a pizza, accompanied by a beer.

The north

One can make a few broad generalizations about the cuisines of Italy, as the food north of Rome tends to differ from that in the southern regions. Butter is preferred as a cooking fat in the north, whereas olive oil and salt pork are used in the south. While flat pastas are the northern preference, tubular pastas are characteristic of the south. You are more likely to find polenta and rice in the north. However, these distinctions only go so far and merely hint at the rich diversity of Italy's gastronomic regions.

Liguria

The northernmost region on the Mediterranean is Liguria and, with its breathtaking rocky coastline and the important port of Genoa, it was traditionally a country of seafarers. Consequently, some of its traditional foods are preserved foods, which could be taken on long voyages, such as dried ravioli, wind-dried cod, preserved anchovies and sardines, and dried beans, in particular, broad beans. Garlic is an important element in Ligurian cuisine, and so are vegetables, fruit and Mediterranean herbs like thyme, marjoram and, especially, basil. Pesto, the paste made by crushing fresh basil, garlic and olive oil, has its origins here, which is why it is known as *pesto alla genovese*. Liguria is a region of fishing villages, and fish is an important element in the diet, but it has never been as plentiful in this part of the Mediterranean as it has in the southern and western parts. As in southern Italy, meat in this poor region is used in small amounts. Scarcity of food, in part a result of Liguria's rocky soil and difficult terrain, has bred ingenuity and great, robust flavours.

Piedmont

An agricultural region producing great wines, wheat, maize, rice and rye, Piedmont's pastures produce beef and veal, and game is popular in the Alpine areas. One of Italy's most renowned delicacies, white truffles, are an autumn speciality of the provinces of Alba and Asti. Hazelnuts, walnuts and chestnuts are used extensively, and

there is a strong coffee tradition, particularly in Turin and Alba. Turin has beautiful, ornate cafés, where people go to drink wonderful coffee and eat home-made ice cream and rich pastries. The pastries are a vestige of the French culinary traditions developed by cooks at the court of the Dukes of Savoy.

The House of Savoy ruled Piedmont from the 15th to the 19th centuries, leaving a legacy of elegance and elaborate style, which is also evident in the region's buttery risottos with saffron, mushrooms and cheese, in rich truffle pastas, and in the polished service of some of Turin's restaurants. But more of the food of Piedmont comes from its strong agricultural, peasant tradition. Meat is plentiful here: *bollito misto*, a boiled meat dinner, which can include up to seven meats, is a popular main course, as are rich Alpine cheeses and filling soups.

Tomato harvest
Grown for a strong flavour, tomatoes in Italy are allowed to ripen on the vine before processing or sale. No country has put the tomato to such profound use in cooking.

Mardi Gras (opposite)
The extravagant carnival celebrations of Venice signal the arrival of Lent, when good Roman Catholics traditionally give up meat.

Valle d'Aosta

Tucked into the north of Piedmont, this Alpine region was once part of the House of Savoy, and it remains a bilingual country of French and Italian speakers. Once the royal hunting grounds for the court, the cuisine of this region is a simple one, which relies on the products of its pastoral mountainsides – wild mushrooms, game, beef, blueberries, raspberries, chestnuts, apples, pears, honey, milk, butter and cheese. One of Italy's most beloved cheeses, Fontina, is produced here.

There is a tradition in Valle d'Aosta called *la grolla*, in which a hand-carved wooden vessel with several spouts, filled with alcoholic coffee made with grappa and sugar is passed around for people to share. *La grolla* is also called *la coppa di amicizia*, the 'cup of friendship', and is a custom that has become quite popular with skiers.

Trentino-Alto Adige

The food of this Alpine region has more Teutonic flavours, understandable because these Tyrolean lands were part of Austria until the end of the First World War. Dumplings, called *canederli*, are much loved, and in the Trentino, apples are used in everything from appetizers to desserts. The food of the Alto Adige, in particular, is really Germanic cooking with Italianate influences. There is a great baking tradition, with dense, dark breads and pastries that use poppy seeds and cinnamon; and the Alpine dairy cows provide lots of butter, milk, cream and cheese.

Lombardy and Veneto

These are Italy's highest-yielding agricultural areas. Lombardy, home of the wealthy city of Milan and the Italian lake district, is known as 'the Italian white belt', because of its love of rice, butter, cheese and cream. This is the home of the classic risotto. This district of lakes produces superb lemons and olive oil. The northern, Alpine province of Lombardy, called the Valtellina, produces the popular *bresaola*, air-dried fillet of beef, which is usually served in paper-thin slices, with chopped greens and slivers of *parmigiano reggiano* (Parmesan cheese).

In Veneto, you can find food from the sea, the plains, the Alps and the foothills. Polenta is the staple of choice, with rice and pasta following close behind. Venice is situated here and was a leading commercial city during the Italian Renaissance. It was also the centre of the spice trade with the Middle East and Asia. Vestiges of its past can be tasted in one of Venice's most beloved fish dishes, *pesce in saor* (also called *sfogi in saor*). This is sweet and sour fish, usually sole, with raisins and pine nuts, which is traditionally eaten at the Festa del Redentore (the Feast of the Redeemer) on 19 July, and at the *sagra* of Santa Marta at the end of July – a festival celebrating nature's fertility. Eastern influences are evident in Venetian desserts like *torta alla turchesca*, a tart containing rice cooked in milk, with butter, sugar, raisins, almonds, pine nuts and eggs. Venice also has a strong pastry tradition. This is where the heavenly dessert, tiramisu, made with mascarpone, sponge cake, whipped cream and semi-sweet chocolate, has its origins.

Venice and the coastal areas of Veneto enjoy abundant seafood from the Adriatic; fish and shellfish are used in *antipasti* (appetizers), risottos and pastas, as well as in main courses. Because

Floating deliveries (*opposite*)
A vast system of canals makes transportation by boat the most effective way of ensuring that food gets to Venetian markets, shops and restaurants.

Fish: a staple food
Only six of Italy's regions are landlocked, and there are lakes in several of these. The result is an abundance of seafood, even in places where the cuisine is meat-oriented.

In a country where there are all kinds of religious festivals, Christmas and Easter remain the most important. On Christmas Eve, everybody eats fish and the traditional focal point of the meal is eel. Christmas Day lunch begins with stuffed pasta in broth, followed by turkey, goose or capon. Christmas in Italy also has its sweet breads, such as panforte *from Tuscany, Roman* pangiallo *and* panettone *from Milan. All these contain spices, nuts and fruits. Easter invariably means lamb. In Sicily, women often bring their lambs to church to be blessed before proceeding with the cooking. Spring vegetables, such as greens, artichokes and asparagus, are a part of the Easter table. Eggs, symbolic of new beginnings, are eaten in many forms, such as chocolate Easter eggs and egg breads.*

Venice had a sailing tradition, salt cod, which could be carried on long voyages, became important in its cuisine, and it has remained so. Inland, meat takes on greater importance; a wide variety is served, often with soft or fried polenta. Another speciality of the interior of the Veneto are cherries, from the area around Marostica, where there is a cherry festival every spring.

Emilia-Romagna

This is Italy's most renowned gastronomic region, and has the country's richest cuisine. Cheese, butter, cream and pork products are key. Some of Italy's most exquisite products come from Emilia-Romagna: *parmigiano reggiano*, which got its name from the provinces of Parma and Reggio Emilia; *prosciutto di Parma* (Parma ham); balsamic vinegar, produced in Modena; and *mortadella*, a sausage, originating in Bologna, that combines pork, spices and, sometimes, pistachio nuts.

Filled pastas are a speciality here. There is an enormous range and most are made with flour and eggs, as opposed to dried pasta, which is

SIGNATURE DISHES

Ragu *The popular meat sauce for pasta.*

Frittata *A flat omelette, which can be plain or filled with herbs or vegetables. In Liguria it is often filled with fish.*

Gnocchi *Potato dumplings, served with pesto in Liguria or butter and cheese in the north.*

Bolito misto *A northern dish of assorted boiled meats, served with* mostarda *(pickled fruits) and other sauces.*

Cotoletta alla Milanese *A breaded veal cutlet fried in butter, typical of Lombardia.*

Pollo alla cacciatora *Chicken cooked in olive oil with rosemary, garlic and tomatoes.*

Cannoli *Sicilian fried pastry cylinders filled with ricotta and chocolate or candied fruits.*

Tiramisu *A dessert made with mascarpone, chocolate and espresso.*

made with semolina and water. Filled pastas from this region are unsurpassed. They can be served simply, in a capon broth, but may also be *alla panna* (in cream sauce), *alla salsiccia* (in a sausage sauce), *al pomodoro* (in a tomato sauce) or with *burro e oro* (a light tomato and butter sauce). Here, different towns will have different names for pastas; in addition to the more well-known tortellini and tortelloni, you can find tortelli, anolini, cappelletti, cappellacci and balanzoni.

Tuscany

South of Emilia-Romagna is one of Italy's most beautiful and well-liked regions. Tuscany produces some of the world's greatest olive oils, but it is also known for its meats, particularly local Chianina beef, which Italians say is unsurpassed in flavour. Other meats common to the region are pork, wild boar, rabbit, lamb, sausage, offal, prosciutto and salami.

Spinach is also associated with Tuscany. The French description *à la florentine* applies to dishes that contain the vegetable, because the Florentine Catherine de Medici loved spinach and took her tastes with her when she went to France. Tuscans still grow abundant and excellent spinach today, and are well known for it, as well as for dried beans, olives and for their unsalted bread. Leftover bread is used for crostini, salads and thick tomato soups.

There is a strong Jewish tradition in Tuscany, particularly around Livorno. Here you can find sweets such as *monte Sinai*, made with almonds and rose preserve, and the sweet bread, *il bollo*, probably brought to Italy by the Sephardic Jews. This group had originally lived in Spain during the Moorish occupation. They left at the time of the Inquisition, and found refuge in Italy. Many of the cooking styles they brought with them had Arab inflections, and these are still evident in several dishes, such as *triglie all'ebraica*, a fish dish traditionally served on the night of Yom Kippur, in which red mullet is cooked with salt, sugar, red-wine vinegar, olive oil, raisins and pine nuts. Other Jewish gastronomic legacies include salt-cod dishes and various sausages and prosciutto made from goose.

Umbria and Marche

A landlocked region that borders Tuscany to the east, Umbria is famous for its pork, and for its pork butchers, called *norcinos* because they originally came from the town of Norcia. A mountainous, forested region, it yields up many black truffles and these are important in the regional cuisine. Italy's *perugina* chocolate comes from the local town of Perugia, and lentils from Castelluccio are prized.

To the east of Umbria lies a little-known region called Marche, which has a long Adriatic coastline, lush, green hills and mountains. This combination of landscapes results in a cuisine that is rich in seafood, as well as cheeses, truffles, mushrooms, olives, grapes and meats. One of Italy's most famous wines, *Verdicchio*, a light, white wine, comes from Marche.

Lazio

Rome lies in the middle of this region and is also at the centre of its cuisine. There is a lustiness to the food here, and pleasure and sensuality are almost palpable. Much of the fat used in the cooking derives from pork, and the vegetables and, especially, the fruit are outstanding. Such a style may have evolved as a reaction against the strong, and otherwise restrictive, presence of the Roman Catholic Church, but it is also inherent in the Church itself.

There is a significant Jewish community in Rome dating back to Roman times. Many dishes based on artichokes, aubergine and fennel began with the Italian Jews. One distinctly Roman dish is *carciofi alla giudea* ('artichokes cooked the Jewish way'). For this dish, artichokes, with their chokes removed, are fried in very hot oil so that they open like a flower. Vegetable dishes, such as risotto with artichokes or asparagus, are common at the Jewish Seder meal, as is the Sephardic dish called *scacchi* – a lasagne, in which the unleavened bread, *matzo*, replaces pasta.

Outside of Rome, the cuisine of Lazio is a pastoral one, where lamb is all-important. Pasta dishes are simple and often flavoured with the local *pecorino romano*, an aged, sheep's milk cheese. Eels from the Lago di Bolsena in northern

Lazio are eaten with – and often cooked in – a popular wine called Est!Est!!Est!!! The food of this region tends to be salty, a legacy of ancient times, when salt was a symbol of wealth. The Romans brought their salt from the Adriatic along the Via Salaria, the 'salt road', which remains an important road between Rome and the Adriatic.

Thin-crust pizza
Traditional Italian pizzas are made with a large, but thin, base and a light topping, and are cooked in wood-fired brick ovens.

The south

The cuisines of the southern regions are simpler than many of the richer, more elaborate northern ones. Originating in poor, dry, mountainous regions, dishes here are geared to drawing lots of flavour out of very little; there is an abundance of garlic-rich, tomato-based preparations here. While the demarcation line in Italy between the land of butter and the land of olive oil and lard is fluid, it seems to be pretty solid when it comes to *peperoncino*, the spicy, dried, hot red chilli pepper that seasons many dishes south of Rome.

Historically, the peasants of southern Italy were the poorest in Europe, disenfranchized people who had to draw what they could from lands that belonged to the Church or to the king

■ SPIRITS: THE AFTER-DINNER DRINK

AN EVENING IN ITALY MIGHT END WITH A SMALL DRINK, SUCH AS GRAPPA, A SPIRIT MADE FROM DISTILLED GRAPE SKINS AND PIPS. IN LAZIO, THE ANISEED LIQUEUR, SAMBUCA, IS WELL LIKED. IT MAY BE SERVED *CON LA MOSCA* ('WITH THE FLY'), MEANING THAT IT CONTAINS A COFFEE BEAN – THE DRINK IS SET ALIGHT TO RELEASE THE FLAVOUR. AMARETTO IS AN ALMOND-FLAVOURED LIQUEUR, SUPPOSEDLY CREATED IN HONOUR OF AN ARTIST, BERNARDINO LUINI, BY ONE OF HIS MODELS.

and nobles. By the end of the 19th century, millions of southern Italians began to emigrate, their only hope of salvation from poverty. Of the 5 million Italians who went to America in the 19th and early 20th centuries, 4 million came from the south.

Because the southern part of Italy is mountainous, villages were isolated from each other until quite recently. Traditions were strong, passed on from one generation to the next, and so were religious beliefs and superstitions. Perhaps this is why there is still a strong festival tradition in southern Italy. Even if the region is not as poor today as it once was, the collective memory of the wolf at the door is vivid, and the pleasure of shutting him out during gastronomic celebrations is palpable.

Abruzzo and Molise

East of Lazio, Abruzzo is a region with a mountainous interior. Long after Christianity took hold in Italy, cut-off areas such as this clung to their pagan rituals. When Christianity did penetrate, in the 8th and 9th centuries, the cultures blended. Luxurious pagan feasts were subsequently used to celebrate Christian festivals, and Abruzzo is known for one of these, called the *panarda*, which occurs during some festivals and wedding celebrations. The *panarda* is a meal that can last days, or at least hours, with as many as 30 courses. The first part of the meal is *magro*, with no meat served, usually the first night of the celebration. Many fish and vegetable courses are served with rosé wine. After midnight, the dishes are *grasso* ('fat') and include various boiled meats,

sausages, soups, pastas, offal and *salumi* (sliced meats). Last, roast kid is served, then cheeses, sweets and coffee.

Abruzzo's small mountain town of Villa Santa Maria, known as 'the village of cooks', has spawned many of Italy's – and, indeed, even the world's – great chefs. The tradition of cooking goes back 400 years here, to a time when the Neapolitan nobility would come to the area to hunt. They were very impressed with the way the young men from the town cooked the game the nobles procured, so they brought them back to serve the baronial families in Naples. Cooks today still go to Villa Santa Maria to train at its culinary institute. So highly regarded are some of the chefs who have come out of this village, that during the Second World War, the German order

BARS: A PART OF EVERYDAY LIFE

The habit of popping into a bar for a coffee and a snack whilst standing at the counter is well suited to the busy lifestyles of city-dwelling Italians. Some bars will be part of a restaurant, others will be places where people can buy stamps, bus tickets, tobacco and newspapers. All bars, however, will have a coffee machine.

Coffee is an Italian speciality and people drink it throughout the day. At breakfast, an Italian might drink: a *caffèllatte*, which is half espresso and half milk; a *cappuccino*, which has more milk foam; or a *macchiato*, which has a tiny spot of milk foam. Later in the morning, an Italian might have a *caffè*, a simple espresso. For coffee with a slight twist, there is *caffè corretto*, which is espresso with a small amount of brandy or grappa. On hot days, the iced *caffèllatte freddo* is refreshing.

went out to spare Villa Santa Maria, because Field Marshal Kesselring had eaten meals prepared by Abruzzan chefs at the Hotel Excelsior in Rome. Every October the town has a two-day festival to honour its culinary traditions, for which the entire main street is transformed into a buffet.

The cuisine of the uplands of Abruzzo and its neighbouring region Molise, has been shaped by a cultural phenomenon called *la transumanza*, which has lasted for centuries. This is an annual migration of shepherds with their flocks from the uplands to the lowlands and the sea. Dishes spawned by this tradition are simple and quickly prepared; they draw upon a range of vegetables and greens that can be gathered from the fields.

Campania

Much of the Italian emigration of the 19th century was from Campania, the home of Naples and Amalfi, and the Italian gastronomic ideal outside of Italy has its origins here: tomatoes, spaghetti, mozzarella, pastries, coffee and, above all, pizza are at their best in Campania.

PASTA: IN MANY FORMS

Recent research suggests that pasta came to Italy from North Africa before the 13th century. It is now 'the' Italian ingredient. Reflecting the variety of cuisines, pastas appear in different guises from region to region. In the Alps, filled pastas include Germanic ingredients such as sauerkraut and beetroot. Sicily's *pasta con le sarde* (with sardines) exhibits Arab influences, containing saffron, pine nuts and currants; and in rural Lazio, pastas are simple, originally so that they could be made by shepherds in the fields – *pasta alla gricia* includes pancetta (salt-cured bacon), pepper and pecorino cheese.

Although it is eaten all over Italy, pizza is still more of a southern dish. The most common varieties eaten here are *pizza margherita*, with a simple tomato, olive oil and mozzarella topping, and *pizza marinara*, which is topped with a tomato sauce flavoured with garlic and oregano, but no cheese. A traditional Neapolitan Christmas Eve pizza is *pizza alla scarola*, topped with *escarole* (a type of endive), sultanas, black olive, pine nuts and capers.

Campania has an elaborate gastronomic tradition, which dates first from antiquity, then from the Spanish Bourbon court cuisine. The Bourbon cuisine was heavily influenced by the court of Versailles, as King Ferdinand's queen, Maria Carolina, was the sister of Marie Antoinette. Cooks from France came to preside over the kitchens of the Neapolitan and Sicilian nobility after the French Revolution. They were called *monzu*, a word derived from the French 'monsieur'. Dishes that have been inherited from the noble families include *sformato Ferdinando*, a stew with meatballs, chicken livers and black truffles; *timballo di maccheroni*, an elaborate pasta mould; *crespelle* (pancakes); and a layered rice cake, called *sartu di riso*. Many of the pastries of this region also came out of these noble kitchens, sweets like *baba*, *sfogliatelle* (puff pastry filled with ricotta and candied fruit) and *zuppa inglese* (trifle). The city of Amalfi reflects a Moorish influence, particularly in its love of lemons and nut-filled pastries. The Arabs brought iced drinks to Italy, and the Italians perfected the art of making *granita* (icy sorbet) and *gelato* (ice cream).

Puglia

The heel of Italy's 'boot' consists of the region of Puglia. This area is very hot, and whereas the rest of the south is mountainous, most of Puglia is flat and fertile and produces abundant fruits, vegetables and wheat. There is a meat and cheese-eating tradition in Foggia, in Puglia's interior, thought to have derived from the shepherds who came from Arcadia in Greece 2400 years ago. Elsewhere in Puglia, fish and seafood are widely appreciated. In the southern part of Puglia, onions replace garlic as a

Reading the
MENU

THOUGH THE INDIVIDUAL ITEMS ON A MENU DEPEND ON WHERE YOU ARE IN ITALY, MOST MENUS HAVE A SIMILAR STRUCTURE.

antipasti

Literally 'before the pasta', antipasti form the first course of a meal. They consist of small dishes, such as salads, grilled vegetables or cured meats. In Emilia-Romagna, you will be able to choose prosciutto from Parma or mortadella from Bologna. In northern parts of Trentino, speck and carne salata (cold meats) will be available. In the south, antipasti may be replaced by minestre (soup).

primi (first course)

While most people outside of Italy see pasta as a main dish, it is customarily the basis of the primi, which is eaten before the meat or fish course. In northern Italy, you could choose a risotto or a polenta dish as an alternative.

secondi (main dishes)

A course based on one of the vast array of meat or fish selections available in Italy. Sometimes it will be served with contorni (vegetables and salads), though the side dish may follow. You might try vegetables drizzled with lemon or olive oil, or something more elaborate, such as carciofi alla Romana (artichokes stuffed with mint and garlic).

formaggi (cheese)

This course precedes dessert. It might be based on cheeses from around the country or local makes.

la fruta e i dolci (fruit and desserts)

Fruit is the most common dessert in Italy, but Italians also make wonderful sweets such as tiramisu, cannoli and, of course, gelato or granita.

Pasticceria
These shops selling elaborate cakes and pastries are a visual delight. Italians might buy *foccacie* (sweet breads) to serve with cream, while *dolci* (little cakes) are eaten with a cup of coffee.

seasoning. Fruit and tomatoes are dried in the sun, the latter sometimes packed in oil or made into a concentrate. The hot, dry climate and flat terrain of Puglia lends itself to large-scale olive production; this is the largest olive oil-producing region in Italy, making a third of Italy's olive oil.

Calabria and Basilicata

The toe of Italy's boot, Calabria, is a spectacular region of mountains and pristine sea, with two coasts, which have made it prey to invasions; its rulers have included Romans, Goths, Byzantines, Saracens, the Spanish and the Austrians.

Peperoncino is a dominant flavour in the cuisine, and Calabria produces excellent vegetables, particularly red peppers, artichokes, courgettes, aubergine and onions. Swordfish and shellfish are enjoyed in coastal areas, whereas lamb, kid, pork sausage, dried beans and cheeses supply most of the protein inland.

Calabria's neighbouring region, Basilicata, is equally poor, even desolate in places. Historically, meat was eaten here only at Christian holidays and weddings, and the meat was chicken or rabbit. Sheep was eaten only when it died of old age. This said, Basilicata's most famous food product is a spicy pork sausage called *lucanica*.

Sicily and Sardinia

Some of Italy's most interesting food comes from Sicily. The cuisine of this island has many influences: Greek, Roman, Arab, Norman, Spanish and Italian. It is the Arab legacy, however, that gives the cuisine of Sicily its individual character. It began in the 9th century, when Muslim Arabs invaded the island. They ruled here 264 years, before the Christian reconquest, but their culture remained intact for a total of 400 years. The Normans, who ruled Sicily after the Arabs, had a very high regard for Arab culture and frequently used Arab cooks in their households. Sweet-making traditions introduced by the Arabs were continued in convents and monasteries.

The Arabs planted citrus trees, almonds and sugar cane in Sicily. They introduced rice and couscous to the island. The fish couscous dish, called *cuscusu*, is a uniquely Sicilian dish. Pine nuts, raisins, orange juice and lemon juice come up time and again in recipes, such as stuffed swordfish rolls, *involtini di pesce spada*. Sweet and sour fish creations, like *triglie con salsa alla menta* (red mullet in mint sauce) and *baccala all'agrodolce* (sweet and sour salt cod) have distinct Arab inflections.

Sicilian sweets are renowned. The Arabs brought sherbet-making and sweet-making skills to Sicily, and their confectionary tradition lived on long after they left. *Cassata alla siciliana*, the local Easter cake, is one of the most well-known Sicilian desserts. It gets its name from the Arabic *qas'at*, the name of the pan in which it is baked. The cake was clearly influenced also by the later presence in Sicily of the Spanish Bourbon court, as it is made with a sponge cake, called *pan di Spagna*, filled with copious amounts of sweetened ricotta cheese, flavoured with cinnamon, candied fruit and semi-sweet chocolate, and elaborately decorated with icing sugar or marzipan. Another famous Sicilian dessert with an Arab heritage is *cannoli*, deep-fried pastry tubes filled with ricotta, sugar, candied fruits, chocolate bits and orange peel. *Seppole di San Giuseppe*, eaten throughout Italy at the festival of St Joseph of Enna, are sweets made of fried pastry dough. They are called *zeppoli* in the rest of southern Italy, and the word comes from the Arabic *zalabiyah*, which means 'fried soft dough'.

As in the Kingdom of Naples, the Bourbon noble families brought in the professional French chefs, called *monzu*. These chefs brought butter to Sicily as well as a refined culinary tradition, which remains in the great banquets held at wealthy households, featuring dishes such as buttered chicken liver mousse, game pâtés covered in aspic jelly, delicate pasta *timbales* filled with meat, and cheese brioches.

Sicilian cuisine has a strong seafood tradition. Fish are plentiful in the waters around Sicily – tuna and swordfish are the most prized. Near Trapani there is an age-old tradition, known as *la mattanza*, in which fishermen in small boats encircle schools of tuna and capture as many as they can. Tuna, swordfish and other Mediterranean fish show up on all restaurant menus, in pasta sauces, rolled and grilled, in various sauces and in soups. However, during the first 40 days of the year, fishing is banned so that the fish can replenish their stocks.

In contrast to Sicily, the nearby island of Sardinia has a pastoral culinary tradition. Bread, lamb, cheese and vegetables are eaten more than fish, due to the fact that many Sardinians traditionally lived inland to avoid the threat of malaria and of pirates on the coasts. Now that Sardinia has a well-developed tourist industry, there are many fish restaurants on the coast, but most of their cooks are from other parts of Italy.

Sardinians produce excellent soft ricotta and pecorino cheese from their many sheep, as well as long-lasting flat breads called *carta de musica*. In the 14th century, the Catalans occupied Alghero, leaving their mark on both the cuisine and the language. Catalan is still spoken here, and the area's culinary heritage includes the use of saffron in dishes, meat pies called *empanadas*, and a mixed meat stew called *lepudrida*. There is also a Moorish legacy in Sardinia as reflected in its sweet almond pastries.

The delicatessen (*opposite*)
Found in most Italian towns, these food stores sell a range of fine foods, such as speciality cheeses, wines, cured meats, sausages and balsamic vinegar.

GREECE

Sitting between Europe and Asia, this is a country with mountainous terrain and over 2000 scattered islands. Its food tastes of the ancient and modern Mediterranean, of Asia Minor and the Middle East.

KEY INGREDIENTS

OLIVE OIL

THYME

GARLIC

BREAD

FILO PASTRY

CHEESE

YOGURT

CUCUMBERS

LEMON

TOMATOES

OLIVES

HONEY

Once a country with its own great civilization, at times Greece has been a part of the Turkish and Byzantine empires. Many of Greece's most beloved dishes, such as *boureki, dolma, loukoumi, soutzouki, moussakas* and *kefte,* derive their names from the Turkish, and Eastern influences can be felt in much of Greek cooking: spices like cinnamon and allspice are popular; raisins, yogurt, aubergine and sesame seeds are used in many dishes; and there is a strong tradition of sweet and pastry-making.

Staple foods

Though rich in Turkish flavours, the foods that make up the backbone of Greek gastronomy – olive oil, bread and wine – have not changed since ancient times, when these foods were held sacred and had their own designated gods. Olives are the most important crop in Greece, and it is the world's third largest olive oil producer. Since ancient times, the olive tree has been an important source of wealth. The Greeks produce dozens of varieties, at least ten of which they export. Few dishes in the Greek repertoire are not seasoned with olive oil. There is an entire category of vegetable dishes called *lathera* (oiled dishes), in which vegetables are stewed in copious amounts of olive oil. They are main dishes, often eaten during Lent, accompanied by bread, wine and olives, and followed by fruit.

Wine, too, has always been a fundamental part of Greek culture, beginning with Dionysus, god of wine, as well as of living things and human emotions. Wine arrived in Greece, probably from Asia, around 5000 BC. The Greeks spread the vine all around the ancient world, east to the Crimea and the Caspian Sea, and west to Andalusia. Southern France, Jerez, Malaga and Sicily all owe their vines to the ancient Greeks. Today, Greece has a huge wine industry, and the country is producing better and better wines. A particular wine associated with Greece is retsina,

The sacred olive (*opposite*)
Long revered by Greeks – so much so that 'I ate bread and olives with him' is the Greek way of saying, 'he is a good friend'.

A fishing nation
The fresh catch of octopus is a common sight in Greek towns. It is eaten widely in dishes such as *htapothi xithato*, a pickled *meze* dish.

which is flavoured by the pine resin added to the must at the start of fermentation. Greece is the only country in the world allowed to produce retsina. Adding the resin to the wine began in antiquity, when the Greeks discovered that the resin helped preserve the wines. Greece's other national drink is ouzo, a liquorice-flavoured liqueur distilled from grape residues.

Bread, crucial to the diet and the culture, has changed little since ancient times, when it was worshipped in the form of Demeter, goddess of the earth, family and property. Special decorative, sculpted breads are made for religious holidays, marriages and births. Nourishing sourdough loaves are standard country food. Barley rusks are common breakfast foods and have been for thousands of years; sesame-covered rings, called *koulouria*, are sold on streets throughout Greece. Flat breads and olive breads also abound.

Cheese and yogurt, mostly made from sheep's milk, are extremely important in the Greek diet, and Greece has a wide range of marvellous cheeses. There are the briny sheep's-milk fetas, but also smoked and aged cheeses, ricotta-like

Seasonal produce
Fruit is usually eaten in season: apples and pears in winter; strawberries and cherries for spring; plums and peaches in summer; and figs and grapes are autumn fruits.

Festive

FOOD

A deeply religious country, Greece celebrates its major festivals with much feasting. At the Easter meal, many traditional dishes are present. The first course is mageiritsa, *a soup of lamb's head and innards with a chicken, egg and lemon sauce called* avgolemono. *The main dish is usually a spit-roasted lamb or goat, served with roasted potatoes. The traditional Easter bread, tsoureki or* lambropsomo, *is a rich, sweet, spicy egg bread decorated with red Easter eggs. Its braids symbolize the Trinity, and the red eggs symbolize the blood of Christ. Special, cheese-filled pastries are served for dessert.*

Mezedes begin the meal at the Christmas feast. The main course usually includes a pitta, filled with seasonal vegetables, and a chicken or turkey dish. A traditional Christmas bread is vassilopitta, or St Basil's bread, which contains a hidden coin – whoever gets the coin in their portion will have good luck. Classic Christmas sweets include deep-fried dough sweets coated with icing sugar, and nut-filled sweets such as baklava and thiples.

cheeses, hard yellow table and grating cheeses, and salted and aged cheeses. In the islands a fresh, unsalted cheese called Myzithra is used in savoury pies and desserts. *Yiaourti* (yogurt) is thick and creamy, made from cow's or sheep's milk. It is eaten in many different ways: baked into sauces; on the side of rice and meat dishes; with honey and fruit or nuts as a dessert; or in cold soups and summer drinks. Strained, it is used as a cheese.

Another important food in Greek culture and gastronomy is honey. A key ingredient in ancient cuisines, it was used not only as a food, but also as an offering to the gods, as a beauty agent and as medicine. Today the wonderful thyme honeys from Mount Hymettus and from Crete are used mostly in syrups for sweets, and as a topping for yogurt – one of Greece's most popular desserts.

Wholemeal noodles have long been eaten in Greece. Popular versions include egg noodles, called *hilopitta*, usually cooked until soft rather than *al dente*. *Trahana*, a hard, pebble-like product somewhat like couscous, is made with yeast, plain or sour milk, yogurt, semolina and eggs, and is widespread, particularly in the north. A Lenten version is made without yeast and with tomatoes replacing the dairy products. *Trahana* is used in soups, added to pies, or is fried and cooked in stock. The Cretan counterpoint is called *hondros*. *Kritharakia*, another popular pasta, is rice shaped, similar to the Italian pasta, *orzo*. *Pligouri*, or cracked wheat, is a staple in southern and north-eastern Greece. The pasta from Anatolia is filled with meat, cooked in stock and served with a yogurt sauce. In Cyprus, ravioli is made and filled with Manouri cheese and mint.

Greek cooking is defined by the seasons. Even in today's world of free trade, Greeks wouldn't think of eating artichokes or tomatoes at the

Greek salad
A model for healthy eating, the traditional Greek salad, *horiatiki salata*, includes tomatoes, cucumbers, feta cheese and olives or onions.

'wrong' time. Artichokes and baby fava beans are springtime foods; tomatoes and peppers are eaten in summer, dried beans in winter. *Horta* (wild greens) gathered from meadows and woods, are eaten throughout the year.

The influence of religion

The Greek Orthodox religion has played an important role in the evolution of Greek food. The country has a well-developed vegetarian tradition, which has evolved because of the fasting calendar of the Church. For 48 days before Easter, 40 days before Christmas, and for shorter fasting periods throughout the year, those observing Greek Orthodoxy must abstain from all animal products, except some fish. On the high holy days like Good Friday, even olive oil is forbidden. This means that for almost half the year meat, cheese, milk, yogurt, eggs and butter cannot be eaten. Many grain and vegetable dishes come in two versions, one of them Lenten.

The Jews of Greece, an influential community, which was all but wiped out by the Holocaust, also made important contributions to the country's cuisine. The communities in the east of Greece were made up of Sephardic Jews expelled from Spain and Portugal in the 15th century, and invited into the Ottoman Empire by the Turks. The culture of these Sephardic communities has changed little over the years, and many of their dishes reflect Turkish influences and the Moorish and Spanish cooking of the 15th century.

SIGNATURE DISHES

Tzatziki *A meze dish of yogurt, garlic, cucumber and dill.*

Htapothi xithato *Pickled octopus meze.*

Dolmadakia *Stuffed grape leaves. Called* dolmadakia yialantzi *when meatless.*

Pitta *These savoury pies are served either as a meze or a main dish.*

Lathera *Literally 'oily', these are vegetable dishes simmered in abundant olive oil.*

Moussaka *Layered baked vegetable dish, usually based on aubergine.*

Kotopoulo yemisto a la polita
'Constantinople-style' chicken, stuffed with a pilaf of raisins, pine nuts, almonds and rice.

Glykos *Spoon sweets made of preserved fruits, nuts or vegetables in syrup.*

typical rice pilaf from this area contains onion, cabbage, tomato, raisins, blanched almonds and cinnamon. Thessaloniki, Greece's second largest city, serves up *mezedes* (see box, below) that are spicier than in other parts of the country. In the north, and particularly the north-east, hot red peppers are commonly used to season dishes. Greeks who returned from Anatolia after independence brought back with them many distinctly Eastern dishes, particularly pastries.

The island cookery in Greece is simple peasant fare, where fish is foremost in importance, served grilled or barbecued, skewered or whole, fried or poached. Islanders claim that their fish soup, *kakavia*, is the ancestor of Marseillaise bouillabaisse; this is probably true, as Marseilles was originally a Greek outpost. As in so many Mediterranean cuisines, the ingenuity of Greek island cookery is generally inspired by poverty. This is not the case, however, on the Ionian islands, particularly Corfu, which have traditionally been rich. There are Venetian and Italian influences in these cuisines, as indicated by veal and rice dishes and the use of Italian sounding names, like *pastitsatha*.

Locally picked herbs
Much of the Greek countryside smells of parsley, dill, fennel and thyme, herbs that grow widely on its hillsides. They are readily available for picking and selling in the market.

Religion and poverty have worked hand in hand to shape the Greek kitchen. In Greece, the poorest country in Europe, meat has only recently become affordable as a daily food, and when it is available, no part of the animal goes to waste. Innards are widely appreciated in Greece, and show up especially at Easter, when a whole lamb or kid is roasted and the innards used for a soup called *mageiritsa*, and for kebabs called *kokoretsi*. The historical paucity of meat has contributed to Greece's rich vegetarian tradition. Consequently, the Greek diet, with its emphasis on vegetables, pulses and grains, its reliance on olive oil as a fat, and its widespread use of yogurt, has been held up as a model for healthy eating by many nutritionists.

A regional flavour

There are some variations in the cuisine of Greece throughout the country. Many dishes in the northern and eastern parts of the country, Macedonia and Thrace, have Eastern and Balkan overtones. Pickling is common in Thrace, where pickled cabbage is often cooked with raisins. A

MEZEDES: DRINKING FOOD

These little savoury dishes are served to guests in homes and in tavernas and cafés. Often they are eaten during an afternoon or evening break from work. The word *mezedes* is Turkish, but the Greeks have their own *meze* tradition. Whereas alcohol is not consumed much in Turkey, Greek *mezedes* are often eaten with wine or ouzo – the Greeks never drink without eating. *Mezedes* can be a slice of bread with olive oil, or an elaborate selection. Roughly, they come in three categories: hot or cooked; spreads and dips; and salads, pickles and vegetable *mezedes*.

Reading the MENU

ALTHOUGH A MEAL COULD CONSIST SIMPLY OF A SELECTION OF MEZE, MORE STRUCTURED COURSES ARE COMMON IN RESTAURANTS.

first course

One or two meze *constitute a good starter, and you can choose some tasty combinations from the three categories of* meze: *hot* meze, *dips, or salads and vegetables. Cooked* meze *might include: savoury pies,* keftedes *(lamb or beef meatballs);* revithokeftedes *(chickpea* keftedes); *or shellfish. Dips and spreads usually feature* tzatziki, hummus, taramasalata *and* melitzanosalata *(aubergine, garlic, olive oil and lemon). Salads invariably include a traditional Greek salad.*

main course

Often a one-dish meal, the main course could be a savoury pie with any number of vegetable and cheese fillings, such as spanokopitta *(spinach),* hortopitta *(wild greens) or* kolokithopitta *(squash). Meat pies are also available, for example* arnopitta *(lamb) or* lagopitta *(rabbit). It could also be a vegetable ragout, a moussaka, or a rice and vegetable pilaf, such as* bourani. *For something a little lighter you can have a soup.*

dessert

Fruit is best eaten in season; you might choose oranges in winter, apricots in spring, melons in summer, or persimmons in autumn. Another healthy dessert is yogurt with fruit, honey or nuts.

drinks

Greek wines go well with meals. The best come from Macedonia, Thrace, the Peloponnese and the Greek islands.

Food through the day

As in most southern European countries, mealtime traditions are in a state of flux as the realities of modern life take hold in major cities. Traditionally Greeks eat an early breakfast, some time between 6 and 8 am, which might include semi-sweet biscuits or barley rusks, called *paximathia*, that can be dipped into drinks. The main family meal is the midday meal, taken between 2 and 2.30 pm. If there are guests, this might begin with *mezedes* eaten with ouzo or wine. One-dish meals, consisting of stews, thick soups or pies called *pittas*, are standard country fare, accompanied by a salad and always by rustic country bread, meant to be dipped into the stew, soup or olive oil of the dish being served. In the islands, lunch is often grilled or fried fish.

If a guest visits in the afternoon, he or she will be offered sweets and a tall glass of cold water, or perhaps a Turkish-style coffee or a cordial. In the past, before women joined the work force, a woman's skill as a housewife was often judged by her ability to make sweets. There is a ritual in the serving of Greek sweets, with special plates, small spoons for preserved fruits in syrup, and ornate trays. Greek sweets include confections; creams; puddings; syrups, called 'spoon sweets' because they are eaten with a small spoon; preserves; cakes; biscuits; honeyed, fried doughs; and stuffed and rolled filo pastries.

Traditional daily rhythms, however, have changed dramatically in Athens, where busy workers often eat nothing at all during the day. According to Greek food writer, Diane Kochilas, lunch for the people 'who sleep by day and live by night...is usually non-existent or is something they can pick up and eat in one hand while talking on the cell phone with the other...' Examples of these include *tiropitta* (filo triangles stuffed with cheese), *spanokopitta* (spinach pie) or sandwiches (smoked turkey and smoked pork are very popular). Many urban Greeks go out to dinner at night, never before 9.30 pm and usually around 10.30 pm, and this is when they eat their main meal of the day.

A strong start
Breakfasts in Greece are taken early and often include mint tea or thick, sweet Turkish-style coffee accompanied by a refreshing glass of water.

THE BALKAN PENINSULA

The name 'Balkan' comes from the Turkish words *koca balkan*, which means 'old mountain'. Though many of the people of this region are isolated, living in out-of-the-way villages, there is a cohesiveness to the cooking.

KEY INGREDIENTS

PAPRIKA

GARLIC

CHILLIS

SAUERKRAUT

POPPY SEEDS

YOGURT

CHEESE

POTATOES

BEANS

CABBAGE

ONIONS

SOUR GRAPES

Romanian cheese
Though feta-like cheeses are popular, hard, yellow cheeses also are made here. They are often made more flavoursome by smoking.

Stretching from the northern Italian and Hungarian borders across mountains and plains to the southern Mediterranean and the Black Sea in the east, the Balkan Peninsula region includes Slovenia, Croatia, Bosnia-Herzegovina, Yugoslavia, Macedonia, Albania, Bulgaria and Romania. Each of these countries does have its own food specialities, but in general, many of the foods and influences of this region are similar.

A taste of history

The Ottoman Turks, who ruled this entire area from the 14th century onwards for 500 years, had the greatest sway over Balkan cuisine, but there are other influences – from the Greeks and Romans, from central and western Europe and from the Middle East. The use of common ingredients, particularly yogurt, feta-like cheese

and hard, yellow, Kashkaval cheese, as well as spices, like paprika, does not stop at borders, which have changed many times over the years.

The Turks introduced many new plants and aromatics to the Balkans, first those from Asia and Africa – okra, spearmint, hazelnuts, flat-leaf parsley and aubergines – and later foods from the New World – beans, maize, pumpkin, squash, potatoes, peppers and tomatoes. The Bulgarians grew vegetables for Turkish garrisons, and became known as the 'gardeners of Europe'. They organized themselves into cooperative companies and worked throughout the continent, growing vegetables, such as green beans, onions, chilli peppers, cucumbers and cabbage. Bulgarians were thus responsible for spreading many New World foods through Europe.

Staple foods

One of most important legacies of the Turks is the *meze* custom. These little dishes, eaten with drinks, such as plum brandy, are served at any time of day or night, sometimes as a welcome to guests or as a first course to a formal meal. Presented on flat, sectioned dishes, Balkan *meze* usually consist of seven or eight items. Cheese and olives are always present.

Of the other staple foods in the region, milk and milk products are essential. Yogurt is eaten every day in some countries, and is used as a souring element for soups and sauces. Other important foods in the Balkans include bread, grains, fruit, soups and seafood. Bulgarians, however, avoid fish, considering it unhealthy to combine seafood and dairy products in the diet.

Soups, particularly *chorba* (sour soup), are an important item in Balkan cookery. Meat-based *chorbas* start nearly all Balkan festival meals. In Bosnia, *chorbas* are served at the end of the meal before coffee. *Chorbas* are soured with vinegar, lemon juice or other citric acid and often include sauerkraut liquor, cooking-apple juice and wine sediment. There are also many non-acidic *chorbas*

Even with the huge changes in diet that have occurred with industrialization and mass marketing, the age-old Balkan cuisines have been preserved in isolated mountainous areas. One much-studied group of people are the centenarians of Smolyan, a district high in the Rhodope Mountains of Bulgaria, where 4 people per 1000 are over the age of 99 (compared to less than 1.5 per 100,000 in the United States). Most are agricultural workers who work 12-hour days, and eat a bulky and frugal diet. Yogurt, dried beans and potatoes are served at almost every meal. Most of their animal protein comes from sheep's milk and cheese; meat is consumed once a week at most. Sugar, spices, tea and coffee are non-existent.

Food through the day

Breakfast in the Balkans can be substantial, consisting of grain porridge, soup, bread, yogurt, cheese and coffee. Lunch is still the main meal of the day. Dinner is usually light, consisting of soup, grains, yogurt or bread. Pastries or syrupy 'spoon sweets', desserts which are eaten with a small spoon, are served to guests along with afternoon tea or coffee, in the Turkish tradition.

Albania

With a large coastal plain, much of Albania is lush, with wheat, rice and maize fields, and citrus, olive and fig plantations. A wealth of fish comes from the Adriatic and from inland ponds, lakes and rivers, with the result that there are many fish dishes to the cuisine. Along the coast, chefs are influenced by the cooking of nearby Italy and create many pasta recipes, such as *kanelloni all toskana*, which looks like a pancake and is filled with minced veal and gratinéed.

Two-thirds of Albania is mountainous, suitable only for sheep and goats. The Ottomans shaped much of the cooking here; staples include bread, cheese, yogurt and pasta. The population is, for the most part, Muslim, but people are fairly relaxed about drinking; *meze* served with raki is a tradition here as it is throughout the Balkans.

Bulgaria

Sofia, the country's capital, is at the centre of the Balkan Peninsula. North is the Danubian plain, which is rich in wheat, maize, water buffalo, cattle, pigs and fruit orchards. Almonds, figs and chestnuts are grown along the Black Sea coast. Few foods are imported besides olives and citrus fruits – home-grown produce being the pride of Bulgarians. In summer, vegetables, salads, uncooked tomato or yogurt soups, yogurt drinks, fresh fruits and compotes are the focus of a meal.

Cooking in Bulgaria is very seasonal, with combinations that are found only at certain times of the year. Meat from older animals or poultry

A prized possession
In a country like Albania, where pasturage is scarce, sheep are important animals, not only for their meat and wool, but also for their milk and milk products.

goes with pulses, cabbage, sauerkraut, potatoes and winter fruit such as prunes, dried apricots and chestnuts. Meat from younger animals is served with spring onions, green garlic, spinach, young fava beans or peas. Bulgarian stews are cooked slowly and gently to melt and thicken the stew juices. The food here is rarely fried; when it is, a minimum of sunflower oil is used.

Bulgarians like red-coloured foods and drinks; they consider them healthy and invigorating. Bulgarian stews are always red from chilli peppers, red wine is preferred over white and red apples over green.

Romania

The majority of the population here is ethnic Romanian, descended from Romanized Vlach people and Roman colonists. A Romanian fondness for piquant spices may be a legacy of their Latin ancestors. The Danube flows along the border with Bulgaria; its fertile Wallachian plain, where Bucharest is situated, is an intensively

Bread is life
Synonymous with food, fertility and life, bread has much symbolism attached to it. Rich, cake-like breads are baked for Easter and Christmas.

SIGNATURE DISHES

Red pepper relish *Grilled red peppers are seasoned with chillis, tomato purée and garlic for this meze dish.*

Cucumber and yogurt salad *A traditional Balkan meze dish.*

Imam bayildi *A regional speciality of aubergine stuffed with onion and garlic.*

Prsut *Matured smoked ham or beef. In Slovenia prsut is often dry-salted.*

Piryan *The name of these rice and vegetable stews come from the Persian biryan.*

Schnitzels *In the Balkans these breaded escalopes are made from beef, lamb or pork.*

Tarhana *Pasta shreds, sometimes made with dried milk or yogurt.*

Katmer *These many-petalled dough sheets are the national pastry of Macedonia.*

farmed breadbasket for maize, Romania's most important staple. This is milled into fine or coarse meal, which is used for polentas, called *mamaliga* and *pasatul*, respectively. These are eaten with cheese, sour cream or butter, or as a substitute for bread. Recently in Romania there has been a shift towards wheat, and the once widespread *turta de malaiu*, a heavy maize bread, is beginning to die out.

Poppies and sunflowers are another big crop. Ripe poppy seeds are used to sprinkle on breads and pastries and as a filling for *cozonac*, a traditional cake baked on Good Friday. Sunflower oil is the most commonly used oil.

Romania has a long tradition of vegetable cookery, particularly during Lent and on the many fast days of the Orthodox Church. Beans, peppers, aubergine, tomatoes, squash and asparagus are widely grown. Fruit is also very important. Cherries, quinces, grapes and apples are cultivated in the foothills of the Carpathians. Grapes are grown for wine, and plums for the national brandy, *tuica*.

As in the other Balkan countries there are two main types of cheese: a feta-like, white cheese and a full-fat, yellow cheese called Kashkaval, which dates from Roman times. The most popular brine cheese is Telemea, which is often spiced with aniseed.

Within Romania there is a variety of regional cuisines. In the maritime province of Dobrogea, many of the fishermen are of Ukrainian descent. They make a Russian-Ukrainian fish soup called *uha*, which is not acidic as most of the Romanian *chorbas* are. Fish is most often spit-roasted or grilled over wood coals.

Food in the northern province of Maramures, which borders Ukraine, exhibits a Russian influence. Here, a beef soup, called *bors de carne*, is popular. Dumplings are called *galusti* (in Russian they are *galoushki*). *Rasol* (boiled beef) is derived from the Russian word *rassol* ('brine'). This part of Romania has a tradition of cattle rearing, and beef is the basis of the cooking.

Transylvania was settled by Saxons from the Rhineland in the 13th century. Some of their culinary legacies include: a baked pudding called *Auflauf*; dumplings known as *Knödeln*; *Gewürzküchlein* (embossed, spiced cookies); and a ring-shaped cake called *Rosenkranz*. South-eastern Transylvania is home to a racial group called the Sekels, who arrived with the Magyars in the 9th century. Sekel food is considered the indigenous Hungarian cuisine. *Szekely gulyas* has been around longer than Hungarian *gulyas* (see page 37) and is made with Old World ingredients like cabbage.

Yugoslavia

Plagued by recent wars, the political boundaries of Yugoslavia and its peoples remain in dispute. Yet each of its regions – Serbia, Montenegro, Kosovo and Vojvodina – has a long-established cultural and gastronomic heritage.

In Serbia the cooking is mainly influenced by Slavonic traditions, though, as is true throughout the Balkans, there are strong Turkish influences. A ripened clotted cream, called *kajmak*, and brined white cheeses made from sheep's milk, called *sir*, are characteristic of Serbian food. The Serbs make a syrupy fruit conserve called *slatka* and, like the Turks, offer it to afternoon visitors with water or Turkish coffee, followed by brandy or liqueurs. The national drink is *sljivovica*, plum brandy, made with fruit from the 'plum belt' of nearly 50 million trees located between Bosnia and Serbia. *Sljivovica* is believed by Serbs to be a cure for almost any ailment. Serbia also produces wine – more than half of all Yugoslavian wine is produced here. A speciality of Belgrade is charcoal-grilled meats. These come in the form of

FILO: THE PRIDE OF BALKAN COOKING

Filo dough was introduced by Ottoman Turks after the fall of Constantinople in the 15th century. As a pastry, it now forms the basis of many Balkan specialities. Importantly, filo is used to make the small turnovers served as part of the *meze* table, but it is also necessary for the large pies or strudels, which are the focal point of many meals. Pastry dishes are always a high point at festivals.

Montenegro, between Serbia and the Adriatic, is a region of rugged mountain ranges. Orthodox Serbs make up the population, but they have their own identity. The highlands are mainly suitable for raising sheep, although maize and potatoes are also grown here. Sheep's milk is made into cheese, butter, yogurt and the salted, clotted cream, *kajmak*. A local speciality is smoked mutton, called *prsuta*. The traditional cooking of the hinterland is much like Serbian cooking, but without the sweet confections or Serbian pork dishes. Along the Dalmatian coast there are vineyards, citrus orchards and olive groves, with trees that are over 3000 years old. Here, as well as on the Dalmatian coast with its fish-based cooking, the tourist industry has introduced a more international cuisine.

Local produce
Despite some commercial food supply, much of the food here still comes direct from the countryside. Even in cities, housewives might rise at 5 am to get the best produce.

cevapcici (skinless sausages or meatballs), *pljeskavice* (meat patties) and *raznjici* (shish kebab). Mint, thyme, paprika and lemon juice are common seasonings.

Vojvodina lies north of Belgrade, between the Hungarian and Romanian borders. Slavs, Serbs, Hungarians, Romanians, Slovaks and Ruthenians all live here. This is the granary of Yugoslavia, its main sugar producer and its stockbreeder for beef and pork. Europe's richest freshwater fishing grounds are here, in the by-channels of the Danube. Because of past connections with the Austro-Hungarian monarchy and Hungary, the cuisine has strong Central European influences, particularly in its cakes and pastries.

Kosovo, south of Belgrade and under Turkish rule until 1913, has long had a largely Albanian population. Orchards, wheat, corn, sunflower and soybeans are cultivated over a large area, as are grapes for wine. In the plains, cattle and water buffalo are raised for milk and meat. The lamb reared in the mountains is particularly rich in flavour. Many Albanian communities still have patriarchal cultures, with villages of only 50 to 90 people where food and bread is made and eaten collectively. The food is served out of *tenxhere* (large cooking pots) or *tave* (baking pans) on low, round tables.

Bosnia-Herzegovina

This republic was settled in the 7th century by Slavs, who converted to Islam during the Turkish occupation. The Bosnian Serbs remained Orthodox and the Croats remained Roman Catholic. The country declared independence in 1992 and a terrible civil war ensued.

There are still many Ottoman cooking traditions here. Vast banquets include many elaborate dishes like a spit-roasted calf, which is, in turn, stuffed with lamb stuffed with chicken stuffed with a raw egg. Although Bosnian Muslims do not, for the most part, observe the Islamic prohibition of alcohol, regularly drinking wine and *sljivovica*, they do eschew pork. The Bosnian *shish kebab* is made with young mutton, veal and lamb. The Bosnians have a tradition of good restaurants, observing a *meze* tradition like that of the other Balkan countries. One long-standing restaurant custom is to serve small amounts of many dishes side by side. This platter is known as *bascarsijski sahan*. It might include a skewer of *shish kebab*, a stuffed onion, green pepper and tomato, small fried meatballs and stuffed vine or cabbage leaves. To serve, the juices from all the cooking pans are mixed together and poured over the dish, and everything is garnished with yogurt.

Croatia

Independent since 1992, the modern country of Croatia includes the old region of Slavonia and the Dalmatian coast. The inland region was under Hungarian rule for 800 years, and for this reason there are many Central European flavours here. The region of Dalmatia was under Venetian rule until the 20th century, when it became connected to Croatia. The Dalmatian coast, with its array of fish and seafood, has southern Italian and Mediterranean overtones to its cooking, though chefs here use less garlic and olive oil and more meat, particularly smoked meats. A large variety of fruit is grown in Croatia, including grapes, figs, olives, maraschino cherries and citrus fruit. Some fine wines are produced in Dalmatia, the best known being a sweet, fruity wine called Prosek.

Macedonia

Originally, Macedonia stretched as far south as Mount Olympus and the Halkidiki peninsula in Greece. At the beginning of the 20th century, Macedonia was partitioned between Serbia, Greece and Bulgaria. It became independent in 1992, and Turks, Greeks, Gypsies, Albanians, Jews, Vlachs, Serbs and Slavs now live here side by side – a mixture which engendered the French word *macedoine*.

Because of its long hot summers and mild springs, Macedonia produces many early fruits and vegetables. It is a centre for grapes, fruits, rice, sunflowers, sesame seeds, aniseed, wheat, maize and opium poppies. Sheep are also important; the yogurt, *ovcho kiselo mleko*, is made from their milk in mountain dairies and is a national staple. The food here is typically Balkan, a mixture of Slavic, Greek and Turkish dishes. Maize meal porridge, called *bakrdan*, is a common peasant dish. Hot red chillis and chilli powder are a signature flavour of country food.

Slovenia

The most northerly and the richest republic of the former Yugoslavia, Slovenia has been independent since 1992. An Alpine region where only 20 per cent of the land is cultivated, much of the region is used for livestock breeding, with fruit and viticulture in the valleys and coastal zones. The Habsburgs dominated this Catholic country from the Middle Ages until the First World War, and Central European cooking traditions prevail. Slavic dishes, like *kasha* (cooked grain dishes), are widely eaten. The *kashas* range from solid polenta-like dishes to porridges with an almost liquid consistency. Another key element in a Slovenian meal is an ancient Slavic meat or vegetable soup called *juha*. Round or ring-shaped leavened breads called *kolac* are also eaten. Pork is popular here; Slovenians make a conserve, called *ded* or *vratnik*, of chopped pork packed into a casing made from the pig's stomach or bladder.

Slovenians take great pride in their strudels, called *stuklji*. This is a legacy of the Austro-Hungarians, but *stuklji* are different from the Austro-Hungarian strudels. The pastry can be stretched like Hungarian strudel pastry, or it can be rolled-out, yeast-raised dough. Savoury fillings include cheese, rice, haricot beans and pork mixed with eggs and pig's blood; sweet fillings include apples, pumpkin, bilberries, walnuts and poppy seeds.

Home-grown honey
In Croatia, where many people still live in the countryside, it is not uncommon to find a wide variety of local honeys sold by the roadside.

TURKEY

There are many shared ingredients and flavours throughout Turkish cuisine. However, just as its capital straddles Europe and Asia over the Bosphorus strait, there is a divide in Turkish cooking, which is both culinary and geographical.

KEY INGREDIENTS

SHEEP'S TAIL FAT

GARLIC

SUGAR

RICE

BULGAR WHEAT

BREAD

LAMB

YOGURT

BEYAZ PEYNIR (WHITE COW'S CHEESE)

DRIED FRUIT

LEMON

NUTS

Turkish 'feta'

Beyaz peynir is one of Turkey's most widespread cheeses. Made from cow's milk, it is stored in brine, and it varies in saltiness and moisture content from region to region.

This is a vast country, stretching from the edge of Europe to the Middle East in the south and to Central Asia in the east. A defining element of the cuisine is contrast: not only taste contrasts, like sweet and sour or sweet and salty, but also contrasts in temperature. Many hot dishes, such as mashed, grilled aubergine, grilled peppers, *kofte* (meatballs) and spicy stews, are served topped with cool, thick yogurt.

A taste of history

According to Nevin Halici's *Turkish Cookbook*, there were three periods in the evolution of Turkish cuisine. The first is the Central Asian period, before 1038, when the Oguz Turks came into Anatolia from Central Asia. These were nomadic people who lived on mutton, horsemeat, mare's milk, unleavened wheat bread and yogurt. *Kebabi* (meat grilled on skewers) may be a legacy of these tribes, as well as of the later warrior Turks, who grilled meat on their swords.

The second culinary period extended into the 13th century, when the religious order of the Sufis was formed. This was the Mevlevi Order, the order of the whirling dervishes, which followed Mevlana Jalaluddini Rumi. They considered the kitchen a sacred place and developed an elaborate set of rules to govern the kitchen and table. Mevlana's guardian master cook, Ates Bazi Veli, was buried in a mausoleum, which, to this day, is a place of pilgrimage for cooks: it is believed that if you visit the mausoleum and take away a pinch of salt, your kitchen will be blessed and your cooking will be beneficial for any illness that may afflict you.

The third and greatest period of Turkish cuisine was the Ottoman Period (1453 to 1923). Food began to take on real importance when Sultan Mehmet II, the Conqueror, captured Constantinople (Istanbul). His magnificent palace, Topkapi, had a kitchen complex that was divided into four main areas: in the most important kitchen, food was prepared only for the sultan; in the second, food was prepared for the sultan's mother, the princes and privileged members of the harem; the other two kitchens were used for the harem, the chief eunuch and members of the palace household. Literally thousands of cooks worked in the Topkapi kitchens, each making his own speciality, such as *helva* (a nut and sugar paste), *corek* (sweet buns), *lokum* (Turkish delight), *kofte* (meatballs) and *borek* (filled pastries).

Culinary cross-fertilization occurred as the Ottoman Empire expanded during the 16th century. The Turks took their dishes to

SOUPS: A MAGIC CURE

Served from breakfast until late at night, soups are all-important in the Turkish diet. Vendors sell it on the street, and every town and village has its soup houses, which specialize in a particular type. The seller of tripe soup, the *icskembeci*, is visited late at night, as tripe soup, *icskembi corbasi*, is supposedly an antidote for drinking too much.

conquered lands in the Balkan Peninsula and the Middle East, and adopted some of the cooking styles of these conquered lands. There was also much trade with Spain, which was at the height of its colonial expansion. Sephardic Jews, who were invited into the Ottoman Empire when they were expelled from Spain, brought New World foods like tomatoes, potatoes, sweet and hot peppers and maize to Turkey. These ingredients quickly became indispensable to Turkish cuisine.

Staple foods

Bread and meat are the most important foods in Turkey. Bread is eaten with every meal; it serves as a utensil and stale bread is added to soups and stews. Towns and regions have unique ways of spicing meat, and dishes are often named for these places, such as the spicy *adana kebabi* from Adana. Sheep are particularly important in the region of Anatolia and every part of the animal is used: the meat for stews and kebabs; the bones for soup; the intestines are stuffed with offal and spices and grilled to make *kokorec*; and the fat from the tail, called *kuyrukya,* is used for cooking. As 99 per cent of Turkey's people are Muslim, pork plays no part in the cuisine.

Aubergine, which came to Turkey via India, is the most widely used vegetable. During the Ottoman period, the Topkapi palace cooks were said to have 40 different aubergine preparations. Dried strips of the vegetable are sold in markets

to be reconstituted, stuffed and fried. It is even made into a sweet jam, called *patlican receli*.

Dairy products are also key. Creamy yogurt is used all over Turkey, as both a sauce and the base for many dishes. Drained yogurt is called *suzme* and is thick like cream cheese. The most widespread cheese is *beyaz peynir,* a cow's milk cheese. Blocks of this white cheese are often stored in brine, like feta. Urfa, in south-eastern Anatolia, is known for a saltless white cheese called *tuzsuz*. The city of Van, farther east, is known for its soft white cheese, *sir move menu,* which is seasoned with local mountain herbs, and stored in earthenware jars underground.

Fruit, either fresh or dried, is used in much Turkish cooking. Some fresh fruits, like quince, sour cherries, pomegranates and apples, are cooked along with meats, vegetables and grains

The daily catch
The Bosphorus strait provides much of Istanbul's fish. Housewives used to buy seafood by calling down from their windows to the boats below.

in savoury dishes. Dried fruit, particularly apricots and currants, are used in a similar way, but are also made into compotes and other desserts. Currants replace sugar in these dishes as a sweetener. *Pestil is* fruit dried into long leather-like strips, called 'fruit leathers' in English.

Turkish people are known for having a sweet tooth. Milk puddings and pastries are eaten throughout the day, washed down with sweet *serbeti* (sherbet drinks). Every town has a person whose job it is to make milk puddings – a legacy of the palace days, when each type of sweetmeat had its own special maker.

A regional flavour

There are seven major gastronomic areas in Turkey. The Marmara region makes up the European part of Turkey. Istanbul is in this region and the city's cuisine is known for being elaborate, with its legacy of sophisticated palace cooking. This region is known also for its fruit, vegetables, cheese and sunflower oil. *Doner kebabi* (meat roasted on a vertical spit) originated in Bursa, while the town of Bolu is known for its chefs, who so impressed the Ottoman nobility who hunted in the region, that chefs from Bolu were brought to work in the palace kitchens.

Much like Marmara, the regions bordering the Aegean Sea produce many vegetables and, consequently, have a tradition of vegetable dishes. They are rich also in fish and seafood.

The regions bordering the Mediterranean are known for meat dishes such as: *acili kebab* (meat roasted with hot peppers); *bulgurlu kofte* (meatballs made with bulgar wheat); and Turkey's spiciest meat skewers, *adana kebabi*. The preparation of *adana kebabi* is dramatic: they are grilled on swords, which, when served, are pulled from the 'sheaths' of meat with great display. Overfishing, pollution and the steepness of the Mediterranean's continental shelf have resulted in a relative paucity of seafood here.

Plentiful produce
Many fruits and vegetables are available in fertile coastal regions. Chillis and tomatoes became popular after being introduced by Sephardic Jews.

Reading the
MENU

ALTHOUGH PALACE BANQUETS DURING THE OTTOMAN EMPIRE COULD INCLUDE OVER 100 DISHES, MENUS TODAY ARE FAIRLY SIMPLE, CONSISTING OF AROUND FOUR COURSES. IT IS POSSIBLE TO MAKE A MEAL OF SEVERAL MEZE DISHES — A GOOD WAY FOR VEGETARIANS TO AVOID MEAT AND FISH-BASED MAIN DISHES.

first course

Cold meze *might include the thick mint and yogurt dip,* haydari, *slices of smoked tuna called* lekerda *or seafood salads, like* ahtapot salatasi *(grilled octopus salad). Hot meze could consist of* ezmes *(vegetable purées),* kizarmis peynir *(grilled cheese seasoned with olive oil and oregano) or the filled filo-like pastries called* boreks.

second course

The meze *course is usually followed by a soup, such as yogurt soup or noodle soup.*

main course

Main courses are generally based on meat or fish. Kofte *(meatballs) or* kebabi *are typical, served with rice or bulgar pilaf. Stuffed pastries and vegetables are also good.*

dessert

Turkish milk puddings are delicious, but if you have a really sweet tooth, honey-soaked baklava are worth a try.

drinks

Although alcohol is forbidden to Muslims, Turkey does have a national drink, raki, *an aniseed-flavoured liqueur. Though usually drunk as an aperitif, it can accompany meals. As for non-alcoholic drinks, there are sweet fruit, ice and water* serbeti *or the yogurt drink* ayran.

Modern-day cave dwellers
The Cappadocian caves, still inhabited, have seen little change to ways of living and eating, with food prepared on the floor and breads baked in communal ovens.

Festive
FOOD

Ramadan, the month of fasting from dawn until dusk, is observed here as it is in other Muslim countries. One special dessert that is eaten throughout this time is gullac, *a dessert made with paper-thin pastry layered with nuts, served in a milk and rose-water syrup. At the end of Ramadan there is a three-and-a-half-day festival of sweets, called* Seker Bayrami. *Sweets made at this time include sugar-coated almonds,* lokum *(Turkish delight) and* corek *(a sweet bun sprinkled with nigella seeds).*

South-eastern Anatolia (Asian Turkey) is a region known for its roasted meats, particularly its extremely spicy, raw *kofte*, called *cig kofte*. A liver sausage called *bumbar dolmasi* is so popular in this region that there is a three-day Bumbar Festival devoted to it.

Eastern Anatolia is Turkey's main grain and cereal-producing area. A mountainous region with a cold climate, dishes here are hearty and rich, with many pilafs and nourishing soups made with grains and beans. The region is known for its butter, yogurt, cheese and honey.

The parts of Turkey bordering the Black Sea are most famous for their anchovies – they are used fresh, salted and dried, and more than 40 anchovy-based dishes can be found here. Among the most popular are a pilaf called *hamsili pilav*, and a savoury dish called *hamsikoy sutlaci*, which literally means 'anchovy village rice pudding'.

Central Anatolia is Turkey's largest agricultural area, a producer of cereals, livestock, fruit and vegetables. The city of Konya competes

with Istanbul to produce some of the best cuisine in the country. A particular speciality is *sac boregi*, cheese-filled pastries cooked on a griddle.

Food through the day

Turkish families eat four meals a day, two main meals and two light meals. The first meal is after morning prayers, before the family elders depart for work. It is a small meal, the name of which in Turkish means 'aviary meal', as it is considered bird-like. Cheese, olives, bread, egg dishes and soup are the norm. At noon there is a small meal, which may consist of leftovers from the previous evening's meal. The most important and substantial meal of the day is dinner, served after evening prayers, which the family always eats together. A small snack, consisting of breakfast foods, fruit, sweet breads and pastries, is eaten just before bedtime. Its name in Anatolia means 'hit the pillow and drop dead'.

The traditional way of eating in Turkey has not changed since the time of the nomads and Topkapi Palace. Meals begin with handwashing,

SIGNATURE DISHES

Cacik *Yogurt and cucumbers with garlic and dill or mint. Served as a salad or a soup.*

Imam bayildi *The name of this stewed aubergine dish comes from a legend that the Imam swooned when he first tasted it.*

Pastirma *Cured veal, encased in a thick, red garlic and spice paste called* cemen.

Kofte *Classic Turkish meatballs, fried and served with yogurt or* cacik *and lemon.*

Cig kofte *Spicy tartare meatballs from the south-east, often served on a bed of parsley.*

Visneli pilav *Cherry pilaf, usually made with sour cherries.*

Baklava *The classic Turkish sweet of layered filo pastry with nuts and a sugar syrup.*

Helva *A rich paste-like confection made with ground nuts and sugar.*

■ TEA AND COFFEE: DAILY REFRESHMENT

THOUGH TURKEY IS USUALLY ASSOCIATED WITH COFFEE, *CAY* (TEA) IS MORE WIDELY DRUNK. IT IS PARTICULARLY POPULAR WHENEVER PEOPLE GET TOGETHER. TRADITIONALLY IT IS SERVED IN TULIP-SHAPED GLASSES, A DESIGN WHICH ORIGINATED IN THE 'TULIP PERIOD' OF THE REIGN OF AHMET III (1703 TO 1730). *CAY* IS SWEETENED WITH LUMPS OF SUGAR, WHICH ARE SOMETIMES PLACED IN THE MOUTH SO THE TEA CAN BE DRUNK THROUGH IT.

COFFEE CAME TO TURKEY FROM YEMEN IN THE 16TH CENTURY, AND THE OTTOMANS SPREAD IT THROUGHOUT THEIR EMPIRE. THICK AND SWEET, TURKISH COFFEE, *KAHVE*, IS DRUNK MID-MORNING AND AFTER MEALS.

then the family elder says grace. Everyone eats from a large serving dish placed in the middle of the table. Napkins may be provided, or there may be a communal napkin that stretches all around the table. Cloths sprinkled with rose-water are passed regularly for wiping the hands and mouth. Though spoons are used for liquid dishes, other foods are eaten with the thumb and fingers of the right hand. Sometimes forks are used, particularly in cities. When eating with the hands, you must consume dishes with gravy or sauce without dipping your fingers in the liquid. This is when bread is an indispensable tool for pulling morsels of food from the common serving dish – usually taken from the edge closest to you. Bread is such an important food in Turkish cuisine, that before any is thrown out, it is kissed and held to the forehead.

If someone leaves the table during a meal, nobody touches the food until he or she returns. At the end of the meal a prayer is said: 'In the name of God, thanks be to God, glory be to God.' Then a final piece of food is eaten, chosen from the farthest end of the serving dish. It is believed that by doing this one is reunited in spirit with friends and family who are away from home.

KIRMIZI BIBER made from dried chilli peppers, ground and roasted with oil, this seasoning comes in varying degrees of heat and oiliness

PARSLEY, DILL AND MINT this triumvirate of herbs is used in large quantities, either individually or together

SUMAC this tangy, deep-red spice, made from ground sumac berries, is used in salads, meat, fish and rice dishes

The tea seller (*opposite*)
Though the elaborate samovar kettle is cumbersome, it allows a seller to bring tea directly to his customers.

Bed of rice
Pickled foods, stews and meats in sauces are commonly on offer, usually served atop a scoop of rice.

AFRICA AND THE MIDDLE EAST

THE MIDDLE EAST

Today's Middle Eastern borders have taken shape only in the last century, and their recent history has been turbulent. Yet these lands are home to some of the oldest civilizations in the world, and their cuisine has been remarkably constant.

KEY INGREDIENTS

FLORAL ESSENCES

RICE

BREAD

YOGURT

CHICKPEAS

LENTILS

OLIVES

AUBERGINES

PEPPERS

TOMATOES

LEMON

POMEGRANATE JUICE

Travelling salesmen
Breads of all varieties are sold on the streets of the Middle East. Flat breads are often used as a utensil or napkin.

The countries of this region are bound by historical, religious and geographical influences that have resulted in attitudes, flavours and eating customs that are unmistakably the same. Geographically, there are two sections to the Middle East. One section borders on the eastern and south-eastern edge of the Mediterranean Sea and includes the countries of Syria, Lebanon, Israel, Jordan and Egypt – though Egypt is, of course, an African country, its history and gastronomy are inextricably entwined with that of the Middle East. The second section is in south-western Asia, has no Mediterranean coastline and includes Iraq, Iran and the countries of the Arabian Peninsula. However, gastronomically, the Middle East divides into three main strands: Persian (Iranian) cuisine, Arabic cuisine and the food of Israel.

The countries of the Middle East are hot and dry; the terrain is rugged, barren, often desert. But there are also great rivers – the Nile, the Tigris and the Euphrates – which have watered the land well enough for people to have cultivated crops for thousands of years. In modern times, dams have been constructed and systems of irrigation developed, greatly increasing the agricultural capabilities of the region. Pasturage being scarce, sheep and lamb have always been favoured over beef.

For hundreds of years the Middle East's strategic position between India and Europe provided the route over which spice caravans travelled. Middle Easterners became rich from the trade in spices and developed their own ways of using them. The decline of some of the Middle Eastern economies coincided with the building of the Suez Canal in the second half of the 19th century, and the subsequent disappearance of the overland caravans from the East.

A taste of history

Middle Eastern food is influenced both by the indigenous Bedouin tribes and by the civilizations that have spread through its lands. The diet of the nomadic Bedouins has always been a simple one based on meat – primarily lamb and mutton – dates and yogurt. The early settled civilizations, such as the Pharaonic Egyptians and later the Jews in Palestine (now Israel) cultivated many fruits, vegetables, beans, bitter herbs, almonds and other nuts. The Arabs and then the Ottoman Turks brought complexity and subtlety to Middle Eastern cuisine, with a love of spices, like cinnamon, ginger and cardamom, and of subtle floral essences, like rose-water and orange-flower water. They also instilled a passion for sweets; all over the Middle East you can find filo-based pastries filled with nuts and sweetened with syrup.

Meeting places
Eating is very much a social affair. This open-air Egyptian restaurant provides the perfect place to meet and swap stories.

The Arabs, who had been Bedouin tribes, learned from the Persians, whose influence on Arabic cuisine can be compared to the gastronomic influence the French have had on other European and American cooking in more recent times. The Ottoman Turks, in turn, learned Persian techniques from the Arabs. Persian cuisine was rice-based and displayed a sophisticated balance of contrasting flavours: sweet with sour, sweet with savoury, hot with cold, or spicy with mild. The Persians used nuts to thicken sauces, and this practice continues throughout the Middle East, changing in character from country to country as to which nuts are favoured: in Iran almonds and walnuts are used; an Egyptian or Syrian cook uses almonds too, but also pine nuts; in Lebanon and Israel sesame paste is preferred; and in Turkey, walnuts are the nut of choice.

New World foods began to penetrate the Middle East in the 16th century. They were made more popular by the Sephardic and Marrano Jewish merchants who had been invited to live in the Ottoman Empire after their expulsion from Spain. Tomatoes, sweet peppers and summer squash are still vital ingredients in the cuisines of the Middle East.

The influence of religion

With the exception of the Jewish state of Israel, Islam is the predominant religion in this part of the world. There are Christians in Lebanon and Egypt, but the food of these countries is influenced most by the Muslim dietary laws, which exclude pork and alcohol. Hospitality is one of the strictest codes of Islam, and cooking and eating are intensely social, marking all important events such as weddings, births, circumcisions and religious festivals.

In Israel, the Jewish dietary laws of *kashrut* prevail, although not all Jews adhere to them. *Kashrut* states that the consumption of blood is forbidden, so meat must be slaughtered and

fins or scales, and this eliminates several types of fish from Jewish diets, including shellfish, shark, eel and squid.

Bread

One of the most important and adaptable foods in the Middle Eastern diet is bread. It serves as food, utensil and napkin, and a meal without it would be unthinkable. There are different names for breads in each country. The nan, *lavash*, pitta and *khubz* are all flat wheat loaves of varying thicknesses and sizes, baked in clay ovens, or on clay or metal griddles. Some breads are flat and dense, while others separate as they bake, forming two thin layers that provide a convenient pocket into which food can be stuffed. In country villages, bread is made in quantity once a week or once a month and allowed to dry and harden. It is reconstituted with water as it is needed. A popular bread in Egypt is the *simit* (also called *smeet*), a sesame-covered bread ring sold from long poles in cities.

RICE: THE BASIS OF IRANIAN CUISINE

Much of Iranian agriculture is village based, with rice featuring highly as a crop. Women are often responsible for planting rice, which has been farmed here for over 3000 years. Rice cooked the Iranian way is called *chelou*. Though often described as plain, steamed rice, the making of *chelou* is an elaborate process involving rinsing the rice several times, boiling it in salted water, then draining it and steaming it in a pan coated with a mixture of butter, powdered saffron, yogurt and water. The rice cooks to perfection, with each fluffy grain separated. To serve, it is mounded onto a platter and garnished with a small amount of saffron-coloured rice. The crowning glory is the *tah dig*, the golden crust of rice that adheres to the bottom of the pan, which is detached from the pan and served separately.

Food through the day

Throughout the Middle East, three meals are eaten daily. Breakfast consists of fresh-baked or reconstituted bread served with cheese, yogurt, fresh fruits and vegetables, honey, preserves, nuts and *belila*, which are sweetened cooked grains. In Egypt, the fava-bean dish *fool medames* is eaten for breakfast, as is sweetened couscous.

Lunch is generally a light meal, including *meze* dishes, felafel or *shawerma* (roasted lamb, cooked on a rotisserie) eaten in a sandwich of pitta bread. Omelettes – called *eggahs* in Arabic countries, *kookoos* in Iran – are also popular midday foods.

The evening meal is the principal meal of the day. Simple family dinners might consist of a one-dish meal, such as a soup, a stew, a bean dish or stuffed vegetables. Bread, yogurt, olives and pickles are always available, no matter what the food. In Iran, cheese might replace yogurt, and fresh raw vegetables and herbs might be included rather than olives. In wealthier families meat will be served several times a week.

Ways of the nomads
Indigenous Bedouin tribes continue to live and eat in much the same way that they did thousands of years ago.

prepared by kosher butchers, who drain the blood from the meat. Animals that 'chew the cud' and have cloven hooves are permitted, because they cannot hold prey, but all others, including pigs, rabbits, horses and beasts of prey, are forbidden. The only fish allowed are those with

■ **TEA: THE SOCIAL DRINK**

LIKE TURKEY, IRAN IS A TEA-DRINKING NATION; EVERY FAMILY HAS A *SAMOVAR*, WHICH STEAMS ALL DAY LONG SO THAT TEA CAN ALWAYS BE OFFERED TO A GUEST. IT SITS ON A TRAY WITH A SMALL BOWL UNDER THE SPOUT TO CATCH DRIPS, CALLED A *JAAM*. THE TEA IS SERVED IN SMALL GLASS CUPS, WITH LOTS OF SUGAR – USUALLY THREE LUMPS. IT CAN ALSO BE SWEETENED WITH PRESERVES, HONEY OR DRIED FRUIT. AN IRANIAN TEA HOUSE IS CALLED A *GHAVAKHANE* – THOUGH THE WORD ACTUALLY MEANS 'COFFEE HOUSE'. THIS IS AN ALL-MALE CLUB WHERE MEN GATHER, DRINK TEA AND SMOKE, WHILE LISTENING TO THE RADIO, WATCHING TELEVISION OR TELLING EACH OTHER STORIES.

HERBS AND SPICES

ZA'ATAR a mixture of sumac, wild thyme and sesame seeds, popular in Arabic cuisine

TAKLIA a spice mixture of coriander seeds fried with crushed garlic, particularly popular in Egypt

DUKKAH an Egyptian mixture of roasted sesame seeds, hazelnuts, coriander seeds, cumin, salt and pepper

QUATRE EPICES an Egyptian mixture of cinnamon, nutmeg, cloves and ginger

HAWAYIJ a Yemeni spice mixture containing black pepper, caraway seeds, turmeric and cardamom

Iran

Directly descended from the food of the great Persian dynasties of the first millennium AD, the cuisine of Iran is the richest of the Middle Eastern cuisines. Butter and oil are used abundantly, often drizzled over rice and used for cooking meat and vegetables. Sour ingredients, such as dried limes, lemon juice and pomegranate and sour grape syrups, are also found in a number of dishes. Yellow split peas are a common thickener for soups, stews and sauces; and dill, parsley and fresh coriander are much loved. The Iranians have long attributed 'hot' and 'cold' aspects to their different foods and Persian cooking seeks to achieve a balance of these attributes.

Rice forms the basis of many Iranian dishes (see box, page 120), and grilled meats often accompany it; the national dish is *chelou kebab*, rice with meat brochettes, which is eaten in households and sold in bazaars. Often, rice is served with a delicate stew called a *khoresh*. This is a dish in which meats, fruits and vegetables come together, subtly seasoned with spices, such as turmeric and saffron, and herbs, like coriander, mint and parsley. The type of vegetable or fruit in the *khoresh* determines its name.

Meat and offal is much prized, as in the rest of the Middle Eastern countries. Lamb and mutton are used in many different ways: threaded onto skewers for grilling; ground and mixed with spices, herbs and other seasonings for *kofte* (meatballs); and stuffed with dried – and sometimes fresh – fruit and a complex mixture of spices. Other meat, poultry and fish will also be stuffed in this way.

Eggs, too, are popular. Amongst the most common Iranian dishes are *kookoos*, thick, fluffy omelettes filled with meat or vegetables or bursting with fresh herbs such as parsley and coriander, served as appetizers, side dishes or main dishes with yogurt, salt and bread. Because they can be served either hot or cold, they are often kept on hand for unexpected guests.

Soups play an important role in Iranian cuisine. The Farsi word for cook is *ashe-paz*, which literally means 'soup-preparer', and the kitchen is called the *ashe-paz khaneh*, meaning 'the place where soup is prepared'. *Ashes* are thick main dish soups that combine meats with vegetables, beans, herbs and spices. Close friends or lovers, in an act of great intimacy, will sip from the same spoon.

Arabic cooking

Those who have enjoyed meals in Middle Eastern restaurants are likely to have eaten Arabic food. Syria and Lebanon, where the capital Beirut was known as the 'Paris of the Middle East' before it was torn apart by civil war in the 1970s, are particularly well known for their cuisines. But throughout the Arab countries, good cooks produce the same types of dishes, tasting of garlic, olive oil, *tahini* (sesame-seed paste), yogurt, lemon, herbs and spices, like cinnamon, cumin and sumac. Particularly memorable are the *meze*, huge appetizer spreads that include salads and dips, *kibbeh* (meat ground with bulgar wheat and seasonings), *labne* (yogurt cheese), felafel, dolmas and savoury pastries.

Beyond the olive-producing Mediterranean region, animal fats and vegetable oils are used instead of olive oil. Some peasant dishes call for sheep's tail fat, called *dehen*, which adds depth and a meaty flavour to dishes that might contain very little meat. Clarified butter is used also.

While the food of Egypt has much in common with that of other Arabic countries, there are a couple of distinctive national dishes. One is *fool medames*, a dish made from cooked, brown-skinned fava beans crushed with garlic, which is served from great brass pots with various garnishes. *Fool* is eaten by Egyptians all day long, as breakfast, lunch, street-food snack and supper. Another Egyptian dish is a soup is made with *melokhia,* a green native to the country, which has a viscous texture when cooked. *Ta'amia* – the name Egyptians give the fava-bean croquettes called felafel in other Arabic countries – are also claimed as a national speciality. According to Claudia Roden, in *A Book of Middle Eastern Food*, both *ta'amia* and *melokhia* soup are thought to have been developed by the ancient Christian Copt sect, to eat during their periods of fasting.

'Beehive' ovens
Traditional throughout the Middle East, these ovens evolved in Egypt and spread to nearby countries. They have kept the same shape for around 3000 years.

SIGNATURE DISHES

Baba ganouj *Meze dish of puréed, grilled aubergine and sesame paste.*

Tabbouleh *Traditionally, a chopped parsley and mint salad with bulgar wheat.*

Felafel *Broad bean or chickpea croquettes served in pitta breads with* tahini *salad.*

Kookoo *These filled Iranian omelettes are richly seasoned with herbs.*

Kofte *Ground meat fingers or balls made from lamb, beef and veal.*

Chelou *Persian steamed rice.*

Khoreshtha *These Persian stews are defined by the fruits and vegetables they contain, rather than the meat.*

Kibbeh *There are over 50 versions of these Syrian meat and wheat paste balls filled with minced meat, spices and nuts.*

The Women's Souk
Markets, such as this famous one in Ibra, Oman, play an important part in Middle Eastern cuisine, since many products for cooking can be purchased in them.

Festive

~~~ FOOD ~~~

The Middle East observes many festivals with foods. At Nourez, the Iranian New Year, a mix of seven dried fruits and nuts is made, called ajeele moshgel goshah, *which means 'unraveller of difficulties'. A cloth is spread in every household, and upon it are placed seven foods or plants symbolizing the seven good angels. The Jewish autumn feast of Sukkot commemorates the time Jews lived in the wilderness in huts, and symbolizes God's protection. It is also a harvest festival, so an abundance of vegetables and fruits are eaten.*

The food of Iraq, which has both Persian and Arabic inflections, has one unique tradition: a grilled river-fish festival called the *masgoof*. Boatmen on the Tigris sell whole fish – grilled on upright stakes and topped with onions and tomatoes – to people sitting in riverside cafés. Diners eat with their fingers, mopping up the juices with Arabic bread.

Sweets are a great delicacy in the Arab countries. Bakers make huge pans of filo-based pastries, like baklava, and these are eaten throughout the day with coffee and tea, and are especially important at weddings and festivals.

■ **COFFEE: FOR ENERGY**

IT IS THOUGHT THAT ONE OF THE FIRST PLACES TO USE COFFEE AS A BEVERAGE WAS YEMEN, WHICH STILL PRODUCES HIGH-QUALITY BEANS TODAY. FROM HERE IT WAS TAKEN TO SAUDI ARABIA. COFFEE WAS POPULAR AMONG THE EARLY MUSLIMS, PARTICULARLY THE SUFIS, WHO FOUND IT ENERGIZING, AND ITS USE SPREAD QUICKLY THROUGHOUT THE MUSLIM WORLD. THICK, SWEET 'TURKISH COFFEE', OFTEN FLAVOURED WITH CARDAMOM SEEDS, IS DRUNK THROUGHOUT THE DAY, EXCEPT IN IRAN WHERE TEA IS THE DRINK OF CHOICE.

Israel

A country of immigrants, Israel has been in search of a cuisine it can call its own for many years. Its most popular and widespread foods are essentially of Arabic origin – felafel, hummus, *tabbouleh* (bulgar wheat mixed with tomatoes, onions, parsley and other ingredients) and *baba ganouj* (an aubergine, tahini and olive oil paste). Israel has many Moroccan foods also, such as couscous, *tagines* and the filo pastries rolled around a spiced meat filling called *cigars*. But, if there is one dish that is purely Israeli, that everybody eats no matter what part of the world they have emigrated from, it is turkey *schnitzel* (breaded turkey cutlets).

The cooking of Israel could be described as a 'fusion cuisine', mixing the foods and flavours of the countries of people's origins: felafels are served in pitta breads with spicy, Yemeni *zhoug* (relishes) and Moroccan *harissa*; and meat and offal combinations are seasoned with hot Ethiopian spices. Wedding buffets might include Ashkenazi (German and Eastern European Jewish) favourites like chopped chicken liver and *latkes* (potato pancakes), as well as stuffed vine leaves and Moroccan *cigars* and *borekas*. At home people cook food from their native lands, so in supermarkets one finds ingredients from Russia, Iraq, Yemen and even from Brooklyn, USA.

Reading the
MENU

THROUGHOUT THE MIDDLE EAST, RESTAURANTS HAVE A MEZE TRADITION AND FEATURE GRILLED MEATS AND PILAFS.

first course

Among the many kinds of meze, *you are likely to find vegetable and* tahini *preparations, such as* fattoush *(bread salad) or* baba ganouj *(aubergines with* tahini*), as well as stuffed pastries,* labne *(drained yogurt) and* kibbeh *(wheat and meat-paste balls). The* meze *menu can be a meal in itself.*

main course

This usually consists of grilled meat, such as shish kebab *or* kofta mehweya *(ground meat on skewers), or* mechoui *(whole roast kid or lamb). Rice pilaf is the common accompaniment.*

dessert

Fruit will be served for dessert, and may be dried fruit, such as dates or figs. A sweet filo pastry, such as baklava, might also be offered.

drinks

Due to the heat and the Muslim religion, alcoholic beverages are not commonly drunk in the Middle East, but are available. In Lebanon there is a local wine. Fruit juices and water are also widely drunk.

However, the food of the early established Jewish communities in Palestine, before there was a State of Israel, has its roots in sophisticated Arab, Persian and Sephardic cuisines. Dishes include delicately seasoned pilafs and pies, gratins, stuffed vegetables and sweet pastries inflected with flower waters, such as rose-petal water and orange-flower water.

This food is a far cry from the food of the original Zionist settlers, who led ascetic lives in collectives called kibbutzim. The kibbutz breakfast, which was eaten after several hours in the fields, consisted of bread, cheese, raw vegetables and olives. This evolved into the standard buffet spread of the Israeli hotel breakfast, a selection including cheeses, herrings, *labne* (drained yogurt cheese), olives, hard-boiled eggs and breads. The breakfast buffet also includes tomatoes, spring onions and cucumbers, served whole for people to make their own salads. These buffet foods, known as 'kibbutz foods', are also eaten as light suppers.

In today's Israel there is a keen interest in food and restaurants, with many chefs exploring foreign foods, ranging from French to Chinese, and also striving to create an Israeli cuisine that melds the many gastronomic cultures present in the country. Much use is made of local produce such as avocados, tomatoes, mangoes and prickly pears. There is also a movement amongst young Israeli cooks to revive the food of their ancestors. The greatest influence has come from the Sephardim, particularly those from Morocco, whose immigrants form the largest ethnic group. Couscous is eaten more than any other dish served in the Israeli army. Sephardic food was once looked down upon in Israel, but now there is much more interest in it.

Deep-fried croquettes
Israelis call felafel their national dish; and here it is made with chickpeas more often than with fava beans, which is the Arabic way.

NORTH AFRICA

The countries of Algeria, Morocco and Tunisia are often called the Maghreb, which comes from the Arabic for 'the West'. Gastronomically, North Africa can be defined as the area where couscous replaces rice as a staple.

KEY INGREDIENTS

OLIVES AND OLIVE OIL

SMEN (PRESERVED BUTTER)

FLORAL ESSENCES

PRESERVED LEMON

HARISSA (HOT PASTE)

GARLIC

COUSCOUS

LAMB

ONIONS

ORANGES

DATES

FIGS

The fruit of the palm
Dates have been cultivated in North Africa for more than 4000 years. This very sweet fruit is much loved here; there is even a festival devoted to dates in Erfoud, Morocco.

High energy grains *(opposite)*
Where food is scarce, grains become an important source of nutrients. North African Berbers were thought to have invented couscous, made using semolina, sorghum or barley.

The countries of the Maghreb are isolated from their neighbours to the east by the great deserts of Libya and from those to the south by the Sahara. The cuisines of each of these countries have distinctive elements, yet they are informed by a common history and culture.

A taste of history

When the coastal areas of North Africa were explored by Phoenician sailors during the first millennium BC, they were inhabited by nomadic Berber tribes, whose diet was – and mostly still is – based on honey, fava beans, lentils, wheat and couscous, which, according to some historians, the Berbers may have invented. The Phoenicians settled in Tunisia and built the great city of Carthage. They brought vines and olives to North Africa and later introduced olives to Rome.

When Rome decided that 'Carthage must be destroyed', it was because a senator held up a luscious, fresh fig from Carthage, symbolizing that this kingdom was so close that a fig could make the voyage without deteriorating. Rome did conquer Tunisia, and later the rest of North Africa. Tunisia became the Empire's breadbasket, supplying Rome with two thirds of its cereals.

The cuisines of North Africa are most influenced by the Arabs, who conquered the area in the late 7th century AD on their way to conquering Spain. They infused the food with sensuality – with spices, aromatic floral essences and delicious sweets. In the 16th and 17th centuries, when the Andalusian Moors and Jews were expelled from Spain and returned to North Africa, they brought back a rich Hispano-Muslim culinary culture that included a paper-thin pastry, called *ouarka* in Morocco, *dioul* in Algeria and *malsouka* in Tunisia. The returning Andalusians also brought chillis, potatoes and tomatoes, which had come to Spain from the New World. Chillis were embraced and became the basis for a seasoning paste called *harissa*, which is particularly important in the cuisine of Tunisia.

The Ottoman Turks, who made North Africa part of their empire in the 16th century, brought a cosmopolitan, Persian-influenced cuisine, the sophistication and subtleties of which are particularly reflected in the cooking of Morocco.

Finally, there is a French influence, stemming from their control of the area during the late 19th and early 20th centuries. Baguettes and croissants are much appreciated, and, whereas traditional North African cooking requires slow cooking techniques, the French introduced sautéing and frying. Also, dishes are often referred to by their French rather than Arabic names.

A taste of Spain
The Andalusian Moors and Jews brought oranges with them from Spain, and the fruit is now particularly popular in salads and in fruit drinks.

The influence of religion

Islam being the religion of the Maghreb, the daily fasting during Ramadan, as well as the feasting at its end, is very important, and pork is not eaten. This distinguishes the cuisines of North Africa and the Middle East from the European cuisines of the Mediterranean, which in other ways share many characteristics, such as a reliance on olive oil, pulses, fresh fruits and vegetables, as well as a love of big flavours.

Sephardic Jewish culture has also left an important culinary legacy in North Africa. Although most North African Jews abandoned the area during the 20th century to emigrate to Israel, France or Spain, Jewish cooking still rates among the four great cooking styles of Morocco, along with the food of Fez, Marrakesh and Tetouan. When the Sephardim and Marranos (Jews who had converted to Christianity to avoid persecution) returned from Spain and Portugal after 1492, they brought their dishes with them. One Sephardic dish that remains popular in Algeria and Morocco is *cassolita*, which contains pumpkin or winter squash, caramelized onions, almonds, raisins, sugar and cinnamon.

There were a considerable number of Marranos on the boats that went to the New World with Columbus, and they retained their contacts in Europe. As a result, it was, by and large, the Jewish merchants based in North Africa who were responsible for spreading New World foods throughout the Mediterranean.

Preserved foods

An important element of North African cuisines, preserved foods have come into common use partially due to the needs of nomadic Berber tribes. The flavours they impart to foods are unique to the Maghreb. Mutton is dried in the sun for *gueddid* (jerky), or cooked, then preserved in its rendered fat to produce *khli*, which is like French confit. Butter is clarified and aged in jars to make *smen*, which is added in small quantities to a variety of couscous dishes and *tagines* (gently simmered stews). Lemons are preserved in salt and are used widely in *tagines* and salads. Tomatoes are dried, tinned and frozen when in season, to be used during Ramadan in *harira*, the soup that is eaten to break the daily fast. Dried figs and dates are all-important, not only in sweets, but as offerings of welcome to guests.

Names of dishes

Many foods in North Africa are called after the manner in which they have been cooked. A *mhammar* is a dish cooked in two stages: first, the meat is cooked with spices in butter, then left to drain overnight; the next day it is browned until crusty. It was once a way to keep meat, before refrigeration; now it is considered a gourmet dish. A *tagine* (a type of stew) is cooked in an earthenware casserole of the same name. This has a conical lid, which traps the steam, resulting in a tender, moist stew. A *qadra* is a rich stew cooked in the bottom part of a *couscousière*, which is also known as the *qadra*.

SIGNATURE DISHES

Slata michwiya *A grilled salad with sweet, hot, grilled peppers, tomatoes and onion.*

Ommok houriya *Tunisian cooked carrot salad with varying garnishes.*

Makhouda *This Tunisian baked egg dish, like a crustless quiche, can have many fillings.*

Kefta *Spiced meatballs, which are usually sausage shaped and grilled on skewers.*

Tagine *A meat and vegetable or fruit stew, traditionally simmered in an earthenware dish with a conical top.*

Marqa *A ragout, usually served with bread.*

Chalada fawakeeh bi ma z'har *Fruit salad flavoured with orange-flower water.*

Kab el ghzal *The name of these almond-paste-filled pastries means 'gazelle horns'.*

Food through the day

Breakfast in North Africa is substantial. Beverages include strong Turkish-style coffee, which is sweet and concentrated, and strong, sweet mint tea (see box, page 132). Another beverage, really a food, that has been eaten since ancient times in Tunisia, is called *bessissa*. This is a bitter mixture of ground grains blended with olive oil and spices. Nuts, fruits and dates, sometimes stuffed with *rigoutta* (soft sheep's milk cheese), are served at breakfast, along with *bouillis* (porridges), cooked cereals or legumes. A typical breakfast dish is *droo*, a slow-cooked porridge made from ground sorghum cooked in water and flavoured with sugar and rose-geranium water or ginger. Other breakfast foods include: *m'halbia*, a creamy rice pudding with raisins; *harira*, a nourishing bean soup; *masfouf*, a fine couscous with milk or cream, sugar and fruits; and *madmouja*, a mixture of stale bread, nuts, honey and olive oil.

Lunch is also hearty, and is eaten late in the day; dinner is usually lighter, unless it involves entertaining guests. A traditional North African meal should last a couple of hours, but in today's world, particularly in the more secularized Tunisia, businessmen and women tend to spend less time at lunch and perhaps more time at dinner. This said, couscous is more likely to be eaten at lunch than at dinner, as it is very filling.

Desserts in North Africa are either very natural – fresh and dried fruit, particularly citrus fruits, dates, figs and apricots – or very sweet. Sweet desserts include pastries made from almond paste, dense pistachio cakes, rich ground-sesame halva and honey-drenched baklava, a legacy of both the Hispano-Muslim culture and the Ottoman Turks.

Special occasions

There is an Islamic saying that goes: 'You open the door to a stranger and you offer your hospitality for three days before you ask the reason for his visit.' Hospitality has been elevated to a high art here. A special occasion requires a banquet, called a *diffa*, and the abundance of the display is a measure of the host's hospitality.

When guests are received for a celebration, the walkway to the house or table may be strewn with rose petals. Upon arrival, the guest is met with dates, nuts and glasses of milk or whey. Before the meal there is a hand-washing ritual. A young family member or servant goes from guest to guest and washes each person's hands with water scented with rose petals or orange flowers. This is important, as it is customary to eat with the thumb and first two fingers of the right hand.

From the moment you sit down, there are little plates of food on the table, but eating never begins before saying the blessing, 'Bismallah'.

Traditional Muslim and Jewish foods are key in festivals of the Maghreb, but they have distinct regional inflections. In Morocco, where dried foods are a staple of the nomadic tribes, kourdess (dried offal) is used in a special couscous eaten at the Muslim festival of Achoura – a festival marking the slaying of Ali, the son-in-law of Muhammad. In Oran, Algeria, a famous fish and rice soup, called caldero, was traditionally eaten by Jews at Rosh Hashanah. Algerian anise bread was eaten to break the fast at Yom Kippur.

Merguez sausage
This spicy sausage may be included in a *mechoui* (meat grill). The cooking of meat is a man's task and meats are cooked outside over wood.

THE SOUKS

The ingredients for all North African dishes can be found in the souks, the food markets that bustle weekly in the countryside, daily in cities. Fruits, vegetables, couscous and dried beans of all sorts are piled high on stall after stall. One vendor will sell pink-tinged sea salt, coarse and fine, while others will offer a multitude of dates and almonds, or amazing displays of green, purple, black and brown olives. There will also be food stalls that sell prepared dishes, grilled or cooked in earthenware *tagines* on braziers. These are prepared by men for other men who are there on business.

Dishes at a special meal are traditionally served in a well-orchestrated succession. After little salads, like *zaalouk* (aubergine salad), chickpeas with cumin or grated raw carrots with orange, comes the beautiful *bastilla*, a complex pigeon pie dusted with sugar and cinnamon. Next are the *tagines* followed by the most important course, which is couscous. The most traditional couscous dish is *couscous aux sept légumes*, which contains seven different vegetables and a broth; but there are literally hundreds of other couscous dishes including lamb, mutton or chicken with vegetables of fruit, or pigeon with onions, figs and fresh favas.

At a really special occasion, such as a wedding feast, there will be *mechoui*, which will follow the couscous, or sometimes replace it. *Mechoui* is grilled meat – most often an entire lamb. Kebabs, meatballs and sausage might also be thrown in.

Towards the end of the meal, platters of fruit are passed and rose-petal water is circulated for hand-washing and rinsing the mouth. Next come mint tea and pastries. The last ritual is to thank God with 'Hamdullah', to which the host responds, 'B'sahatkoum', meaning 'to your health'.

Morocco

Although Morocco shares many culinary traditions with the other North African countries, its food tastes different. The cuisine of Morocco is richer and the haute cuisine more refined than those of Tunisia and Algeria. Moroccans love spices as much as the Tunisians and Algerians, but the spice culture here is a more subtle one. Among the defining spices you will find saffron, nutmeg, cinnamon, cumin, cloves and paprika.

Moroccan dishes mix sweet with savoury: *tagines* often combine meat with fruit, such as lamb with prunes or quince, or chicken with apricots; couscous is served with fish, raisins, sugar and saffron; and salads include carrot and orange salad, or orange and olive salad. These dishes represent the marriage of two of Morocco's riches: salt from the Mediterranean and Atlantic and sugar from the Arab merchants, who had the world monopoly on sugar until the Age of Discovery, when Europeans began to plant sugar cane in their new tropical colonies.

One ingredient that is unique to Morocco, because the trees are indigenous, is *argan* oil. This is a very rich-tasting, nutty oil from the fruit of a tree that grows in arid, misty regions. It is

Flat breads
(opposite)
In North Africa, where much food is eaten with the hands, unleavened flatbreads are important for enfolding or scooping up food.

obtained from the pits of the fruit, after goats, who feed on the leaves and fruits, excrete them. The most widely eaten dish made with this oil is a rich ground-almond and honey confection called *amlou*, made in the Souss region in the south, where there are vast groves of *argan* trees.

A regional flavour

Morocco has three gastronomic centres: Fez, Marrakesh and Tetouan. The cooks of Fez are particularly known for their skill at making the pigeon pie, *bastilla*. There is also a sweet, dessert version of the *bastilla*, called *knaffa*, made with milk and almonds. Essaouira, on the Atlantic coast, is also an important culinary town, particularly for its fish. Essaouira once had a large Jewish population; their specialities include sweet meatballs served with fish, and a fish dish called *tasira*, made with conger eel, raisins, onions and cinnamon.

In the mountainous northern and central regions and in the south, the cuisine is more rustic, with couscous dishes based on grains like sorghum and barley rather than semolina. The nourishing bean soup, *harira*, is a typical breakfast eaten in the Moroccan countryside. Specialities of the southern Souss region include tiny birds called *ehyells*, cooked with raisins and onions, and delicious *tassergal* (bluefish) caught off the coast. In the Pre-Sahara and outlying oases, Arab tribesmen eat meat such as camel, gazelle, hedgehogs, jackals and desert foxes, with flat bread baked in the sand.

■ MINT TEA: A CHOICE DRINK

THE NORTH AFRICAN DRINK OF CHOICE IS SWEET MINT TEA, WHICH IS POURED FROM HIGH INTO SMALL GLASS CUPS. IT IS DRUNK IN THE HOME, IN SHOPS AND IN CAFÉS. IT IS SOMETIMES ACCOMPANIED BY SWEET PASTRIES, AND IS ALWAYS ATTENDED BY MUCH CONVERSATION. THE FESTIVAL OF *ID AL FITR*, WHICH CELEBRATES THE END OF RAMADAN, IS MARKED BY MINT TEA SERVED WITH HUGE TRAYS OF FILLED PASTRIES.

BREAD: MORE THAN A FOOD

Bread, used for dipping and as a utensil for scooping up foods, is all-important to North African meals, and the only food not eaten with it is couscous. The first task of the day for every housewife is to make the dough and take the formed loaves to the local bakery on a tray. This tray joins many others to be baked for the midday meal. Breads are flat and round, with a springy, spongy texture. Sourdough is often the only leaven used. In the south, breads are often baked like tandoor breads, in a clay oven.

Algeria

The largest country of the Maghreb, and the second largest in Africa, Algeria's food is less understood than the food of its neighbours, partly because the country has closed in on itself since independence from France in 1962, and because of the civil war, which began in 1990. What we have learned about the food of Algeria has been learned largely from foreign émigrés.

Algerian food, like that of Morocco and Tunisia, has a mixture of Arab, Andalusian, Berber and European influences. Many of its dishes are a legacy of its once large Jewish community. In the eastern part of the country, the food is like that of Tunisia: spicy, incorporating *harissa* and cayenne. In the western part of Algeria, according to food historian Clifford Wright, sauces are slightly sweet and thickened, reflecting a European influence. In central Algeria one finds both traditional Arab and Hispano-Muslim influenced couscous, *keftas* and skewered foods. In addition to hot red peppers, Algerian cuisine includes black pepper, cumin, ginger, aniseed, wild parsley and cloves. Algerian-style couscous is steamed over broth and often mixed with diced carrots and peas, which have been sautéed in butter.

Tunisia

Tunisia marks the dividing line between the eastern and western Mediterranean. The easternmost country of the Maghreb, its cuisine is distinct in that of all the countries of the Arab world, both to its east and west, Tunisia is the only one with an extensive fish cuisine. This is not only because it has a long coastline, but, more importantly, because it has a wide continental shelf, necessary for fish to breed and feed. Although there is much fish to be had in Algeria and Morocco, there is not the variety or abundance that you find in Tunisia. A widespread use of *harissa* also distinguishes this cuisine.

Pasta and hard-crusted, white breads are also popular in Tunisia, which has always been explained by the country's proximity to Italy. Recent research, however, suggests that hardwheat pasta was actually invented in Tunisia around the 11th century and reached Italy later, in the Middle Ages, by way of Sicily, Tunisia's closest European neighbour. In any case, the proximity of Italy and the influence of Italy's colonial presence in North Africa has assured the continued importance of dried pasta, which takes on many shapes and is served with complex, spicy stews.

A regional flavour

There are differences between the cuisine of the south of Tunisia and that of the north, around Tunis. The cooking of the north tends to be richer, with more meat and more animal fat in general. But the real regional distinction is between the food eaten in the desert, home of the Berbers, and that eaten on the coast, where most of Tunisia's population lives. The coastal cuisine is vibrant and spicy, with a tremendous array of fish and vegetable dishes. In the inland areas, where water is scarce and the land infertile, the mainly Berber cuisine is more a diet of sustenance; people rely on simple, nutritious foods, such as mixtures of grains and dried beans, and on the nuts and fruits – dates, figs and oranges – that grow in desert oases.

An oil unique to Morocco
Goats are attracted to the *argan* tree by its fruit. Berber women gather the goats' droppings and extract the indigestible *argan* nuts to make oil. Harvested *argan* nuts are used also.

AFRICA

Africa, the second largest continent in the world, is a land of great geographical contrasts. Moving through vast deserts, tropical rainforests, grassy plateaus and wide savannahs, the foods change with the landscape.

KEY INGREDIENTS

SUGAR

SORGHUM

MILLET

FISH AND SHELLFISH

BEEF

CASSAVA

SWEET POTATOES

PLANTAINS

OKRA

GREENS

DATES

PEANUTS

Grinding millet
Grains form the basis of many African staples. Millet is an ingredient in such foods as couscous, bread, mash and beer.

One in eight of the world's population lives in Africa. Traditionally the peoples of Africa have been farmers and herders, but in recent decades famine, wars and poverty have resulted in migrations to urban areas, with one in five people now living in or around cities. The most densely populated areas are along the northern and western coasts, but the cuisines of this area are very different from the rest of the continent, so are discussed separately (see pages 126 to 133).

A taste of history

African cultures have been influenced greatly by outsiders. The Arabs brought Islam to North Africa in the 7th century, and the religion became established in many of the countries of Central Africa and West Africa as well. Europeans brought Christianity in the 16th century, and it became established throughout the rest of the continent. However, there are still many African peoples who practise early animist religions.

According to food writer Jessica Harris, African foods changed tremendously because of the ingredients introduced by Europeans during the Age of Discovery. The coconut tree arrived from South-east Asia, and sweet potatoes, maize, cassava, pineapple, guava and peanuts came from the Americas. As a result of the slave trade, the foods of parts of the Americas are very similar to African foods, both because of an exchange of ingredients, and because of African cooking techniques and tastes.

Throughout the 19th century, and early part of the 20th, Europeans ruled most of the countries of Africa and they left culinary, as well as linguistic, influences when they eventually departed: French cooking methods are used in some of the dishes of West Africa; the crusty rolls introduced to Mozambique and Angola by the Portuguese are still eaten for breakfast in cities; and in Kenya the British left their taste for garden vegetables and summer fruits. The indentured labourers from India and Malaysia, brought by the colonial powers to Eastern and Southern Africa, have also left their mark; rice, samosas and curries are not unusual on menus throughout these countries.

Staple foods

The food in Africa varies from region to region, yet there are important similarities in staple foods throughout the continent, namely: the reliance on grains and starches, which serve as a bed for everyday stew-like dishes, called *sauces*, made from meats and vegetables; the wholesale adoption of certain ingredients from the Americas, such as chillies, cassava, maize, peanuts and tomatoes; and the widespread use of greens, okra and beans.

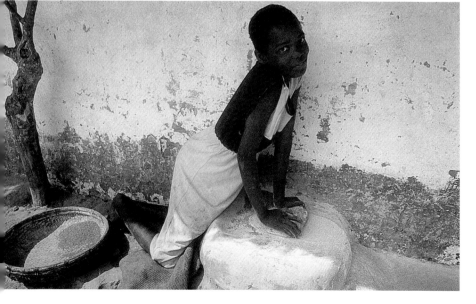

Grains and beans played a major role in African cuisines long before the arrival of the Europeans. In the Middle Ages, Arabic travellers reported that the people of the area that is now Mauritania and Mali ate beans and a type of millet known as *dukhn*. Africans also ate forms of sorghum, wheat and rice, which were, and still are, made into thick porridges, pancakes, fritters, bread and puddings, and served topped with *sauces*. Beans included kidney beans, black-eyed beans, broad beans, chickpeas and lentils. Yams – not to be confused with sweet potatoes – were also an important element in the various African diets. Dried or salted meat and fish were eaten when fresh types were not available. They were – and still are today – combined with vegetables and cooked in *shea* butter (a vegetable butter), sesame oil, peanut oil or palm oil. Dishes were seasoned with *melegueta* pepper (also called 'grains of paradise'), ginger and aromatic spices imported from North Africa. Salt was used sparingly. People drank water, either plain or sweetened with honey, or fresh or soured milk – from goats, sheep, camels or cows.

The Portuguese brought maize, white potatoes, tomatoes and cassava, and the tiny incendiary chilli peppers that had developed in Asia via the New World. These are now all African staples.

Throughout Africa, beer is drunk widely. It is made with millet, or with other regional starches like plantain or wild grains. A light beer called Star beer is popular in the former British colonies. In South Africa wine is produced and drunk widely by people of European descent.

Food through the day

Throughout Africa, there is African food, and there is European food, a legacy of the colonial powers, notably in the hotels and restaurants. English food is part of the gastronomic landscape in South Africa, Nigeria and Kenya, with English-style tea an afternoon ritual.

The main meal of the day, at midday, is a one-dish meal with a grain or starch base accompanied by a *sauce*. This *sauce* may be made from meat, fish, poultry or beans and vegetables,

and is usually seasoned with chillis and onion. Food is served from a large bowl, on a mat on the floor. Men and women often eat separately, and in most countries, silently. People eat with wooden spoons or with the right hand, taking pieces from the part of the bowl that is just in front of them. It is up to the host or hostess to make sure that the food in the bowl is regularly redistributed so that everybody has something to eat. The guests get the choicest morsels. In West and Central Africa milk is the main food eaten for breakfast, either fresh or cultured. The evening meal may also consist of milk, or a grain or starch, and broth or vegetable *sauce*.

Patterns of eating are different in the cities and countryside. In cities, lunch is the main meal of the day, whereas nomadic peoples usually do not eat at midday. Their main meal, however frugal, is the evening meal. It usually consists of cooked grains served with fresh or soured milk and, occasionally, meat or a soup made with meat, water, salt and spices.

The Gambia, smoking fish
Much of the fish that is eaten in West Africa is smoked. In countries where there are few refrigerators, it is an important method of preserving food.

West Africa and Central Africa

Mauritania, Senegal, The Gambia, Guinea-Bissau, Guinea, Sierra Leone, Liberia, Ivory Coast, Ghana, Togo, Benin, Nigeria, Cape Verde, Mali, Niger and Burkina Faso are the countries of West Africa. All but the last three countries, which are landlocked, have west coasts bordering the Atlantic Ocean.

Cameroon, Equatorial Guinea, Gabon, Congo, Zaire, Central African Republic and Chad make up the mostly steaming, tropical Central Africa. All but the last two countries extend west to the Atlantic Ocean and, with the exception of Chad, rainforests make up most of the landscape in these equatorial countries.

Nomadic herding dominates the northern, drier areas, the major livestock being cattle, sheep, goats and camels in the desert and semi-arid regions. Cash crops include cocoa, oil palms, cashews, coffee and bananas. On the coasts and along rivers, fish is an important part of the diet. Subsistence farming is the way of life for most of the population in the tropical regions, growing crops like millet, rice, peanuts, sugar cane, pulses and palm oil.

The style of eating grains or starches topped with a *sauce* or stew is similar across the region, but the staple bases vary from country to country or ethnic group to ethnic group. In Niger, Mali, Burkina Faso and parts of Nigeria, Ghana, Ivory Coast, Cameroon and Chad, millet is the most widely eaten staple, although sorghum, maize, and various wild grains are also appreciated. The grains are ground into flour, cooked into a mash, or made into couscous or patties, then topped with milk or a meat-based *sauce*.

Cassava and plantains are more important staples in the other rainforested Central African countries. Tropical fruits, like pawpaw and mangoes, are eaten with meats and eggs. Ostrich eggs, one of which can feed six people, are a great delicacy. Peanuts and sesame seeds are important foods, and chillis and salt the main seasonings. In the tropical rainforests there are still many tribes who live a hunting and gathering existence; wild

A staple from South America
The cassava root is collected, grated and dried in the sun. It is ground into a meal, for use in dishes like *fou fou*.

In Ethiopia eating is stratified; the country still has an upper class with an aristocratic tradition. The types of foods served by wealthy families are much the same as those served in humbler households – often bread with stew – but the quantities are vast in comparison, and the variety of dishes is much greater.

main course

In hoteli *(small restaurants) simple meals are
offered in huge portions. These consist of large
servings of a starch, such as potatoes, rice or the
Kenyan maize mush called* ugali, *accompanied by a
chicken, goat, beef or vegetable stew. One of Kenya's
speciality dinners is called* nyama choma, *a roast
meat feast including chicken, beef, game or lamb.
There are bars specializing in* nyama choma *served
with beer and accompanied by vegetables, most
often* sukuma wiki *(greens).*

dessert

Fruit is the most commonly eaten dessert.

drinks

*Chai (tea) is the national beverage, served
sweetened and with milk. You could also drink*
maziwala *(fermented milk), coffee or* bia *(beer).*

---

game, mushrooms, greens and insects may be
supplemented by cultivated beans, peanuts and
vegetables such as okra.

In Senegal the most widely eaten staples are
rice and millet. Millet is often ground and made
into couscous. The Yoruba people of the area eat
a variety of basic staples, including yams, cassava,
plantain, beans, maize and rice. The starches are
pounded and cooked into a paste, then eaten as
the base of a stew or sauce. The Igbo of South-
west Nigeria subsist primarily on yams and
cassava, with vegetable sauces.

North-eastern and central East Africa

Sudan, Eritrea, Ethiopia, Djibouti and Somalia
form North-east Africa. Kenya, Uganda, Rwanda,
Burundi, Tanzania, Zambia and Malawi are found
in central East Africa. The cuisine of Egypt, with
its Arabic influences, is more closely related to
the foods of the Middle East, so is discussed
elsewhere (see pages 118 to 125).

Sudan is a desert country watered by the Nile.
In the dry north the people are Arabic-speaking
Muslims, and in the south they are of African,
non-Muslim descent. In southern Sudan, where
there is more rainfall, the country is covered in
swampland and rainforest, and in the central
region by savannah and grassland. Subsistence
agriculture dominates the economy, though
cotton, gum arabic, sesame and peanuts are
important cash crops.

Eritrea, Ethiopia, Djibouti and Somalia make
up the region known as the Horn of Africa. These
countries are among the poorest in the world,
and have suffered terribly from drought, famine
and civil wars in recent years. The dry, stony
lands of Eritria, Somalia and Djibouti are
populated by mainly pastoral peoples to whom
the borders established by previous colonial
powers mean very little. Ethiopia has an
agricultural economy, with most of the
population involved in subsistence farming.
Coffee is the country's biggest export crop; it is
grown mainly in the mountains of Kaffa province,
from where the drink got its name. Coffee is also
important within these countries, particularly in
Ethiopia, where it is served to honour guests and
elaborate rituals accompany the preparation of
the drink (see box, page 140).

The largely nomadic populations of Somalia,
Sudan, Djibouti and Eritrea subsist mainly on
meat (from camels, cows, sheep and goats),
butter and milk, both fresh and soured. Somalia
is a mainly Muslim country, so no pork and very
little game is eaten. Some grain and gathered
plants are also consumed, as well as fruits such as
dates. Tea, sweetened with sugar, is the most
important beverage. Farmers who live along the

A source of two oils
The fruit of the oil palm,
grown in West Africa,
yields a reddish orange
palm oil, which is used in
cooking, as well as palm
kernel oil, a major
ingredient in margarine.

■ TEA: THE QUENCHING LEAF

THROUGHOUT WEST AFRICA, TEA IS THE BEVERAGE OF CHOICE. WHEN GUESTS COME TO VISIT, THE RITUAL OF THE 'THREE TEAS' IS PERFORMED. AFTER FIRST RINSING THE POT, THE HOST OR HEAD OF THE FAMILY HEATS THE TEA GENTLY OVER A FIRE. WHEN THE TEA IS READY, HE ADDS SUGAR, LEAVES IT FOR A FEW MINUTES, THEN POURS THE TEA BACK AND FORTH BETWEEN A GLASS AND THE POT TO SWEETEN THE TEA THROUGHOUT. THE HOST THEN TASTES A BIT AND, WHEN IT IS READY, HE SERVES IT IN SMALL GLASSES TO HIS GUESTS IN ORDER OF THEIR RANK. THEY PARTAKE THREE TIMES, THE TEA BECOMING PROGRESSIVELY SWEETER AND LIGHTER. AROMATICS OR MEDICINAL HERBS ARE OFTEN ADDED TO THE THIRD SERVING. A SAYING GOES: 'THE FIRST TEA IS BITTER LIKE LIFE; THE SECOND TEA IS SWEET LIKE LOVE; THE THIRD TEA IS SMOOTH LIKE DEATH.'

HERBS AND SPICES

BERBERE this red flavouring is an essential ingredient in Ethiopian cuisine, particularly in mutton dishes. It is an aromatic and very hot paste, combining pungent chillis and long pepper, as well as black pepper, ginger and fenugreek, and the sweeter cinnamon, cardamom, cloves and allspice

two major rivers, the Scebeli and the Giuba, raise beef, goats, sheep and poultry and grow maize, sorghum, millet, beans and vegetables. In the coastal towns and cities of the north-eastern African countries fish is widely consumed, and there is a relatively varied diet that is influenced by Indian Ocean trading partners.

Of the countries of North-east Africa, Ethiopia has the most distinctive cuisine; it is known for the cooking of the highlands, where the dominant ethnic group is the Christian Amharas. During the early centuries of the first millennium, Ethiopia had extensive contacts with southern Arabia, and also with Coptic Christians, whose religion was adopted in the 4th century. Today the population is mixed religiously, with a large proportion of both Muslims and Christians. The Coptic Christian Church has many fasting days on which no meat or animal products can be eaten, so the Ethiopian repertoire is rich in vegetarian dishes. However, there is also an array

of meat dishes cooked in copious amounts of butter, such as the favourite festival dish *kitfo,* which is a deliciously spicy beef tartare.

A great variety of fruits and vegetables are cultivated in Ethiopia, despite the fact that the country has recently suffered terribly from famines. Its principal grain is *teff,* a small millet-like grain, which is the basis for *injera,* the country's staple food. *Injera* is a thick, pancake-like sourdough bread with a spongy texture. It is often eaten in combination with *wat,* a meat stew flavoured with red pepper. *Injera* is not only a food: it also serves the function of plate and utensil. Accompanying dishes are placed on it – it is sometimes the only plate there is – and a bit of the bread is torn off, wrapped around the food and eaten. A custom at dinner parties is for one diner to select and wrap a choice morsel of food and to feed it to a fellow diner as a token of esteem or affection.

The flavours of Ethiopian dishes are spicy and complex: hot chillis, spices and herbs, like fenugreek, cardamom, ginger, peppercorns, cinnamon, holy basil, mint, onion and garlic, are widely used. Several of these are included in the fiery paste called *berbere,* served at all meals (see below left).

Alongside the typical Ethiopian foods served in restaurants, many Ethiopian restaurants today feature dishes like spaghetti and meatballs – a legacy of the Italian colonial period.

Africa's most dramatic highlands run through Central East Africa, from Uganda in the north to Malawi in the south, forming part of the Great Rift Valley. Much of the rest of the country is covered in savannah, with large areas converted into protected game parks, such as the Serengeti and Masai Mara. The rural population is made up of subsistence farmers and herders, particularly in the lower, less fertile country; in the highlands tea and coffee are an important source of income.

The Masai people, who live in the area of Kenya south of Nairobi, and in the bordering region of Tanzania, are nomadic herdsman who raise humpbacked zebu cattle. They live on its milk and its blood, and very occasionally their meat, but they never eat the meat of their animals on the same day that they drink their milk. Along the Great Rift Valley runs a chain of salt and freshwater lakes, including Lake Albert, Lake Nyasa and Lake Tanganyika. People living along these shores subsist on fishing, and in Malawi fishing has grown into a huge industry. The main source of protein here is a small fish called the *usipa*, which is dried before use.

The same types of crops that serve as staples in West Africa feed the people of central East Africa: sweet potatoes, cassava, millet, maize, rice, plantains and bananas. Most often these are served in the form of thick porridges or dumplings, and are accompanied with the stew-like *sauces* made with meat, beans or fish and vegetables and cooking oil.

Southern Africa

Angola, Namibia, Botswana, Zimbabwe, Mozambique, Swaziland, Lesotho and South Africa make up Southern Africa. There is great variation in the landscape of this part of Africa with vast swamps, woodlands, grassy savannahs, tropical forests, fertile farmlands and the high mountains of South Africa. The Namib Desert runs along the Atlantic coast of Namibia and the semi-arid Kalahari covers much of Botswana, so the agricultural economies of both these countries are based mainly on herding. Much of the world's mineral wealth – gold, copper, uranium, coal and diamonds – originates in Southern Africa.

Zimbabwe and South Africa have rich farmlands, and South Africa exports many fruits and vegetables to countries in the northern hemisphere. South Africa also has a thriving wine industry, which was begun with cuttings brought to the country by Protestants fleeing France in the 17th and 18th centuries.

Of the Southern African countries, South Africa has the most varied cuisines. Mirroring the country's former racial policies, there is 'White' South African food and 'Black' South African food, as well as distinctly British elements and distinctly Afrikaner elements. The international hotel cuisine and the dishes served on the South

African railway have traditionally been English-influenced, whereas South African home cooking reflects the Afrikaner traditions.

The most interesting cooking of this entire region is known as Cape Malay cooking. Centred in Cape Town, Cape Malay cooking is a marriage of Dutch and Malaysian culinary traditions. The first European settlers here were sent by the Dutch East India Company to grow and provide food and water for their ships sailing around the Cape of Good Hope between Holland and the East Indies. The Dutch soon began importing slaves to Cape Town from India, Ceylon (now Sri Lanka), Madagascar, Mozambique and the Indonesian islands. Those from the East were mostly Muslim, as are their descendants today, and with them came spices, condiments and many gastronomic festive rituals. Curries, *sambals* (mixtures of chillis and spices), chutneys, *bredies* (slow-simmered vegetable stews) and elaborate *birianis*, joined the Dutch repertoire of

Mopani worms
Actually caterpillars, these are a delicacy throughout Southern Africa. Often eaten as a snack with beer, they are cooked by boiling and sun-drying or by covering them with ash.

COFFEE: THE ETHIOPIAN RITUAL

AN ETHIOPIAN HOST WILL ALWAYS HONOUR HIS GUESTS BY ROASTING COFFEE IN FRONT OF THEM. THE BEANS ARE ROASTED IN A TIN SAUCEPAN CALLED A *MIGHAT* OVER A CHARCOAL BRAZIER, THEN BREWED IN A ROUND-BOTTOMED, CLAY POT CALLED A *JABANA*, WHILE FRANKINCENSE OR MYRRH ARE BURNED ON A PIECE OF CHARCOAL.

Making *ugali* (opposite)
Ground maize is all important to the Kenyan diet. This Giriama woman is making it into the staple mash, *ugali*.

Sun-dried meat
Seasoned with salt, spices and vinegar, *biltong* is dried in the sun and air – a traditional form of preservation.

buttered vegetables, *frikkadels* (meatballs), and baked goods, like custard tarts, waffles, pies, biscuits and pancakes. The French Huguenots, Protestants who arrived in the 17th and 18th centuries, contributed a wine-making and drinking tradition to the mix.

The Afrikaners were great pioneers, establishing vast farms and mines throughout South Africa and Namibia. Pioneer foods that evolved over the years include: a dried meat sprinkled with salt, vinegar and spices, called *biltong*, which is eaten both as a snack and as the basis for a main dish; *boerewors*, sausages which the pioneers made out of minced meat, cubed pork fat, spices and vinegar; and the *braai* (a South African barbecue), in which various meats are cooked over a wood fire. Vegetable and fruit preserves, important mainstays for the pioneering Afrikaners, remain popular foods.

In the 1860s many Indians were brought into Natal Province along the East Coast to work in the sugar plantations. Although the same spices had arrived earlier with the Cape Malays, the Indians used them in different proportions. Curries permeate South African cookery, but a curry from Durban is hotter than a Malay curry.

The diet of 'Black' South Africa is much like that of the rest of Africa, in that it is based on grains or starches topped with a stew or sauce. Here the mainstay is *mealie* (maize) ground and made into a kind of mash mix called *foo-foo*, which the Dutch call *pap* and the Bantu call *putu*.

The waters off the South African coast are rich with seafood. The tails of South African spiny lobster, called *kreef*, served braised or curried at home, are shipped all over the world, and local fish such as *kingklip* and *snoek* (barracuda) are enjoyed in coastal areas. *Ingelegde vis* (pickled *snoek*) is an important Cape Malay dish, as are fish *birianis* and a dish made with dried *snoek*, onions and potatoes, called *snoeksmoor*.

SIGNATURE DISHES

Fou fou *Called many different names, these mashes, made with yams, maize, cassava, millet or potato are staples everywhere.*

Thiebou dienne *A rice and fish stew, which is the national dish of Senegal.*

Le to sauce baobab *A combination of a mash made from grains and a stew made with baobab leaves, smoked fish and chillis.*

Mechoui *Lamb is roasted in a pit for this speciality of Mauritania, Chad and Sudan.*

Wat *Hot peppers flavour this Ethiopian stew.*

Sosaties *Spicy kebabs from Zimbabwe and South Africa made with lamb or mutton.*

Biltong *This South African jerky is made from beef, venison or large game birds.*

Gesmoorde kreef *Braised spiny lobster popular in South Africa.*

ASIA AND AUSTRALASIA

INDIA

In spite of the diversity of geography and peoples on this vast subcontinent, a recognizable Indian cuisine has evolved, which maintains a strong identity because of the complex way spices and seasonings are used.

KEY INGREDIENTS

CORIANDER

CUMIN

CHILLIS

GINGER

MUSTARD SEEDS

TAMARIND

TURMERIC

BASMATI RICE

BREAD

DHAL (LEGUMES)

ONIONS

PICKLES, CHUTNEYS AND RELISHES

India is the world's second-most populated country, and almost a fifth of the world's population lives on the Indian subcontinent, which also includes Pakistan, Bangladesh, Nepal, Sri Lanka and Butan. Bounded on the north by the Himalayas and on the north-west by the Hindu Kush mountains, and with the Arabian Sea to the west and the Indian Ocean and Bay of Bengal to the east, India's landscape and climate vary from that of very high, snow-capped mountains to hot, tropical rainforest with a monsoon climate. Almost three-quarters of India's population lives in villages, yet its major cities, New Delhi, Calcutta and Bombay, are teeming with people, many of whom live – and therefore eat – on the street.

The influence of religion

India is a deeply spiritual country with a long and often turbulent history. Home to three of the world's major religions, Buddhism, Hinduism and Sikhism, the other important faiths in India include Christianity, Jainism (an indigenous faith that grew out of Hinduism) and Islam, which arrived in India at the end of the 10th century with the Muslim invasion from Central Asia.

India's cuisines are intricately tied up with these many religions. Hindus, who are by far the largest religious group – making up around 80 per cent of the population – do not eat beef. Nor do Sikhs, many of whom are strict vegetarians. The second largest religious group, Muslims, who make up around 12 per cent of the population, eschew pork and alcohol. And the small Jewish community that still exists in India – mostly in Bombay and to a lesser extent in Calcutta – adheres to the Jewish dietary laws. Another minority are the Parsees, of Iranian decent, whose

Zoroastrian religion shares the Hindu prohibition of beef, but allows other types of meat.

Today, somewhere between 20 and 30 per cent of India's population is vegetarian, a legacy of its Hindu and Buddhist tradition. The origins and spread of vegetarianism were both spiritual and economic in nature. Around 600 BC, as the Hindu belief in the transmigration of souls took hold, so, too, did vegetarianism. The avoidance of meat was a basic tenet of a pious, non-violent and ethical life, but it also made economic sense to keep animals, rather than kill them for food. Early on, the Indians realized that cows were much more valuable alive than dead, because much more in the way of food could be obtained from the milk of a cow than from its flesh. Milk and its resulting products, like *ghee*, curds, yogurt, buttermilk and cheese, have been the most highly esteemed foods in India since ancient Vedic times. Moreover, cattle were the only draught animals that could work efficiently in India's hot monsoon climate, pulling a wooden plough through sodden fields and not requiring the pasturage needed by asses and horses.

The spread of vegetarianism in India was facilitated by its sheer abundance of vegetable foodstuffs. Such a wide variety of fruits, vegetables, grains and legumes could be grown that an interesting, varied vegetarian diet was possible as far back as 1000 BC. Many of India's legume-based dishes, particularly those of southern India, were probably eaten by the earliest inhabitants of the Indus Valley. Of course, the diet of the poor was a very simple and austere one, and it remains so today, but the wealthy classes and the Brahmin priests, to whom vegetarianism became a symbol of piety, and thus prestige, could eat very well.

All Hindus and Sikhs in India believe in the sanctity of the cow and eschew beef, but they do not necessarily deny themselves other meats, such as chicken, goat or seafood. Brahmin and Jain Hindus, however, are strict vegetarians: they eat no meat, poultry, fish, shellfish or eggs, and some will not even eat food that resembles meat or evokes the colour of blood, such as tomatoes, beetroot and watermelons. Nor do they use onions and garlic – stimulating seasonings associated with meat. The spice asafoetida, which has a flavour evocative of onions, is an important ingredient for these vegetarians. The Jains have such reverence for life of all kinds that they will not farm the land, for fear of killing insects. As a result, they have become one of the great merchant classes of India.

Among the Hindu populations of India, there are regional exceptions to the vegetarian traditions. The Hindu Brahmins of Kashmir, called Kashmiri Pandits, have a history of being passed back and forth between Muslim and Hindu conquerors, resulting in forced religious conversions. During long periods of Muslim rule, meat, particularly lamb, became important in

their diet, and has remained so. However, they still do not use garlic and onions, as the Kashmiri Muslims do. In Bengal, Hindu Brahmins eat fish; indeed, fish are so abundant here that they are called *jal toori*, meaning 'cucumbers of the sea'. Also the Bengali Hindu Brahmins eat meat on special occasions, such as the festival of Durga Pooja, when animals are ritually sacrificed to the Goddess Durga, or Kali. The flesh of these sacrificed animals is eaten because it is considered pure and holy.

Staple foods

The world's most widely cultivated cereal, rice, probably originated in India, where it was cultivated more than 5000 years ago, later spreading through China and into Persia. Alexander the Great is known to have brought it to Greece after his conquests of northern India in 327 BC. After China, India is the second largest consumer of rice in the world, and one-third of all arable land is given over to growing this grain.

Over the entire Indian sub-continent, from Pakistan – where the much prized basmati rice is grown – to Sri Lanka, long-grain varieties are

Street eating
Ways of eating are uncomplicated: leaves may be used as plates, and food is eaten with the right hand.

generally preferred. Common types include basmati and patna. Rice flour is used to make breads and sweets, such as the popular rice and lentil cakes, called *idli*.

Rice may be boiled, steamed or fried; it is flavoured with all kinds of herbs and spices, including turmeric and saffron. In the south, as one enters the more tropical climates of Kerala and Tamil Nadu, it is often flavoured with coconut. Rice is cooked with vegetables and meats and made into pilafs, *birianis* and kedgerees. It is garnished with nuts and dried fruit and, for the most auspicious occasions, it is even decorated with gold leaf; such is the value of this grain, that it is considered fitting that rice and gold share the same plate.

A typical Indian family can spend as much as a third of its monthly food budget on milk and milk products. Cows have been worshipped since ancient times and cow's milk, called *doodh*, is enjoyed as a beverage, and is served cold with spices in summer, and warm with saffron and cardamom in winter. Milk is used to enrich savoury sauces, and is incorporated into many desserts and sweetmeats.

Buttermilk is one of the most popular drinks in India. It is used to make sweet drinks called *chach* or *lassi* and savoury drinks called *mattha*. Buttermilk is also combined with vegetables, grains and legumes in moist salads, and is used for cooling soups.

Dahi is a thick, creamy yogurt, usually made from buffalo milk, and is present in one form or another at just about every Indian meal. *Dahi kadi* (yogurt cheese), made by draining yogurt in a cheesecloth bag, is a speciality of the west-coast states of Gujarat and Maharashtra.

Desi ghee (Indian butter), also called *makkhan*, made from yogurt or yogurt cheese, is popular in northern and western regions. It is eaten for breakfast with local breads, such as *makka ki roti* (a maize and radish bread), or millet bread made with chillis. *Desi ghee* is melted also and then folded into lentil dishes and mustard purée, to

Where fish are plentiful
Fishing is a major occupation for men on the coast. Women sell the fresh catch that day.

make a classic dish of the Punjab region. Butter is made from yogurt, or from clotted cream made from yogurt, and has a characteristic sour flavour. *Usli ghee* (clarified butter) is the favourite cooking fat of Indian vegetarians, particularly in the north. It has a pale yellow colour and a nutty flavour. It keeps for quite a long time. Fresh cheeses, called *chenna* or *paneer*, provide an extremely important source of protein in India. *Chenna*, made by curdling milk and separating the creamy curds, is used in the sweets of Bengal and in other sweetmeats and desserts. *Paneer*, which is pressed *chenna*, is used in a wide variety of savoury dishes.

Rabadi (thickened milk sauce), *khurchan* (milk flakes) and *khoya* (milk fudge) are sweet products made from slowly boiled milk. They are used in popular Indian sweetmeats and candies. *Malai* (clotted cream), made from milk or yogurt, is used as a topping for fruit and as in ingredient in sweetmeats, such as the classic Bengali dessert called *ras malai*.

Spices

These have been at the foundation of Indian cooking since ancient times. Black pepper, in particular, was for a long time one of India's most valuable commodities. Southern India is spice country: mustard, turmeric, black pepper, asafoetida and ginger were all in use here during the 1st millennium BC, as were several spices that had been introduced by Indonesian traders, including cinnamon, nutmeg, mace and cloves. Spice merchants from the south-western Indian coast traded with Rome, and later with Arab merchants, who introduced coriander, cumin and almonds. Spices and herbs have several functions beyond seasoning. Some are used as aromatics, some for colour, some as souring agents, and some thicken or tenderize dishes. Many contribute more than one attribute to a dish; for example, saffron adds both colour and a marvellous savoury flavour. The Indian cook knows how spices interact, not only with the food, but also within the human body.

nut, lime paste, fennel seeds, cardamom and cloves, are chewed after dinner, also serving the function of refreshing the palate. Fenugreek seeds, when soaked in water, are often added to heavy, starchy and leguminous dishes because they, too, are known to aid the digestion. Black salt and lemon juice increase blood circulation and stimulate the appetite, so they are routinely sprinkled onto *chat* dishes, which are spicy north Indian appetizers.

Spices are also important to the religious life of Hindus. Part of the balance and harmony that Hindus strive for has to do with body temperature, and this is affected by spices, according to their holy scriptures. Some spices generate internal body heat, and are recommended for cold weather; these are known as 'warm spices' and include bay leaf, black cardamom, cinnamon, ginger powder, mace, nutmeg and red pepper. Other spices are said to take body heat away; known as 'cool spices', these include fennel, cloves and green cardamom. Certain spices are good for inducing perspiration; this is why many Indians drink hot tea laced with spices during hot weather.

A regional flavour

India's many cuisines have been influenced in different ways by regional cultural and religious factors, as well as by local geography and climates. Invaders, including Aryans, Persians, Greeks, Central Asians and Europeans, have all played their part, as have trading partners as diverse as Greeks, Romans, Arabs, Chinese and Indonesians. The Central Asian Muslims had the most widespread and lasting effect, particularly in the north of India.

Through the islands of South-east Asia, Indians made contact with China, an important trading partner for hundreds of years; oranges, tea, peaches, lychees and soybeans were all introduced by the Chinese.

The Europeans left their mark by bringing New World foods, such as the chilli and potato. The influence of the Portuguese, who arrived with Vasco de Gama in 1498, can still be detected in certain dishes in the south, particularly in Goa,

Fertile plains
Wheat, maize, millet and barley are gathered and transported by hand in the fertile northern plains south of the Himalayas.

Spices and herbs have medicinal properties, which have been documented in ancient Hindu scripts and are still highly regarded. Asafoetida and ginger root, for instance, are known to counteract flatulence and colic, so they are traditionally added to lentil and other leguminous dishes. Herbs and spices that stimulate digestion, such as betel leaf and betel

BREADS: A DELICIOUS DIVERSITY

The staple of northern and central India, even more so than rice, Indian breads are flat breads, and most of them are unleavened. The exception are the delicious tandoor-baked nans, which are made commercially. Other breads are made daily in homes. In addition to plain wheat breads, an array of stuffed and spiced breads are made, some of them meals in themselves. Breads made with millet flour are popular in north India, and in southern India, breads are often made with rice flour or a combination of fermented legumes and rice.

The basic skillet-baked wholemeal flat breads are called *roti* or chapatti. Besan *roti* are made from chickpea flour and are a speciality of north-west India. They are usually seasoned with cumin seeds and onion. *Makki ki rotis* are made with radishes, and are a speciality of the Punjab Sikhs.

Poppadom are crisp, paper-thin wafers made from mung beans or *urad dhal* (black gram beans), sold dried, then roasted, grilled or fried at home. They can be plain or seasoned with cayenne pepper, black pepper or garlic.

One of the great treats of India are *poori*, deep-fried, puffed breads. *Khas khas ki poori* are seasoned with cumin seeds or poppy seeds, while *aloo poori* are mixed with sweet potatoes and spices.

Nan are flat, yeasted breads, baked in a hot tandoor oven. There are many versions. *Pathiri nan* are rice-flour bread, and are a speciality of the Malabar Muslims. *Dhebra nan* are a millet and squash bread made with chickpea flour, chillis, ginger and garlic, and are a local Gujarat speciality. *Paratha* is rich, flaky wholemeal bread, sometimes stuffed to make *aloo paratha* with potato, *palak paratha* with spinach, or *phool ghobi paratha* with cauliflower.

a Portuguese colony for 150 years. More widespread still is the contribution the British made to the whole cuisine in the form of Anglo-Indian dishes. During the nearly 200 years that the British ruled India, Indian cooks created dishes especially for their British masters. These include a popular meat cutlet dish, called *gosht tikka*, kedgeree (a breakfast dish consisting of rice, fish, boiled egg and butter) and the well-known soup, mulligatawny – a name that comes from the Tamil language of southern India and literally means 'pepper water'.

Northern India

This part of India has very cold winters and hot summers, when the mercury can rise to 49°C. Basmati rice is grown in the foothills of the Himalayas and eaten widely, but bread is the most important staple. This fertile area, which is irrigated by the Indus and Ganges rivers, provides rich soil for growing all sorts of grains.

North Indian cuisine, as compared to the cooking of southern India, has evolved widely over the centuries, due to the influence of invaders who entered India from Central Asia through the Hindu Kush passes. These nomadic, meat-eating cultures found the land to be similar to the high, arid country they had come from, and continued to raise sheep in the cool foothills of the Himalayas. Lamb thus became an important part of the north Indian diet, particularly in the disputed region of Kashmir – a magical area of terraced gardens and lakes, with walnut and fruit orchards and highly prized saffron crocuses. Goat and chicken are the other main meats of northern India.

The food of the north was particularly influenced by Muslim tribes, who eventually established the Moghul Dynasty in 1526, with Delhi as their capital. The Moghuls ruled for 200 years, and, as well as building many lavish palaces, fortresses and mosques, which have become emblematic of India, they introduced a highly refined and sensual cooking style, which was deeply inspired by Persian culture. Eventually the Moghuls embraced local herbs, spices and cooking styles, and the combination of foods and cooking techniques evolved into a lasting, sophisticated cuisine known as Moghul cooking. The Persian origins of many of the better-known Moghul dishes are clearly recognizable, both in name and substance; they include: saffron-specked, ornately garnished meat pilafs called *biriani*; braised meat and vegetable dishes, known as *korma*; grilled or fried small pieces of meats in a kebab; pot-roasted meat or vegetables, known as *dum*; *halwa*, the sweet, nut and fruit-based desserts; and meatball-based dishes called *kofta*. Moghul flavourings are delicate and the dishes are rich, like those of their

Persian antecedents. The spices used are mild and evocative – cinnamon, cardamom, mace, nutmeg, cloves and saffron. Sauces are silky, laced with yogurt, cream and *usli ghee*, the main cooking fat of northern India. Fruits, nuts and nut butters are used in savoury dishes.

The tandoor ovens that are used in the north for baking breads and for roasting meats also originated in Persia, but it was in north-western Peshawar, after the Moghul period, that the method of cooking skewered, marinated meats in the ovens was invented. This is known as Tandoori food, and it is one of the most popular cooking styles of India.

Despite the profound influence of the meat-eating cultures that have settled in north India, the states with the highest percentage of Indian vegetarians are the north-western Indian states of Gujarat, Rajasthan, Punjab-Itaryana and Uttar Pradesh. This is due to the prevalence of Hinduism and Buddhism in these states.

Outside of India, in England particularly, much of the cooking of north India is known as Balti cooking, a name deriving from the region of Baltistan, a remote area of the Himalayas, which was absorbed by Pakistan in 1947. Following partition, many Baltistanis emigrated to Britain, and a great number of them created restaurants. Their food became commonly known as Balti food. However, it is also known as *karahi* cooking, a *karahi* being the two-handled, wok-like pan that is widely used in the region.

The north-eastern edges of the Himalayas, the mountains of Assam and Darjeeling, are cool and wet, ideal for growing tea. Tea came to India from China, but it was the British, who ruled India during the 19th and early 20th centuries, who created the great Assam and Darjeeling plantations. India eventually surpassed China as the number one tea-exporting country.

Bengal

The Ganges River flows eastwards from the northern plains into the fertile lands of Bengal, eventually emptying into the Bay of Bengal. An important rice-growing region, this area is hot and humid. Coconut palms abound, and fish and shellfish, both freshwater and ocean, are the most important source of protein here. Fish is even eaten by Brahmins, the highest Hindu caste, who, in other parts of India, are the strictest of vegetarians. The main cooking fat of Bengal is the piquant mustard-seed oil, a product of the lush mustard plants grown throughout the region. Mustard is an important spice in Indian cooking also, as it is used in garnishes, seasonings, curry powders and pastes.

The drink of choice
A third of the world's tea comes from India, but it is still picked by hand. *Chah* (tea) is widely enjoyed here, often drunk spicy and hot, so that it induces sweating and so cools the body.

The food of Calcutta, in west Bengal, includes many milk-based sweets and fried snacks. The Bengali love sweets, a taste that was encouraged by the Portuguese, who colonized the area in the 16th century and brought with them many egg-sweet specialities. Two minority communities in Calcutta have distinctive cuisines. One is the Hakka Chinese, who probably came to the area around 100 years ago. Hakka Chinese food includes many stir-fries, steamed dishes and soups seasoned with soy sauce, ginger and fresh coriander. The Hakka are Buddhists, and, although theirs is a vegetarian tradition, chicken, pork, duck and seafood are popular. The other interesting minority cuisine is that of the Armenian Christians, who came to Calcutta in the 17th century after a sojourn in Persia. Some of their specialities, such as their *mis* and *khasho* (lamb and vegetable soup) and *mis pilau* (lamb and vegetable pilau) originated in Armenia, while others, such as the greens omelette known as *kookoo*, came from Persia.

Western India

The cooking of the western province of Gujarat, south of Rajasthan on the Arabian Sea, has a very strong vegetarian influence, due to the historical presence of the Jain Hindu sect, who have been in Gujarat since the 6th century BC. The Jains are the strictest of vegetarians, so two thirds of the population here are vegetarian. Bread is the staple, and lentil and other legume dhals, as well as vegetables cooked in sesame oil, are widely eaten. Other characteristic foods are savoury fried snacks, which can travel well on religious pilgrimages. The soil in this part of India is very rich, producing cotton, millet, barley, legumes and a wide variety of vegetables.

Southern India

At different times wet, dry and humid, southern India has a monsoon climate. Rice is the principal staple here, and is widely cultivated. With the exception of the cooking of Hyderabad, which was founded by Muslim royalty in 1589 and has always been a centre of Moghul cooking, southern culinary habits were less influenced by

the Moghuls than those in the north. Spicing here is hotter and less subtle. Indeed, it is sometimes fiery, as it was through the southern ports that the chilli pepper found its way into India from the New World, introduced by the Portuguese. As black pepper had been used here for thousands of years, the chillis met with immediate acceptance and quickly worked their way into the southern India spice repertoire.

Except for along the coasts, where fish is eaten widely, Hindu vegetarian practices are strong and long-standing in southern India. Pulses play a major role in the cuisines of this region, not only in the form of dhals, but also as the basis for flat breads made with a combination of ground, fermented legumes and rice. These types of breads, known as *dosas* and *rotis*, are much more common in the south than wheat-based breads.

The eastern plains of southern India are wide, flat and fertile, providing the population with an incredible assortment of vegetables and tropical fruits. Date palms yield not only dates, but also a

Fried snacks
(opposite)
Served on most busy streets, snacks are an everyday food. There is a huge variety, including *bhajis* (chickpea-flour-coated vegetables) and *samosas* (filled pastries).

Pulses: the vital protein
With a largely vegetarian population, peas, beans and lentils are a good source of energy. There are more produced in India than anywhere else in the world.

Fresh vegetables
Indian markets abound in colourful vegetables. In the home they may be cooked simply, by frying them in spices, or puréed or mashed and fried.

Reading the MENU

INDIAN DISHES ARE NOT SERVED IN COURSES, BUT AT THE SAME TIME — DESSERT INCLUDED — ON A ROUND TRAY CALLED A THALI.

main dish

There is always one food on the thali based on a protein. For non-vegetarians the choice might include grilled kebabs, a biriani, or a fish dish, such as masala jheengari (prawns with spices and onions). Vegetarian main dishes are based on vegetables, cheese or legumes.

side dishes

Dhals (puréed legumes), raitas (yogurt salads), chat (salads), light soups and simple vegetable dishes are served on the side. Several raitas and vegetable dishes may be served, but only one dhal.

staples

The starches of the meal come from rice, rice pilafs or breads. Breads are favoured in the north, rice in the south.

desserts

These are for the most part sweet, milk-based puddings or custards.

drinks

Indians usually drink cold water with their meals, although in restaurants beer is popular. Fruit punch and yogurt or buttermilk drinks are also served.

delicious, dark-brown, unrefined sugar and syrup from its sap, called palm jaggery and jaggery syrup. These are used in the special confections of the region.

The daily diet of the tropical coastal regions consists of fish and shellfish cooked with coconut and rice. The most popular fish are the pomfret, a white fish, and bombil, a small, transparent fish, which is sold dried and also called Bombay duck. To a great extent, coconut milk replaces dairy milk here, forming the basis for many curries. Coconut oil and sesame oil are the main cooking fats. Banana trees provide abundant fruit, as well as platters in the form of leaves.

Goa was a Portuguese colony during the 16th and early 17th centuries, and its cuisine reflects both Portuguese and Hindu tastes and sensibilities. European influences include: the addition of vinegar as a seasoning; the widespread use of pork in vindaloos, sausages and *feijoadas*; and the popularity of egg sweets

SIGNATURE DISHES

Samosas *Stuffed, deep-fried turnovers. Most popular are* aloo samosa *(potato-filled) and* keema samosa *(meat-filled).*

Dhal *Puréed legumes are present at most Indian meals.*

Seek kebab *These are India's most popular kebabs, made with minced lamb dipped in herbs and spices.*

Biriani *Elaborate pilafs in which layers of rice and meat or vegetables dotted with saffron are steamed and served on a platter.*

Mughalai korma *A Moghul braised chicken dish, served with yogurt, spices and cream.*

Tandoori chicken *Chicken is cooked on a spit in a clay oven for this now widespread dish, which originated in the north. The meat may be served dry or with a sauce.*

and other desserts, which incorporate abundant coconut and sugar. Some of these same influences can be seen in the food of the eastern state of Maharashtra.

Food through the day

The main meals in the home are lunch and dinner, with more emphasis on the midday meal. Throughout the day, however, there are other meals and traditional snacks worth noting, including brunch, *tiffin* and high-noon tea.

Breakfast is simple, with many regional variations. In some areas, people might eat nothing more than bread smeared with butter, with which they drink a cup of milky, spice-laced tea. In Bengal, people customarily eat vermicelli pudding with cardamom-scented bread. In the south, coffee with steamed milk is preferred, taken with crepes or dumplings and hot sauces and chutneys. In Gujarat, millet bread with green chillis and chutneys are common breakfast fare, and, in Kashmir, shortbread seasoned with fennel, berries and green tea are typical.

In southern India, people rise very early and work in the fields until around 9 am, when they eat a full lunch. Then, sometime between noon and 3 pm, they might eat a light meal called *tiffin*, which can be quite elaborate, but usually is more what Westerners would perceive as a light lunch. For the English community during the British Raj, *tiffin* was an important family meal, and in the 19th century quite a large one. *Tiffin* dishes are usually grain-based, and may include rice pilafs and stuffed breads, *dosas* (crepes), *idli* (dumplings), *opma* (semolina pilafs) and noodles.

Most Indian meals consist of many dishes, all served at the same time – including dessert. The foods are served in small cups called *katoori*, which are placed on a large, round tray called a *thali*. In southern India, a large banana leaf might replace the *thali*. Food is customarily eaten with the right hand only.

There are several elements to an Indian meal. For non-vegetarians, a main dish would include meat or fish, while for vegetarians it would consist of vegetables with a protein, such as legumes or a dairy product, in a rich sauce. There may be several side dishes, including a vegetable dish, a rice dish, a dhal, perhaps a soup, a vegetable salad, a yogurt *raita*, chutneys, pickles and bread. Bread sometimes replaces rice, particularly in the north, where it is used to scoop up foods, which are generally drier than southern foods. In the south rice serves as a mop for the gravies and sauces that characterize the regional cuisine. Desserts are, for the most part, sweet, milk-based puddings or custards.

Eating practices are highly ritualistic. The purity of the food is of utmost importance. In each region, the position of food on the plate or banana leaf is specific, based on age-old belief systems, religious taboos and regional needs. Food has six tastes: sweet, sour, salty, bitter, pungent and astringent. All of these must be present if a meal is to be balanced, as each of these tastes exerts a different action on the body's humours. Texture is also important.

Indian sweetmeats
There is much confectionery in India, particularly in Portuguese influenced areas. Sweets are made using rice flour, milk, vermicelli, sago and almonds.

CENTRAL ASIA AND THE CAUCASUS

Landscape and climate have determined much of this region's eating habits. Central Asia is, for the most part, barren, so a nomadic lifestyle predominates, and the diet is largely based on foods that are portable and quickly made.

KEY INGREDIENTS

SHEEP'S TAIL FAT

FERMENTED BUTTER

CORIANDER

SESAME SEEDS

LAMB

BEEF

YOGURT

DRIED CHEESE

CHICKPEAS

APPLES

POMEGRANATES

DRIED FRUITS

Hot potato seller
In Tibet, 'the land of snows', cooked snacks, such as baked potatoes, are very popular.

Geographically, this is an enormous region, stretching from the Middle East to Mongolia and China's Xinjiang Province, through Afghanistan and northern Pakistan. It is an area of high mountains and grasslands, of inhospitable deserts and occasional oases, of intense winds and of extremes of heat and cold. This part of the world has long been populated by nomadic herdsmen who use the sparse pastures for sheep, yaks and goats. The herds provide meat and milk for nourishment, and wool for trading. Grains are cultivated by semi-nomadic people who live in villages and also tend herds. In the warmer areas wheat is grown, whereas barley is the main staple in the colder high-altitude places, such as Tibet.

In oases and valleys, fruit and vegetables are farmed, and most families possess chickens, as well as sheep and goats. In Tajikistan, valleys are fed by melted snow from the mountains. A variety of melons are grown here, as well as pistachios, peaches and other tree fruits.

The influence of religion

Islam is the main religion of Central Asia, and has been since the 8th century AD. Many ancient Islamic cities exist in this part of the world; Samarkand, Bukhara and Tashkent were key points for merchants travelling the Silk Road that stretched from China through to the Middle East and Europe, and these cities became important market towns.

The urban food of Central Asia, and the cooking of the more fertile areas such as the Hunza Valley of Pakistan and the valleys of Tajikistan, reflect the early unity of these places with the Persian Empire. Although Central Asian countries and their cities have been isolated from each other and from Persia (now Iran) for a few hundred years, their rice dishes, soups and recipes combining meat with fruit, show Persian influences. However, the rustic foods of Central Asia, with chillis, cumin and black peppercorns, tend to be more robustly spiced than the more subtle Persian versions.

In the latter part of the 20th century, much of this area was under Soviet control and many religious practices were suppressed – Islamic eating rituals had to be carried out in secret. Independence in the early 1990s brought a revival of Islamic customs.

Until the Jewish emigrations to Israel of the 19th and early 20th centuries, a community of Iranian-speaking Jews, known as the Bukharan Jews, inhabited many towns in Uzbekistan. They were a prosperous merchant class until the Russian Revolution, and were known for their good food, hospitality and legendary feasts.

The Bukharan merchants were largely self-sufficient for food: they kept cows for milk and chickens for eggs; stored preserves, sheep's tail fat and dried fruits in large cellars; distilled their own arrack; and made a boiled-down grape syrup called *shini*, as well as tomato juice and wine. They lived closely with the Muslims, and their dining habits were similar, eating food at low tables, on a floor strewn with cushions or blankets. Bukharan Jewish food was rich in meat, with vegetables eaten only in meat stews. Their most prestigious dish was *pilof*, a rice dish with carrots, chopped onions, raisins, chicken and meat. Rice, being highly regarded, was reserved for special occasions. Bukharan flavours were subtle; food was seasoned mostly with salt, pepper, garlic, turmeric, saffron and coriander.

Tibet

If there is one grain that characterizes Tibetan food, it is barley. The local flat bread, *amdopali*, is made from barley and named after the large north-eastern region, Amdo. High-altitude nomads eat barley in the form of *tsampa*, which consists of barley that has been roasted or parched, then milled to a flour. *Tsampa* is sprinkled into Tibetan tea flavoured with aged butter and salt or soda, to produce a dry porridge, which is eaten in small lumps.

In the Changtang region of Tibet, people live at elevations ranging from 4500 to 5500 m. The nomads, called Goloks, herd sheep, yaks and goats. In the winter, men travel to salt pans near the northern edge of the region to gather salt, which they trade for barley. Dried mutton or yak meat is a staple in these thin-aired regions, as is dried cheese, which is cut into small squares and threaded, for easy storage and transportation.

Another Tibetan staple is milk from *dzi* (female yaks). *Dzi* produce milk year-round in cold high altitudes, unlike goats and sheep, which produce for only a few months a year. The Tibetans make butter, cheese and yogurt from the milk. The butter, which ferments over time, is stirred into tea, and is also used to protect hair and skin against the cold dry air.

Mongolia

Like the rest of Central Asia, this is a land where herding and the nomadic life determine the way people eat. Meat, noodles and dairy products are the main foods. Local herbs and grasses are used as seasonings. Vegetables are scarce – cabbage, turnips, onions and carrots being the most widely eaten. Meals during the day are light, and leftovers from the evening meal make a common breakfast, along with milky tea. Cheese, yogurt and dried meat are the principal foods eaten in the day. The main meal is usually at night, when shepherds return to the communal *yurts* (tents).

Mongolian 'bundle' is a feast dish, in which a goat is killed in the Muslim way, by slitting its throat and hanging it to bleed. The meat and bones are removed from the skin, which is left intact. Special rocks are collected from a riverbed,

Cheese cubes
For easy portability, cheese is dried, cut into squares and then it is reconstituted by soaking or boiling. It has a smoky taste, because it is dried near cooking fires.

Breakfast soup

In cold, windswept Mongolia, noodles in broth make a warming start to the day. This is typical of the area's light breakfasts.

Uzbek bread stall *(opposite)*

Far more than a staple food, bread is sacred in Uzbekistan. Traditionally it should be placed flat side up and should never be cut with a knife.

then heated on a fire until very hot, and layered inside the goatskin together with the meat and herbs. All of the openings in the goatskin are then sewn up with metal thread, and the stuffed skins are set over a flame. The stones cook the meat from the inside, while the flames cook it from the outside. The result is an incredibly aromatic and tender combination. It is the custom to eat sausage and offal while the 'bundles' cook. The drippings make a delicious bouillon, which is also eaten at the feast.

FLAT BREADS: THE REGIONAL STAPLE

For the most part, food in Central Asia is very simple. Flat breads form the basis of most meals. Nomadic people make thin, unleavened breads, which cook quickly over an open fire. Settled people bake leavened flat breads, called nans, in home or village tandoor ovens. The breads are dipped in tea or yogurt, and served with grilled or wind-dried meat.

Every region has a specific flat bread. In Afghanistan the breads are yeasted nans made with wheat and yogurt. In Turkmenistan the breads are called *choerek* – as in Turkish – and are made from sourdough. Often breads contain milk and fat, to keep them moist. In the Hunza Valley of northern Pakistan, flat breads are made from sprouted wheat and apricots. The people here, the Hunzacots, are known for their longevity, which may be due to their healthy diet of yogurt, apricots and wheat.

Armenia and Azerbaijan

Lying between the Black Sea and the Caspian Sea, the Caucasian Republics of Armenia, Azerbaijan and Georgia have long formed a link between Europe and Asia, between the Christian and Muslim worlds. From the 17th to the late 20th century, they were under the geo-political shadow of Russia. Gastronomically, however, they have been more influenced by Turkey and Iran. This is particularly true of Armenia and Azerbaijan, where the food tastes Middle Eastern.

Armenia was occupied by the Ottoman Turks from the 16th century until after the First World War, and its food has much in common with that of Turkey. Many of Armenia's soups, salads, pilafs, *meze* (small savoury dishes), *kofta* (meatballs), *manty* (dumplings) and sweet and savoury pastries are virtually identical to those of Turkey and the Middle East. But there are some variations. One major difference is that Armenia is a Christian country, and pork appears now and then in the cuisine, such as in pork and wheat *koftas* and in *khorovadz khozi miss*, grilled skewered pork with pomegranate sauce. Wine, also, is much appreciated, and the brandies from Armenia are highly regarded. Wine-making and the production of rose-petal preserves are two of the country's most important industries.

Armenia can be divided into two gastronomic regions: Caucasian Armenia and Middle Eastern Armenia. The food eaten in Caucasian Armenia tends to combine fruit with meat, and to use coriander as a seasoning. In Middle Eastern Armenia, seasonings mirror those found in Turkey, with parsley, dill and mint featuring regularly. Spices are used in both parts of the country, but their presence is not as intense as it is in Turkey and the Middle East. Trout, from the high-mountain Lake Sevan, is a speciality of Caucasian Armenia. It is grilled on skewers and served with lemon, tarragon and pomegranate seeds. Thin flat bread, called *lavash*, is the staple, eaten with every meal, and Turkish breads, such as *pideh* and *simit* are popular. Baklava is a favourite sweet, and the Armenians make unique coffee cakes and rich shortbread biscuits.

Mongolian dumplings
Rolled meatballs, known as *buuz* are popular on special occasions, such as the lunar new year, Tsagaan Sar. They are left outside overnight to freeze, then cooked by steaming.

In contrast to Christian Armenia, Azerbaijan is a Muslim country, where the food has much in common with that of Iran, its southern neighbour. Thick soups, much like Iranian *ashes*, are enjoyed, and *pilov* (pilaf) is the most important Azerbaijani dish – there are over 40 varieties in the country's repertoire. The Caspian Sea provides access to abundant sturgeon, which are now diminishing, sadly, due to overfishing; both the fish and its roe are prized.

Food through the day

Breakfast here is simple, often consisting of just bread and cheese, or soup or yogurt. Lunch is also moderate, and based on the same foods. It is dinner that is the main meal.

■ WINE: AN AGE-OLD GEORGIAN DRINK

VITICULTURE IS AN ANCIENT ART, THOUGHT BY SOME TO HAVE ORIGINATED IN GEORGIA – IT HAS BEEN PRACTISED HERE AS FAR BACK AS THE 4TH MILLENNIUM BC. GEORGIANS WORSHIP THE VINE: THE *MARANI* (WINE STORAGE SHED) IS LIKE A SHRINE IN THE YARD, AS HIGHLY REGARDED AS THE HEARTH IN THE HOME. THE TRADITION OF REPEATING TOASTS AT GEORGIAN FEASTS IS JUST ONE ILLUSTRATION OF THE IMPORTANCE OF WINE IN THIS COUNTRY'S CULTURE. GEORGIA PRODUCES MANY WINES, WHICH ARE HIGHLY REGARDED IN FORMER SOVIET TERRITORIES.

Dinner is served in courses. The starter may be simple *meze*, such as roasted almonds, olives, bread or *basterma* (cured and dried meat, coated with spicy paste). Alternatively, more complex *meze* may be served, such as *midia dolma* (stuffed mussels), cold vegetable salads or *baba ganouj* (a grilled aubergine purée). In some places aniseed-flavoured *oghi*, or raki, is drunk. The second course is usually a soup, often enriched with egg and lemon or a yogurt and garlic sauce. The Armenians enjoy a cucumber and yogurt soup, called *jajik*, in hot weather. Main courses generally consist of meat, chicken or fish, served with rice or bulgar *pilav* and vegetables, such as artichokes, courgettes or green beans. Lamb is by far the most popular meat, and it may come in the form of kebabs, stews, casseroles, *koftas*, hot *boeregs* (pastries) or meat-filled dolmas. Dessert is usually a compote or fruit and cheese, followed by coffee or tea. At special occasions, richer pastries, like baklava, are served. Wines are drunk with meals in Armenia, and brandies or cherry cordial complete the meal.

Almost all meals in Armenia are accompanied by a plate of fresh herbs, which might include mint, coriander, tarragon, dill, basil, parsley and chives, and a pile of thin Armenian bread, called *lavash*. The amount and mix of herbs that a diner adds to his dish determine the final flavours.

Georgia

Of the three countries of the Caucasus, Georgia has the most unique cuisine. Myths about the origins of the land all revolve around feasting and food. Its cuisine has long been highly regarded, and Georgian restaurants are favoured in far-flung cities of the former Soviet Union.

A taste of history

Georgia has been a Christian enclave surrounded by Muslim foes for over 1000 years, and has had a difficult history, with a seemingly endless series of invasions and subjugations. An Arab invasion in the mid-7th century led to 400 years of Arab rule. This was followed by a brief period of Georgian rule until the Mongols invaded in 1225. It was next subjugated by Tamerlane, then the Ottoman Turks, and, in the late 16th century, Georgia was split in half by Turkey and Iran. In the 18th century it turned to Christian Russia, to protect it from its Muslim neighbours. Although Russia had guaranteed Georgia's sovereignty, by 1801 the country had been incorporated into the Russian Empire, and later, the Soviet Union, where it remained until 1991.

As a result of all these exchanges, Georgian cuisine has developed both Middle Eastern and Mediterranean elements. The pilafs of south-east Georgia, and the regional dishes that combine meats stewed with fruits, echo Iranian cooking, but with a distinctive, tart Georgian taste; Georgians are more apt to include pomegranates or sour plums in a stew than the sweeter quince or prunes favoured by their Iranian neighbours. The stuffed vegetables of the Black Sea coast resemble the dolmas of Turkey. But, unlike other Ottoman-influenced cuisines, Georgia never developed a *meze* culture, nor a strong interest in sweets, with the exception of a few holiday foods.

There are also influences from Central Asia, evident in the wonton-like dumplings called *khinkali*, typical of Georgia's mountainous zones. The same Central Asian Mongols left their mark on the cuisines of both Georgia and northern India, and striking similarities can be found in the cuisines of both countries. The Georgian word for bread, *puri*, is the same as the Hindi. Georgians bake their marvellous flat bread in a clay oven called a *tone*, which is the same as the Punjab tandoor. Georgia's emblematic chicken dish, chicken *tabaka*, is made in a cast-iron skillet called a *tapha*, which is related to the north Indian skillet, the *tava*.

However, despite all these influences, the country has retained a strong autonomy and a proud national identity, which is very much linked with its reverence for the earth and, in particular, the vine (see box, opposite). Georgian

HERBS AND SPICES

IMERETIAN SAFFRON whereas most saffron is made from crocuses, this saffron, popular in Georgia, is made from marigolds

KHMELI-SUNELI a mixture of fenugreek, coriander, garlic, chillis, pepper, savory and marigold. It can be bought in hues ranging from pale green to amber

NIGELLA these nutty, peppery seeds are a common seasoning for Central Asian breads

cooking is distinguished by its use of walnuts, the richness and nuttiness of which are balanced by souring agents like *matsoni* (yogurt), pungent cheese, *machari* (immature wine), vinegar or fruit juices. *Tklapi*, sheets of dried, puréed fruit (known as 'fruit leathers' in English) are used in many dishes. Other flavours that characterize Georgian cuisine are that of coriander, summer savory and Imeretian saffron (see box, top right).

Meat skewers
Caucasian kebabs are much like those eaten in Turkey. They are usually made from lamb and grilled over a coal fire.

Staple foods

Bread, vegetables and grains are all-important in the cuisine of Georgia. This is due in part to the strict fasting calendar of the Georgian Orthodox Church. As in the Greek Orthodox Church, religious Georgians must abstain from meat, eggs and dairy products for six months of the year. Vegetables comprise by far the greatest part of the Georgian repertoire, with over 100 kinds of greens used, including sarsaparilla, nettles, mallow, ramp and purslane. They are cooked, marinated, dried, eaten fresh, and steeped in

Local traders, Turkmenistan
Market towns provide a focus for the sale of produce. Many herdsmen are only semi-nomadic, relying on agriculture as well as on their flocks.

water for a drink. A selection of herbs and greens is always placed on the table; a plate might include coriander, dill, tarragon, parsley, basil, spring onions, summer savory, *tsitsmati* (false-flax, similar to rocket) and some radishes.

Khachapuri, Georgian cheese bread, is the country's closest thing to fast food. It is ubiquitous, and has many regional variations: round, rectangular and boat-shaped; yeasty and thick-crusted; or layered and flaky. In the Adzharian version the yeast bread forms an open 'boat' containing abundant cheese and butter. The crust is torn off at pointed ends and dipped into a liquid centre.

A regional flavour

Nearly 80 per cent of Georgia is mountainous, resulting in self-contained regions that have little contact with each other. The Caucasus Mountains separate the country from Russia to the north, and the treacherous Likhi Range runs down the middle, essentially dividing the country into western Georgia, which borders on the Black Sea, and eastern Georgia, which has a dry, windy and hot climate.

Western Georgia enjoys high rainfall and hot temperatures. The food here is spicier than in the eastern part of the country; dried hot chilli peppers are much loved, and maize is preferred over wheat. Maize was introduced via Turkey in the 16th century, and it quickly supplanted millet, which was then the staple grain. Maize cakes, called *mchadi*, are eaten widely. Red kidney beans, tomatoes and green beans – all New World foods – are local favourites.

Adzharia, on the south-west coast of the Black Sea, is a fertile area renowned for its citrus groves and tea plantations. Plums, apricots, figs, pomegranates and olives are among the many foods which are cultivated on every inch of land. Much of the food in Adzharia has Turkish influences, but seafood does not comprise an important element in the cuisine. Georgians prefer freshwater fish, obtained from rivers and high-altitude lakes. In Batumi, Adzharia's major city, grilled meat is more popular than fish, even though Batumi is right on the Black Sea. The reason that fish has never played a great part in this cuisine is because in the past people flocked away from the coast to the highlands to escape both malaria and the Turkish slave trade.

To the north and east of Adzharia are the provinces of Imereti, Samegrelo and Guria. This is the Georgian heartland, where rolling green hills stretch towards the Likhi Range in the east. Its hub is the city of Kutaisi. Here the food is even hotter than on the coast. The region has always been known for its honey, honey-infused vodka and wild fowl, particularly pheasant.

In the east of Georgia, Tblisi, the capital, is a city of many nationalities; Armenians, Iranians, Kurds, Jews, Greeks and Russians live and worship side by side. Here, Eastern sweets, such as halva and sugared almonds, are found, and parlours sell syrup-based fruit drinks, which are much like Middle Eastern *sharbats*. However, some of the flavours of these drinks are uniquely Georgian: emerald-coloured *tarkhuna* is made using tarragon and ruby-red *khakhuri* is made from grapes. Armenians dominated the local population for many years, but had little influence on the cuisine, leaving their mark on only a few dishes, such as *hashi* (tripe soup), *bozbashi* (lamb soup), *borani* (vegetables with yogurt), *lavashi* (thin bread), *nazuki* (spice bread) and *gozinaki* (candied nuts).

In the rest of eastern Georgia the food is more subtle, with a cuisine based on fresh ingredients and spare seasonings. Mountain people in the southern Caucasus rely on mutton, cheese and pickled sarsaparilla. Bread is stuffed with minced meat, often kid, called *kubdari*, a speciality of the Svanetti region. The eastern town of Pasanauri boasts the best *khinkali*, though here they are usually filled with lamb, while a mixture of beef and pork, or cheese and greens is used elsewhere. Bear, thought to be a preventive against rheumatism, is eaten in this part of Georgia.

Food through the day

Georgians are flexible with their mealtimes. They like to sleep late, so breakfast is generally a mid-morning meal. Breakfasts are hearty and savoury, consisting of omelettes, yogurt, cheese and salad greens. In the afternoon, coffee and tea are served, accompanied by a copious spread. A more substantial meal is eaten at night.

However, what really determines eating and mealtimes in Georgia is hospitality; whenever guests arrive, a big, festive meal is served. If they happen to arrive in the middle of the day, then that's when the feast will occur, and a light snack will be served at night.

A traditional style
People in Central Asia eat in much the same way as they have for centuries, sitting on the floor and using the right hand, and sometimes bread, to pick up food.

CHINA

A steady flow of emigration has ensured that China's food is enjoyed across the globe, whether it is the formal banquet cuisine or simpler street cooking, which displays many of the same flavours, textures and techniques.

KEY INGREDIENTS

GINGER

SOY SAUCE

SESAME OIL

OYSTER SAUCE

HOISIN SAUCE

RICE

NOODLES

FISH AND SEAFOOD

PORK

SOYBEANS

SPRING ONIONS

PEANUTS

The People's Republic of China is the most populous country in the world, and the third largest, after Russia and Canada. Its civilization goes back more than 7000 years, and, up until the 20th century, a succession of emperors ruled. It became a republic in 1911 and, in 1949, a communist state. Over time, Chinese gastronomy has developed into a sophisticated style of cooking which ranks, with French haute cuisine, as one of the greatest in the world.

China is a country of mostly rugged terrain, with broad alluvial plains flanking its great rivers, the Yellow River in the north and the Yangtze River in central China, and also its southern coast. It is a country of geographic contrasts: tropical rainforest in the south-east; frozen glacial Himalayan caps in the south-west; near-frozen tundra in the north; and harsh deserts that occupy central and western China. Its dramatic natural landscapes are home to some of the world's highest mountains, in the Himalayas, and one of the world's lowest depressions, Turfan. Natural disasters have been frequent here, with flooding along the Yellow River, typhoons in the south, and droughts, plagues and earthquakes in other areas. Yet through all of this, Chinese peasants have continued to work and reclaim the land, transforming it to meet their needs by draining, irrigating, terracing, deforesting and reforesting.

A taste of history

The Chinese have always been interested in new foods, and have borrowed from the neighbouring cuisines of South-east Asia and the Middle East. By the end of the Han Dynasty, around 220 AD, a comprehensive agricultural development policy was in place, which would be maintained throughout China's history. Great irrigation systems were developed, and gourmet food became ritually sanctioned. As the empire expanded under the Han, plants such as grapes and alfalfa were brought back from Central Asia, and noodle technology developed. During the seven centuries that followed the Han Dynasty, more crops were introduced from the west and south, including tea, spinach, sugar beets, lettuce, almonds and figs. Central Asian rulers and travelling Buddhists encouraged the use of dairy products, which have maintained their popularity only in northern and western regions.

Beginning in the 16th century, foods from the New World, particularly the peanut, sweet potato, chilli pepper, tomato, guava, papaya and

jicama, found their way into the country via Portuguese and Spanish traders. Peanuts and chilli peppers found particular favour as condiments and seasonings.

Traditional Chinese medicine emphasizes the role that nutrition plays in maintaining good health. Medical practice and food are closely linked, resulting in an impressively diverse diet, in which many highly nutritious foods are eaten for primarily medical reasons.

Staple foods

Although only 15 per cent of the land in this vast country is suitable for farming, every inch of this land is cultivated. Crops are planted along roads and railroad tracks; one type of crop is planted between rows of another; and there is extensive terracing. Agriculture is intensive and employs two-thirds of China's population. The people of China draw on a spectacular range of plant and animal species for their cuisine, and the country

is the world's largest producer of carrots, watermelons, pears, cucumbers, rice and sweet potatoes. Its other principal crops include wheat, maize, millet, barley, *kao liang* (a type of sorghum), peanuts, soybeans, cotton, tobacco and tea. Pigs and poultry are commonly raised and provide the staple meats of the cuisine. Both inland and marine fishing are also important.

An intricate cuisine

Although China's cuisine is regional, with tremendous variations from one area to another, it has several unifying factors that distinguish it from other cuisines. The drive for balance inherent in all aspects of Chinese life is evident in the country's gastronomy. The philosophy of Yin and Yang – the idea that in every aspect of life there are two opposing forces, male and female, dark and light, soft and hard, which must be balanced – has had a profound effect on Chinese cuisine. Cooks here naturally combine sweet

Chopsticks
These eating utensils were developed in China about 5000 years ago. Chinese chopsticks, traditionally made from bamboo, are rectangular with a blunt end.

Banquets
(opposite)
Highly decorative arrangements are used at formal feasts, such as this dish, arranged to resemble a peacock.

Egg dishes
'Tea eggs' *(top)* are hard-boiled and soaked in tea to create a delicate marbled effect, while 'thousand-year-old eggs' *(bottom)* are made by being coated in an ash, rice or lime mixture and left for up to six months.

flavours. Sometimes textures are created through cooking techniques, while at other times they are inherent in the foods themselves, such as in sharks' fins or birds' nests. Different parts of an animal, for example, the cheeks of a fish or the innards of a pig, are appreciated in great part for their texture, and different parts of the same animal may be cooked in a variety of ways to achieve the best results.

Since ancient times, the cutting-up of ingredients has evolved into a complex art in itself. The size and shape of the pieces depends on the texture of the food and the degree of cooking sought. The thickness of the pieces influences how they will be seasoned.

Fats are considered great delicacies in China. This is, in part, due to the fact that grains – rice in the south and wheat and millet in the north – constitute the bulk of the Chinese diet. The flavours of grains are greatly enriched by fats, and both animal fats, from pork, duck and chicken, and vegetable fats, primarily from sesame seeds and peanuts, are used.

The main cooking methods in Chinese cuisine are boiling, steaming, braising, sautéing, deep-frying and stir-frying, and these are used throughout the country. The cleaver is the ubiquitous tool, and the wok the national cooking utensil. Soy sauce is used everywhere as the main seasoning.

Food through the day

The Chinese are united by an interest in and commitment to good cooking and good food. Food is used to mark cultural exchange, calendric and family events, social transactions and ethnicity. At social events, food delineates the social relationships of the eaters.

Although every part of China has particular customs of preparation and cooking, there is a similarity throughout the country in people's eating patterns. Breakfast is usually casual, consisting of bowls of noodles or *congee* (rice porridge). Lunch is eaten at midday either with the family or, as is more often in cities, at a noodle stand. Dinner is generally considered the main meal of the day and is eaten with the family

with sour, meat with crunchy vegetables, a pungent sauce with a neutral wrap, a fiery meat dish with plain, white rice. Gastronomic pleasure is above all an aesthetic pleasure: colours must satisfy the eye; the cook must strive for subtle perfumes rather than overpowering aromas; and scent and colour must complement each other. The cook must also attempt to maintain a balance between the five basic flavours – sour, sweet, bitter, hot and salty.

Another peculiarity of Chinese cuisine is its emphasis on texture. Some foods are appreciated purely for the way they feel, rather than their

SIGNATURE DISHES

Hot and sour soup *This peppery vegetable and pork soup often contains poultry blood.*

Ants climbing a tree *The classic Szechwan stir-fry of pork and glass noodles.*

Mapo doufu *A stir-fried bean curd dish with pork, from Szechwan.*

Yangchow fried rice *This popular rice dish mixes prawns, eggs, onions, ham and peas.*

Peking duck *This dish of crispy, fattened duck is served with Mandarin pancakes. The head, tongue and feet are served separately.*

Mantou *These steamed buns – a legacy of the Mongols – are a northern staple.*

Lacassa *A brothy, Macanese noodle dish containing local prawn paste.*

Steamed dumplings *Made with wheat.*

---

alternating mouthfuls. Soup is sipped from time to time. At some meals, a fish dish is served as the main dish, followed by a noodle dish or fried rice. After a diner has eaten enough of the main dishes, he or she usually drinks a bowl of hot soup, which is thought to aid digestion.

Banquets

Chinese ceremonial meals follow a rigid format, in which a series of courses – anywhere from 10 to 24 – is served, one after the other. Ingredients and dishes vary from region to region, but the formula is always the same, usually consisting of the following courses.

Leng pan is the opening appetizer. It is a cold platter, eaten in a leisurely way while the cook prepares the dishes that are to follow. It usually contains cooked meats and seafood, pickled vegetables and crisp, fried nuts. The platter is designed in an ornate way, with the food arranged in decorative designs, which might depict a dragon, a phoenix, a panda or flowers.

Peking pancakes
Made with wheat flour dough, flat breads accompany many northern Chinese dishes such as Peking duck and *mu-shu* pork (with 'golden' noodles).

---

at around 6 or 7 pm. Between meals, snacks are eaten frequently, the last one being after dinner, at about 8 or 9 pm.

A typical Chinese meal consists of rice or another grain, noodles or pancakes with a few dishes. The number of dishes depends on the number of people and the economic status of the family, but usually displays a variety of ingredients, including meat, seafood, bean curd, eggs and vegetables. There are usually fewer dishes served at lunch than at dinner. A soup is generally served, both as a beverage to accompany the meal, and as a palate cleanser.

The Chinese table is usually a round one, which facilitates the sharing of dishes. Each place setting has a rice bowl, a saucer and a pair of chopsticks. The rice bowl is for the *fan* (see box, page 171), and the saucer is for the accompanying dishes. All the dishes are served together, in no specific order. Each diner receives a full bowl of rice, and throughout the meal uses chopsticks to help him or herself to small portions of food from the platters on the table. The rice and various dishes are eaten in

Deep-frying
Cooked in the all-purpose wok, deep-fried foods include egg rolls and dumplings.

The first part of any banquet consists of a series of toasts to the guest of honour, the hosts and other guests. Small dishes, called *jiu cai,* are served to offset the effect of the alcohol. They are savoury dishes, such as stir-fried beef or prawns. Anywhere from one to four courses may be served with the toasts, depending on the extravagance of the banquet.

Soups and pastries may follow. They are served also between the subsequent sections of the banquet, to cleanse the palate and to alert the diner that a new phase of the banquet will begin.

The focal points of a meal are the *da cai* (the main dishes). As many as four may be served, and they are lavish, consisting of preparations such as Peking duck or roast suckling pig. Drinking and toasting continue and reach their climax at this point.

Next come the *fan cai*. As with the more everyday version (see box, page 171), these are vegetable, egg or bean-curd dishes, served with rice. Rice is often served as a symbolic gesture to signify that if the guest has not had enough food, he can fill up on rice.

Dessert generally consists of fresh fruit. Tea and hot towels will then be offered, and, according to tradition, the host will apologize for the meagreness of the meal.

Festive FOODS

The New Year festival is a major holiday in China, with a full schedule of food-related rituals, symbolizing renewal, both for the living and for the ancestral spirits.

On the 30th day of the 12th Moon (the equivalent of New Year's Eve), a family reunion meal takes place and offerings are made to gods and ancestors. Places are set for ancestors at the banquet table. Every dish has a name which symbolizes health, honour and riches. For example: 'broth of prosperity' is a chicken soup with dumplings and pigeon eggs representing gold and silver ingots; seasoned pork shoulder is called 'mist of harmony'; a dish combining sea cucumber, squid and seaweed is named 'jade of ink, gold of darkness'; and bean threads are called 'silvery strands of longevity'.

The dinner begins late in the afternoon and includes four to eight dishes of vegetables, chicken, fish, shellfish and pork – many families, especially in the north, slaughter a pig and make sausages at New Year. Cold plates include pig's-feet jelly, roasted peanuts, thinly sliced jellyfish skin in vinegar and soy sauce and green apricots or kumquats preserved in sugar. Delicacies such as sea cucumber, shark's fin, bird's nest and lion's heads (see page 171) are also served.

Other popular dishes, served at the banquet, or over the next few days, include jiao zi, small filled dumplings. Sometimes these contain surprises symbolic of long life and prosperity, such as copper coins, gold, silver and gems. The dumplings are dipped into vinegar and sesame oil and accompanied by pickles, sliced salted eggs, sliced fermented eggs and roasted peanuts. Also served is 'eight precious rice', consisting of sweet, sticky rice with eight other ingredients including lotus seeds, almonds, sliced red dates, candied fruits, sweet-bean paste and brown-sugar syrup.

Marriage foods

Ingredients and dishes have important symbolic functions at Chinese weddings. On the day of the wedding, the bride's family traditionally serves the groom with a bowl of soup containing an unbroken egg, which has been soft-boiled. The groom is supposed to break the egg, symbolizing the bride's departure from her family. The bride makes another soup for the groom's family, which contains a pig's heart, to show that they are all 'of one heart'. Wild goose is often eaten as a symbol of marital harmony and fidelity, as geese mate for life and migrate together.

Fruits and nuts are other important wedding foods, which are customarily folded inside a marriage quilt. Many names for fruits and nuts sound or are spelt the same as words implying children and good fortune. For example, the second syllable in the word peanut, *sheng*, is a homonym for the word for 'birth'; and the word for date, *zao zi*, has the same sound as the word for 'early arrival of a son'.

Northern China

This large area includes the provinces of Inner Mongolia, Honan, Shantung, Shansi, Shensi and Hopei. Beijing (formerly Peking) is located in the last of these and is the centre of one of the country's best-known cuisines. The majority of people of this region live on the alluvial plain of the Yellow River and in its surrounding hills. The land is intensively farmed, agriculture here being dominated by wheat, maize, sorghum, rice, cotton and sesame. The main vegetables found in these northern provinces are Chinese cabbage, cucumbers and celery. Northern China is where many key varieties of plant foods originated, including millet, soybeans and peaches. Sheep are native to this region and may have been domesticated here independently of their domestication in the Middle East.

Although Shantung has a temperate climate, the overall climate of the north is harsh. Beijing experiences extremes of heat in the summer and cold in the winter. In the spring, periodic sandstorms blow in from the Gobi Desert.

There are two main cooking traditions in the north: the imperial food of Peking, and the food of Shantung and Inner Mongolia. The imperial cooking of Peking evolved over hundreds of years and through the succession of great dynasties. It is elaborate and expensive, characterized by lavish banquets and complex or rich dishes, such as Peking duck – though this dish dates only from the 19th century. Many of the area's refined recipes were brought to Peking cuisine by chefs from Shantung, who liked the more pungent flavours of garlic and leeks. However, the day-to-day food of Beijing is considered plain and robust.

The foods of Inner Mongolia and Shantung are 'the backbone of northern cuisine' according to Yan-kit So, in *Yan-kit's Classic Chinese Cookbook*, and they reflect their Mongolian

Peking duck
This dish is created by pumping air between the skin and flesh of the duck. It is then blanched and coated in honey and hung until the skin is hard and dry, and finally it is roasted.

Eastern China

This area covers the lower Yangtze valley and the Yangtze delta area, and includes the coastal provinces of Kiangsu, Chekiang and Anhwei. This is a fertile, temperate area where land and water meet, yielding up rich agricultural products, particularly wheat and rice, as well as abundant seafood.

Eastern China is densely populated and prosperous, with a rich, decorative and slightly sweet cuisine, which is little known outside of China. In contrast to Peking cooking, garlic is seldom used, and oil is used abundantly, as is sugar, sweet bean paste and rice wine. Shellfish, particularly prawns, and Shanghai crabs, known for their yellow roe, are much loved. A long Buddhist tradition has led to the creation of many wonderful and subtle vegetable dishes. The best vinegar in China, dark Chekiang vinegar, and Shao-Hsing rice wine, are specialities of the region. It is also known for Chinjhua ham, a special cured ham with pinkish-red flesh and a savoury-sweet flavour.

The eastern school of cooking is known as Shanghai cooking, but there are other culinary centres in this part of China, such as Hangchow, Yangchow, Suchow and Wuhsi. The *hung-shao* (red-braising) method of cooking originated in the eastern region and has since spread throughout China. For this, ingredients are cooked slowly in a mixture of thick, dark soy sauce and rice wine, which is then reduced and spooned over the main ingredient. High-quality ingredients are prized here – as they are throughout China – and seasonings are used to accentuate natural flavours. Delicate vegetables are paired with delicate fish or meats, such as baby cabbage hearts with crabmeat or prawns, to bring out their natural sweetness.

There was a strong European presence in Shanghai in the 19th century, which left its gastronomic mark on the city in the form of cakes, breads, pies, sweets and other Western snacks, and lavish cold appetizer platters, which are a legacy of the Russians. As a result, Shanghai's cuisine is the most eclectic of China's

Roadside noodles
Though most are now made by machine, it is still possible to see noodles being hand-stretched on the street. Once cooked, they are served with vegetables, fish or meat.

heritage. Whereas pork and chicken are favoured elsewhere in the country, this region has a large number of lamb and mutton dishes. Two particular favourites are Mongolian barbecue and Mongolian 'firepot'. The first of these is said to have originated with Mongolian warriors who would sit around a fire, each grilling his meat. The 'firepot' is also communal and is built around a simmering pot of stock, in which people cook thinly sliced pieces of lamb and vegetables.

cuisines, incorporating ingredients from East and West. However, the region's most classic dishes rely on purely local ingredients. These include crisp, stir-fried prawns, eel cooked in oil, Yangchow fried rice, 'lion's heads' (giant pork meatballs with cabbage and fresh dried prawns) and 'west lake fish' with a sweet and sour sauce, which comes from Hangchow.

Southern China

This type of cooking, which includes Cantonese cuisine, is centred in the southern coastal provinces of Fukien and Kwangtung, where the climate is sub-tropical and the land, of the Pearl River delta and the coastal plains, is fertile. Agriculture flourishes here, and rice, the region's staple food, is harvested twice a year. Sweet potatoes, maize, taro, wheat and vegetables, particularly leafy greens, are also cultivated, as are tropical fruits, oranges, peaches and tea. Fish and shellfish, particularly crabs, crayfish, prawns, scallops and clams, are abundant and contribute to the variety of Cantonese cuisine.

This region's cooking is the most refined, varied, and indeed famous, in China. Its exports do not, for the most part, do it justice, because it is a cuisine that relies primarily on the quality of the ingredients. No other cooks in China are as demanding as the Cantonese when it comes to freshness, range and quality of ingredients. Cooks here are highly skilled in their use of cooking temperatures and split-second timing.

Cantonese food is not highly seasoned, and it is at its best when it is simple: boiled prawns, steamed fish, steamed or stir-fried vegetables, clear soup, fried oysters and boiled chicken are but a few examples. Success lies in the harmonious blending of different flavours. The combinations may be simple, but Cantonese cooks have evolved an elaborate set of rules as to which combinations can be formed. Of the dipping sauces and seasonings used at Cantonese tables, the ones most often found include soy sauce, oyster sauce, chilli sauce, very hot mustard, vinegars, sesame oil and white pepper. Black beans are also a distinctive flavouring.

The Cantonese use the full range of Chinese cooking techniques and have a tremendous variety of dishes, but they are known for the quality of their stir-fries, particularly for the aromas, or 'wok fragrance', which they achieve when cooking these dishes. They are also known for the quality and variety of their dim sum, the small, stuffed noodles or pastries eaten as snacks, luncheons and late breakfasts. The Chinese love of snacks and light bites is most evident in this part of the country.

In addition to the Cantonese, there is an ethnic group in Kwangtung called the Hakka, who produce a cuisine that is simple and straightforward. The Chinese appreciation of the many textures of offal is evident here, and the Hakka are known for their skill with livers, kidneys, tripe and cow spinal cord, stir-fried with

FAN CAI: THE BASIC COMBINATION

There are two elements to the Chinese meal: the *fan* and the *cai*. *Fan* refers to the staple, the most substantial part of the meal, which could be rice, noodles, millet or steamed breads. In general, breads and noodles are more common in the north, whereas rice is the staple in the south. The word *fan*, which literally means 'cooked grain' or 'cooked rice', is also used to denote, simply, 'food'. *Cai* is the complementary dish, the stew, or meat, fish or vegetable preparation. In day-to-day eating, there is always more *fan* and less *cai*, whereas festive meals emphasize, and so include more, *cai*. In small snack foods, such as dim sum or dumplings, the *fan* and *cai* are combined into one dish.

vegetables. The Hakka specialities include salt-baked chicken, beef balls, chillis, aubergine, bitter melon and a fish paste seasoned with onion and ginger, which is used to stuff fried bean curd.

In Fukien province, north of Kwangtung, there is a great emphasis on soups and one-dish preparations ranging from thin, clear soups to thick stews and rice *congees* (a sort of rice cream porridge). Noodles are popular, and the region is known also for a type of thin pastry or dough skin called *yen pi*, which consists of pounded and finely chopped meat mixed with flour or cornflour. Lard is used widely as a cooking fat here, and there is a fondness for deep-frying, as well as slow simmering and long steaming. Specific dipping sauces are used according to the dishes being served, such as garlic crushed in vinegar with poultry and sweet malt syrup with fried rice balls. Another popular ingredient in Fukien is poultry blood, which is boiled or roasted and served with the bird. The cooking of shark's fin and bird's nest is at its best in Fukien.

Cooking fires
In some homes, such as this farmhouse in Guizhou, traditional cooking stoves made of stones are still used.

Central China

Known as the 'spicy zone' of Chinese cooking, this region, which encompasses Szechwan, Hunan and Yunnan provinces, has always been a place of spicy food, even before the introduction of the chilli pepper in the 17th century. Chilli, garlic, black and brown peppers, cassia, star anise, five-spice (see box, page 168), fresh coriander and dried citrus are important ingredients in these cuisines. While some dishes here are delicately spiced, others, particularly those cooked in the 'village style', are fiery.

The cuisines of the central provinces were influenced during the medieval days of the silk route by the cuisines of China's trading neighbours to the west. Walnuts and broad beans were introduced from Iran, and halva-like desserts became popular.

Of these provinces, the cuisine of Szechwan is the most distinctive, influencing those of many of its neighbouring regions. Szechwan is the most populous province of China and a fertile rice-bowl. A land of high mountains and deep gorges around the Yangtze, Szechwan is humid and rainy in the summer and mild in the winter, making its climate suitable for year-round agriculture. Rice, wheat, rapeseed, maize, bamboo shoots and citrus fruits, particularly tangerines, are the main crops.

Good Szechwan cooking is not just hot, but brings a number of flavours into play, including salty, sweet and vinegary. The Szechwanese feel that the heat of the chilli awakens the taste buds allowing the full range of flavours to be appreciated. Specialities of Szechwan include hot and sour soup, fragrant and crispy duck, twice-cooked pork, many fish dishes and *ma po* (bean curd). Another popular dish is tea-smoked duck, in which several cooking techniques are employed: the duck is first marinated, then smoked, steamed and, finally, stir-fried.

Pickled vegetables and bamboo shoots are important in Szechwan cooking, and a strong Buddhist influence has resulted in many vegetarian dishes. The Szechwanese are also fond of broad beans and pastes made from them.

Smoking and barbecuing are frequently used cooking methods in the region, predominantly with spareribs. Another cooking method used here, as well as in Beijing, is splash-frying. This involves hanging the ingredients over a pot of boiling oil and letting them cook in the constant splashes of oil.

The cooking of Hunan is centred on rice, noodles, pork, cabbage, white radish, river fish and mountain foods, such as bamboo shoots, funghi, game, wild roots and herbs. New World foods, such as maize and sweet potatoes found their way to this region along with the chilli pepper. Maize cakes and white potatoes are also popular, the latter a result of French missionary activity in the 18th and 19th centuries. A wide range of fruit is eaten here, and pine nuts and ginkgo nuts are particularly popular.

Yunnan cooking draws heavily on the cooking of Szechwan, but it is less spicy. It is also influenced by local minorities, particularly by the Tibetan and quasi-Tibetan peoples who live there, and by its proximity to India. For example, dairy products, particularly yogurt, are popular. China's finest hams come from Yunnan, which also produces sausages, brawn, bacon and other cured pork products.

Western China

The Xinjiang Province of western China is home to one of the driest and most inhospitable deserts in the world, the Takla Makan desert. There is little, if any, rainfall here, but in the oasis towns, intensive irrigation produces melons, tomatoes and a variety of other fruits and vegetables.

The majority of people in Xinjiang Province are Urghurs, a Turkic population. Consequently, the food of this region has more in common with the food of Central Asia (see pages 156 to 163) than with the food of the rest of China.

Fresh vegetables
An important part of the Chinese meal, vegetables are appreciated both for their flavours and textures.

■ TEA: OF ALL FLAVOURS

PROCESSED IN DIFFERENT WAYS ACROSS THE COUNTRY, THERE ARE MANY VARIETIES OF TEA IN CHINA. THESE INCLUDE THE DARK TEA, *TIT-KOON-YUM*, FROM FUKIEN, AS WELL AS SCENTED CHRYSANTHEMUM AND JASMINE TEAS. MOST TEAS ARE SERVED AFTER MEALS. *PU-ERH*, FROM YUNNAN, IS BELIEVED TO HAVE MEDICINAL VALUE AND IS OFTEN DRUNK AFTER EATING RICE.

ONCE AN EXPENSIVE PRODUCT, TEA USED TO BE A SYMBOL OF MARRIAGE. IF A WOMAN ACCEPTED A GIFT OF TEA FROM A SUITOR'S FAMILY, IT MEANT THAT SHE ACCEPTED THE OFFER OF MARRIAGE. SOME WOMEN STILL RECEIVE A SO-CALLED 'TEA-GIFT' ON THEIR ENGAGEMENT.

In this region, wheat is the main crop and staple food, eaten mainly in the form of flat breads, dumplings and noodles. Flat breads, sometimes called *uighur nan*, are baked in tandoor ovens and seasoned with cumin seeds and onion, garlic and sesame seeds.

Grilled kebabs – called *shashlik* in Central Asia – are made here with lamb and mutton. In the oasis towns of the Takla Makan Desert, spice-encrusted kebabs are the most popular street food. These are made using skewered pieces of meat rubbed with cumin, black peppercorns and cayenne, which are quickly grilled. The spicy kebabs are generally served with mint-seasoned yogurt, nans and stir-fried peppers. In contrast to the rest of China, pork is not an important meat in Xinjiang Province due to the Muslim religion.

Macao

Until its handover to China in 1999, Macao was the oldest European settlement on the South China coast, with a history of 450 years of Portuguese rule. Many of today's Macanese are descended from the Portuguese sailors and merchants who settled in South-east Asia in the 16th century and married women from Indonesia, Malaysia, India, Japan, Thailand, the Philippines and eventually China. The Portuguese men wanted Portuguese dishes; their wives and servants learned to accommodate them using Asian ingredients. The cuisine that evolved is a fascinating fusion cuisine, in which soy sauce and olive oil often show up in the same dish, and Chinese dim sum may be accompanied by Portuguese *vinho verde*.

The regional dish, *galinha portuguesa*, has a purely Macanese character; as with a Portuguese dish, its preparation begins by sautéing chicken in pork fat or olive oil with potatoes and onions, and the dish contains other Mediterranean ingredients, like chorizo and olives. But then Malaccan and Goan ingredients, such as ginger, curry paste and coconut milk, are added.

Many ingredients used in Macanese cooking come from Portugal's other former colonies: hot piri piri peppers from Mozambique; sweet potatoes, peanuts and kidney beans from Brazil; and saffron and spices from Goa. One of Macao's signature dishes, *galinha africana*, hails from Angola. Still others are pure Portuguese: *bacalhau* (salt cod) graces restaurant and hotel tables all over Macao; sweet egg pastries, like *pastéis de nata* (egg tartlets) and *barriga de freiras* (meaning 'nun's belly') are common.

In the latter half of the 20th century, the Macanese left this colony in droves. The population of Macao is now 97 per cent Chinese, and the pervasive food culture here today is Cantonese. Authentic Macanese food is easier to find in Portuguese than in Chinese restaurants; but mostly, it is cooked in the home.

Bok choy
(opposite)
The whole of this vegetable is used in Chinese cookery and has a pleasant, mild flavour.

Steaming
An efficient method of cooking, as basket steamers can be layered on top of a pan of rice, so that all parts of the dish will be ready at the same time.

China **175**

INDONESIA

Though there are regional variations throughout the islands of Indonesia, certain types of dishes are common, including curries, satays, fried-rice and coconut-milk based dishes, and food cooked in banana leaves and bamboo tubes.

KEY INGREDIENTS

GINGER

GALANGAL

CHILLIS

FISH AND SHELLFISH

BEEF

TOFU

TEMPEH (FERMENTED SOY BEAN CAKE)

RICE

SWEET POTATOES

COCONUT

CANDLENUTS

PEANUTS

Roadside foodstalls
Known as *warung*, foodstalls selling *satay*, rice cakes and snacks wrapped in banana leaves are widespread.

Indonesia is the world's largest archipelago, with somewhere between 13,000 and 17,000 islands, of which only about 6000 are inhabited. Its population of around 216 million people, speaking over 250 different languages, is the fourth largest in the world. Jakarta, its capital city on the island of Java, has a population of over 9 million, which makes it the largest city in South-east Asia. Sixty per cent of Indonesia's population lives on Java. The other major islands are Sumatra, part of Borneo, Sulawesi, Irian Jaya, Bali and Timor. With over 160 million Muslims, Indonesia is the world's largest Muslim country.

A country of abundant rivers and fertile, volcanic land surrounded by a warm ocean, food here is plentiful. Rice, maize, cassava, sweet potatoes and peanuts, as well as vegetables, herbs and fruits are grown throughout the islands. The eastern islands are drier and less fertile; here maize, sweet potatoes and yams are the staples. Everywhere, the ocean provides a large variety of fish and seafood.

SIGNATURE DISHES

Sambals *These are relishes or condiments, which accompany many Indonesian dishes.*

Sambal goreng udang *This condiment consists of shrimp in a sour and spicy sauce.*

Gado gado *Vegetable salad arranged in layers and served with a peanut sauce.*

Asam pedas *A dish of fish or meat cooked in a hot and sour sauce.*

Gulai *This stew has either a coconut-based sauce or a tart sauce with palm sugar.*

Satay *Strips of meat or fish are skewered, coated with spices and grilled for this national dish, served with a peanut sauce.*

Nasi goreng *This is fried rice with chicken, shrimp, vegetables and spices.*

A taste of history

If any part of Indonesia has determined the course of its history and its gastronomy, it is the Molucca Islands in eastern Indonesia, known to Europeans as the Spice Islands, the name purported to have been given by Marco Polo. Polo was the first recorded Westerner to visit the islands. The treasures that they bear – pepper, nutmeg, mace, cinnamon, cassia, cloves, ginger, turmeric and other spices – were being traded by Indonesian seamen along the African coast as early as the 1st century AD. Around this time, and possibly earlier, Indian merchants conducting trade with China set up outposts on Sumatra, Java and Borneo. By the 5th and 6th centuries,

Throughout Indonesia selamatan (feasts) are frequent. The centrepiece of the table is nasi kuning, a platter of yellow-tinted rice steamed in a cone-shaped bamboo dish. At the end of Ramadan cakes and spicy fruit salads are prepared, and rice in woven palm leaves is served with many dishes.

Indian culture was well established here, with Hindu and Buddhist priests and monks, and many settlers who followed the traders.

In the 11th century, Arab traders supplanted the Indian merchants, and Islam became the major religion. In addition to exporting spices, the Arab traders introduced spices such as coriander, cumin, caraway, dill and fennel, all of which are used in Indonesian cooking today. *Satay*, the skewered marinated meat and fish, which is widely eaten here and in neighbouring countries, is probably a legacy of the Arabs, too.

In the 16th century it was the Portuguese and Dutch who battled for supremacy over the spice trade. The Dutch East India Company eventually triumphed and Indonesia remained a Dutch colony until 1949.

A regional flavour

Though many Indonesian dishes are common throughout the archipelago, there are distinct regional differences. Much of the food of Indonesia, particularly on the western islands, has a strong Malaysian influence, while the cuisine of the eastern islands in the Pacific have Polynesian overtones. Sumatran food is quite substantial, with strong Arab and Indian influences. Lamb and beef dishes, as well as pilaf-type rice dishes, are popular.

Fruits of the tropics
(right)
Pineapples are just one of the fruits found in abundance on these tropical islands. These are being sold as a snack on a beach on Lombok.

A rich source
(previous page)
The waters around Indonesia provide many types of food, including this seaweed, being gathered in Bali.

RIJSTTAFELS: A COLONIAL IMPORT

Many Westerners have been exposed to the Indonesian buffets called *rijsttafels*, a Dutch word meaning 'rice table'. The origins of this custom lie not with the Indonesians, but with the colonials, who used to display their wealth by giving huge banquets, at which tremendous platters of rice were surrounded by up to 60 or 70 different dishes, all of them carried in by servants. When Indonesia gained independence, the *rijsttafels* were quickly abandoned, and can now only be found in restaurants in Holland and luxury tourist hotels.

The food of Java is more subtle, with sweet, sour and hot flavour combinations. Fermented bean curd, called *tempeh*, is an invention of the Javanese and an important Indonesian food. The food of west Java is simple and less highly flavoured, with meats and fish wrapped in banana leaves to be grilled or steamed, and many raw vegetable salads. The Javanese have a sweet tooth, and make a number of cakes and sweets.

In Bali, the majority of people are Hindu rather than Islamic, so pork is eaten much more than beef. Balinese food is spicy and lively.

Food through the day

Indonesians eat rice-based meals three times a day. Breakfast is usually a fried-rice dish, or rice with fried egg or plantain. At about 1 pm families gather for a late lunch that usually consists of rice and two or three meat and vegetable dishes. Vegetables are often cooked and dressed in a coconut milk and peanut sauce. Dinner is the main meal of the day, generally eaten at dusk. It consists of rice and four or five cooked dishes, including a hot spicy curry, a couple of vegetable dishes, a fish dish, and perhaps fritters. Fresh fruit is served for dessert.

MALAYSIA

The cuisine of Malaysia reflects its ethnic mix. Chinese and Indian influences are the strongest, yet Malaysian cooking also bears many similarities to that of Thailand, with its widespread use of chillis and coconut milk.

Malaysia consists of Peninsular Malaysia, which sits on the peninsula south of Thailand, and East Malaysia, located on the island of Borneo, over 600 km across the South China Sea. Both parts have densely forested interiors flanked by coastal plains. A polyglot culture of ethnic Malays, Chinese, Indians, Eurasians, Punjabi and Portuguese, all with a common language of English, Malaysia enjoys a high standard of living by South-east Asian standards, with a steadily expanding industrial sector.

A taste of history

Malaysia's beginnings are in the 3rd and 4th centuries, when, along with Indonesia, it made up the Hindu Javanese Empire, Srivijaya. With its strategic position between India and China, Malaysia was a very important destination for Indian and Chinese merchants, who traded silks, spices and porcelain along the Straits of Malacca. The indigenous Malays adopted the traders' Buddhist and Hindu traditions, and, in the 11th century, Indian converts brought Islam, too, which became and remains the chief religion.

The Portuguese arrived in Malacca in 1511, establishing a government that ruled for 100 years. The Dutch followed, then the British, who colonized Malaysia and anglicized it. Britain ruled until the country's independence in 1963, during which time it established the rubber and tin industries, which were worked by Chinese and Indian immigrants. Today's population of 21 million is mainly ethnic Malay, Indian, Chinese and Eurasian. Also, many Malaysians have Indonesian origins, which has resulted in a blend of recipes and styles in several dishes.

KEY INGREDIENTS

GHEE (CLARIFIED BUTTER)

CURRY LEAF

REMPAH (CHILLI PASTE)

ROJAK (SPICY SHRIMP PASTE)

COCONUT MILK

GALANGAL

BEAN CURD

RAMBUTAN

STAR FRUIT

DURIAN

MANGOES

Street food
Almost everyone stops to eat at the food stalls lining the streets of most Malaysian towns and cities. They serve rice and noodle dishes, satay and regional specialities.

Festive
~~~~ FOOD ~~~~

The most important Malaysian festival is Ramadan. At its end people feast on rendang *(dry curry) and on* ketaput, *a compressed rice dish. Malay-Indians celebrate Deepavali, the Festival of Lights, and in Penang a spring festival called Thaipusam is celebrated, in which altars are carried to a favourite deity. The Malay-Chinese celebrate Chinese New Year with traditional Chinese foods.*

A varied cuisine

As well as being shaped by Chinese, Indian, Thai and Indonesian cuisines, further influences came from the Portuguese, who introduced foods from the New World, and from the *nonya/baba* culture (see opposite), which began to evolve in the 19th century as the result of intermarriage between Malay women and Chinese immigrants. The result of this entire mixture is that Malaysian cuisine simultaneously reflects Confucian principles, Indian Vedic rules and Muslim dietary laws. In the course of a day, you could have a rich lunch, featuring folded, fried griddle breads, called *murtabaks,* and fried Chinese noodles, later followed by a lighter, healthier dinner of *chapattis* and mung-bean stew. One meal might include

'The king of fruits'
Though the flesh of the durian is creamy and slightly sweet, its smell is so strong that it is banned in several public places and on most airlines.

separate dishes from a number of origins, and even in one dish, several influences might come together; for example, *laksa*, a curried noodle dish, brings together noodles from China, curry from India and the indigenous coconut.

These varied cultural influences carry through into the way that people eat in Malaysia. The meals of the Malay-Chinese are eaten using chopsticks, whereas ethnic Malays and Malay-Indians eat with the fingers of the right hand. In a Western-style restaurant, the table might be laid with forks and spoons. Generally knives are not on the table, because the Malaysians consider them to be a sign of aggression.

Texture is important in Malaysian cooking, so dishes often combine crunchy and soft, rough and smooth and sticky and slippery elements. The five flavour centres of bitter, sweet, sour, salty and pungent are well represented and, as in the other cuisines of South-east Asia, colours and aromas are as important as flavour. Malaysia also has a rich vegetarian tradition, influenced by its Buddhist and Hindu populations. Buddhists of Malaysia do not eat meat on feast days, and Hindus do not eat it on Fridays.

REMPAH: THE NONYA PASTE

At the heart of many Malaysian, Indonesian and *nonya* dishes is *rempah*, an aromatic paste of pounded 'wet' and 'dry' ingredients. *Nonya* women stake their reputations on the quality of their *rempahs*, which they learn to make at a young age.

The 'wet', or fresh, ingredients that go into *rempah* include chillis, garlic, candlenuts, prawn paste, herbs and galangal (a member of the ginger family). The 'dry' ingredients include spices, such as coriander seeds, cumin, cloves and cinnamon.

To begin, the 'wet' ingredients are pounded in a *batu leong* (a pestle and mortar) or on a *batu giling* (a flat, granite slab), then combined with the 'dry' ingredients into a paste, which must be as smooth as possible. The next step, called *tumis,* is when the paste is fried, until oil, usually slightly red from the chillis, begins to seep out. The *rempah* is now ready to be used.

SIGNATURE DISHES

Satay *A favourite snack food, appetizer or main meal of cubes of meat grilled on skewers. Usually served with a peanut sauce.*

Murtabaks *Folded griddle breads, sometimes filled with meats.*

Roti chanai *'Handkerchief' griddle bread.*

Laksa *This creamy curried noodle dish contains fish, prawns and fish balls.*

Rendang *An Indonesian-style curry with a coconut-based sauce, which is cooked with the meat until it is absorbed.*

Indian mee goreng *Noodles with tofu, eggs, pork or lamb and spices.*

Lontong *A meal consisting of compressed rice, sauces, sambals (hot mixed seasonings) and vegetables cooked in coconut sauce.*

Nonya cuisine

Among the most complex and fragrant in the Malaysian repertoire, *nonya* dishes are reminiscent of Thai cooking; they incorporate *rempahs* (see box, above) tempered by coconut milk. They are cooked mainly in the home by women (*nonyas*; men are *babas*), and are difficult to find in restaurants. Using Chinese stir-frying, braising and steaming techniques, they combine the robust flavours of Malaysian spices with Chinese ingredients, such as noodles, soybean pastes, tree ear mushrooms and lily buds.

Food through the day

Malaysians eat three meals a day and rice is almost always included, even at breakfast. A typical meal consists of rice served with soup, two curries and a few vegetable stir-fries. Fruit is eaten for dessert, and in Malaysia, fruits are exotic: rambutan, duku, langsat, star fruit and mangosteen are all on offer. Sweets, mainly starchy cakes made from sticky rice, coconut and sugar, are eaten at afternoon tea.

CAMBODIA

Spicier than Vietnamese and subtler than Thai, the food in Cambodia bears many similarities to the foods of its neighbours, Vietnam and Thailand, but it also contains distinct Chinese and Indian influences.

KEY INGREDIENTS

PRAHOK (FISH PASTE)

PHAHOK (SPICE MIX)

PEANUT OIL

MINT

GINGER

LEMONGRASS

CORIANDER

CHILLIS

RICE AND RICE NOODLES

PORK

FISH AND SHELLFISH

BANANAS

Wok cooking

Many Cambodian dishes are prepared in a *chnang khteak* (wok). Here pancakes are being cooked in oil.

Cambodia consists mainly of a large, alluvial plain drained by the Mekong River. South-east Asia's largest lake, Tonle Sap, is in the middle of this mountain-flanked plain. Important crops grown in Cambodia include rice, maize, vegetables, peanuts and tobacco.

A taste of history

From the 1st to 6th centuries, Cambodia was part of the Indianized state of Funan, and there are still Indian legacies in the cuisine, such as the use of spice mixes – though these seem to be becoming less important. This empire was supplanted in the 8th century by the Cambodian people, the Khmer, who built their own powerful empire. At its centre was Angkor Wat, a vast Hindu temple in the northern jungles. However, in the 15th century, the empire fell to the Siamese (Thai), and then later to the Vietnamese and eventually the French, becoming part of French-ruled Indo-China until 1953. There is still a French influence in the cuisine, particularly in the consumption of freshly baked breads.

Cambodia's recent history has been a painful one; between 1975 and 1979 it was ruled by Pol Pot and the Khmer Rouge, a revolutionary group, which killed more than a million Cambodians and caused widespread emptying of the country's cities. Many fled to refugee camps in Thailand, where they developed Thai tastes, particularly a fondness for sweet foods, which they brought back with them when they returned.

Staple foods

The Khmer people place a lot of importance on rice, especially after the suffering they have had to endure in recent years. Steamed rice is commonly eaten, but also rice in other forms.

During the water festival between October and November, unhusked rice is soaked in water before it matures, grilled and then pounded. The pulp is mixed with the juice and pulp of unripe coconut. Rice flour and sticky rice are used in cakes and desserts, such as banana fritters.

Fish is a major source of protein here, both freshwater from the country's many rivers and Tonle Sap Lake, and salt-water fish from the Gulf of Thailand. It is prepared in a number of ways; probably the most widespread is by poaching in an aromatic broth seasoned with a tart ingredient, like lemongrass or lime juice. As in the other South-east Asian countries, preserved fish is the basis for widely used seasonings, such as: dried fish and prawns; sugared, flaked fish; the fermented fish sauce *tuk trey*; and the very strong fermented fish paste *prahok*, of which there are salty and sour versions.

SIGNATURE DISHES

Samla mchou banle *An acidic fish soup with tomatoes, cucumbers and galangal.*

Sngao chrouk *A sour fish, chicken or crayfish soup, with lemongrass, lime or tamarind, spring onions and garlic.*

Samla mchou croeng *A sour soup including the basic spice mixture,* phahok.

Samla kako *A salty, thick stew made with chicken or crayfish.*

Phoat khsat *A speciality of Phnom Penh. With a name meaning 'royal rice', this includes chicken, pork, crayfish and rice.*

Festive

~~~ FOOD ~~~

Ceremonial and festive meals in Cambodia are elaborate. In rural areas, cattle, pigs and poultry are sacrificed for marriage banquets. Villagers make gifts of rice, vegetables and fruit to the families, and up to ten different dishes will be served at the banquet, including curry, coconut milk soup, stuffed duck, meat or chicken sautéed with vegetables, and pork or veal satays. Wedding meals are less elaborate in cities; they are often Chinese meals prepared by Chinese chefs, either at home or in restaurants.

Cambodians enjoy a wide range of meats, such as pork, water buffalo, beef, poultry and duck, as well as wild animals such as boar, deer, birds, snakes, frogs and toads. Meat and fish are often grilled on skewers – like *satay* – then wrapped in edible leaves and dipped in sauces, as is the practice in Vietnam and Laos.

Soups are the most common everyday food in Cambodia. They often combine meat or fish with vegetables and seasonings in an aromatic broth, which is always seasoned with kaffir lime leaves and an acidic ingredient, such as lemongrass, lime juice or tamarind. Some soups are very salty.

In this poor country, where 95 per cent of the population is Buddhist, vegetables and local herbs are all-important. Almost every family grows its own lemongrass in a pot. Hot and spicy salads are widespread.

Food through the day
Class and lifestyle in Cambodia determine the ways people eat. In cities, many people eat Western-style, at a table, whereas in the countryside, people sit on the floor and dishes are placed on a mat in the middle. A single dish, such as a spicy soup served with vegetables and rice, will feed a family of modest means. Meals are more varied for wealthier families and for those who live along riverbanks, where fish, shellfish and greens are plentiful. Such meals generally consist of a soup and rice served with two or three dishes, such as a stir-fry, a grilled meat or fish dish, and a salad, served simultaneously. Rice and accompanying dishes are eaten with the fingers, and spoons are used for soup. Condiments, such as salt, pepper, kaffir lime slices, chillis and fish sauce are set on the table in small bowls. Along with rice, packed lunches for factory and agricultural workers might include grilled fish, fish cakes, pickled vegetables, stuffed frogs or small birds wrapped in lotus leaves.

The way the food is to be cooked determines how it is cut. If vegetables are going to be used for a soup, they are often crushed or flattened before cutting. If they are to be used raw to accompany dishes they are split in two. When beef is used in curry, it is cut into large pieces, but for an acidic soup it is cut into smaller pieces; for stir-frying it is sliced, and for use in a salad it is thinly sliced. Pork is ground for stuffing, and thinly sliced for frying, but if it is to be caramelized, larger pieces are used.

LAOS

A landlocked country, Laos has Vietnam to the east, Cambodia to the south, Thailand to the west and China to the north. While these countries have exerted a strong influence on the food of Laos, some of its specialities remain unique.

KEY INGREDIENTS

DILL

SOM PA (FISH PRESERVE)

SOM MU (PORK PRESERVE)

NAM PA (FISH SAUCE)

GINGER

STICKY RICE

FISH AND SHELLFISH

PORK

WATER BUFFALO

LETTUCE LEAVES

PAPAYA

MANGOES

Lettuce leaves
Many dishes are served with these greens, which diners use to create their own spring-roll-type packages.

A mainly Buddhist country, the population of Laos comprises some 60 ethnic groups. The largest ethnic group are the Lao, who inhabit the north bank of the Mekong River and the surrounding plains and valleys, as well as portions of south China and Thailand. In fact, most of the Lao population lives in the lowlands along the Mekong River, where the capital, Vientiane, is located. Outside the lowlands the land is mountainous and thickly forested. The former royal capital, Luang Prabang, is in the mountains to the north, where many other ethnic groups, such as the Mon, live.

A taste of history

When the Lao people arrived from Yunnan, China, in the 13th century, the country was part of the Khmer Empire. By the 17th century, a powerful Lao kingdom, Lan Zang, held sway over much of South-east Asia, but by the early 18th century the Siamese (Thai) had gained control. Their rule lasted until the French arrived in the 19th century and made Laos a protectorate in

French Indo-China. Though it became independent in 1953, French foods have remained: baguettes are common in the larger towns, and the French added tossed salad to the traditional raw vegetable repertoire.

Since the mid-1970s, Laos has been an isolated communist state, and one of the poorest countries in the world. Around 75 per cent of its people are subsistence farmers, growing mainly rice, as well as maize, vegetables, tobacco, sugar cane and cotton.

Staple foods

Surprisingly for a landlocked country, *pa* (fish) is one of the most important foods. It is fished from the rivers, lakes and ponds, but also from the irrigation canals in the paddy fields. In his book, *Fish and Fish Dishes of Laos*, food writer Alan Davidson lists some 80 species of fish that are eaten in Laos, the best-known of them being the huge *pa boeuk*, a member of the catfish family, which is prized for its delicate white flesh and particularly for its roe – Laotian 'caviar'. Sadly, this fish appears to be on the brink of extinction. Freshwater prawns, water-snails, frogs and algae are also used by Laotian cooks.

As in other South-east Asian countries, fish sauce, *nam pa*, is used in almost every Laotian dish. A related fermented fish product, also found in northern Thailand, is *padek*. This is a strong-smelling, fermented fish sauce with chunks of fermented fish still in it, as well as rice powder and husks. Because of its strong smell, families keep their jars of *padek* outside on a veranda. Sometimes only the pieces of fermented fish are used in a dish; sometimes both liquid and solids are used; and in other dishes only the liquid is included.

Although a third of the rice eaten in the country is ordinary white rice, Laotians prefer to eat glutinous, sticky rice. Rolled into balls, the rice serves as a utensil and is used either to pick up more solid foods, or to mop up liquids. Sticky rice is also used for deep-fried rice cakes, which are sold widely in Laotian markets. Rice is sometimes ground into flour for use in cakes and *galettes* (round, flat cakes, which can be sweet or savoury). It is often roasted before being ground, and then used as a thickener in other dishes. *Khao poon* (rice vermicelli) is popular and is the main ingredient in the national dish – also known as *khao poon* – which is an elaborate pork and noodle dish served in a piquant sauce.

Pork is by far the most widely eaten meat in Laos, and every part of the animal is used – fried pork skin is an ingredient in many dishes. Water buffalo is also very popular. Its meat is eaten raw, dried or cooked in a number of ways, and the dried skin of the water buffalo is widely used. Beef is hardly known, but poultry and duck are highly esteemed foods. Chicken is the choice for special feasts, and the giblets are considered great delicacies. Game birds, such as quail and wild chicken, are also popular. One traditional Laotian dish, called *laap*, is made with raw chicken or duck, finely chopped and mixed with spices, broth and rice grains – it is not unusual here for foods, including meat, to be eaten raw.

Other Laotian dishes that are not found in neighbouring South-east Asian countries are creamy, spicy purées, which are generally served in lettuce leaves. Stews can also be thick and creamy, the thickeners often being puréed aubergine – the small round, green South-east Asian type – and ground, roasted rice.

The stuff of life
Rice, shown here being harvested from a paddy field, is the foundation for all Laotian meals. Sticky rice is more common in the north, while long-grain rice is widespread in the south.

A baçi is a ceremony held to mark special occasions, such as a birth, a journey abroad or the arrival of a distinguished visitor. It is presided over by a Buddhist monk or a local 'magic man'. The table is laid with a symbolic tree, usually made with banana leaves and flowers, which is surrounded by special foods, such as eggs and rice. After prayers, the person being honoured has symbolic foods placed in his or her hand, and cotton strings tied around his or her wrists. Guests tie strings around their own wrists, which are not removed for at least three days.

Local delicacies
Rat on a stick is available in markets, as are ants' eggs and stuffed frogs.

Food through the day

Two Laotian concepts of life apply to daily meals. One is the notion of *piep*, meaning 'prestige' or 'rank'. The other is that of *lieng*, referring to the idea that by feeding, we are giving nourishment. In practical terms, this means that at a family meal, the father and the mother, who traditionally have the highest rank in the family, always take the first bites of food, called the 'first tasting', followed by the other members of the family in descending order of age. Throughout the meal, nobody should help himself or herself to a dish at the same time as somebody else, nor go in front of a person of higher rank, as this would cause that person to lose prestige.

A guest also must observe these rules. For example, he or she must not begin to eat before first being invited to by the hosts, and may not continue to eat after the others have finished. If the guest is still hungry, another member of the household must continue eating, too. It is polite to leave something on the plate at the end of a meal, otherwise it would indicate that the host

SIGNATURE DISHES

Foe *This rice noodle soup is eaten as a snack or sometimes for breakfast.*

Som khay *The roe of the huge* pa boeuk *fish is considered the Laotian 'caviar'.*

Tam maak hung *A pounded spicy salad made from shredded papaya, lime juice, chillis, fish sauce and lettuce leaf paste.*

Lap *A common dish of minced, sometimes raw, meat, poultry or fish mixed with sticky rice, lime juice, green onions and chillis.*

Khao poon *Rice vermicelli, served with a number of accompaniments and sauces. The Laotian national dish.*

had not provided enough, and this would mean that the host's *piep* would suffer. For this reason, the host tries to provide more than enough food in a broad array of dishes.

Food is generally served on a low, round bamboo table, and diners sit on the floor. All the dishes are served at the same time, on platters of various sizes. People have individual bowls for soup and baskets of sticky rice. Chopsticks are not part of the Laotian tradition; spoons are used for soups and stews, and sticky rice is used for eating more solid foods. People also eat with their fingers, often wrapping food in edible leaves. Morsels wrapped in leaves are dunked into a sauce. A typical basic sauce served with rice, *jaew som*, is a mixture of garlic, chilli peppers, fish sauce and coriander leaves pounded together. Sometimes ground peanuts are added, reflecting a Thai influence.

Laotian cooking methods can be quite intricate. Chicken and fish, for instance, are often boned before cooking and ingredients are ground using a mortar and pestle to just the right consistency. Cooking methods include searing, frying, steaming, grilling and stewing.

MYANMAR

A richly spiced and varied style of cooking, the gastronomy of Myanmar integrates elements from Chinese and Indian cuisines. Thai influence is particularly evident in the Burmese fondness for hot chillis and coconut milk.

Myanmar, previously known as Burma, changed its name when it gained independence in 1948, following a period of Japanese occupation during the Second World War. Before that it was under British rule for over 200 years. Since gaining independence, it has had a policy of political and economic isolation, and has consequently become one of the world's poorest nations.

Populated 2500 years ago by peoples from the Central Asian and China-Tibetan regions, Myanmar has been highly influenced by its Chinese and its Indian neighbours. Integrating elements from these two cuisines, Burmese cooks enhanced the subtle flavours of Chinese cooking, which was considered too bland, and reduced the oiliness of south Indian cuisine, which was considered too rich and strongly flavoured.

The influence of religion

Buddhism is by far the most important religion, practised by 95 per cent of the population, resulting in a strong vegetarian tradition. Not all Buddhists are vegetarian, but the religion prohibits the killing of animals, and so the butchers in Myanmar tend to be Chinese and Muslim. The Chinese-Burmese are the pork butchers, pork being the most popular meat in Myanmar and central to many delicious dishes.

Staple foods

Rice is eaten in large quantities at most meals. Usually, it is simply boiled, but fried rice dishes of Chinese and Indian origin are also eaten, as are rice-flour pancakes. For special occasions, rice is cooked in coconut milk.

KEY INGREDIENTS

GHEE (CLARIFIED BUTTER)

BLACHAUNG (SHRIMP PASTE)

CHILLI

COCONUT MILK

RICE

CHICKPEA FLOUR

RICE-FLOUR PANCAKES

FISH AND SHELLFISH

PORK

LIME

A key staple
Fish is the most widely eaten food after rice, particularly in the interior and the western coastal areas. Both salt and freshwater fish are eaten, along with shellfish.

SIGNATURE DISHES

Mohingha *This thick, fish and noodle soup may be garnished with fritters, fish cakes, crispy onions or hard-cooked eggs.*

Mandalay mishee *A long-noodle salad with pork, fritters and vegetables.*

Payagyaw *These yellow-pea fritters are just one type of Myanmar's many fritters.*

Let-thoat son *This vegetarian main dish includes tofu, hot chillis, several types of noodles and five different vegetables.*

Htamin lethoke *An assortment of rice, noodles and various cold vegetables, such as cooked potatoes and bean sprouts.*

On no kyauk swe *A chicken curry in coconut-milk sauce, served with fresh noodles, fried noodles and other garnishes.*

SEASONING: THE RICHES OF THE CUISINE

A variety of spices and condiments are used in the richly varied Burmese cuisine, including ginger, turmeric, nutmeg, cumin, fennel, cloves, lemongrass and chillis. Salt plays a very important role, as it does in most tropical cuisines, both for preserving food and for seasoning. In the highlands and inland areas, salty flavours come from granular salt, but in the rice-growing and coastal areas they are more likely to come from the fish sauce *nam pya ye* and the prawn paste *ngapi*.

Meat, poultry and fish are the major sources of protein, and curries are the most popular type of dish. The national dish, *mohingha*, made in various versions throughout the country, is a creamy fish curry with rice vermicelli, served with an array of garnishes. The Burmese love fritters, too, which they make with beans or split peas, *besan* (chickpea flour), curds, meat, prawns, fish and vegetables.

The Burmese distinguish six savours, as opposed to five in Chinese cuisine and four in the West. These are: sweet, acid, salty, spicy, astringent and bitter. A meal should be a feast, bringing pleasure, satisfaction and good flavours; colour, aroma and texture are also important elements in the Burmese meal.

Food through the day

Meals are traditionally eaten twice a day, the first between 6 and 10 am, the second between 4 and 5 pm. This is changing in the cities, such as Rangoon and Mandalay, where three meals are now customary. Meals are usually eaten around a small, round, low table and the tendency is for people to leave the table as soon as they have finished eating. The Burmese generally eat in silence; conversation is reserved for tea, which follows the meal.

Breakfast can be a rich soup, like *mohingha*, or rice with boiled beans, fish sauce and sesame oil. Sometimes it includes fritters. Some people in towns and cities, however, have adapted a more Western-style breakfast. The main meal of the day consists of rice and a few cooked dishes, such as a meat or fish stew or a curry, a dish of sautéed vegetables and soup, which is served throughout the meal as a beverage. Soups are light and served at room temperature. They usually contain local herbs and greens.

A great deal of care is given to cooking in this tropical climate, where food goes off quickly. Sometimes dishes are twice-cooked, first stewed, then fried. The first step in many dishes is to heat oil with onion, chilli, garlic and ginger, and this is undertaken with great precision as this mixture determines the eventual flavour of the dish.

Hands-free transport (*opposite*)
Carrying food on the head is a traditional technique, widely used by the mainly rural population of Myanmar.

THE PHILIPPINES

Filipino cooking has elements of Malaysian, Spanish and Chinese cuisines. Its origins and tropical location are reflected in a fondness for coconut milk and tamarind, and a love of garlic, tropical fruits and vegetables.

KEY INGREDIENTS

ACHIOTE (ANATTO SEEDS)

PATIS (FISH SAUCE)

RICE

EGGS

PORK

PALM HEART

YAMS

SWEET POTATOES

CASSAVA

TOMATOES

CHOCOLATE

The Malay influence
Souring agents, such as this vinegar, are essential ingredients in Filipino cooking.

The Philippines comprises over 7000 volcanic, tropical islands, stretching from south of Taiwan to east of Borneo. Half the population is engaged in agriculture – rice, maize and coconuts being the principal crops – and most live on the island of Luzon, where the capital, Manila, is located.

Like other South-east Asians, the Filipinos eat with their hands and use dried fish and fermented fish sauces and pastes to flavour dishes. It is a rice-based cuisine, but noodles are also very important. The Filipinos have their own version of spring rolls, which are made with egg and called *lumpia*. Also, the sweet snacks and puddings of the Philippines are much like those of Malaysia and Indonesia.

There are also South Pacific influences here. The Filipinos learned to cook with yams, taro and sweet potatoes from the Pacific islanders, from whom they also adopted the tradition of eating *lechón* (see picture, opposite).

A taste of history

The original Filipinos were of Malaysian descent, but 400 years of Spanish occupation, beginning in the 16th century, coupled with a great deal of Chinese immigration, has produced a race of mixed Chinese-Malay-Spanish ancestry. One island, Mindanao, in the south, was very influenced by Malay Muslim traders and it remains Muslim today, in a country where 92 per cent of the population is Roman Catholic.

Soon after the Spanish arrived, Manila became an important centre for trade between Latin America and Spain and China and the other countries of South-east Asia. Many of the New

SIGNATURE DISHES

Lumpia *Egg rolls, often including heart of palm, which may be a starter or side dish.*

Tamals *These banana-leaf or maize-husk packages are filled with rice, coconut milk, ground peanuts, achiote and slivers of meat.*

Bibingka *Grilled rice cakes wrapped in banana leaf packages.*

Puto bumbong *For this dish, violet-coloured rice, sprinkled with coconut meat and brown sugar, is cooked in bamboo tubes.*

Champorado *A sticky rice dish flavoured with chocolate.*

Adobo *A dish consisting of chicken, beef or pork marinated and cooked in seasoned palm vinegar.*

Asado *Meat simmered in soy sauce with bay leaves, onion, tomato and peppercorns.*

Festive
~~~ FOOD ~~~

Christmas is by far the most important holiday in the Philippines. Many traditional foods are eaten, most of them based on rice. Makeshift stands materialize outside churches everywhere, to satisfy the appetites of people leaving early-morning mass with bibingka *(fragrant grilled rice cake packages),* puto bumbong *(violet-coloured* pirurutung *rice cooked in bamboo tubes) and other rice-treats, such as* suman, *glutinous white rice steamed in a banana leaf or palm-leaf package. People enjoy their snacks with the hot ginger tea,* salabat.

World foods that found a foothold in Asia were introduced via the Philippines. It was during this period that Chinese immigration transformed the population and what they ate; rice production increased, and stir-frying joined the array of Filipino cooking methods, which also include grilling, stewing and deep-frying.

The Philippines remained in Spanish hands until 1898, when the islands passed to the United States as a result of the Spanish-American War. After a struggle for independence led by the middle classes, this was a bitter disappointment. The country did not become independent until 1946, following a period of Japanese occupation during the Second World War.

The Spanish influence makes the food of the Philippines unique within South-east Asia. The Spanish introduced several foods, such as chorizo, and from Mexico, tomatoes, as well as the root vegetable *jicama* and chocolate – Filipinos still drink rich hot-chocolate regularly. The Spanish also brought *achiote* (anatto seeds), which Filipino cooks use to give an orange hue to a popular meat stew called *kari kari*. Dishes such as Spanish omelettes, *calderata* (goat stew) and *bacalao a la vizcaína* (Basque-style salt cod) have obvious Spanish origins, and non-Muslim Filipinos learned to cook using olive oil and lard. Other dishes have Spanish names, but their origins are probably Filipino/Malay. *Adobo*, for example, is one of the most popular dishes on the islands, and is considered by many to be the national dish. To make it, chicken, beef or pork is marinated in palm vinegar, lots of garlic and spices, then simmered with soy sauce in the marinade. The souring is typical of South-east Asian cuisines, even though the name of the dish is the same as that of Spanish and Mexican dishes. In general, there are more Western elements in Filipino cooking than in any other Asian cuisine. The food tends to be much blander than in other South-east Asian countries.

Food through the day

The Filipinos eat three meals a day. A favourite breakfast dish is garlic fried rice. Meals are informal, consisting of a main dish and several accompanying dishes. Fish is common at meals, as both salt-water and freshwater fish from the islands' rivers are abundant.

The Spanish colonialists also left a tradition called the *merienda*. This is a late-afternoon break, in which tapas-like snacks and sweets are served with drinks or tea.

SINGAPORE

Although Singapore imports most of its food, it is renowned for the cuisines of its diverse immigrants who have settled here over the years. Four distinct cooking styles are represented: Chinese, Malaysian, Indian and *nonya*.

KEY INGREDIENTS

GHEE (CLARIFIED BUTTER)

GINGER

CURRY LEAF

ROJAK (SHRIMP PASTE)

REMPAH (CHILLI PASTE)

LEMONGRASS

KAFFIR LIME LEAF

GALANGAL

BREADS

NOODLES

FISH AND SHELLFISH

CHICKEN

Off the tip of the Malay peninsula lies the small island-state of Singapore, which has the busiest port in the world, and one of the densest populations. Enjoying one of the world's strongest economies, most of its 3.5 million people enjoy a high standard of living.

Singapore began as an important trading settlement on the shipping route between India and China, and remains the port through which Malaysia's large export trade goes out. Three quarters of Singapore's population is Chinese, the rest are Malay and Indian.

Chinese influences

Many of the Chinese in Singapore arrived in the early 1800s, from Penang and Malacca in Malaysia and from southern China. The southern Chinese brought with them cooking ingredients such as soy sauce, ginger, garlic, green onions,

peanut and sesame oils, dried black mushrooms, bean curd and fermented soy products, along with their woks, cleavers, steamers and clay pots. They clung to their traditional cooking techniques, and continued to make the dishes they had always made in their native countries. As well as everyday Chinese cooking, the art of dim sum and Chinese banquet food became part of Singapore's cuisine.

At one huge hawker centre (see box, below) in Singapore, the food is practically all food of a Chinese ethnic group called the Teochew, from Guangdon province. It is subtle and light, with an emphasis on fresh fish and vegetables. Specialities include braised goose, Teochew cake (a crisp rice skin wrapped around a sweet bean paste), steamed fish with sour plums, glutinous rice balls filled with ground peanuts or sweetened yellow beans served in a sugar syrup.

HAWKER CENTRES

Of particular interest in Singapore is the street food, which is some of the best in South-east Asia; Singaporeans eat it regularly and are passionate about it. However, the food is not actually sold on the street, as it is in other Asian countries; the restrictive government requires that street food is sold only in highly regulated hawker centres, which are food courts consisting of floors of Asian food stalls built into markets and apartment buildings. Open from lunchtime through to dinner and beyond, they are nearly always busy, packed with people of all walks of life.

Chinese, Indian and Malaysian foods of all kinds are to be found in the bustling hawker centres, and there are stalls specializing in *satay*, noodles, fried rice, turtle soup and exotic fruit juices, to name but a few. Stalls in the Chinatown food centre sell every kind of Chinese food imaginable. Little India curry houses serve spicy, tamarind-infused south Indian curries on banana-leaf 'plates'. In the Muslim market, hawkers are practised in the art of *birianis* and charcoal-grilling, and lamb, goat, chicken and prawn *satays* are often eaten side by side.

Malaysian influences

The cuisine of Singapore's northern neighbour is also influential. Particularly popular are curries, redolent of the Malaysian spice blend called *rempah* (see page 181). All the ingredients typical of Malaysian cuisine are used, such as lemongrass, kaffir lime leaf, curry leaf, galangal, turmeric, ginger, tamarind and prawn paste. Malaysians in Singapore, influenced by local Indian cooks, also accent their food with spices such as cumin, coriander, cardamom, cloves and fennel seeds. As in Malaysia, most of the Singaporean Malays are Muslim, and therefore do not eat pork. They concentrate instead on mutton, beef, fish, shellfish and chicken.

Indian influences

The art of spicing food has infiltrated all of Singapore's cuisines, and Indian food here is highly regarded. Most of the Malay-Indians are Tamil, from Madras and Kerala in south-west India, but northern Indian cooking is also represented. Southern Indian cooks have brought dishes such as *mee goreng*, an Indonesian-style, fried noodle dish, and wonderful flat breads and *rotis*, such as *roti prata*, a flaky, griddle-fried bread served with a thin curry sauce. Slightly sour pancakes called *dosay*, and a steamed bun, made with black-skinned lentil and rice-flour batter, are popular breakfast breads. Another popular snack is *murtabak*, a griddle-fried *roti* stuffed with spiced minced mutton or beef, eggs and onions.

Nonya cuisine

There is a great resurgence of interest in *nonya* cooking in Singapore (see also page 181). The group is locally referred to as Peranakan, or Straits Chinese. The Straits Chinese are known for their *tok panjan* (meaning 'long table'), an extravagant style of entertaining in which an assortment of soups, *gulais* (curries), *mee* (noodle dishes), *sambals* (condiments) and other dishes are laid out on a long table. People take turns at sitting and sampling the food. The *nonya* are also known for their elaborate, multi-layered cakes called *kueh*, made from glutinous rice flour, coconut and brown sugar.

SIGNATURE DISHES

Chinese hokkien *Also called 'pork rib tea soup', this is a typical breakfast soup with spare ribs and sweet spices.*

Nasi lemak *This dish of rice simmered in coconut milk is often eaten for breakfast*

Laksa lemak *Nonya-style noodles, served with a coconut sauce.*

Hokkien mee *Noodles with shrimp, minced cuttlefish, garlic, Malaysian lime and blacan (pungent shrimp paste).*

Chilli crab *A dish of crab, stir-fried in its shell with a sweet and sour tomato sauce.*

Hainanese chicken rice *Poached chicken served with aromatic rice, a light soup, Chinese vegetables and three dipping sauces.*

Nasi goreng *Malaysian/Indonesian fried rice, with egg, meat, vegetables and spices.*

Chinatown

The food sold in Singapore's Chinatown includes dishes that stall-owner families brought with them from China four generations ago, and which back in China remain unique to their native villages.

THAILAND

Although it has many Chinese and Indian influences, the cuisine of Thailand is simple and unique, with a sense of refinement that stems from the pure flavours of its fresh, natural ingredients.

KEY INGREDIENTS

LEMONGRASS

CHILLIS

NAM PLA (FISH SAUCE)

LIME JUICE

ASIAN BASIL

PALM SUGAR

RICE

FISH

BEEF

BEAN CURD

COCONUTS

PEANUTS

Fish and rice – foods that are to be found in waterways, gardens, farms and forests – are the backbones of this simple cuisine; a Thai idiomatic expression for feeding oneself translates as 'eat rice, eat fish'. Thailand never developed a grand court cuisine like that of China. The only difference between peasant cuisine in Thailand and the cooking of its aristocrats, lies in the elaborate fruit and vegetable carvings favoured by the aristocracy, which may take the form of flowers, crabs, leaves, boats or figures from Thai mythology.

A taste of history

The original T'ai tribes came from the Yunnan region of South China. They migrated into the area that is now Thailand in the 13th century, after China fell to the Mongols. At that time, Thailand was populated by Buddhist Mon and Khmer tribes, whose languages and governments had much in common with those of India.

The T'ai eventually supplanted the Khmer and the Mon, and established the kingdom of Sukhothai. Rather than impose their Chinese culture on the region, they adapted local Hindu dialects and Buddhist and animist beliefs. The kingdom continued to expand and thrive, and by the mid-15th century the Siamese had created the greatest rice-producing area in the world. The Siamese had a highly developed court, and a capital city, Ayuthia, of around a million inhabitants, which was an important centre of trade between India and China.

The arrival of Portuguese traders in the 16th century marked the beginning of Siam's relations with the West. The kingdom was threatened time and again with colonization by the French and British in the 19th century, but adroit diplomacy

SIGNATURE DISHES

Ma uon *With a name meaning 'fat horses' in Thai, these are a common snack of ground meats steamed in banana leaves.*

Tom yam *These watery, broth-like soups, seasoned with lemongrass, kaffir leaves and galangal, are an essential at every meal.*

Pad thai *This widespread dish of thin noodles fried with egg, bean sprouts and tofu, is topped with a characteristic sprinkling of peanuts.*

Mee krob *Crisp-fried noodles with chicken, pork and vegetables.*

Kao pad *A dish of fried rice with pork, eggs, prawns or crab and vegetables.*

Gaeng keo wan gai *A green chicken curry made with chillis and coconut milk, which gives it a slightly sweet edge.*

enabled it to retain its independence. In 1932, after a bloodless coup, Siam went from being an absolute monarchy to a constitutional one. It changed its name to Thailand in 1939.

Thailand's heavy May-to-October rains are partially responsible for the lush vegetation of the country's alluvial plains, jungles and deciduous forests. Its economy is heavily agricultural, with the planting and harvesting of rice dictating the rhythm of rural life. It is the world's largest exporter of pineapples, and a major producer of rice and rubber. However, in recent years manufacturing, particularly electronics, has surpassed agriculture in importance.

A regional flavour

Central Thailand and the higher plateaus of the north-east make up the region of Issan. The fertile plain in this area dominates the country and forms Thailand's rice bowl. Northern Thailand, called Lana Thai, is mostly highlands and mountain ranges, and it is here that many of the country's rivers originate. The western and southern region of Thailand, called Pak Thai, comprises mountains, jungles, strips of rice fields and white beaches lined with palms. Here, the cultivation of coconuts is a thriving industry, and the bordering Gulf of Thailand and Andaman Sea offer up a wealth of seafood.

In the remote northern forests, hill tribes hunt deer and occasionally wild buffalo and pheasant. These north-eastern tribes prefer short-grain, glutinous rice to long-grain rice, a legacy of the T'ai tribes from whom they are descended. The food here is dry and eaten with the fingers, or sticky rice is pressed into balls and used to scoop up the food. One of the signature dishes of north-eastern Thailand, *laab*, a mixture of raw chopped beef, ground rice, herbs and spices, is quite similar to a dish eaten in Yunnan Province, and marks the Chinese ancestry of these tribes.

Chinese influences

The concept of balancing five different types of flavour – bitter, salt, sour, hot and sweet – has come to Thailand from China. Nowhere is this balancing act more evident than in bitter hot-and-sour soups, such as the prawn soup, *dom yam gung*. In Thai cooking, sweetness comes from palm sugar, coconut sugar or wild honey; saltiness comes from prawn paste or *nam pla* (fish sauce) – stronger than the Vietnamese version; acidity comes from lemongrass, tamarind or lime juice; and spiciness comes from chillis that are often hotter than a Western palate can handle.

The chilli pepper came to Thailand with the Portuguese, after the discovery of the New World. The Thais already loved the spice of black pepper, so chillis were well received, and they thrived in the fertile soil. The Spanish introduced other foods via the Philippines; these included the chiku fruit, tomatoes and tapioca.

Stir-fry cooking in a wok, called a *kata*, is one of the three important cooking techniques in Thai cuisine, the others being grilling and stewing. Some dishes, such as *pla brio wan*, a whole fish served with a soy and ginger sauce, are almost identical to Chinese dishes. The Thai fondness for duck and the importance of noodles in the diet, probably stem from China. *Mee krob*, one of the most beloved dishes in Thai cuisine consisting of fried noodles with meat, seafood and bean sprouts, is much like a Chinese chicken salad with crispy noodles. Pork and poultry butchers in Thailand tend to be ethnically Chinese; and certain pork dishes, such as pork-stuffed omelettes, probably have Chinese roots.

Bustling markets
The buying and selling of flowers, produce and vegetables is a regular scene in Thai cities, whether the markets are on water or land.

Reading the
MENU

THAI MEALS CONSIST OF THREE TO SIX DISHES, ALL ACCOMPANIED BY RICE. THERE IS NO PARTICULAR ORDER AND STRUCTURE TO COURSES.

soups

Soups are generally thin and broth-like and may include rice or noodles, as in kao dom (rice soup) or sen mee nam gup (noodle and pork soup).

rice and noodle dishes

These are often based on fish or meat. You might choose, for example, pad thai, kao pad tamada (red fried rice with prawns) or mee krob (crisp-fried noodles with chicken, pork and vegetables).

curries

Besides green and red Thai curries, you might find a gaeng mussaman (Muslim curry) or puu phat phong karii (stir-fried crab with curry and eggs).

fish

Pla brio wan (fried fish with ginger sauce) and poo cha (crab cakes) are popular fish dishes. Plaa phao, fish roasted in banana leaves and served with a seafood sauce, is a great way to enjoy Thai fish.

salads

Tangy, sometimes spicy vegetable salads are called yam, and might include plaa meuk (squid), wun sen (bean sprouts) or ma-muang (green mango).

desserts

Tropical fruits are a favourite dessert, though custards and egg sweets are also available.

drinks

Beer, water, fruit juices and iced tea are all drunk with Thai meals.

Indian influences

Thai curries have some things in common with their Indian counterparts. As in southern India, coconut milk is used to dilute the fire of chillis. There is also a Thai Muslim curry known as *gaeng mussaman*, which was brought to Thailand by Indian immigrants, and uses an Indian-tasting spice blend of star anise, cinnamon and cloves. Other Thai curries, however, use distinctive spice pastes including chillis, galangal and lemongrass. Indian and Arab merchants were responsible for introducing other popular seasonings into Thailand, such as cardamom, coriander, cumin and spices from the Spice Islands, namely nutmeg, cloves and mace.

Food through the day

Traditionally, Thais eat three meals a day; rural people eat breakfast before going to the fields and lunch in the fields, then a substantial dinner in the evening. Breakfast is often a rice soup called *kao dom*, in which rice is cooked in water and a number of other ingredients, such as pork, dried fish, smoked meat, eggs and boiled or pickled vegetables, are added. The soup is seasoned with *nam pla*, ginger, chillis, onion flakes, fresh coriander and green onions. This same soup is also a favourite late-night snack.

Dinner generally consists of a minimum of three dishes: a curry or soup, a meat or fish dish and a sautéed vegetable dish. Rice is provided in individual dishes, and each diner takes portions from the large bowls of soups, stews and stir-fries on the table. At formal meals individuals receive their own servings, which might include a soup, a steamed dish, a fried dish, a sauce, a salad and a curry, all accompanied by rice. One of the dishes served at dinner is always spicy, and on the table there are bowls of *nam pla*, chopped garlic and chopped chillis with lime juice. Dessert can be fresh fruit, a sweet cake or pudding, or both. Thai custards and sweets that combine eggs and palm-sugar syrup, are descended from Portuguese sweet-making traditions. Popular fruits are mangoes, pineapples, citrus and bananas.

HERBS AND SPICES

PRIK KAENG KIO green curry paste contains green chillis, garlic, coriander leaves, cumin, onion, galangal, lemongrass and the shrimp paste, *blachan*

KAENG PED red curry paste is much hotter, as it gets its colour from red chillis. It also uses red onion rather than white, and the stems of coriander rather than the leaves

MUSSAMAN CURRY PASTE is a milder paste, introduced by Islamic traders, containing star anise, cinnamon and cloves

The banana seller (*opposite*)
Tropical fruits, sold throughout Thailand, make popular desserts.

Green papaya salad
Hot, sweet and sour *som tam*, including lime juice, fish sauce and garlic, is a favourite on Thai streets.

VIETNAM

With a coastline longer than that of California, Vietnam wraps itself around the eastern side of South-east Asia. Its three geographic regions – the North, South, and Centre – have varied histories, which bring a diversity to its cuisine.

KEY INGREDIENTS

CORIANDER

CULANTRO

MINT

CHILLIS

SUGAR

NUOC MAM (FISH SAUCE)

RICE

NOODLES

FISH AND SHELLFISH

BEEF

PORK

BANANAS

Mixing flavours
At meals each diner has a bowl of rice, onto which he or she places foods selected from the array on the table.

The natural landscape of Vietnam is impressive, with the Red River in the North, the fertile Mekong Delta in the South and rice paddies everywhere, irrigated by swamps, lakes and canals. These same waterways, and the country's long coastline, provide the Vietnamese with an abundance of seafood, the most important source of protein and the basis of the everyday seasoning, *nuoc mam*, fermented fish sauce.

The other major influence on the cuisine is religion. Of the Vietnamese population, just over half is Buddhist, and this is evident in the importance of vegetarian dishes. These are based mainly on rice and soy – eaten in the form of bean curd – sprouts, beans, milk and sauce.

A taste of history
Although the delicate, sophisticated cuisine of Vietnam is unique, echoes of its ancient nemesis, China, which occupied the country for around 1000 years between 111 BC and

939 AD, are evident in some of the country's cooking techniques and flavours, especially in the northern regions where the Chinese had the most influence. Here can be found a large number of dishes that are stir-fried or that make use of exotic Chinese ingredients, particularly in dishes prepared for festive events. A further Chinese legacy is the use of chopsticks; Vietnam is the only South-east Asian country where chopsticks are used by the entire population.

During the period of Chinese occupation, an important trade relationship existed between China and India, and this is how Indian flavours found their way into the cuisine of southern Vietnam. Indian traders, priests and merchants

SIGNATURE DISHES

Banh xeo *Sizzling rice-flour crêpes stuffed with pork or chicken and shrimp.*

Cha gio *Rice-paper spring rolls with noodles, pork and crabmeat or shrimp.*

Cuon diep *Lettuce rolls filled with prawns, meat and noodles.*

Chao tom *Shrimp paste on sugar cane.*

Pho ga *Ginger chicken and noodle soup, served with thin strips of chicken.*

Hu tieu *Rice vermicelli and chicken broth soup, which is also known as 'Saigon soup'.*

Thit kho nuoc dua *A dish of pork cooked with coconut water.*

Bo bay mon *A restaurant speciality of seven beef dishes. The first is always beef fondue with vinegar, the last is beef rice soup.*

established several outposts along the Mekong Delta, and these developed into towns that were culturally and religiously Indianized. The peoples of this region were eventually absorbed into an Indianized state called Funan.

The central part of Vietnam, Champa, where Hue is located, was fiercely independent even during Chinese rule. Hue later became the seat of the kings of the Vietnamese empire, Annam. The ancient royal cuisine has echoes in today's decorative presentation of foods.

The Portuguese were the first Europeans to arrive in Vietnam, in 1516, and they introduced chilli peppers. But it is the French who have had the strongest Western influence on the culture and cuisine, bringing new ingredients, cooking methods and ways of eating. The French first came as Catholic missionaries, but soon sent soldiers, and by 1883 Vietnam was a French protectorate within Indo-China, with its capital in Saigon. This lasted until 1954.

A regional flavour

Vietnam's geography also designates the regionality of its cuisines. The climate in the north is colder than in the south and the variety of foods and spices is consequently smaller. Black pepper and ginger are the most

widely used seasonings. Crab and shellfish are popular in this area, but fish is less common.

In the centre the food is spicy; chillis are widely used, as is shrimp paste and the fish sauce, *nuoc mam*. Game from the highlands is enjoyed by the wealthy, and the presentation of food is decorative – a legacy that dates back to the ancient court cuisine of Annam.

The cuisine of the south is the most varied and refined, with more ingredients used than in the centre or north, and a preponderance of locally produced sugar and sugar cane. The French influence on the region is reflected in the use of Western vegetables like potatoes and asparagus, and in the popularity of coffee drinks, crusty French bread and croissants. The French also inspired the Vietnamese in their execution of fish and meat pâtés, which are quite refined. Restaurants in this part of Vietnam often serve dishes in French-style courses, rather than all at once. The Indian legacy in the south is also in evidence, with curry a popular dish.

In 1954, following the partition of the country into communist North Vietnam and democratic South Vietnam, there was a huge migration of North Vietnamese to the south. They brought many of their Chinese-style dishes with them and this was when the beef and rice-noodle soup, *pho bo* (see box, page 200), arrived in the South; it quickly became Saigon's most popular street and noodle-shop meal.

A taste of France
Colonial rule has left its mark on Vietnamese cuisine: travellers are often surprised to find baguettes sold widely on street corners.

Festive

~~~ FOOD ~~~

The lunar new year, Tet, was traditionally celebrated for one month, but is now more often celebrated for three days. Foods eaten at Tet include steamed rice cakes, known as banh chung, *and a pork stew, called* thit heo kho.

■ **TEA: A FRAGRANT RITUAL**

THE MOST WIDELY DRUNK BEVERAGE IN VIETNAM, TEA IS MADE EVERY MORNING FOR THE DAY, AND CONSUMED MORNING, NOON AND NIGHT. THE MOST POPULAR TEA IS FROM BLAO, AND THIS IS GROWN ON PLANTATIONS IN THE CENTRAL HIGHLANDS. BLAO TEA IS OFTEN MIXED WITH DRIED FLOWERS, SUCH AS JASMINE, ROSES, LOTUS BLOSSOMS AND CHRYSANTHEMUMS. LOTUS BLOSSOM TEA IS THE FAVOURITE.

A TRADITIONAL VIETNAMESE WAY OF ENTERTAINING IS TO INVITE GUESTS FOR TEA, SNACKS, AND POETRY. GUESTS ARE SERVED STRONG TEA IN TINY CUPS AND ARE REQUIRED TO COMPOSE A POEM AFTER FINISHING THEIR CUPS. THERE IS MUCH COMPETITION TO CREATE THE BEST POEM.

Staple foods

Rice, Vietnam's most important food, takes the form of steamed rice and rice noodles. Fruit and vegetables are plentiful and important, as meat is scarce and expensive, and certain fruits when unripe are eaten as vegetables; these include papaya and bananas. Bananas are the most widely eaten fruit and their leaves are indispensable for cooking. Lychees, longans, mangoes and rambutans are also widely eaten.

Although meat is still a luxury for most Vietnamese, it is becoming more available as the country develops economically. Pork and duck are popular, and beef is a favourite, a legacy of the French, whose predilection for *boeuf* and *bifsteck* influenced Vietnamese tastes.

Food through the day

The Vietnamese eat three meals a day. Rice or soup are common breakfasts in Vietnam. There are many breakfast-only places in Hanoi and Ho Chi Minh City (Saigon) serving the popular breakfast soups. Traditionally, 'Hanoi soup' is

pho bo (see box, below) and 'Saigon soup' is a mixed meat, shrimp and noodle soup called *hu tieu*. *Pho bo* is popular now all over Vietnam.

Dinner, eaten at dusk, is the most important meal of the day. Family meals in Vietnam are simple but refined, often consisting of a soup, a simmered main dish and a stir-fried dish, all placed together on the table with abundant rice. The dishes are eaten in no particular order, but with a desire to mix flavours and textures, going from salty to sour, from sweet to spicy and from soft to crunchy. Dipping sauces and condiments also grace the table; the food is dipped into the sauces or condiments are added to the bowl. Some dishes, eaten with the fingers, are wrapped in pancakes or lettuce leaves, then dipped into sauces. If any dessert is served, it is fresh fruit.

Vietnamese meals are animated, and the more people the merrier: the sharing of culinary pleasure is an important concept. Meals require a lot of preparation, which is accomplished mainly by women, who work in an open, outdoor kitchen where everybody can see them, so that they don't feel isolated.

Special occasions

Meals for parties and special occasions are more elaborate, with more dishes served. Many of the dishes require hours of preparation, and this is an indication that the guests are important. Ingredients are added to rice to give it flavour and colour. Soups are made with expensive ingredients like beef, and they are served as an individual dish.

Unlike family meals, party dinners are served in courses. Drinks are served first, with appetizers. Then comes soup, followed by several main dishes and a decorative rice dish. There is fruit for dessert, followed by tea.

PHO: VIETNAM'S FAVOURITE MEAL IN A BOWL

One of the biggest treats for a Vietnamese family is an outing to a noodle shop to eat *pho bo*, often called, simply, *pho*. This is an aromatic beef broth filled with noodles, sliced beef, onions and coriander, and garnished with Asian basil, bean sprouts and the fragrant saw-leafed herb, culantro.

Pho originated in Hanoi around the turn of the century. Before the French occupation, beef was hardly eaten, as cows and buffalo were valued as beasts of burden. But the French loved beef, and so the meat began to appear in the markets, eventually catching on with the upper-class Vietnamese. One theory suggests that *pho* was created by cooks who made *pot-au-feu* for the French and that the word *pho* comes from the word *feu*. But the soup has Chinese elements, too, which had been part of the cuisine long before the French arrived.

KOREA

Sensible eating and nutritional balance are the foundations of Korean cuisine. It is based on rice, vegetables, fish and meat, and flavour and colour are of the utmost importance, resulting in a diet that is both healthy and attractive.

KEY INGREDIENTS

GINGER

RED CHILLI PEPPERS

GARLIC

SESAME SEEDS AND OIL

KOCHUJANG (RED PEPPER PASTE)

RICE VINEGAR AND WINE

FISH AND SHELLFISH

BEAN CURD

BEEF

PORK

RICE

SEAWEED

Though the country has been divided politically since 1948 into communist North Korea and democratic South Korea, these divisions do not exist gastronomically, although South Korea has been much more prosperous than the North and has a greater abundance of food. Korea is surrounded on three sides by water, and mountains run down its centre. To the west is the Yellow Sea, to the east the Sea of Japan, and China borders the peninsula to the north. Thousands of islands flank the west and south coast, resulting in fertile grounds for shellfish and sea vegetables. The waters off the east coast are deeper and colder, with great catches of deep-water fish, squid, cuttlefish, as well as prawns, oysters and shellfish of all kinds.

Korea's climate is temperate, with four distinct seasons. Winters are harsh, particularly in the North, and summers are long and humid. Because of the difficult winters, Koreans have a long tradition of preserving vegetables, fish and meat by salting and pickling. These foods, called *kimchi* (see box, page 204), are made to last out the winter, and have become signature dishes of Korean cuisine, present at every meal.

Squid snacks
Harsh winters have made it necessary to preserve many foods in Korea. Seafood is plentiful, and dried squid makes a very popular dish.

SIGNATURE DISHES

Pajon *This green onion pancake is eaten on streets across the country.*

Nakchibokkum *Stir-fried baby octopus is a favourite Korean snack.*

Twoenjang-tchigae *This soybean-paste soup makes a common everyday food.*

Chongol *A meat and vegetable hotpot, which is prepared at the table.*

Pibimbap *A classic one-dish meal combining rice with vegetables and often some meat.*

Pulgogi *This marinated barbecued beef dish is the most well-known of the Korean* gui *(grilled meat dishes).*

Naengmyon *Cold noodles served in a broth, garnished with beef and Korean pear.*

A taste of history
Koreans are descended from the Mongolians, and ancient Korea was culturally advanced, with three kingdoms existing at around the first century: Koguryo to north, and Paekche and Silla in the south. It was Silla, with the aid of China, that eventually conquered the other two kingdoms and established a unified country. In the 10th century the Koryo Dynasty was founded. This lasted until 1392 and was followed by the Yi Dynasty, one of the longest in history, with 26 kings. Throughout these centuries, two distinct types of cooking developed: a complex, elegant court cuisine, for which a wide variety of seasonings and spices were used, and a simpler,

more robust peasant home cooking. During the Yi Dynasty special dishes evolved – such as the many-layered hotpot, *shinsolla* – that were prepared uniquely for the royal family.

Korea modernized in the 17th and 18th centuries, after the Europeans began to arrive. They brought with them Roman Catholicism, which became widespread, and New World foods, such as sweet potatoes, tobacco and chillis – now an essential Korean ingredient. New systems of irrigation and farming techniques brought widespread cultivation of crops, such as rice and ginseng. As farmers and merchants became wealthy, a middle class developed.

Staple foods

For centuries the basic diet in Korea has consisted of rice and *kimchi*. Rice is the principal staple, and the rhythms of daily life revolve around its planting and harvesting. The casual Korean greeting, 'Pam mogosoyo?' means literally, 'Have you eaten rice?' and the verb *papporihada* means 'to earn one's daily rice', with much the same connotation as 'breadwinning'. Plain,

steamed rice counterbalances the strong flavours of preserved vegetables and pickled fish. Noodles, a symbol of longevity, are also widely eaten, particularly at lunchtime, and on streets all over the country noodle stands provide this classic Korean fast food.

As well as being a food, rice forms the basis of several alcoholic drinks. *Makkolli*, for example, is a frothy, milky-white beverage. *Ju* is a rice wine that comes in several varieties: *tong dong ju* is country rice wine; *nong ju* is farmer's wine from the South; *chung chong ju* is Korean sake, served warm in china carafes; and *pob ju* is the highest quality rice wine, the best coming from Kyongju.

Every Korean home has a *jang* terrace, a stone area outside a country house, or a section of an apartment balcony or roof, where large earthenware jars are kept. These contain the three most important seasoning elements of Korean kitchen: *kanjang* (soy sauce), *twoenjang* (fermented soybean paste) and *kochujang* (red pepper, soybean and glutinous rice paste). The number of jars on a *jang* are an indication of a family's wealth.

Eating on the go
Street food is everywhere in Korea. Favourites include steamed mussels served in their shells, soups with *kimchi*, rice cakes in red-chilli sauce, pancakes and roasted chestnuts.

KIMCHI: THE KOREAN MAINSTAY

Consisting of pickled and preserved vegetables, fish or meat, or a combination of these, *kimchi* is the national dish and a centuries-old staple. The food is fermented in large earthenware jars, which can be left outside buried in the ground or insulated in straw huts for months. Cabbage is the most classic of the preserved vegetables, but each region has its own variations. *Kimchi* in Seoul and Kyonggi-do province includes abalone, ginkgo, pine nuts and pickled raw fish. North Korea's Pyongyang regional speciality is a radish water *kimchi*, called *tongchimi*. Spices and salt are used sparingly here because the water in North Korea is said to be very pure, so the *kimchi* is not very salty. In the southern Cholla and Kyongsang-do provinces, the *kimchi* is made with more salt and more chilli to assure preservation in hotter weather. In Kyongsang-do pickled fish is usually added.

The most popular meat in Korea is beef. It is marinated with soy sauce, garlic, sesame oil and ginger for *pulgogi* (a grilled meat dish) and *kalbi* (braised short ribs), and used as a base for stews and soups. Pork is popular in the North. The main source of protein, though, is fish, which is eaten fresh, dried or preserved. Tofu (soybean curd) is also an important source of daily protein.

A regional flavour

North and South Korea divide naturally into distinct geographic regions. In the North are high mountains and deep valleys, lined with pine, fir, spruce and cedar forests. The soil is thin on the high plateaus, but western river plains support large fruit orchards and a wide variety of crops, including rice, maize, millet, barley, wheat, soybeans and sweet potatoes.

The flatter plains of the South are dedicated to agriculture, and rice, millet, sorghum, barley, fruits, vegetables and nuts are grown. The steep mountains that run down the spine of the country are a rich source of wild vegetables, herbs and funghi, as well as roots, such as ginseng, one of Korea's most important products.

Although culinary habits are much the same throughout North and South Korea, there are regional specialities. The farther south one travels, the hotter and spicier the food becomes. Korea's foremost gastronomic centres are in the Cholla province, in the south-western corner of the country. The food of Kwangju is hot and fiery. Nearby Chonju is famous for a vegetable medley called *pibimbap*, and the number and variety of its *panchan* (side dishes).

Korea also has a tradition of vegetarian temple cuisine. When the Yi Dynasty followed the Koryo Dynasty in the late 14th century, and Buddhism was replaced by Confucianism, Buddhists were persecuted, and monks fled to the mountains, where they foraged for foods. A temple cuisine evolved, which grew out of the monks' use of edible wild plants, roots and herbs. A possible legacy of the earlier Koryo Dynasty, which was Buddhist and vegetarian, is the idea that butchers are outcasts and to be treated with disdain; there are still elements of this in modern-day Korea.

Food through the day

The nutritional balance of Korean cuisine is evident in everyday eating habits. As in other Asian countries, meals include five flavours: salt, sweet, sour, hot and bitter. Salt is provided by soy sauce, salty bean paste and preserved fish and vegetables. Beet sugar, honey and sweet potatoes are used to sweeten food, while chilli peppers and mustard are heat sources. Vinegars are used as souring agents, and ginger and other roots are regarded as bitter. The Koreans also follow a gastronomic tradition that a meal should include five colours: red, green, yellow, white and black.

Breakfast and dinner are the main meals of the day, similar in nature and equal in importance – a traditional Korean breakfast can consist of up to 20 dishes. Even Korean picnics can be elaborate, with special burners transported to the picnic spot for cooking hotpots and barbecues. Today, with many women working outside the home, a number of urban Koreans have begun to eat Western-style breakfasts.

A typical family meal consists of a large variety of dishes, seldom fewer than seven. Poorer people, however, normally eat one-dish meals with rice. There is no concept of a 'main

dish' at a meal; all of the dishes, both light and substantial, are served at the same time, except at formal banquets. Dishes made up of many components are presented in compartmented lacquer dishes. *Panchan* (side dishes) are a unique feature of Korean food and a meal is often judged by the variety of its *panchan*.

At a meal, each person has a lidded rice bowl, traditionally made of metal, filled either with plain rice or rice mixed with other grains and vegetables. Spoons and chopsticks are used for eating. *Kimchi* is always present, as are *guk* or *tang* (soups) and raw or lightly cooked vegetable dishes called *namuls*. These are often eaten with *jon* (fritters) and with other side dishes, such as salted fish or seasoned, toasted seaweed. Seaweed in many forms has always been an important element in the Korean diet. Substantial meat or fish dishes are eaten in small bowls. Balance is important at a meal: no single food or flavour should dominate: hot, spicy food and strong, salty *kimchis* are balanced by rice; batter-fried *jon* are accompanied by crunchy vegetables; and fresh raw fish complements barbecued meats. A meal normally ends with fresh fruit.

Formal dinners may include as many as 13 courses. The rice and soup will be served last, after the succession of other dishes. This is meant to imply that the fillers (rice and soup) are hardly needed after such sumptuous hospitality.

Tea urns
Normally served in pottery vessels, tea is drunk with most Korean meals. It is most commonly made with roasted barley.

Festive

~~~ FOOD ~~~

A baby's first birthday is a major celebration. The child is placed near a table, on which there is rice, noodles, books, coins and calligraphy brushes, all symbolizing the future. A feast follows, with seaweed soup and chalttok (sweet rice with beans) – dishes symbolic of longevity.

JAPAN

Of all the cuisines of Asia, Japan's has been the least touched by outside influences, having until recently kept its doors closed to foreigners. Despite a current vogue for Western foods, traditional, highly stylized cooking persists.

KEY INGREDIENTS

RICE

NOODLES

GINGER

SEAWEED

SESAME SEEDS

SOY SAUCE

RICE VINEGAR

WASABI (HORSERADISH)

FISH AND SHELLFISH

BEAN CURD

MISO (BEAN PASTE)

MUSHROOMS

Rice-planting festival
A celebration that is both a ceremony for a good harvest and fun for rice workers.

A chain of several thousand islands makes up Japan, the most important of which are Honshu, Hokkaido, Shikoku and Kyushu. Stretching for some 2500 km off the coast of mainland Asia, the northern islands have a temperate climate, with cold winters, while the southern islands enjoy year-round warmth. More than three-quarters of the land in Japan is hilly or mountainous, leaving only about one-tenth suitable for agriculture. Yet Japan manages to produce enough rice – its staple grain – to meet all its needs. The Japanese word for 'boiled rice', *gohan*, also means 'a meal'. Rice is intensively cultivated using modern machinery, and many of the farmers in Japan have other sources of income as well.

A taste of history

The country's earliest inhabitants came from Siberia and the Korean peninsula. They developed a cult of fertility of the land and of the spirits of the countryside. Later, people migrating from southern China merged their clan worship with this nature worship, resulting in Japan's oldest principal religion, Shintoism, a formalization of nature worship. Although Buddhism, which arrived from China in the 6th century, eventually supplanted Shintoism as Japan's most important religion, Shintoism remains at the heart of the Japanese ethos; it can be linked to many of today's harvest celebrations, as well as to the country's reverence for plant life.

The Japanese diet, which relies on simple ingredients, like fish, vegetables, rice, fruits and sea vegetables, has changed little through the centuries. It has always been somewhat austere, even in the highest imperial court of ancient Kyoto. Japanese cuisine embodies an acute awareness of the seasons and, more than anything else, it requires the freshest of ingredients. Its flavours are characterized by subtlety and, unlike other Asian cuisines where combinations and blends are emphasized, individual flavours and textures are of the greatest importance in Japanese cooking. Buddhism, which prohibited meats, and thus animal fats, further influenced this aesthetic.

The cuisine itself may have remained frugal, but presentation is refined and of the utmost importance. Garnishes are carefully chosen to represent nature and the seasons, both of which are reflected also in the composition of each dish. There is meaning and tradition behind each serving plate and bowl. Such style and etiquette began to flower during the golden age of Japanese culture, the Heian Era, from 794 to 1185 AD – an era named after the capital of the imperial court. A feudal period followed, in which the *samurai* ('warrior class') flourished, and the culinary arts of the nobility filtered down to the lower classes.

Historically, Japan has always been an isolated country. Much of its cuisine has developed within the country, but there are a few exceptions, in particular, the introduction of tea and soybean products from China in the 6th century, and later the introduction of vegetable oils and frying techniques by European traders. In the 16th century, the Portuguese were the first Europeans to set foot in Japan, and from them the Japanese adapted the technique of frying fish in batter, which became known as tempura. The word comes from the Latin word *tempora*, referring to the *quattuor tempora* – the Ember Days of the Roman Catholic Church when meat is forbidden and batter-fried fish was an alternative. European traders, including the Dutch and the Spanish, also introduced potatoes and hot red chilli peppers into Japan.

At the end of the 16th century, when Jesuit missionaries began to follow the European traders, the Japanese closed their country to foreigners. Not until the mid-19th century, when Japan began to industrialize, did the cuisine begin to borrow from the Western diet. Beef, pork and poultry began to appear on the menu – pork also represents the Chinese influence in Japan – and the vegetarian tenets of Shintoism were relaxed. The Japanese studied Western methods of raising livestock and began to rear Kobe and Matzuzaka beef, widely regarded as the finest beef in the world.

Staple foods

Despite this influx of meat, fish has always been the main source of protein in Japan, where the waters are rich in every form of marine life. The Japanese have the largest fishing fleet in the world; and they catch and eat more seafood than any other country. Fish farming is also widely practised. Seafood is present in one form or another at every Japanese meal, be it cooked fish, *sashimi* (raw fish) or the dried bonito tuna flakes that flavour Japanese broth. Seaweeds are also very important, particularly *kombu* (kelp), a basic ingredient in Japanese soup stock, and *nori*, paper-thin strips of seaweed, which are used as a wrapping and garnish for many foods.

Soybean products, particularly tofu (bean curd) and miso (fermented soybean paste), constitute Japan's other main sources of protein. *Miso shiru*, broths thickened with miso paste, are the most common Japanese breakfast, and are eaten at other meals as well. There are hundreds of different styles of miso, ranging from light and sweet to dark and savoury. Lighter pastes are

SUSHI AND *SASHIMI*: DELICACIES OF A SEAFOOD-BASED CUISINE

Also called *nigiri-zushi*, which means 'hand-shaped sushi', sushi consists of vinegared rice topped with raw fish or shellfish. It is often served dipped in soy sauce. *Sashimi*, in contrast, consists of raw fish or shellfish cut in different styles to enhance the appearance of the fish. The hot horseradish *wasabi*, often accompanies it. *Iwashi no miso ae*, a speciality of Nagasaki, is a sardine *sashimi* mixed with spring onions in tart miso sauce.

There are several varieties of sushi in Japan. *Oshi-zushi*, for example, meaning 'pressed sushi', is a speciality of Osaka. *Maki-zushi* is 'rolled sushi', for which seafood, vegetables or pickles are placed on a layer of rice and rolled in a sheet of *nori* (seaweed), which is then sliced. *Fukusa-zushi*, meaning 'silk-square sushi', is wrapped in a square of paper-thin omelette. *Inari-zushi* are stuffed bean curd pouches, which are deep fried.

Many different types of seafood are used to make sushi and *sashimi* in Japan. Some of the most widely available include: *shime-saba* (vinegared mackerel); *ika* (squid); *maguro*, the red meat of tuna; *anago*, a sea eel, which is boiled then grilled; *odori* (live shrimp); and *akagai*, a ribbed clam with red meat.

Low table seating
In a casual setting, men sit cross-legged and women sit on their knees, with their legs to the side. At formal meals, both genders kneel symmetrically.

preferred in the south-western part of the country, and darker pastes in the north-east. Each family has its own style of miso soup, and when a woman marries, she gives up her own style for that of her husband's family. *Shoyu* (soy sauce) is also a very important seasoning in the cuisine.

In addition to rice, the Japanese eat vast amounts of noodles. According to Shizuo Tsuji, author of *Japanese Cooking: A Simple Art*, more noodles are consumed in Japan each day than any other dish, despite the fact they do not have a place in formal Japanese cooking. They are the most popular fast food lunch eaten by workers. *Soba* (buckwheat noodles) are associated with Tokyo and northern Japan, as buckwheat is a cold weather crop, and *udon* (wheat noodles) are eaten in Osaka and southern Japan. Traditionally, *soba* are the last thing eaten on New Year's Eve, and they are called *toshi-koshi soba*, meaning 'the year is passing'.

Reading the MENU

THE FORMAL JAPANESE BANQUET, RYROI-YA, IS DIVIDED INTO COURSES ACCORDING TO THE METHOD OF PREPARATION. THERE IS A VERY STRICT SEQUENCE OF DISHES, WHICH CAN BE GROUPED INTO A BEGINNING, A MIDDLE AND AN END. THE FOOD IS ALWAYS IN SEASON AND IS NOT OVERWHELMED BY OTHER FLAVOURS. BASIC SEASONINGS, SUCH AS DASHI OR SOY SAUCE, ARE USED SUBTLY. THE FOOD IS EXTREMELY LIGHT; EVEN WHEN IT IS DEEP-FRIED, CLOSE ATTENTION IS PAID TO THE TEMPERATURE OF THE OIL SO THAT LITTLE IS ABSORBED BY THE FOOD.

beginning

To start the banquet there is an assortment of seasonal delicacies made from fish, shellfish, sea urchins, squid or vegetables, served in tiny portions, known as zensai. These are followed by suimono (soup) and then sashimi (raw fish).

middle

The central section of the banquet consists of four types of dishes: yakimono are grilled foods, which are usually prepared on skewers, but may also be pan-grilled; then come the steamed foods, called mushimono; these are followed by nimono (the simmered foods); and finally the deep-fried foods, agemono. These four dishes could be replaced by nabemo, a one-pot dish.

end

For the finale of the banquet you will usually eat gohan (boiled rice), miso-shiru (miso soup) and tsukemono (pickles). These three may be served together.

To follow the banquet there may be green tea and possibly fresh fruit, though fruit is not always present.

A regional flavour

Although there are preferences for different types of noodles in the north and south of the country, on the whole, Japanese cooking is not regional by nature. The strict requirements of harmony, beauty of presentation and freshness of ingredients are spread throughout the country.

However, this is not to say that there are not regional specialities, or food that has not been influenced by outsiders. One eclectic style of cooking, in which Chinese and European influences are evident, is called *shippoku ryori*. Its home town is Nagasaki, which has been particularly influenced by the cooking of China. As such, this region is known for its pork dishes and for its sardine cookery. Tsuchiura, on the island of Honshu, is known for a freshwater fish, called *wakasagi* (pond smelt); Sandai is known for its *kaki-miso* (oysters cooked in miso); and Izumo, which boasts a 300-year-old noodle shop, is known for its *soba*. The cuisine of Kyoto is considered to be very refined, and its vegetarian temple cookery is highly regarded.

Food through the day

Breakfast and lunch are quick, light meals in Japan, the main meal being dinner. The most common breakfast consists of miso soup, rice and pickled vegetables. Noodle dishes are among the most common lunches. The other type of widely eaten lunch comes in a multi-compartment lunchbox called a *bento* box, filled with various cold dishes.

Another popular lunch is *eki-ben*, meaning 'station lunch'. These are boxed lunches sold on railway platforms; particular stations are known for the type of food and the container it is served in. In Tokyo the *eki-ben* are very often *chirashi-zushi* (meaning 'scattered sushi'), consisting of bite-sized pieces of seafood and vegetables, shredded omelette and seasoned mushrooms strewn over the top of vinegared rice. In Osaka, you find *maze-zushi*, which translates as 'mixed sushi', as the fish and vegetables are mixed in with the rice. *Maze-zushi* is used also as a stuffing for *inari-zushi* (deep-fried bean curd pouches) or *fukasa-zushi* (omelettes).

The evening meal, eaten at low tables with chopsticks, is the main meal of the day. Rice, served with fish, poultry, meat or vegetable side dishes, is the focus of a typical family meal. One-dish meals, consisting of hotpots with fish, meat or tofu, and vegetables served with rice, are also very common. In poorer households rice, miso soup and pickles constitute a meal.

At a formal Japanese meal, it is the tradition never to serve a large amount of any one thing. Instead, the Japanese banquet consists of many small portions served in a particular order – as in

SIGNATURE DISHES

Hoenso no goma-ae *A starter of spinach in a nutty sesame dressing.*

Miso-shiru *A thick, white miso-based soup, including dried fish, shellfish and seaweed.*

Dengaku *Tofu, vegetables or fish are coated with miso, skewered, then grilled.*

Teriyaki *A dish of grilled or pan-fried fish or meat, glazed with a sweet soy sauce.*

Tempura *These batter-fried fish and vegetables are served with a dipping sauce.*

Yakimono *These grilled foods are cooked quickly over a high heat, so that they are crisp on the outside, but moist inside.*

Shabu-shabu *For this dish paper-thin slices of beef and vegetables are cooked in broth at the table and served with sauces.*

A winter stew
The hearty hotpot *oden* includes fish paste, tofu and vegetables cooked in kelp stock.

TEA: A DRINK FOR ALL OCCASIONS

ALONG WITH THE RICE WINE, SAKE, GREEN TEA IS THE NATIONAL BEVERAGE IN JAPAN. TEA-GROWING IN JAPAN BECAME SUCCESSFUL IN THE 12TH CENTURY AND FLOURISHED WITH ZEN BUDDHISM. PRIESTS INITIALLY CONSUMED POWDERED GREEN TEA AS A STIMULANT DURING ALL-NIGHT PRAYER, BUT AS THE RELIGION EVOLVED, TEA DRINKING IN THE CONTEMPLATIVE STYLE BECAME A SYMBOLIC RITUAL OF THE NOBLE AND WARRIOR CLASSES.

THERE ARE TWO MAJOR TYPES OF GREEN TEA: LEAF TEA AND POWDERED TEA. OF THE TWO, LEAF TEA IS LESS EXPENSIVE. *BANCHA*, THE LOWEST GRADE OF LEAF TEA, IS SERVED EVERYWHERE AND COMPLEMENTS MOST FOODS. *SENCHA*, OF MEDIUM GRADE, IS DRUNK WHEN ENTERTAINING GUESTS AND IN EXPENSIVE *SUSHI* RESTAURANTS, AS IT GOES WELL WITH RAW FISH. *GYOKURO* (MEANING 'JEWEL DEW') IS THE HIGHEST QUALITY LEAF TEA. RARE AND FRAGRANT, IT IS DRUNK BY ITSELF SO ITS FLAVOUR CAN BE APPRECIATED.

POWDERED TEA IS EXPENSIVE, AND MAKING IT CORRECTLY REQUIRES SKILL. TEA IS NEVER PREPARED WITH BOILING WATER, NOR IS IT STEEPED TOO LONG. *MATCHA*, OR *HIKI-CHA*, IS POWDERED TEA FROM THE CHOICEST PLANTS. RESERVED FOR SPECIAL OCCASIONS, IT IS THE TEA OF THE ZEN TEA CEREMONY.

the menu on page 208. Each dish demands much time and reflection in its presentation. The extravagance of the hospitality is linked to the variety of dishes, and the artistry of the chef is reflected in the balance and subtlety of flavours. A cook's skill can be judged by the two seemingly simplest items on the menu: the *wan* (literally 'soup bowl') and the *sashimi* (see box, page 207).

The *wan-sashi* are the high points of a Japanese meal. They illustrate the chef's talent for balancing subtle flavours and choosing the freshest of ingredients. The *wan* consists of the clear soup, *suimono*, which is served after the appetizer in covered lacquer bowls, and sometimes again, midway through the meal, to refresh the palate if the banquet is very long. A strict formula is adhered to when making the *suimono*. It consists of *dashi* (the basic stock made with kelp and bonito tuna flakes) plus three solid ingredients to lend flavour and colour. The first of these is a bite-sized piece of chicken, egg, shellfish, bean curd, boiled sliced vegetable, fish fillet or part of the fish head – the eye is given to the guest of honour. Secondly, there is a vegetable to complement the first ingredient, such as a couple of strips of boiled burdock to go with a jowl of fish. Finally, there is a garnish to add fragrance, which is often not meant to be eaten, such as trefoil, a sprig of sancho pepper leaves, or a couple of slivers of lemon or citrus rind.

There is also a simplified basic formula for meals served to guests at home, called *ichiju*, meaning 'soup and three'. This meal consists of soup and three main dishes: *sashimi*, *yakimono* (a grilled dish) and a simmered dish, called *nimono*. These are followed by rice, pickles, tea and often fruit. The courses are served in small separate dishes or bowls. As at a formal banquet, presentation is all-important; flavour alone is not enough. The whole meal must be an orchestrated composition, however humble it may be.

Japanese chopsticks
Unlike the blunt Chinese versions, chopsticks in Japan are tapered to a point, perhaps to help the removal of bones from fish.

The Buddhist 'way of tea' *(opposite)*
The complex tea ceremony is rooted in the precepts of Zen Buddhism. Harmony, respect and purity are an integral part of it.

AUSTRALIA

A true fusion cuisine, modern Australian food is characterized by the drawing together of the ingredients and cooking styles of its recent immigrants with the traditions of the country's original settlers and indigenous people.

KEY INGREDIENTS

BUTTER

FISH

YABBY (A CRUSTACEAN)

MARRON (A CRAYFISH)

LAMB

BEEF

KANGAROO

EMU

CHEESE

WARRIGAL GREENS (LIKE SPINACH)

MACADAMIA NUTS

BUNYA NUTS

Bush oranges
Many of Australia's native fruits are gathered by Aborigines from the wild.

Though it has a population of about only 19 million, Australia is one of the world's largest countries – nearly the size of the United States. Bounded by the Indian and Pacific Oceans, it is a land of many climates, which enjoys rich soils, pure waters and abundant sunshine. Much of the country is above the Tropic of Capricorn, while other parts, such as Sydney, are more temperate. Australia's vast interior is sparsely populated and extremely dry and hot. This landscape is particularly suited to livestock farming, and with about 150 million sheep, it is the world's largest wool-producing country.

About 85 per cent of Australians live along the coasts, where the major cities are located. The waters here provide abundant seafood, while inland waterways are home to unique crustaceans, the most well known being yabbies, a freshwater crayfish. Other popular fish include snapper, King George whiting, abalone and shrimp. Oysters are prized, and widely eaten.

A taste of history
Up until the European invasion about 200 years ago, the country was inhabited by Aborigines, a food-gathering society, which had been in Australia for somewhere between 50,000 and 70,000 years. Their diet was based on kangaroo meat, wild seeds, nuts, fruits and vegetables. Although they were never farmers, they practised a kind of management of their resources through controlled burning of vegetation, selective irrigation and regulation of the undergrowth. They scattered the seeds of the fruits they ate, and always left a few nests alone when gathering eggs. Rather than eating everything from a catch, they kept excess fish in special traps.

The Aborigines ate most of their foods raw. Certain foods were leached in running water to remove toxins, then pounded or roasted. Foods that were cooked were roasted over an open fire. The seeds of wattle and kurrajong trees were roasted on coals, ground to a flour, mixed with water and baked into cakes. Today, many modern Australian chefs have begun to incorporate some of the indigenous ingredients into their cooking.

Captain James Cook arrived in Botany Bay in 1770 and claimed the country for Britain. Although many of the earliest settlers were prisoners transported from overcrowded British prisons, it was the Europeans who brought wealth and industry to the country, by introducing agriculture, grazing and mining. Grains, wool and minerals became major exports.

For the first 200 years of Australia's modern history, its cuisine was modelled after the cooking of England. Native fruits, vegetables, nuts and seeds, which had long been used by the Aborigines, were largely ignored. The early 19th-century immigrants, who worked in the outback

as shearers, drovers and diggers, were paid in sugar, flour, tea and meat, in the form of mutton slaughtered ' on the shearing stations. The so-called 'bush-tucker' diet, which evolved from this payment, consisted mainly of slabs of grilled meat – mutton, kangaroo, emu and wild goat – a heavy bread called 'damper', which was baked in ashes and eaten with butter or oil, and a very sweet tea, boiled above an open fire in a tin can called a 'billy'.

In the mid-19th century, immigrants were lured to Australia from the British Isles with the promise of 'meat three times a day'. In response, farmers started producing wheat, milk, sugar, fruit and vegetables as well as wool. The industrialization of food storage and distribution enabled the mass-production of preserved foods, such as tomato sauce, biscuits, jams and chocolates. As settled communities began to thrive towards the end of the 19th century, a style

of home cooking developed, which was no longer focused on tinned goods, but based on plain, good English cookery, such as meat roasts and vegetables, puddings and cakes. People bought food from local stores daily, or from 'carters' who went from house to house. It was not until after the Second World War, with the proliferation of refrigeration and cars, that supermarkets came into being.

After the Second World War there was a huge influx of immigrants, first from Mediterranean Europe – mainly Italians, Greeks, Cypriots, Spanish, Maltese and Lebanese – and then, right after the war, from Eastern Europe. Italians make up Australia's second largest immigrant group after the English and Irish, while Melbourne has the third largest Greek population in the world. As these communities increased, so did the production of their traditional foods. Mediterranean foods, such as Lebanese and

A cuisine of the sun
Reflected in both their food and the places where they serve it, modern Australian chefs produce bold, exciting dishes that blend native and imported flavours.

SIGNATURE DISHES

Steak Diane *Fillet of steak, pounded thin and pan-fried in butter.*

Meat pies *Also called 'four and twenty meat pies', these are the Australian fast food.*

Shearer's casserole *Lamb's fry with tomato sauce and bacon.*

Angels on horseback *A dish of grilled oysters wrapped in bacon.*

Damper *The original Australian bread, made in the outback with flour and water and baked on hot ashes.*

Lamingtons *Small, sweet sponge cakes, which are dipped in chocolate and rolled in desiccated coconut.*

Pavlova *A dessert of meringue topped with whipped cream and sliced fruit, such as bananas and kiwi fruit.*

A fusion cuisine

Recently, a large second wave of immigration has occurred in Australia, with people coming mostly from Asia, but also from countries such as Chile and Iran. A particularly large influx of Asian immigrants occurred in the 1980s, and this has greatly influenced the cuisine of the country. There are now Asian supermarkets in every city, with ingredients from India, South-east Asia and China readily available. Australian chefs have begun to see that the cuisines of Asia are more relevant to their country's climate than the cuisines of northern Europe and now include Asian dishes on most menus.

As the population has evolved, Australian cooking has come into its own. A true fusion cuisine, it is characterized by the drawing together of the ingredients and cooking styles of its newer immigrants with those of its original settlers and indigenous people. It includes influences from the Mediterranean, Asia and California and from the French tradition of nouvelle cuisine. Australia is a prosperous

New world wines
There are about 750 wineries in Australia, which produce reds and whites that rival the best European wines.

Syrian *tabbouleh,* hummus and *pita* bread, Greek salads, olives, sun-dried tomatoes and peppers, and Italian pizza, pasta and bread, are now an integral part of the gastronomic landscape. Indeed, in the 1990s, Australians were the largest per capita consumers of olive oil outside of the Mediterranean region.

country, and its people and chefs are well travelled. The resulting gastronomy is informed by foreign inspiration and uses an abundance of native ingredients, such as tropical fruits, herbs, cheeses, wines, high-quality meat and seafood. It is a cuisine of the southern sun, where freshness of ingredients is emphasized and chefs are bold. This is a far cry from the cooking of the early settlers, when tinned and bottled ingredients were the norm, and dining out was limited to steak and chips or a mixed grill at a pub.

A regional flavour

Although Australia is vast, it does not have regional cuisines. Many different areas do, however, have local specialities. Queensland is known for its mangoes, mud crabs and Moreton Bay bugs (similar to flathead lobsters), as well as a number of varieties of reef fish, including red emperor, coral trout and pearl perch. Macadamia nuts, once known as Queensland bush nuts, are indigenous to the continent. The island of Tasmania off the south coast, produces abundant apples and very highly regarded farmed salmon. This island is the seafood capital of Australia, and the cool seas that surround it have abundant deep-water fish, such as trevally, blue grenadier, rock lobster, deep-sea crabs and scallops. Barramundi fish come from the Northern Territory and Queensland. Also from the Northern Territory come kangaroo, crocodile and buffalo. Sydney has wonderful seafood, particularly oysters, sea bream and yellowfin tuna. Olive groves, providing a small olive oil industry, have been planted in South Australia, and wild olives also grow here.

Australia has a large dairy industry, and since the 1970s it has been producing high-quality cheeses, particularly on the islands of Tasmania, King Island, in the Bass Strait, and Kangaroo Island, off South Australia. The principal cheese states on the mainland are New South Wales, Victoria, South Australia and Western Australia. Most of the classic European cheeses are produced, as well as goat cheeses and special Australian cheeses, including True Blue, Mersey Valley and Mialawa Blue.

MEAT: FOR THE 'BARBIE'

Usually of excellent quality, meat is abundant in Australia, and is widely eaten. Lambs graze on lush south-eastern and south-western pastures, and the Sunday roast leg of lamb remains a classic dish. The Australian 'barbie' (barbecue) is a cherished tradition and the classic eating mode for big events. Its roots lie in the days when 'bush-tucker' was common, but it has evolved considerably since then. Modern Australian chefs, who use indigenous herbs and flavourings, now make widespread use of native animals, using their meat not only for steaks, but also for preserved products like prosciutto. Kangaroo, emu and venison are now widely eaten meats, and even camel steaks are making an appearance on modern Australian menus.

Food through the day

Although Asian immigrants may still follow the eating habits of their native countries, most people eat in a Western fashion here. In the Anglo-Irish tradition, breakfast can be large, with porridge or eggs and bacon. Alternatively, it may be a lighter continental breakfast of coffee or tea served with bread or a pastry. Lunch, which used to be a large meal, is now rather light, with dinner being the main meal of the day. The British Sunday lunch tradition persists in Australia, and this is when many people entertain – such lunches tend to be all-afternoon affairs.

NEW ZEALAND

With its roots firmly in the traditions of its 19th-century European settlers, the cuisine of New Zealand is beginning to evolve as it is touched by a new wave of immigrants from Asia and by the fashions of modern-day Europe.

KEY INGREDIENTS

BUTTER

FISH

TOHEROA (A NATIVE CLAM)

GREENSHELL MUSSELS

OYSTERS

LAMB

BEEF

CERVENA VENISON

CHEESE

KUMARA (TYPE OF SWEET POTATO)

KIWI FRUIT

Located about 1500 km to the south and east of Australia, New Zealand consists of two large islands, North Island and South Island. The major cities, Wellington and Auckland, are on North Island, which has a warm, damp, mild climate and is home to about three-quarters of the population. South Island is colder, with glaciers, mountains and rain forests.

These conditions make New Zealand a fertile country; three-quarters of its exports are agricultural products. The land is particularly suited to raising cattle and sheep – there are 20 sheep for every person in the country. Indeed, New Zealand is one of the world's largest exporters of wool, meat and dairy products.

A taste of history

New Zealand, which was a British colony from 1840 to 1907 and gained full independence in 1947, has only been populated for around 1000 years. It was first inhabited by the Maori, who came from Polynesia and today make up about a tenth of the population. Their diet was based on seafood, birds and the cultivation of gourds and *kumara*, a type of sweet potato. One Maori tradition, which is still used at celebrations today, is the *hangi*. Much like other South Pacific pit feasts, this involves cooking meat, shellfish and vegetables in woven baskets buried in the ground for several hours with hot rocks.

The majority of people in New Zealand are of British and Irish descent, and the country's food is mostly derived from the 19th-century cooking styles of these immigrants. Unlike neighbouring Australia, New Zealand has not experienced a large influx of immigrants from Europe, but has become home instead for a large number of people coming from South-east Asia. The cuisine of New Zealand, particularly restaurant cooking, is beginning to reflect these new elements in the population.

There is also a very large Polynesian community in New Zealand, mostly on the warmer North Island. These peoples have adopted the mainstream New Zealand culinary habits, but also they eat their traditional foods on special occasions. There is a Polynesian market in Auckland on Saturday mornings where shoppers can buy South Pacific foods such as *puha* (a wild green) and fish.

Staple foods

Meat, particularly beef and lamb, are in plentiful supply and of a high quality in New Zealand. It has been estimated that, in comparison to Americans, who eat an annual average of 0.5 kg of lamb per head, New Zealanders eat 10 kg of lamb per head – around 20 times the amount. It is often prepared in the British tradition as a Sunday roast, served with roasted potatoes and

KIWI: DELICATE FRUIT

New Zealand is the world's largest producer of kiwi fruit, a vine fruit that was introduced from China around 1900, when it was known as the Chinese gooseberry. It was later renamed after New Zealand's national flightless bird. Kiwi fruit is grown in orchards divided by hedges or trees to protect the vines from strong winds.

vegetables. However, lamb and beef also make regular appearances on barbecues, which are a common sight at parties and outdoor events.

In addition to meat and dairy products, New Zealand is a large producer and exporter of orchard fruits. Because the country is in the southern hemisphere, it can export fruits, such as peaches, apples, apricots and strawberries, to northern customers during their off-season. One fruit dessert claimed to have been invented in New Zealand – though also claimed by Australia – is the pavlova, a meringue filled and topped with whipped cream and fresh fruit, often kiwi fruit. It was named in honour of the Russian ballet dancer Anna Pavlova.

Seafood is another important food in New Zealand, much as it is in Australia. The surrounding waters are pure, and oysters are loved and widely eaten. Bluff oysters are harvested from deep beds between South Island and Stewart Island. At the north end of South Island they are known as Nelson oysters. More common varieties of oysters are farmed also and are known as Pacific oysters.

Although New Zealand is quite isolated, it is a prosperous country, and its young people are great travellers, saving up their money for the

WINE: A RECENT TRIUMPH

AN IMPORTANT ELEMENT IN NEW ZEALAND'S GASTRONOMY, WINE IS ALSO A GROWING EXPORT. BIG AND VIBRANT, NEW ZEALAND WINES NOW RANK AMONG THE TOP NEW WORLD WINES. MOST WINES IN NEW ZEALAND, PARTICULARLY REDS, ARE PRODUCED ON THE WARMER NORTH ISLAND, BUT THE MARLBOROUGH REGION ON SOUTH ISLAND IS KNOWN FOR ITS CHARDONNAY AND SAUVIGNON BLANC. IN CONTRAST TO EUROPE, WHERE WINES ARE NAMED AFTER WHERE THEY ARE PRODUCED, NEW ZEALAND WINES ARE LABELLED ACCORDING TO GRAPE VARIETIES, FOR EXAMPLE, SHIRAZ OR CABERNET SAUVIGNON.

'Big OE' (overseas experience), which usually involves travelling for long periods via Australia, Asia and the Middle East to Europe. The flavours they soak up along the way work their way back into both home and restaurant cooking in New Zealand, with the help of the media and local and imported television shows. Consequently the country has branched out from the traditional British style of 'meat and three veg', and, while fusion cooking is not quite as widespread and vibrant as it is in Australia, pasta, grains and Asian foods have caught on.

THE AMERICAS

THE UNITED STATES

This, the richest country in the world and one of the biggest, has always been a nation of immigrants. Few of the dishes commonly thought of as 'American', hot dogs, hamburgers or pizza, are native to the United States.

KEY INGREDIENTS

SUGAR

KETCHUP

BEEF

CHICKEN

BACON

MAIZE

POTATOES

SHELLED BEANS

SWEET ONIONS

TOMATOES

SALT

PEANUTS

Cook out
Chow time for cowboys of the Wild West (as well as for contemporary ones) often consisted of rice and beans cooked on an open fire.

What is fascinating about American food is the way it is in a constant state of flux. This is because of the changing face of its population. The newer the immigrant community, the more authentic its cuisine. In the areas these groups settle, new flavours gradually make their mark, until, eventually ethnic foods, from bagels to burritos, find their way into the mainstream, where they are often corrupted into versions that bear little resemblance to the originals.

A taste of history

The earliest American gastronomic traditions have their roots in British cooking, coupled with Native American foods such as maize (known as 'corn'), beans, turkey and squash. The 18th, 19th and early 20th centuries brought waves of immigrants from Northern Europe, Eastern Europe, Italy and Russia. The African slaves, brought here between 1600 and the mid-19th century, had a tremendous influence on the cooking of the South. Later, in the last half of the 20th century, another tide of immigrants started arriving from Asia, Latin America and the Caribbean, and foods from these parts of the world have become more popular than ever.

Mechanization and industrialization of food preparation have had a tremendous impact on the tastes of Americans, particularly since the outbreak of the Second World War, when women joined the workforce in greater numbers. Although there has been a reaction to packaged foods in recent decades, with growing health food and farmers' movements, many families still rarely prepare food using fresh ingredients.

To many, today's American food, indeed American culture, means fast food; the Big Mac, Kentucky Fried Chicken, Coca-cola and Pepsi

are all hugely successful brand names known around the world. Having grown out of immigrant street-food traditions – hamburgers and hot dogs have their roots in Germany, tacos originate in Mexico, and American pizzas stem from their Neapolitan cousins – these foods do comprise an important part of American cooking. The United States is also a country of unique geographic regions, and each one has its history, its culture and its gastronomy. The fast-food restaurants that flank the endless network of freeways criss-crossing the country tell only one story of eating in the United States.

Food through the day

By and large, Americans eat large breakfasts, medium-sized lunches and moderate dinners. Meals are eaten early: breakfast between 6 and 8 am, lunch around noon or 1 pm, and dinner between 5 and 7 pm. In big cities, like New York and Los Angeles, mealtimes stretch in both directions, particularly in restaurants where dinners are served until late at night. In fact, it could be said that Americans, with their 24-hour fast-food restaurants and profusion of snack foods, eat all day long, and that set meals are becoming less and less common.

Traditional 'Yankee breakfasts' reflect the days when farmers needed to be well fuelled to work in the cold, rocky fields. They consisted of thick Canadian bacon and fried eggs with molasses doughnuts, jonnycakes or hasty pudding – all stick-to-your-ribs foods. Similar breakfasts of bacon and eggs, cereals and pancakes, are daily foods in the central farming states.

Lunches tend to be eaten out of the home, at least on work days. Sandwiches, soups and salads, as well as fast foods, like hamburgers and hot dogs, are popular lunchtime meals that are often eaten on the job, or on the run.

When families do sit down to a meal together, that meal is dinner. It is the main meal of the day, eaten around 6 or 6.30 pm. People often have a snack, like ice cream, before going to bed.

The north-east

This, the oldest part of the United States culturally, has cuisines both old and modern. The country's first settlers established their homes here. They were Europeans, who brought with them dishes and cooking methods from their home countries, but had to adapt to a new environment, often with the help of Native Americans. The north-east is also home to the modernity and diverse cultures of New York City.

New England

A land of rugged coastlines and rocky but fertile soil, New England was home to one of the earliest groups of British settlers. The *Mayflower* landed on Cape Cod, perhaps unintentionally, in 1620, with about 100 middle-class English passengers who were fleeing religious persecution. Their settlement, the area that is now Plymouth, Massachusetts, was on the site of an abandoned Native American village, whose population had been decimated by disease. The few survivors introduced the pilgrims to unfamiliar foods, such

as maize, beans, squashes and pumpkins, and helped these pioneers to survive their harsh first winter (see side panel, page 226).

The Native Americans of New England dried maize and ground it to meal, called samp, which they made into a mush. This staple sustained early settlers, who called it hasty pudding, after the oatmeal porridge they had eaten in England. The settlers also made fried or baked cakes from the meal, called jonnycakes or journey cakes.

With its long coastline and rich shoals, New England has always been a land of seafood. It was the vast schools of cod that drew the earliest

Food on the go
Many Americans take their meals on the run, consuming a wide range of hand-held items like orange juice and brownies.

Europeans, as far back as the Vikings, to eastern Canada and New England. Before the Pilgrims settled in the area, fishermen had already set up temporary camps along the coasts for salting and drying cod. As well as becoming an important staple, salt cod became big business for New

PUSHCART FOOD: FROM AROUND THE WORLD

Many different types of street food are sold from pushcarts on street corners throughout New York City. Pretzels, one of the most common snacks served in this way, have their roots in Germany, as does the classic and most long-standing New York quick lunch – the hot dog. Italians, too, have made a strong mark. New York pizza may not resemble its Neapolitan counterpart, but it is a firmly established food of the city.

England. Throughout the 17th, 18th and early 19th centuries there was a steady exchange, between the Caribbean and New England, of salt cod for molasses and rum, by-products of the sugar industry. Molasses and maize meal come together in New England's signature bread, Boston brown bread, which is steamed rather than baked, because the early New Englanders had no ovens. Molasses is also a key ingredient in another New England dish, baked beans. Served with brown bread, they are a traditional Saturday night and church supper.

The early settlers were amazed by the abundance and size of the local fish, and ate it almost exclusively during their first years. The mudflats along Cape Cod were teeming with clams, mussels, oysters and all manner of shellfish. The Native Americans taught the Pilgrims their method of cooking shellfish, by building a wood fire on a layer of rocks, then covering the hot rocks with a bed of wet seaweed

when the wood burned away. The shellfish were placed on the seaweed and covered with another layer, and they would steam open from the heat of the rocks. This evolved into today's clambake, mixed shellfish served with corn on the cob. The products of the land and the bounty of the sea are married in another of New England's most beloved dishes: chowder is a creamy fish or shellfish stew, seasoned with salt pork.

New Englanders also brought fruit trees from Europe, and they thrived. Apples became a major crop, and cider a favourite drink. Wheat and rye were also planted, and wheat and fruit come together in many New England dishes, such as pandowdy and cobbler, baked desserts in which the fruit is covered with a biscuit topping.

New York City

The most populous city in the United States, New York City, was founded by the Dutch on the island of Manhattan and has become home to immigrants from all corners of Europe, followed by Chinese and, most recently, immigrants from the Caribbean, Latin America and Russia. The flavours of New York are those of just about every cuisine in the world. However, they also reflect the trends of the day, as food is an object of fashion as well as sustenance in the United States, and New York is one of its great centres.

The city has a significant Jewish population, mainly of Central and Eastern European descent, whose gastronomic influence is reflected in its many delicatessens, kosher restaurants and bakeries specializing in German and Eastern European pastries. The bagel, a hard-crusted, doughnut-shaped bread that was once considered a Jewish speciality, has now become one of the most widely eaten foods, not only in New York, but throughout the country.

The Pennsylvania Dutch

This group of people were descendants of German religious radicals, who began to settle in Pennsylvania at the end of the 17th century – the description 'Dutch' comes from the German word 'Deutsch'. They were, and remain today, farmers who lived off the land and worked hard to

produce abundant, high-quality food. Their cooking is pure and nourishing, but not austere. Pork is their meat of choice, and they use every part of the animal; in addition to hams and sausages, they stuff the stomach with sausage and vegetables to make hog's maw, and pickle the feet in cider vinegar for souse.

The Pennsylvania Dutch have a sweet tooth and are known for their many cakes, pies and biscuits. They also make dark German-style breads, and pickle all manner of fruits and vegetables in sweet-and-sour brine.

The South

If there is one regional cuisine that is known to any degree outside of the United States, it is Southern cooking. Complex and rich, the food of the South has three major influences: that of the Native Americans, who cultivated maize and beans; that of the Europeans, particularly the

English and the French, who made fortunes as growers of rice and cotton; and, most importantly, the influence of the African slaves, who were essential to the economy of the region before the Civil War. Although the economies of the Southern states were ruined by the war's outcome, the gastronomic customs and the associated hospitality did not die out.

The region known as 'the South' stretches from Maryland to Florida on the east coast, and from the Ohio River valley of Kentucky to the Gulf of Mexico. Bounded by the Atlantic and the waters of the Gulf, and permeated by waterways, this subtropical region is rich with seafood, particularly shellfish, like shrimp and crab.

The early European settlers here sometimes lived on oysters alone, but surf and turf now come together in many seafood stews, like gumbos, which might combine sausage and shrimp. Another signature dish from this part of the South, muddle, is a sort of bouillabaisse,

A varied cuisine
As a country built on immigration, America's wide range of fast food reflects its varied heritage.

are purely African in origin; others, like tomatoes, chillis, peanuts and sweet potatoes had made their way to Africa in the 16th century with the Portuguese slavers, and had become established ingredients in the West African diet. Rice had been introduced into Africa by the Arabs, and it then became crucial to the cuisine of the Carolinas. This never could have happened were it not for the know-how of the West African slaves, who were experts at cultivating and cooking the delicate grain. As the slaves worked as cooks at the plantations, their tastes and cooking techniques blended with those of the Europeans to shape 'Southern cooking'.

Two key ports, Charleston and New Orleans, became the centres of important sub-cuisines within the South: the Lowcountry cooking of South Carolina; and Cajun and Creole cooking of Southern Louisiana. The cuisines evolved out of mixed traditions but, in particular, they were shaped by the refined cooking styles of France and the robust flavours of Africa.

Lowcountry cooking

The coastal plain that stretches from near the North Carolina border to the Georgia state line and inland to the foothills of the Blue Ridge Mountains is known as the Lowcountry. The early settlers, French Huguenots and English, who had already made fortunes in the Caribbean, created vast plantations here for rice, indigo and cotton, importing enormous numbers of slaves to do the work.

The cuisine that evolved was an aristocratic one, heavily influenced by French country traditions, but even more so by the stewpot cooking of Africa. Its cornerstone was rice. Called 'Carolina Gold', it was once considered the best rice in the world, in the words of John Martin Taylor, the 'caviar of the early 19th century'. With the Civil War and the abolition of slavery, the Carolina rice industry collapsed, yet rice remained a staple food. A typical Lowcountry meal, be it veal roast and butter beans or shrimp gumbo, is served on rice. Rice is the basis for signature dishes like hoppin' John, a New Year's Day dish of rice and beans served with greens.

Bushels of peaches
California is the centre for the cultivation of produce of all kinds. Peaches are just one of the fruits grown in abundance in California's Central Valley and transported across America.

Market day (opposite)
Home-grown produce like pumpkins, chillis and squashes are popular buys at farmers' markets.

combining simple vegetables with abundant fish and eggs cooked on the top. Like the chowders to the north, it is seasoned with bacon.

Native American ingredients like maize were an essential part of the mix. Used in both its fresh and dried form, maize has long been an important staple. Dog bread, also called corn pone, are griddle cakes made simply with maize and water. Dried maize, soaked and de-hulled, is called hominy, which is coarsely ground to make grits, a breakfast favourite.

Chicken, too, is important. Most Southern chicken dishes are long-simmering affairs that use old hens that are no longer valuable as laying hens. The exception is Southern fried chicken, which is made with tender young chickens and is considered a special dish, reserved for Sunday lunches and holidays. The crispy deep-fried chicken is one of the South's major contributions to American gastronomy.

Many of the key ingredients associated with Southern cuisine came with the slaves from Africa. Some, such as okra and black-eyed peas,

Thanksgiving is traditionally held to commemorate the Pilgrims' survival of their first, harsh winter in America.

The cooking is intended to honour the foods that the Native American's gave the Pilgrims, allowing them to last that first winter; roast turkey, maize, sweet potatoes and pumpkin pie.

Sugary doughnuts
Brought to America by German immigrants, doughnuts in many shapes are a favourite American snack.

Louisiana

The majority of people in Louisiana are of Cajun French descent. They arrived over 200 years ago when the French were expelled from Acadia, in Canada, by the British. The people grew what they could in this unfamiliar climate. Hot peppers were easily cultivated, and the food they made gradually took on a spicy character. Cajun cuisine also uses the French technique of the roux to thicken seasoned dishes, such as gumbos, jambalayas (rice stew), *boudin blanc* (pork and rice sausage) and *étouffées* (crayfish or prawns in a cayenne sauce).

The African and Afro-Caribbean influence on Cajun food is even stronger than the French, particularly in its key ingredients, like okra, field peas, yams, sweet potatoes, peanuts and sesame seeds. Cajun stews are spicy, soup-like and served over rice.

The Creole food of New Orleans, to the east, is much more European and aristocratic. It has its roots in the period of aristocratic Spanish, and then French rule. Whereas Cajun food is country food, based on locally grown produce, Creole food is city food, based on the market. It includes many traditional French dishes.

Miami

This tropical state has its own set of flavours, and they are Caribbean in nature, Cuban in particular. When Fidel Castro took power over 40 years ago, many Cubans emigrated to nearby Miami. Now the city has a large and thriving expatriate community; there are many Cuban markets and restaurants featuring dishes like *ropa vieja* (Cuban shredded beef) and *moros y cristianos* (black beans and rice).

More recent immigrants to Miami have come from other Caribbean islands, like Haiti and the Dominican Republic, bringing their Creole foods with them. The warm waters off the coast of Florida are rich with fish and shellfish, which are often paired with tropical salsas, spicy mixtures of fresh fruit or vegetables and chillis.

The south-west

The flavours of Texas, New Mexico and Arizona have many Mexican overtones. These states were all part of Mexico until 1848, and remain border states with large Hispanic populations. Ingredients we associate with Mexican food, such as chillis, tortillas, lime, avocados and *tomatillos*, are used throughout the south-west.

The Mexican-infused cooking of Texas has long been called 'Tex-Mex' food, and has had an impact on Mexican-style cooking throughout the rest of the United States and around the world. Tex-Mex food is richer and less nuanced than Mexican food; its signature tortilla-based dishes like enchiladas, tacos and nachos tend to use crisp-fried tortillas and be topped with copious amounts of cheese. Tex-Mex food is often quite spicy as well; Texas holds an annual jalapeño-eating contest.

The people of this part of the country also love barbecues. A Texas barbecue is a slow meal, smoked over chippings of mesquite wood. A selection of meats is used, and beans, potato salad and a puffy, white bread, called Texas toast, are served on the side. The meat is continually basted during the cooking with a 'moppin' sauce', a spicy sauce that contains no sugar; then, before eating, it is covered with a 'soppin' sauce', the sweet and sour tomato-based sauce used commonly throughout the South.

The food of New Mexico and Arizona shows many traces of the early Spanish settlers, who called this area New Spain, and held large land grants when this area was still part of Mexico. There is also a strong Native American cooking tradition. The Pueblo tribes are great breadmakers. Beehive-shaped adobe ovens, called *hornos*, sit in front of houses in the Pueblo villages. Flat breads are baked on the floor. They are made from wheat and often contain pine nuts or sunflower seeds. The best-known Native American bread in New Mexico is called frybread; these are deep-fried flat breads served with soups and stews, or stuffed with ground meat and salsa. The Arizona version, lighter and often dusted with sugar and drizzled with honey, is called *sopaipillas*.

Chilli peppers are one of New Mexico's most important crops. New Mexico chillis are moderately hot, and can be green or red, fresh or dried. Houses are adorned with strings of red chillis set in the sun to dry. They are used in the sauces that top enchiladas, and in New Mexico chilli (see box, above).

The central states

Within a century of making their homes in a new land, the pioneer spirit of early settlers drove them west across the country. Land was plentiful and fertile, and the farms of the Heartland were quickly established, while farther west the harsher landscape was more suited to cattle herding. Both of these occupations led to a simple, hearty style of cooking.

The Heartland

America's Heartland begins in western Pennsylvania and extends through the Midwestern states to the Rocky Mountains. The earth is dark and rich and the land bounteous, yielding up much of the world's food: grains, vegetables and tree fruits, as well as meat and dairy products from vast herds of cattle.

The Midwest was settled first by New Englanders, who began migrating west in the 1700s. They had learned to use maize from the Native Americans, and it so thrived in this flat, fertile country with its hot summers that the region evolved into America's 'corn belt'. Today, farms are highly mechanized, and the region is the world's top producer of maize and wheat.

The flavours of the Heartland epitomize American home cooking and are rooted in farm produce and dairy products such as eggs, chickens, pigs, fresh fish and game. Farmhouse cooking is straightforward and hearty. It is a copious cuisine where meat is usually at the centre of the plate, but the produce of the farm, cooked simply and preserved in winter, is abundantly present. Baked goods, a legacy of immigrant cultures and a reflection of community spirit, are also an important aspect of eating in the Heartland.

The Midwest is much more complex than its basic meat-and-potatoes image. It is an amalgam of the cuisines of its many settlers. In addition to European immigrants, Southerners came here after the Civil War to farm the rich soils of the Mississippi Valley and the Ohio River Valley, so it is not surprising that there are aspects of Southern cooking in much of the area's foods.

Pecan pie
'As American as apple pie' is a well-known phrase, but blueberry pie, pumpkin pie and, of course, rich, Southern pecan pie, could also fit the description.

Outdoor fare
Camp fires, barbeques, clambakes, picnics and tail-gate parties are all popular American get-togethers with food at the centre.

German immigrants, too, have had considerable influence on the eating habits of middle America. They established sausage shops, bakeries and breweries in Milwaukee, and are responsible for Wisconsin's considerable cheese-making industry. Rhineland Germans from Pennsylvania migrated west, creating Mennonite, Amish, Dunkard and Moravian communities that were devoted to living off the land, producing and preparing high-quality food.

Many of the people who settled in the Midwest were fleeing religious persecution. Their communities grew up around their church, which has remained a focal point of Midwestern culture. The 'church supper' has engendered popular dishes that are easy to stretch for a crowd, like potato salads, coleslaws, macaroni and cheese, fruit pies, cobblers and cakes.

One of the most well-known Midwestern foods is Kansas City barbecue. Different from its Southern counterpart, Kansas City barbecue is usually made with beef brisket rather than pork. The meat is coated with a dry rub (a mixture of spices and sugar), before being smoked, and the sauce is added at the end or served on the side. The most common way of eating Kansas City barbecue is in a sandwich, slathered with sauce, and served with coleslaw.

The West

As you move west from Missouri, Iowa and Minnesota, you are still in the Heartland, but the states are more sparsely populated, with less impact from immigrants on the cuisine. By the time you reach the Rockies, the food is plainer and less exuberant. This is cowboy country. Meat, particularly beef, is much loved. Freshwater fish from mountain streams is abundant as well. It is prepared simply, usually pan-fried or grilled. Potatoes are the vegetables of choice, and beans, Texas chilli (see box, page 227) and biscuits (here meaning small savoury breads) are also appreciated, a legacy of the days when cattle were herded on long drives. Each drive had a cook, whose domain was called the 'chuck wagon' and who had the power to determine the desirability of the outfit he worked for. Black, pot-brewed coffee and whiskey were the beverages of choice.

A few immigrant communities did bring their foods to the Rockies. Basque shepherds were brought here to herd sheep in Idaho and Nevada, and today you will find Basque restaurants in unexpected places, like Winnemucca and Reno in Nevada, serving up lamb stews and *piperades*.

The Pacific states

The youngest states – California, Oregon, Washington, Alaska and Hawaii – are those that border the Pacific Ocean. Cuisines here are young as well. Chefs in these parts have led the way in creating a 'fusion cuisine' with Asian, American and Mediterranean flavours coming together on the same plate. The cooking of these states accommodates their youthful, health-conscious populations; food is fresh and light.

Agriculture here is big business. Oregon and Washington are large producers of tree fruits, particularly apples and pears. Much of Hawaii was once bought up by the Dole fruit company, which planted acres of pineapples, but today, a lot of this land is used for sugar cane. California, however, is the state with the highest agricultural yield in the country; its intensively farmed Central Valley is a once-dry area that has been transformed by irrigation. Vegetables and fruits of all kinds, like citrus fruits, cherries and apricots, as well as nuts and olives, are produced in great quantities. In addition to the giant, mechanized farms, there is a growing farmers' market movement here, where smaller producers sell organically raised fruits and vegetables.

The Pacific Ocean, from Hawaii to Alaska, is as bounteous as the land it borders. From northern California to Alaska, the cold waters yield up rich catches of halibut, salmon and shellfish. In warmer waters, fish like *mahi-mahi*, tuna and swordfish thrive. Freshwater fish are also abundant in the rivers and streams of Washington, Oregon and Alaska.

California is at the helm of contemporary cooking in the United States. Like Louisiana, it is one state that can attach its name to a style of food. But, unlike the older, Southern state, Californian cuisine has its origins only in the last 50 years. With an exuberant style, which emphasizes fresh, seasonal ingredients and bold tastes and combinations, California cooks have been seduced by Mediterranean foods, which are at home in this warm, sunny state. They often reinterpret dishes using local ingredients. Thin-crusted, oven-baked California pizza, for example, might be topped with local goat's cheese, wild mushrooms or smoked salmon.

California also has a large Hispanic population. They are, for the most part, recent immigrants, but the state itself was once part of Mexico. It was populated in the early 18th century by Spanish missionaries, who brought with them foods such as beans, tortillas, avocados, chillis, olives and wheat.

A large Asian population is also evident; many Chinese came to work on the railways and in the gold mines in the 19th century, and have since continued to arrive. The Chinese cuisine in the state was at first Cantonese, but in recent decades immigrants have come from other regions of China, such as Hunan and Szechwan. There are sizeable Japanese and Korean communities as well, particularly in Los Angeles.

Hawaii's native cuisine is South Pacific in nature. Taro root is a staple, and seafood an important food. Contemporary Hawaiian chefs emphasize local ingredients and Asian ingredients like soy sauce, ginger and spicy tropical salsas. The islands are a natural home for Pacific Rim cuisine and fusion cooking.

Cooking crabs
Crabs of all sizes are provided by the abundant waters of the Pacific, and are well suited to the fresh, light cooking of the Pacific states.

CANADA

Originally based on British and French pioneer cooking, including a smattering of native ingredients – such as fish, game and berries – Canadian cooking has developed in recent years in response to a renewed wave of immigrants.

KEY INGREDIENTS

MAPLE SYRUP

WHEAT

FISH

SALT COD

PORK

BACK BACON

BEEF

VENISON

CARIBOU MEAT

POTATOES

SEA VEGETABLES

ICEWINE BERRIES

Canadian salmon
Both Atlantic and Pacific salmon are fished in Canada. The chinook and sockeye varieties are considered, by some, to be the tastiest.

Although the third largest inhabited country in the world, the population of Canada is quite small, about a tenth that of the United States. This is because much of the country is within the Arctic Circle and uninhabitable. Most people live in towns and cities around the Great Lakes and the St Lawrence River. The rest live in coastal areas and in farms and villages in central Canada.

The northern third of Canada is tundra and ice, remaining frozen for nine months of the year. The native peoples who live here have a diet based on protein and fat, as the only vegetation consists of lichen, grasses, shrubs and trees. Baked goods introduced by the British pioneers, such as bannocks, are common here. Central Canada is the country's main farming area, dominated by wheat and cattle; Canadian wheat is considered to be the highest-quality wheat in the world. Sunflower and canola (rapeseed) are other important crops. Around the Great Lakes, Ontario and Erie, delicate tree fruits, like peaches, plums, pears and cherries, are grown.

A taste of history

Canada was inhabited by native American and Inuit peoples when French fur traders began to settle the country in the 17th century. The British followed, and eventually took control of Canada, in 1763. They drove the French out of the Maritime Provinces, and gave the land to New Englanders and English immigrants. But the French remained, mostly in the province of Quebec, which is still French-speaking. In recent years, immigrants have come from Eastern Europe, South-east Asia and South America. All of these peoples have contributed to the eating habits of Canada, though their influence is mostly limited to the areas in which they settled.

A regional flavour

In the Maritime Provinces, the abundant, but diminishing, stores of North Atlantic seafood, such as lobster, salmon, cod and shellfish, are the dominant feature of the cooking. With the exception of potatoes and fiddlehead ferns, vegetables are of minor importance, although sea vegetables, like the pungent and briny seaweed dulse, are used. The local berries – blueberries, cloudberries, partridgeberries and cranberries – are plentiful and widely eaten. Moose, deer and caribou are important game foods in the northern areas.

Maritime food has much in common with the food of New England. This is due partly to the ingredients that the two regions have in common – for example fish, cranberries and maple syrup – but also to the fact that the provinces were settled by New Englanders after the French were expelled. Fish and shellfish chowders here are rich and hearty. Maple syrup sweetens pancakes and the fried, maize meal

SIGNATURE DISHES

Cretons de Québec *A pork-based pâté.*

Tourtière *A traditional Christmas pork pie.*

Pâté à la rapure *Grated potatoes are layered with meat in this Nova Scotian pie.*

Fish and brewis *This dish from Newfoundland is made with salt cod, hardtack, potatoes, onions and fatback pork.*

Baked, stuffed lobster *A delicious dish popular in Nova Scotia.*

Grands-pères au sirop d'érable *Also called 'maple grandfathers', these are dumplings boiled and served in maple syrup.*

Bannocks *Introduced by the English and Scottish, these are griddle-baked oat cakes.*

Cipâte aux bleuets *An unusual three-crusted blueberry pie, with a pastry heart.*

Butter tarts *Raisin-filled cakes.*

cakes called jonnycakes. Salt cod, once big business in Newfoundland, is the basis for a regional dish called fish and brewis, made with salt cod, hardtack (dried bread), potatoes, onions and fatback pork (fat from the back of a pig).

In Quebec, food is mainly French in character. Dishes that have counterparts in New England tend to be more highly seasoned in French Canada, reflecting the less austere nature of French cooking. Chowders, for example, include bay leaves, celery leaves, carrots and thyme. However, some traits of New England cookery have remained: the black iron kettle, which once hung over an open hearth and now sits on a stove, is the focal point of French-Canadian cookery.

In Toronto, Canada's fastest growing city, contemporary Canadian cooking has come into its own. Here, there is an emphasis on fresh, local ingredients and a melding of the foods of the city's many immigrant groups. You can buy food from almost anywhere in the world in Toronto, and the many neighbourhoods include a thriving Greektown, Little India, Little Italy and Little Portugal.

Moving through central Canada, and the provinces of Manitoba, Saskatchewan and Alberta, the farm cooking here is a legacy of the pioneers – wholesome food where meat takes centre stage. British Colombia has tastes of England, particularly in its capital, Victoria, where afternoon tea is a tradition. Vancouver has an altogether different cuisine, mainly due to its large Asian population. Here, in the city's Chinatown, there are bustling markets selling Asian foods, and noodle shops line many of Vancouver's streets. British Colombia is influenced also by its neighbour to the south, especially by the 'fusion cooking' of California.

Toronto street market
In Canada's fastest growing city, you can buy food from almost anywhere in the world.

CENTRAL AMERICA AND MEXICO

The cooking of Central America and Mexico reflects, like their peoples, a mixing of cultures, as these are countries where European, particularly Spanish, flavours are combined with Native American foods.

KEY INGREDIENTS

GARLIC

CHILLIS

LIME JUICE

RICE

MAIZE

BEANS

SQUASH

ONIONS

TOMATOES

AVOCADOS

BANANAS

CHOCOLATE

Eating on the go
Though everyone stops at lunchtime for a full meal, breakfast may be eaten on the go, at a café or food stall.

Despite the Spanish conquest, it is generally the countries that had the strongest native civilizations, namely Mexico and Guatemala, that have the region's most complex and individual cuisines today. That of Mexico is particularly varied and inspired.

However, the different styles of cooking in each country do not mean that Mexican and Central American foods are not linked; they are tied by a common ingredient: maize. Indigenous to the Americas, maize has always been the staple here, both before and after the 16th-century Spanish colonization. The other native foods that link these countries are beans, chilli peppers, tomatoes and squash. The Spaniards introduced rice – along with many other foods – and it, too, has become a mainstay throughout this part of the world. As well as foods, the Spanish brought Christianity, which remains the major religion.

Central America

This region can be divided into three geographic zones: a fertile Pacific plain, where bananas and sugar are widely grown and much of the land is owned by foreign fruit companies; the central highlands, where coffee is grown and cattle raised; and the forested north-east, which is not well suited for agriculture.

While native beans, rice and maize dominate much of this region's daily foods, each of the Central American countries has its dictinctive specialities. Nicaragua's most famous dish is the maize-based *nacatamal*. This is a tamale, which is filled with meat or vegetables, wrapped in a maize husk and cooked by steaming. El Salvador's most popular dish is the *pupusa*. These are stuffed maize tortillas, which are a legacy of the Native American population. The Spanish influence is noteworthy in two popular El Salvadorean dishes, *gallo en chicha*, capon cooked in wine, and *la semita*, a pineapple torte. *Casamiento* is a mixture of rice and beans that is eaten daily. Despite El Salvador's long Pacific coastline, seafood does not play a great role in the country's cooking.

The cuisines of the tropical Central American countries of Panama, Nicaragua, Belize and Honduras have Caribbean overtones. Coconut milk, plantains, bananas, *achiote* (anatto seeds) and cassava are widely used. These cuisines have been somewhat influenced by the Native American groups who populated them before the arrival of the Spanish, but not nearly to the same extent as the cuisines of Guatemala and Mexico.

Costa Rica's population is mostly non-Native American; consequently its cooking has very little native influence and is not too spicy. It is based mainly on beef, chicken and fish, supplemented by rice, maize, beans and local fruits.

Belize, half of which is covered in tropical rain forest, was a British colony until 1981, and its population is descended from many ethnic groups, including Caribs, Africans, Mayans, Asians and Europeans. The character of its food is Caribbean, including coconut milk and plantain, with many English overtones. Its main staples are rice and beans.

Guatemala has the largest Native American population of the Central American countries. About half of its people are direct descendants of the Maya. The Mayan Guatemalans live, for the most part, in highland villages, subsisting on the same foods as their forebears, such as maize, beans, squash and some turkey. The cooking of the highlands is one of the three cuisines of Guatemala. There is also a colonial Ladino cuisine reflecting a mixture of Spanish and Mayan foods and techniques. This is based in the major cities of Guatemala and Antigua. Finally, there is the cooking of the tropical Caribbean coast, centred in Livingston, where indentured labour from India and Africa, brought to work on the sugar plantations, left their mark. Here the cooking is based on seafood, coconut milk and bananas, more Caribbean in nature than Mayan or Ladino. The African-influenced Caribbean food is known as Garifuna food.

Food through the day

Breakfast is usually early, consisting of coffee, beans and tortillas, and if they can be afforded, eggs and cheese. As in Spain, many people

FONDAS: A VARIETY OF FOODSTALLS

Markets in Mexico are some of the most popular eating places. Among the colourful stalls selling all manner of produce, are food stands called *fondas*. Some sell simply drinks such as juice, *aguas frescas* (fruit-and-water drinks) and frothy *licuados* (blended milk, sugar and fruit drinks); others serve substantial cooked dishes, such as soups, roasted meats and beans and tortillas. Still others might specialize in *masa*-based *antojitos*, such as tacos, enchiladas and tamales. In Puebla most of the *fondas* at one market are devoted to the local sandwich speciality, *cemitas*. Other market stands sell *nieves*, ice creams, made with every fruit under the Mexican sun.

observe the tradition of having a mid-morning snack, called *merienda*, consisting of coffee and a sweet pastry. Lunch, eaten at about 1 pm, is the main meal of the day, as it is in South America. This is a time when everything comes to a halt; working lunches are unheard of. Dinner, in contrast, is a light meal, usually eaten at around 7 or 8 pm. It often consists simply of a soup or a bean dish, and tortillas.

Mexico

It may come as a surprise to many that the cuisines of Mexico are as varied as the cuisines of France or Italy. Yet, like French or Italian cooking, no matter what the regional differences are, the food has a national character; everywhere, it is distinctly Mexican. A large country (about a third of the size of the United States), with long coastlines bordering on the Pacific to the west and the Gulf of Mexico and Caribbean to the east and south, Mexico is a land of high mountains, deserts, jungles, coastal plains and plateaus. The diversity of its plant life is astounding, as is the spectrum of flavours that characterize its food.

A taste of history

When the Spaniards arrived in Mexico in 1519, they found that the Aztecs had already developed a sophisticated court cuisine, based on ingredients that the Europeans had never seen before: maize, chillis, beans, tomatoes, avocados, squash, turkey and chocolate, as well as little dogs. Foods were simmered in tomato and chilli sauces or in chilli sauces thickened with pumpkin seed, called *pipians*, and were eaten with maize tortillas, as they are today. The other maize-based dishes that we associate with Mexico, such as tamales, date from this pre-Colombian era. Cortés and his men were enchanted with many of the native fruits, like pineapples and papaya, and were so enthusiastic about chocolate that it gained quick acceptance in Europe, unlike many of the other New World foods such as tomatoes and potatoes.

It did not take the conquistadores long to defeat Moctezuma, the Aztec emperor, and to lay waste to the beautiful Aztec capital city, Tenochtitlan, on the site of which Mexico City now stands. What ensued over the next three centuries of European subjugation was a mixing of indigenous and Spanish bloodlines and cultures, known as *mestización*. Gastronomically, this found expression in the evolution of a cuisine that brings together foods and traditions from the New and Old Worlds.

The Native Americans of Mexico readily incorporated European foods and cooking techniques into their diet. Spices, such as cinnamon, black pepper and cloves, herbs, such as thyme and bay leaf, and sesame seeds, almonds and citrus fruits, all brought in by Spanish traders, are foods now associated with Mexican cooking. The Spanish introduced such basics as wheat, chickpeas and onions. Meat, which had been a luxury in pre-Colombian Mexico, became a widespread commodity after the Spaniards brought in cattle, chickens and pigs, all of which thrived in the New World. It is hard to imagine Mexican cuisine without the pig, every bit of which is important, from the lard used as a cooking fat, to the skin that is crisp-fried and eaten as a snack.

Before the arrival of Europeans in Mexico, cooking oils and fats were not used; dishes were stewed or roasted rather than fried. Frying, so prevalent in Mexican cooking today, is a Spanish legacy, as is the widespread use of vinegar marinades, called *escabeches*, both in Spain and in Mexico. The Native Americans had no cows or other beasts of burden, thus the presence of milk and its by-products – the wonderful cheeses and creams that flavour, garnish and enrich Mexican dishes – also reflect this mixed heritage.

Spanish gastronomy had been greatly influenced by Arab traditions – the Moors had occupied Spain for 700 years and were only expelled shortly before the discovery of the Americas. This filtered through to Mexican cuisine and is most evident in the country's love of sweets, particularly the Arab invention, marzipan. The widespread use of spices like cinnamon, cumin, anise and cloves, also reflects Hispano-Arab gastronomic traditions.

Staple foods

What gives Mexican cooking its unmistakable identity are the indigenous ingredients, particularly maize and chillis (see box, page 236). Maize is the country's staple, consumed mainly in the form of flat griddle-baked tortillas, which are made from ground maize that has been treated with slaked lime to break down the kernel shells and render the maize more digestible and nutritious. The maize-dough basis for tortillas and tamales is known as *masa*, and this is often used as a thickener in stews and soups.

Another important staple is the dried bean. In southern Mexico black beans are preferred, whereas in the north a light brown pinto bean is prevalent. Beans, along with chillis and tortillas, have been standard daily foods since well before the Spanish conquest.

One ingredient that typifies the taste of Mexico is the rather tart tomatillo, a small, green, husk-covered fruit, which is related to the gooseberry. The tomatillo, which is also known as the Mexican green tomato, even though it is not related to the tomato, is used in marvellous stews and for many sauces, both cooked and uncooked. Mexicans love crisp white and red onions, which they sprinkle, plain or pickled, over many foods. Many other dishes are garnished with the well-known fresh tomato and chilli sauces called salsas.

Not only ingredients, but certain cooking techniques give Mexican food its particular

Agave (*opposite*)
Produced mainly in the western state of Jalisco, Tequila is made from the sap of the agave plant (*top picture*). The hearts of the plant are baked (*below*) before the juice is fermented and then distilled to produce this popular drink.

Tamales
These neat packages consist of *masa* dough wraps, spread on maize husks. Tamales are filled with meat or vegetables and steamed.

SIGNATURE DISHES

Sopa de tortilla *A Mexican chicken soup topped with chillis, lime juice and cheese.*

Pozole *This hominy soup is either* verde *(green), with pork, chicken and tomatillos, or* rojo *(red) with pork and dried red chillis.*

Frijoles de la olla *Cooked beans in broth.*

Enchiladas *These tortillas include various fillings, such as chicken or pork.*

Frijoles refritos *Refried beans are often used to top* tostados *(toasted tortilla chips).*

Pescado a la veracruzana *Fish, usually snapper, served in a seasoned tomato sauce.*

Gallo en chicha *A dish from El Salvador, also known as 'Monday rooster', as it often uses the losing bird of the Sunday cock fight.*

Rondón *Nicaraguan beef in coconut milk.*

character. Many of the seasonings, like garlic, chillis, onions, tomatoes and spices, are toasted on dry griddles before being incorporated into dishes, which gives the food a unique dimension. Blended sauces are often seared in hot oil, then simmered, adding a smoky aspect to the food.

A regional flavour

According to Mexican food writer, Rick Bayless, in *Authentic Mexican*, the country can be divided into six distinctive gastronomic regions: central Mexico; southern Mexico and, particularly, the state of Oaxaca; west-central Mexico; the southeast state of Yucatan; northern Mexico; and the Gulf states, particularly Veracruz.

Central Mexican cooking reflects a clear mix of European and native traditions. Puebla, for example, is famous for its marzipan sweets and its rich egg-based pastries. The pastries are a legacy of the French, who had a presence in this part of Mexico in the 19th century. The same city is the namesake for the local dish, *mole poblano*, a rich, complex sauce made from ground chillis and nuts, herbs, spices and chocolate, which is usually served with turkey.

CHILLIS: A VAST ARRAY

The variety of chillis on display in every market in Mexico is tremendous. Different types are popular in different regions: the jalapeño and its smoke-dried version, the *chipotle*, are widely used in the state of Veracruz – the capital of which, Jalapa, gives this chilli its name. The fiery *habanero* is a speciality of Yucatan, whereas the *poblano* gets its name from the state of Puebla. Chillis are used in their dried and fresh states, and there are different names for each form; the dried *poblano*, for example, is called *chilli ancho*. Dried chillis are often rehydrated and ground, for use in stews and thick, complex sauces, like *moles*, *adobos* and *pipians*.

The cuisine of southern Mexico has more of a Native American flavour. Oaxaca is famous for its *moles* (chilli and nut-thickened sauces), made with the state's astounding variety of dried chillis. The chocolate is magnificent in Oaxaca; people bring cocoa beans, sugar and almonds or cinnamon to local mills, where the ingredients are ground into rich mixtures for hot chocolate and *atoles* (*masa*-thickened hot drinks). Wherever you go in southern Mexico, the sweet aroma of maize *masa* is ever present.

In the western states, many of the dishes commonly associated with Mexico – such as fried tacos filled with *carnitas* (stewed and crisp-fried pork), *pozole* (hominy stew) and red chilli enchiladas – are popular foods. In the state of Michoacan, where numerous cattle graze on the green hillsides, cheese and particularly cream are much loved. Cream enriches soup and is spooned over enchiladas and sweet, maize tamales, a speciality of this state.

Yucatecan food is descended from the Mayans, and is unlike the rest of the food of Mexico. It is characterized by red *achiote* seasoning (a paste made from annatto seeds), which is rubbed over fish and meats before they are cooked. Many dishes are cooked in banana leaves. The Spanish influence can be tasted in several of the region's vinegar-sauced dishes, and here, as well as in Veracruz, olive oil is used in some of the cooking.

The food of northern Mexico is rustic. Grilling and roasting are widely used cooking techniques, for fish along the coasts and for steaks everywhere. Shredded barbecued meat fills both maize and wheat tortillas.

Some of the most interesting food in Mexico comes from the Gulf states, particularly Veracruz, which was where the Spanish conquistadores landed in 1521. Veracruz remained the main east-coast port of Mexico, its gateway, until the era of the airplane, and its food retained many Spanish characteristics. Olive oil is widely used and capers and green olives are important ingredients in many Veracruzana dishes. The jalapeño and the hot, smoky *chipotle* are the most widely used chillis here. Seafood is abundant;

scrambled with chillis, tomatoes, onions and tortillas for *migas*; or mixed with refried black beans for *huevos tirados*. Eggs may be served in combination with refried beans, which are cooked beans that have been mashed and thickened in hot lard.

Lighter breakfasts might consist of brioche-like rolls or sugar-sprinkled pastries eaten with fruit. Coffee is generally the beverage of choice, but hot chocolate is also very popular, particularly in southern Mexico. Hot chocolate is made from the sweetened, cinnamon-laced chocolate, which is melted and brought to a froth in hot water. Mexican Indians enjoy hot *atoles*; chocolate, nut, pineapple and strawberry are among the most popular *atole* flavours.

The main meal of the day is the midday meal, the *comida*, eaten between 1 and 4 pm. The traditional *comida* begins with an appetizer such as cactus salad or prawn cocktail, or with a *antojito* (a *masa*-based dish, such as *quesadillas* or enchiladas), followed by a light soup. A rice dish sometimes follows, and then comes a main dish based on meat or fish. The main dish may consist of a stew. Dessert is often a sweet pastry or flan, or fresh fruit, followed by coffee.

The midday meal often stretches into the evening, but light meals are served at night. Sometimes this will be nothing more than a pastry and hot chocolate, coffee or herb tea. *Tortas* make another popular supper. These are nourishing sandwiches made on round white rolls called *bolillos* and filled with meat or cheese, tomatoes, chillis, avocados and lettuce.

There are many regional variations on the sandwich in Mexico, all with different names: in Veracruz a flaky bread called *pambazo* is used for a sandwich of the same name; the sandwich of Puebla is the *cemita*, made on a crusty roll and filled with cheese, avocado, pickled *chipotle* peppers, meat and a peppery green, called *papaloquelite*; and Oaxacan *molletes* are buttered rolls slathered with refried black beans, toasted and sprinkled with cheese.

huachinango a la veracruzana, red snapper cooked in a pungent tomato sauce flavoured with capers, green olives and pickled jalapeños, is one of Mexico's best-known fish dishes. There is a Caribbean/African element in the cooking of coastal, tropical Veracruz, with a widespread use of plantains and coconut. This is because the population here is descended, in part, from African slaves who were brought over by the Spanish to work in the sugar plantations.

Food through the day

Breakfast in Mexico is a substantial meal, one that offers up some of the country's most beloved dishes. Eggs are prepared in a number of ways: they are fried and served over tortillas with a tomato and chilli sauce, to make *huevos rancheros*;

HERBS AND SPICES

CORIANDER Mexican soups are invariably garnished with lime juice and chopped coriander

EPAZOTE this is a native herb which has an earthy, astringent taste

AVOCADO LEAVES in southern Mexico these are used to impart an aniseed-like flavour to beans

OJA SANTA another leaf with a complex aniseed-like flavour, used in Veracruz and southern Mexico

Mexican breads

Aside from the more widely known maize-based tortillas, there are many other breads and rolls, made with different grains, which are widely used in a variety of sandwiches.

THE CARIBBEAN

The beautiful islands of the Caribbean, with their white beaches, lush rainforests and crystal-clear waters, are home to an equally rich cuisine, with delicious seafood, spicy seasonings and tropical fruits.

KEY INGREDIENTS

ACHIOTE (ANATTO SEEDS)

CHILLI

MOLASSES

RICE

FISH

KID

CHICKEN

OKRA

PLANTAIN

CASSAVA

CALLALOO (GREENS)

COCONUT

Caribbean snappers
There are many varieties of this popular fish caught off the Caribbean islands – by far the most esteemed is the red snapper.

Tropical fruit
(opposite)
Bananas and especially their leaves have a strong presence in Caribbean cookery, but the fruit originally came from the Canary Islands and was introduced by the Portuguese.

The Caribbean islands stretch from just off the coast of Florida down to South America. This was the 'New World' that Columbus discovered in 1492. When they arrived here, the Spanish explorers found lush, tropical lands, which were inhabited by three native tribes: the Tainos, who disappeared from memory within a generation; the peace-loving Arawaks, who were both hunters and cultivators; and the fiercer Caribs, who ate mainly meat, including human flesh.

A taste of history

The staple foods and seasonings of the Arawaks and Caribs remain important in the Caribbean, although the native peoples were all but wiped out by slavery and European diseases. The Arawaks grew cassava and maize, foods that the

Europeans had never seen, and both tribes seasoned their foods with incendiary chillis, called *aji*, which the Europeans mistook for pepper. The Arawaks ate many wild animals, trapping iguanas, armadillos, turtles and a type of guinea pig, called *hutia*. The stick-framed grill the tribes used for cooking was called a *barbacoa* – the original barbecue.

Many of the ingredients we associate with island cooking were brought by the European explorers: rice came from Asia; breadfruit arrived with Captain Bligh; and sugar cane came with Columbus on his second voyage. As sugar became increasingly important, one of its by-products, rum, grew in importance as well. Rum and the many cocktails made with it, are still the most popular drinks of the Caribbean.

Because the climate resembled that of their homelands, the Africans brought over as slaves for the plantations could grow the foods they were used to, and were encouraged to do so in their 'slave gardens'. Okra, yams, sweet potatoes, greens and beans of all kinds soon became major Caribbean foods. The slaves and their descendants cooked them in the African manner, in earthenware and cast-iron pots, or over charcoal, wrapping foods in banana leaves. They produced dishes like *coocoo* and *funghi*, which are mashes related to West African *fufus* and *foutous*.

After the emancipation of the slaves, workers were brought in from India and China. They brought new cooking styles and ingredients, such as *pak choi* (the vegetable bok choy). The Asian influence is evident in some of the most popular Caribbean dishes: *colombo de porc* is a curried, Martinican dish, which combines south Indian spices with pork, the typical meat of the Caribbean and a legacy of the Spanish.

'Stamp and go'
Salt-fish fritters are popular throughout the Caribbean. In Jamaica, they were named 'stamp and go' after a command used by 17th-century English sailors.

HERBS AND SPICES

ALLSPICE also called Jamaican pepper, this spice is native to the island. It is highly aromatic, with a clove-like smell. It is used in the French Antilles to season seafood *blaffs* and Creole blood sausage

JERK this characteristic Jamaican paste is made from onions, chillis, allspice, garlic, thyme and black pepper. It is commonly used to season pork or chicken before grilling

SEASONING this mixture of chives, fresh thyme and other herbs is a common addition to the dishes of Barbados

Staple foods: seafood
Spiny lobster, crayfish and conch are abundant in the Caribbean's emerald sea. Sea turtle is also an important meat, most often used to make turtle soup, but also for turtle steaks; it is farmed in the Cayman islands, the original name of which was Las Tortugas ('the turtles'). Salt cod is eaten everywhere, most often made into deep-fried cod-cakes. It is a legacy of the plantation era, when New England salt cod merchants traded their low-end product for sugar, molasses, tobacco, cotton and salt. The salt cod was an inexpensive protein source for the slaves, who worked in the fields for 16 hours a day or more.

A regional flavour
What distinguishes the foods of one island from the next is the nationality of its former or present colonial power. The French Antilles (Guadeloupe, Martinique and St Barts) offer French-Creole cooking at its best, with *crabes farcies* (breadcrumb-stuffed crabs), *boudin créole* (allspice-seasoned blood sausage) and *blaff* (spicy, poached fish).

SIGNATURE DISHES

Acras de zieu noi's *Black-eyed bean fritters from Martinique.*

Callaloo *A thick soup of greens and okra, which has different names on each island.*

Coocoo *This maize meal mush, eaten with fried and steamed fish, is also called foofoo.*

Run down *A Jamaican dish of preserved fish in coconut milk, served with plantains.*

Curried prawns and dumplings *Also made with crab, this dish is a legacy of the Indians who worked on the plantations.*

Rice and peas *Depending on the island the 'peas' used in this dish could be kidney beans, yellow lentils or black-eyed beans.*

Ropa vieja *A Cuban dish combining leftover roast with tomatoes, onions and peppers.*

Spain left its mark on the cuisines of Cuba and Puerto Rico; *lechon asado* (roast suckling pig) is a signature dish on both islands. The Puerto Rican seasoning, *sofrito* (a mixture of onions, green peppers and garlic sautéed in lard) is also Spanish in character. One of Cuba's national dishes, *ajiaco*, is a sort of cross between a traditional Spanish stew and a Caribbean pepperpot. Spanish cuisine comes together with African influences in other Cuban dishes, such as *moros y cristianos*, a mixture of rice and black beans.

In the former and present British West Indies, there has been a melding of British and African foods seasoned with Asian spices. Curry goat and jerked pork (a spicy, barbecued pork dish) are signature dishes of Jamaica. In Barbados, flying fish (a pan-fried, breaded fish) is a national dish.

Dutch influence in the Netherlands Antilles (Aruba, Curaçao and Sint Maarten) is evident in the local *rijsttafels* (Indonesian buffets) and dishes like *keshy yena* (Edam cheese stuffed with meat, shrimp or chicken). Aruba and Curaçao have Dutch-Creole culinary traditions, which include dishes like deep-fried, breaded conch and *sopito* (a fish soup flavoured with coconut).

SOUTH AMERICA

The cuisines of this continent vary from country to country, but all reflect a blending of indigenous and European cultures and, in many cases, a three-way mix including African ingredients.

This, the fourth-largest continent in the world, has a range of landscapes. About 60 per cent of the land is covered in vast, grassy plains where the climate is temperate. The Andes mountains stretch the length of its western side. The west coast has one of the most desolate deserts in the world, while much of the Caribbean and north-east coasts, as well as vast stretches of the interior, are covered in tropical rainforests. Much of the land is unable to support agriculture, and about three-quarters of the South American population live in cities, many in slums.

A taste of history
All of the societies of South America were shaped by the Spanish and, in the case of Brazil, the Portuguese, when they began colonizing in the 16th century. The native ingredients that the conquistadores found, such as potatoes, squash, maize, chillis, tomatoes, beans and cassava (known also as manioc and yuca), have remained defining elements in the cuisines, but many of the countries' flavours and cooking techniques were shaped by the Europeans as well as by African slaves, who were brought over to do the Europeans' work. Much as the word 'Creole' is used to refer to a person of European or mixed European and African heritage born in the New World, this kind of food is often called a *comida criolla*, meaning 'Creole cooking'.

A regional flavour
South America can be divided geographically and gastronomically by the Andes – the longest unbroken mountain chain in the world over 3000 m in height – which runs down one side of the continent. The Andes were home to the great Native American civilization of South America,

the Quechua, more commonly known as the Inca – a word meaning 'king' or 'royal family' in the Quechua language. When the Spaniards arrived in South America, the Inca Empire covered all of Peru and Ecuador, most of Bolivia and Chile, and the north-west corner of Argentina. The Spaniards noted that 'no one went hungry in that land'; every subject was given enough space to grow food for his family, plus he was required to cultivate lands of the state. The Quechua had terraced the mountains and invented an ingenious system of aqueducts so that even the highest slopes could be cultivated.

The high altitude of the Andes played an important role in the Quechua development of freeze-drying, air-drying and salting techniques

KEY INGREDIENTS

RICE

MAIZE

FISH AND SHELLFISH

BEEF

BEANS

POTATOES

SQUASH

PLANTAINS

TOMATOES

COCONUT

AVOCADOS

BANANAS

The *feijoada*
This Brazilian favourite is a rich black-bean and meat stew, which is served with rice and orange slices – its name comes from *feijão*, the Portuguese for 'beans'.

for preserving foods. The Quechua still use dehydrated and freeze-dried potatoes, called *chuño* and *papa seca*, respectively. These preserving techniques ensured that there would always be enough food throughout the Inca Empire of 12 million people. Surplus food was stored, and if there was a drought or crop failure, it could be transported to the stricken area by llamas, the much revered Peruvian pack animal. Both llamas and alpacas, a close relation, were reared for meat, too, which could be air-dried; called *charqui*, this is still a Quechua staple. The main source of Quechua meat was *cuy* (guinea pig), and this is also still eaten.

The southern part of this continent is a land of geographic and climatic contrasts, from the tropical interior of Paraguay to the glaciers of Patagonian Argentina and Chile. The region's most outstanding feature is the large, fertile plain called the pampas, which stretches across Argentina and Uruguay. The world's richest expanse of agricultural land, this is South America's breadbasket. With its gently rolling grasslands, the pampas also provides abundant grazing for Argentina's vast cattle herds and Uruguay's huge flocks of sheep.

The indigenous peoples of Chile, Argentina, Uruguay and Paraguay were not as numerous as those in northern South America when the Spanish arrived, nor did as many survive the subsequent waves of European immigration. Consequently, the cooking in this part of South America, particularly in Chile, is more European in nature. Local ingredients, however, give these cuisines their own unique character.

While the Creole cuisines of the Andean countries reflect the marriage of European and Native American traditions, those of the tropical countries of South America, in particular Colombia and Brazil, are strongly infused with African elements introduced by slaves. Although many died under the extremely cruel working conditions, their rich religious and gastronomic traditions survived.

Feast for the senses
South American streets are lined with the flavours, colours and smells of its food: orange juice is freshly squeezed by vendors and market stalls spill into the road.

Food through the day

Mealtimes in South American countries once resembled those of Europe, with small, early breakfasts of cheese, fruit and bread or pastries with butter, avocado or marmalade, followed by long midday meals and late suppers. With urbanization and modernization that has changed. Lunches are now often lighter, and in the evenings, people eat a larger meal. In cities, the evenings are when people tend to socialize. In Santiago or Buenos Aires, for example, dinner is late, between 9 and 10 pm, and the meals are European in nature.

The exceptions to this pattern are Brazil and rural districts, where lunch is still the main meal of the day and is long, usually lasting from about 12.30 to 2 or 3 pm. People might use this time not only to eat but to bathe and rest. Dinner in such areas will be a light supper. It might consist of coffee, bread, cheese, possibly a soup or leftovers from lunch.

Peru, Ecuador and Bolivia

When the Spanish arrived in Peru, they found a food system based on potatoes, maize, tomatoes, peppers and guinea pig. Although the Spanish rapidly subdued the Quechua nation and killed many of its subjects, the descendants of the Quechua are numerous, and they maintained much of their language and culture. The influence of the Quechua is the dominant factor in the cuisines of these three Andean countries, particularly Peru. Its highly developed cuisine is considered by many to be the most refined cooking in South America.

The Quechua domesticated and bred various grains. Some strains of South American maize, called *choclo*, have kernels as big as cherry tomatoes. Another strain, called *mote*, has even larger kernels. Referred to as the 'snack of the Andes', *mote* is carried around by Quechua people in sacks and nibbled on throughout the

day. The original tribes also cultivated a high-protein grain called *quinoa*. It thrives at high altitude, and is still an important staple in Peru.

The coastal zone of Peru is a desert, where rainfall can be absent for years on end. However, about 50 rivers trickle down from the Andes and these support oases, which are watered by irrigation ditches. Here, crops can thrive year round, and every inch of soil is cultivated. Before the arrival of the Spanish, indigenous populations inhabited and cultivated this land. They were ruled by the Inca in the high Andes, who sent highland products to them on trains of pack llamas. The Spaniards decimated these coastal societies. Then, gradually, the Spanish established haciendas, and recruited native people to work them.

As the oases thrived, the Spanish landowners established a rich, aristocratic society. The Creole cuisine that evolved in the great houses here was at first very Spanish; but Native American elements inevitably crept in. Two of Peru's signature dishes, *ceviche* and *escabeche*, are direct results of the marriage of local ingredients with Spanish foods; fish or other ingredients are marinated in lime and/or lemon juice for *ceviche*,

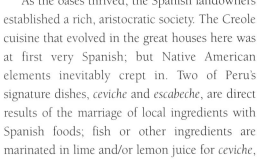

Peruvian 'chillis'
Aji are related to Mexican chillis, but the strains are different. A bright red, very hot *aji* is popular in the mountains of southern Peru.

Reading the
MENU

IN PERUVIAN COASTAL CITIES MENUS ARE MORE ELABORATE AND FEATURE MORE SEAFOOD THAN MENUS IN THE MOUNTAINOUS AREAS.

aperitif

Peruvians make a delicious spirit called pisco, *which might be drunk in cocktails or straight and slightly warmed. It might be accompanied by* anticuchos, *small pieces of spicy, grilled beef heart.*

first course

Appetizers include dishes like causa a la limeña *(potato cake),* humitas (tamales) *and various kinds of* ceviche *(marinated raw fish).*

soup

A formal meal features soup after the appetizer. This can be a meat broth or a thick chupe *(chowder) of shellfish, milk, vegetables and poached eggs.*

main course

This might be a fish dish, such as tuna or sea-bass or a meat dish, such as steak à la chorrillana, (smothered in onions and hot peppers). Many dishes combine meat with sauce and rice or the rice-like grain, quinoa. If a dish has the word arequipeño *in the title, it will probably be spicy.*

dessert

This course is usually fresh fruit, though restaurants will offer pastries and ice creams. There are many sweets made in South America, but they are usually eaten with coffee as a snack.

drinks

Beer and wines are on most menus. Water and a drink called chicha morada, *made from cherries, lemons, pineapple and purple corn, are also drunk.*

and in vinegar for *escabeche*. An old custom of these households involved a special stew course. The stew was not really meant to be eaten, but was brought out and quickly taken away again, to show that the servants were being well fed.

The staple food of the high sierra, where maize does not grow well, is the potato. Today, the indigenous peoples of Peru, Ecuador and Bolivia cultivate about 30 varieties, with colours varying from purple to creamy white. The poorest Native Americans eat them boiled and with *aji* (native Peruvian chilli). Richer embellishments marry potatoes with cheese, which the Spanish taught the Native Americans to make. Probably the most well-known Peruvian potato dish is *causa a la limeña*, a filled potato cake, which is decorated with ingredients such as hard-boiled eggs, olives, prawns and maize.

The cold Pacific waters of this area, fed by the plankton- and mineral-rich Humboldt Current, have always provided Peru with abundant seafood. Quechua runners used to run fresh fish from the ocean to Cuzco, the Inca capital, along the Inca Trail – a series of mountain roads, which stretched the length of the Andes. Some of the marine life that feeds on the plankton here, such as *conchita*, a pink and white scallop, and *corvina*, a relative of the sea bass, are unique to Peru.

The cooking of coastal Ecuador, where desert gives way to rainforest, is of a more tropical nature. Peanuts are widely used, and bananas and plantains are important staples. The leaves are used for wrapping and steaming foods, and crisps are made from green bananas or plantains. Cooks in Ecuador use banana flour as a base for breads and pastries. There are many banana desserts, the most popular being fried ripe bananas, with sugar and brandy or rum.

In the 19th century, immigration from Italy, China and Japan brought new culinary traditions into Peru. Many of the country's sauces are soy-based, and ginger – which was, in fact, introduced by the Spanish – is widely used. Immigration continued in the 20th century, and Peru's cuisine continued to evolve. Today, there is even a Peruvian nouvelle cuisine, referred to as *novoandina*, meaning New Andean.

Chile

Although the Inca Empire extended through much of Chile, the cooking of this country does not reflect the strong Native American influences inherent in the cuisines of its Andean neighbours to the north. This may be because the inhabitants of Chile, when the Spaniards arrived, were not natives, but fierce nomadic tribes who lived mainly on grilled meats. Chilean cuisine is informed largely by the cooking of Spain and France, with other European influences. However, like the other countries of South America, local ingredients – particularly beans, its abundant seafood and the strain of maize known as *choclo* – give it a character of its own.

Chile is a skinny country, over 4000 km long and rarely more than 200 km wide. The northern coastal Atacama Desert is one of the driest places on earth, and mountains shoot up within sight of

Chocolate

As in Central America, to the north, chocolate is a favourite in Ecuador, where it is enjoyed as a hot drink. Cacao is a major export.

the sea. However, Chile's Central Valley, south of Santiago, is extremely fertile, with vineyards, grain fields, vegetable farms, orchards and rich grazing lands. This allows Chile to be a major supplier of fruits and vegetables to North America and Europe during their winter months.

A unique cuisine linked with rodeo traditions exists in the Central Valley. This is a varied version of *comida criolla*, which combines native ingredients, like beans, maize, chillis, tomatoes and seafood, with the beef, lamb, pork and chicken that Europeans introduced. The vegetables are as present as the meats; as opposed to the meat-based gaucho food of Argentina, or cowboy food in North America. *Porotos* (beans) are particularly important. The typical Chilean bean stew, a national dish called *porotos granados*, almost always contains three kinds of beans: borlotti or pinto, navy and lima.

Because of Chile's coastline and the rich plankton of the cold Humboldt Current, fish and shellfish are abundant and form the basis of much of the country's gastronomy. It is both a fish-eating and fish-exporting nation. Santiago's central market displays a wonderful array of seafood. Specialities include enormous sea urchins and abalone.

By and large, Chilean food is not hot, but an orange-red flavouring called *color*, which is made by heating garlic and paprika in melted fat and cooking oil, is widely used in the cooking. Some *colores* are mild; others, made with chilli, are hotter. Another popular sauce is called *pebre*; this is made with onions, vinegar, olive oil, garlic, chilli and coriander.

Chile is a wine-producing and wine-drinking country. Vineyards were established here by the Spanish shortly after their arrival, but it was not really until the late 20th century that the rest of the world took interest in New World wines. Accordingly, exports have been increasing over the last few decades, but this has led, according to some wine writers, to overproduction and falling standards. Most of the country's vineyards are based in the Central Valley, and growing conditions vary here from east to west, from sunny and dry to damper areas.

Argentina, Uruguay, and Paraguay

Neither Paraguay nor Uruguay, both meat-loving countries, have cuisines that are particularly different to the rest of South America. Uruguay eats much like its neighbour to the south, Argentina. Grilled beef is ubiquitous, but even more important are sheep – it is the second biggest wool exporting country in the world.

Paraguay has the largest proportion of native Americans remaining in southern South America. The northern grassland and forest, called the Gran Chaco, is inhabited by the Maca and the Guarani, whose language, along with Spanish, is still widely spoken. In the tropical forests of Paraguay, cassava is a staple. The country's most

Street food (opposite)
Buying meals off the street is so popular that it can account for up to a quarter of household spending in South America.

Lunch on the go
Today, at least in cities, the midday meal is not very big, perhaps consisting of a moderate serving of meat, fish or pasta and rice, or, for many office workers, a quick sandwich or pizza.

■ **YERBA MATE: THE ENERGY DRINK**
PARAGUAY IS THE HOME OF THE STIMULATING HERBAL TEA, *YERBA MATE*, THAT IS ENJOYED THROUGHOUT URUGUAY, PARAGUAY AND ARGENTINA. THE TRADITIONAL WAY OF PREPARING AND SERVING *YERBA MATE* IS TO PUT THE LEAVES IN A DRIED GOURD, AND TO ADD BOILING WATER. IT IS THEN DRUNK OUT OF THE GOURD WITH A *BOMBILLA*, A WOODEN OR METAL TUBE WITH A SPOON-LIKE STRAINER AT ITS LOWER END. THE GOURD MAY BE SHARED AS A SIGN OF HOSPITALITY.

Festive

~~~ FOOD ~~~

A pre-Hispanic tradition, called the pachamanca ('earth oven') is still a popular Andean feast for special occasions. A circular hole about 1.5 m wide is dug and lined with stones. These are topped with wood, straw and more stones, and a fire is lit. When the stones are red-hot, the pit is lined with moist green leaves and herbs, upon which are placed meats, such as chickens, guinea pigs or whole pigs or goats. Casseroles, vegetables and tamales (filled maize packages) are added. More stones are set on top, and the pit is sealed with earth and decorated with flowers. Several hours later the pit is opened up and the foods are removed for the banquet.

Asado (meat roast)

At these events, meat is impaled on crossed iron rods, which are thrust into the ground at an angle to a fire. As the meat roasts, the fat runs down, basting it.

typical soup, *bori-bori*, is a simple meat broth with dumplings made of maize meal and cheese. This is thought to be a legacy of one of Paraguay's large immigrant groups, the German Mennonites, who came from Canada in the 1920s.

In Argentina, meat is eaten at almost every meal. The cuisine here is a beef-lover's dream; the scent of grilled steaks is the national aroma. When the Spaniards arrived, there were Native Americans living on the pampas, but the great Quechua civilization of the Andes had not settled there. The Spaniards found the land perfect for their herds of cattle, and they could turn the heavy sod with their ploughs in order to plant wheat and other temperate-climate crops.

Most people in Argentina today are of European descent. The Spanish were the original colonizers, and there were other waves of Spanish immigration in the 19th and early 20th centuries. In the 1860s, there was a large immigration of Welsh people, settling in the pampas and the southern plains of Patagonia to raise sheep. The other large group of European

SIGNATURE DISHES

Aji de gallina *A spectacular Peruvian* aji *dish of chicken seasoned with chillis.*

Tamales *With different names in each of the countries, these filled maize packages can be found across South America.*

Chupe de porotos *A bean chowder, made with three kinds of beans.*

Carbonada criolla *Argentinian beef stew made with squash and vegetables, often baked in a pumpkin.*

Arroz con coco *Rice in coconut milk.*

Vatapa *A mixture of bread, dried prawns, peanuts and cashews, which is served as an accompaniment to Bahian dishes.*

Acaca *this custard-like Brazilian dish, with coconut milk and* dende *oil, is steamed in banana leaves.*

immigrants were Italians, who escaped the poverty of Italy in the 19th and early 20th centuries and came here to work for the wheat harvest. Many of the early wine-makers in Argentina were of Italian descent. Buenos Aires is filled with Italian restaurants.

Many of Argentina's traditional foods derive from the gauchos, herdsmen of mixed Native American and Spanish descent, who live a nomadic life on the pampas. Their diet traditionally consists almost solely of meat, often the flesh of half-wild cattle, which is boiled or grilled over an open fire. The only vegetable in the gaucho diet was boiled or roasted pumpkin.

Cooking meat over a wood fire, whether in the country or city, is still extremely popular. The open-air *asado* (meat roast) is a long-standing tradition at big events like fairs and political rallies. Whole, split carcasses of sheep, goats and pigs, as well as slabs of beef and large sides of beef ribs, are prepared for such events. For less festive affairs and cooking at home, people grill smaller cuts on barbecues.

Colombia, Venezuela and the Caribbean coast

These northern countries fall into more than one climatic and gastronomic zone. Although there are long, tropical Caribbean coasts and jungles here, the Andean ranges extend into both Colombia and Venezuela.

Bogotá, Colombia's capital, is located in a valley almost 3000 m high. Potatoes thrive here and many traditional Bogotá dishes are based on them; a favourite is *papas chorriadas*, boiled potatoes with a sauce of spring onions, tomatoes, cheese, coriander, chillis and cream. But even in Bogotá, the proximity of the tropical lowlands can be tasted in its widespread use of tropical and semi-tropical foods, like plantains and avocados.

The geography of the Colombian-Venezuelan Andes results in many valley communities, which are isolated from each other and have, therefore, formed distinct cuisines. The most well known of these styles of cooking, and a source of great local pride, is that of the Cauca Valley, where the cities of Medellin and Cali are located. The climate in this lower area is semi-tropical, and cassava, plantains and bananas replace potatoes as the staples. Banana leaves are used to wrap tamales, which are called *hallacas* in Colombia and Venezuela. Plantain crisps, called *tostones*, are a favourite snack.

The food and culture of the tropical lowlands of Venezuela and Colombia are African-influenced. Some of the people here are almost pure descendants of African slaves. There are also still jungle dwellers, either of Native American, African or Mestizo descent. Small patches in the jungle are cleared to plant cassava, plantains, maize and beans and to hunt for monkeys, tapirs, deer, birds, turtles and ants. On the coast, fish is eaten and is an important source of protein.

One of the most vivid examples of the African influence on Colombian cooking is the widespread use of coconut, which came to South America from Africa – and to Africa from Asia. Coconut meat and milk are used in many recipes, both sweet and savoury. Rice cooked in coconut milk, *arroz con coco*, is a signature dish of

BAIANAS DE TABULEIRO: BAHIAN WOMEN WITH TRAYS

All over Salvador de Bahia in Brazil, *baianas da tabuleiro* sell the street food, *acaraje* – black-eyed pea fritters, filled with dried shrimp and *melegueta* peppers. The women are descendants of slaves who sold foods for their owners, and many still wear the traditional cooks' dress: layers of petticoats, lacework blouses, turbans and glass beads.

Many of the *baianas da tabuleiro* are initiates of the Candomble religion, which has survived in north-eastern Brazil. The faith places much emphasis on food, and the *iya basse* (ritual cook) plays an major role in all ceremonies. Many of their foods began as ritual offerings.

Cartagena and its environs. The coconut milk gives the rice a brown hue and rich texture. It is served as an accompaniment to almost every kind of dish, including the rich boiled dinner called *sancocho*, which is like a Caribbean bouillabaisse, containing fish, seafood and local vegetables. There are many versions of *arroz con coco*, even a dessert version with chocolate.

Empanadas
These savoury pastries are filled with meat, and sometimes vegetables such as greens.

HERBS AND SPICES

MELEGUETA PEPPER also known as *malagueta* pepper, *atare* and 'grains of paradise', this is not a true pepper, but the seeds of a cardamom-like plant, which are spicy and can be used in the same way. It is used mainly in the cuisine of Brazil

Needle fish (opposite)
Seafood, a mainstay of Brazilian cuisine, is caught off the sandy beaches of the country's long Atlantic coastline.

The cooking of the three other Caribbean countries in South America – namely Guyana, Suriname and French Guyana – is also Afro-Caribbean in nature, but with an interesting twist, particularly in Guyana. The food here is infused with many features from India. This is due to waves of immigration in the 19th century, when people from India came to work as indentured servants on the plantations after slavery was abolished. Curries and *roti* are among Guyana's favourite foods.

Brazil

This is the largest country in South America, and it covers almost half the continent. There are deserts in the north-east, rainforests in the north and west, and rolling grasslands in the south. With its varied climate and rich farmlands, almost anything can be grown in Brazil. The country produces large quantities of soybeans, sugar cane, cotton, oranges, bananas and cocoa beans, and is the world's largest coffee exporter. The coffee culture here is widespread and people drink strong, black coffee all day long.

The gastronomy of Brazil differs substantially from the rest of South America, because of the country's history. It was not colonized by the Spanish, but by the Portuguese, who came in search of land, not gold. Naturally, this has had an effect on the cuisine. Many of Portugal's signature dishes, such as *caldo verde*, and the egg sweets made in Portuguese convents, are popular foods in Brazil.

The Portuguese ruled Brazil from the 16th to the 19th centuries. They planted huge sugar plantations in the north-east, and imported vast numbers of African slaves to work them. Brazilian culture, gastronomic and otherwise, has been greatly influenced by these slaves, particularly in the states of Bahia, Pernambuco and Maranhao. According to food writer Jessica Harris, Bahia and its capital city, Salvador de Bahia, which was the original capital of Brazil, is 'the spiritual home of much Afro-Brazilian food'.

The most important ingredients introduced by African slaves in Brazil are palm oil, called *dende*, and the *melegueta* pepper (see box, left). *Dende* oil gives Afro-Brazilian food its characteristic reddish-yellow colour, its strong, pungent aromas and its rich flavours and textures. Also important were the introduction of okra and the greater use of bananas, plantains, coconut oil and coconut milk.

Native to the Amazon region, cassava was widely eaten by the local inhabitants before the Portuguese arrived. It remains one of the most important staples in Brazilian cuisine. The starchy root is dried and ground into a flour called *farinha*, which is sprinkled onto moist dishes to soak up sauce. Special shakers called *farinheiras* can be found on most restaurant tables. Toasted *farinha*, called *farofa*, is eaten as a popular side dish.

Rice and black beans are also important staples throughout Brazil. The Brazilian national dish, *feijoada* is a rich black-bean and meat stew. The standard meal for poorer Brazilians is black beans and rice topped with *farinha*.

RECIPES

SOUPS

Soup au pistou *(France)*
Caldo verde *(Portugal)*
Borshch *(Russia and Eastern Europe)*
Miso soup *(Japan)*
Hot and sour soup *(China)*
Hanoi soup/pho bo *(Vietnam)*
Saigon soup *(Vietnam)*
Tortilla soup *(Mexico)*
Clam Chowder *(The United States)*

STARTERS AND SALADS

Marinated herring salad *(Russia and Eastern Europe)*
Tapenade *(France)*
Pipérade *(France and Spain)*
Frisée, egg and bacon salad *(France)*
Grilled duck breast salad *(France)*
Red pepper relish *(The Balkan Peninsula)*
Tzatziki *(Greece)*
Tunisian carrot salad *(North Africa)*
Bulgar wheat and parsley salad/tabbouleh *(The Middle East)*
Baba ganouj *(The Middle East)*
Spring onion pancakes *(Korea)*
Spinach with sesame dressing *(Japan)*
Caesar salad *(The United States)*

VEGETABLES, PULSES AND DAIRY

Braised red cabbage *(Germany)*
Artichoke ragout *(France)*
Greens with raisins and pine nuts *(Spain)*
Georgian cheese bread *(Russia and Eastern Europe)*
Pirogi *(Russia and Eastern Europe)*
Spanokopitta *(Greece)*
Cherry pilaf *(Turkey)*
Iranian herb omelette *(The Middle East)*
Stir-fried Chinese broccoli *(China)*

Mee goreng with prawns *(Malaysia)*
Cooked black beans in broth *(Mexico)*
Chilean bean and winter squash stew *(South America)*
Rice cooked in coconut milk *(South America)*

FISH

Gravlax *(Scandinavia)*
Mussels steamed in white wine *(The Low Countries)*
Clams in a cataplana *(Portugal)*
Turkish grilled swordfish with dill sauce *(Turkey)*
Crab cakes *(USA)*
Red snapper à la veracruzana *(Mexico)*
Caribbean curried prawns *(The Caribbean)*

MEAT AND POULTRY

Veal porkolt *(Russia and Eastern Europe)*
Sauerbraten *(Austria and Germany)*
Flemish beef and beer stew *(The Low Countries)*
Alsation tarte flambée *(France)*
Poulet basquaise *(France)*
Paella valenciana *(Spain)*
Ragu *(Italy)*
Rabbit with tomatoes, sage and white wine *(Italy)*
Persian stew with peaches *(The Middle East)*
Bulgar wheat and lamb koftas *(The Middle East)*
Couscous with chicken, lemon and olives *(North Africa)*
Lamb and prune tagine *(North Africa)*
Moghul-braised chicken *(India)*
Szechuan-braised tofu with pork *(China)*
Pork adobo *(The Philippines)*

Barbequed beef *(Korea)*
Chicken jambalaya *(The United States)*
Green enchiladas with chicken *(Mexico)*
Jerk chicken *(The Caribbean)*
Callaloo *(The Caribbean)*

DESSERTS, CAKES AND BAKES

Scandinavian fruit soup *(Scandinavia)*
Swedish honey and spice biscuits *(Scandinavia)*
Black bread *(Russia and Eastern Europe)*
Sachertorte *(Austria and Germany)*
Linzertorte *(Austria and Germany)*
Cherry clafoutis *(France)*
Apple and prune tart *(France)*
Pecan pie *(The United States and Canada)*
Brownies *(The United States and Canada)*
Pavlova *(Australia and New Zealand)*

SOUPS

SOUP AU PISTOU

This Provençale spring vegetable soup is like a minestrone, enriched with pesto.

SERVES 8

FOR THE SOUP

225 g dried borlotti or 225 g white beans soaked and drained

1 large onion, chopped

6–8 garlic cloves, minced or crushed

4 L water

1 bouquet garni of a bay leaf, thyme and parsley sprigs and Parmesan rind

250 g green beans, trimmed and broken into 2-cm pieces

2 medium courgettes, scrubbed and diced

2 large carrots, chopped

2 celery stalks, chopped

2 leeks, white and light-green part only, cleaned and sliced

2 medium turnips, peeled and diced

450 g new potatoes, diced

450 g tomatoes, peeled, seeded and chopped or 1 x 425 g tin

50 g soup pasta, such as macaroni or small shells

salt and black pepper to taste

FOR THE PISTOU

2–4 large garlic cloves, to taste, peeled

50 g packed fresh basil leaves

75 ml extra virgin olive oil

1 small tomato, peeled and seeded (optional)

90 g grated Parmesan, or a mixture of Gruyère and Parmesan

50 g grated Parmesan or Gruyère for sprinkling

salt and black pepper, to taste

1   Combine the dried beans and 2 L of the water and bring to the boil. Skim off any foam, add the onion, 2 garlic cloves and the bouquet garni. Bring to the boil, reduce the heat, cover and simmer for 1 hour.

2   Set aside half the green beans and half the courgettes. Add the remaining water, garlic and vegetables to the pot and bring to the boil. Add salt to taste (be generous). Reduce the heat, cover and simmer for 1 hour. Adjust seasonings.

3   While the soup is simmering, blanch or steam the green beans and courgettes, about 5 minutes, until tender but bright, and set aside.

4   Meanwhile, make the pistou. To make it in a food processor, use one fitted with a steel blade. Drop in the garlic and process. Scrape down the sides of the bowl, add the basil and salt and process again, until finely chopped. Scrape down the sides once more. Next, drizzle in the olive oil with the machine running, then drop in the tomato, if using. Process to a paste. Add salt to taste and stir in the cheese. To make the pistou in a mortar and pestle, pound the garlic with the salt to a paste. Add the basil, a handful at a time, and grind. Add the optional tomato and work to a paste with the basil. Drop by drop, work in the oil. Stir in the cheese.

5   Add the pasta to the soup about 10 minutes before serving and simmer until cooked *al dente*. Add pepper, taste and adjust salt. Stir the blanched or steamed green vegetables into the soup and heat through.

6   To serve, stir the pistou into the pot or into the individual bowls or let people stir in their own. Sprinkle with Parmesan or Gruyère.

CALDO VERDE

In Portugal, the most popular greens for this national dish are turnip tops and Galician cabbage, but kale works well, too.

SERVES 6

30 ml olive oil

1 medium onion, chopped

1 large garlic clove, finely chopped

900 g floury potatoes, peeled and thinly sliced

2 L water

175 g Spanish or Portuguese chorizo, sliced thin. Use mild Italian sausage if chorizo unavailable.

450 g turnip greens or kale, stems trimmed

salt and black pepper, to taste

1   Heat 15 ml of the oil over a medium heat in a large, heavy-based pan and add the onion. Stir for about 3–5 minutes, until tender. Add the garlic and cook for a further 30 seconds. Stir in the potatoes and water, bring to the boil and add 2 tsp of salt. Reduce the heat, cover and simmer for 30 minutes, until the potatoes start to fall apart.

2   Meanwhile, prepare the greens and sausage. Stack the leaves, about 6 or 8 to a stack, roll them up tightly and slice crossways thinly. Sauté the sliced sausage gently over a medium-low heat in a frying pan for about 10 minutes, until the fat runs out. Drain off the fat.

3   Mash the potatoes in their pan and stir in the sausage and greens. Simmer for 5–10 minutes, until the greens turn bright green and tender. Season to taste. Stir in the remaining olive oil to serve.

BORSHCH

A gorgeous red-hued, warming winter soup originating in the Ukraine.

SERVES 4–6

FOR THE BEEF STOCK

450 g beef shank or brisket

2 L water

2 carrots

2 onions

FOR THE SOUP

4 medium beetroots with greens, the beetroots peeled and quartered and the greens stemmed and coarsely chopped

2 garlic cloves, thinly sliced

1 L water

2 tsp. fruit sugar

15 ml white wine vinegar

15 ml vegetable oil

2 medium onions, chopped

2 small or 1 medium turnip, chopped

2 carrots, sliced

25 g fresh mushrooms, trimmed and chopped

250 g cabbage, shredded

2 bay leaves

10 sprigs fresh parsley

3 allspice berries

6 black peppercorns

4 tbsp chopped fresh parsley

salt and black pepper, to taste

250 ml sour cream, to serve

1 Place all the ingredients for the stock in a large saucepan and simmer for 2–4 hours. Remove from the heat and strain through a cheesecloth-lined sieve. Measure out 1 L of the stock and season to taste. Freeze any remaining stock to use in another dish. Shred the meat and set aside. Add it to the soup before serving if desired.

2 While the stock is simmering, combine the beetroots, garlic and water in a pan and bring to the boil. Add 1 tsp of salt and the sugar, reduce the heat and simmer, uncovered, for 30 minutes. Stir in the vinegar. Remove the beetroots from the water using a slotted spoon, and set aside the cooking water. Rinse the beetroots with cold water and slice them into matchstick-sized pieces.

3 Heat the oil in a large, heavy-based pan over a medium heat and add the onion. Cook for 3–5 minutes, until just tender, and add the turnip, carrots, sliced beetroots, mushrooms, cabbage and beef stock. Tie the bay leaves, parsley sprigs, allspice berries and peppercorns together in a piece of muslin and add to the pan with 1 tsp salt. Bring to the boil, reduce heat, cover and simmer for 40 minutes.

4 Add the beetroot greens and simmer for another 10 minutes. Stir in the reserved beetroot cooking water and season to taste. Remove the muslin bag. Heat the soup through, and sprinkle on the parsley. Serve with a generous spoonful of sour cream.

MISO SOUP

Primarily a breakfast food in Japan, miso soup can be served as a starter also. Seasonal vegetables can be added for variety.

SERVES 4

1 L dashi or water

60 ml miso

4 small or 2 large mushrooms, cleaned and thinly sliced, or 2 shiitake mushrooms, sliced

100 g tofu, drained and diced

2 spring onions, chopped

a pinch of ground shansho pepper (optional)

4 stalks mitsuba, chopped

2 tbsp chopped fresh chives

75 g squash, diced and steamed until just tender

1 Gently heat the dashi or water in a saucepan and keep at a very low simmer. Put the miso in a bowl and add 15–30 ml of the warm liquid. Whisk until the miso is softened and blended with the liquid. Gradually add the softened miso to the pan. Do not boil, as this can change the flavour.

2 Add the remaining ingredients to the pan. Bring to just below boiling point and remove from the heat. Sprinkle on a little pepper to serve.

HOT AND SOUR SOUP

This soup has become one of the most popular Chinese dishes in the West. The black pepper gives a hot flavour and the rice vinegar provides the sour.

SERVES 4–6

5 ml soy sauce

5 ml dry sherry

4 tsp corn flour, dissolved in 20 ml water

10 ml sesame oil

100 g pork fillet, cut into matchsticks

10 Chinese mushrooms, stems discarded

25 g cellophane noodles

1.5 L chicken stock

250 g tofu, drained and cut into matchsticks

1 tsp fruit sugar

$1\frac{1}{2}$ tsp ground black pepper

30 ml soy sauce

45 ml rice vinegar

2 medium eggs, beaten

2 tbsp finely chopped spring onions

2 tbsp chopped fresh coriander

salt, to taste

1 Mix together the soy sauce, dry sherry, half the dissolved corn flour and 5 ml of the sesame oil. Season with salt and black pepper. Toss the pork in the mixture until thoroughly coated. Cover and refrigerate for at least 15 minutes – longer if possible.

2 Cover the mushrooms in hot water and soak for 20 minutes. Drain, then squeeze out any excess liquid. Cut into thin strips. Cover the cellophane noodles in warm water and soak for 5 minutes. Drain, then cut them in half.

3 Bring the chicken stock to a simmer in a large saucepan and stir in the pork and marinade. Use chopsticks to stir and separate the mixture.

4 Simmer for 2 minutes, then stir in the mushrooms, cellophane noodles, tofu, sugar, 1¹⁄₂ tsp ground black pepper and soy sauce. Bring back to a simmer and stir in the rice vinegar and remaining dissolved corn flour. Taste and correct salt.

5 Drizzle the beaten eggs into the soup, stirring with chopsticks to create thin strands. Stir in the spring onions, coriander and remaining sesame oil to serve.

HANOI SOUP

This signature dish of Vietnam is also called pho bo.

SERVES 6

3 kg oxtails or meaty beef bones

450 g braising beef, in one piece, trimmed of fat

6 L water

7.5-cm piece of ginger, unpeeled

1 large onion, quartered

45 ml fish sauce

1 tbsp fruit sugar

6 star anise

5 whole cloves

1 cinnamon stick

1 tbsp black peppercorns

1 tbsp salt

450 g thin rice noodles

225 g beef sirloin, slightly frozen to make cutting easier

50 g chopped fresh coriander

3 shallots, sliced paper-thin and separated into rings

25 g fresh Asian basil leaves

4 spring onions, chopped

200 g beansprouts

2–4 serano or bird chillies, seeded and finely chopped

3 limes, cut into wedges

salt and black pepper, to taste

1 Place the bones and braising beef in a very large pan and cover with water. Bring to the boil and cook for 5 minutes. Drain, and rinse the meat and bones thoroughly. Clean the pot, then return the bones and beef to the pot and add the water, or enough to cover. Bring to a gentle boil. Simmer gently for 30 minutes, skimming often.

2 Scorch the ginger and onion quarters by holding them directly over a gas flame with tongs and turning until charred on all sides. If using an electric hob, heat in a dry, heavy frying pan or on a grill until charred. Rinse briefly, then add to pan.

3 Add the fish sauce and sugar to the pot. Bring the water back to the boil, then simmer it over a low heat, partially covered, for 2–3 hours, until the meat is very tender. Skim the water often. Remove the meat from the pot and transfer to a bowl. Cover with water and allow to rest for 15 minutes. (This prevents it from drying out.) Drain the meat, wrap it tightly in plastic wrap and refrigerate until shortly before serving.

4 Tie the spices and peppercorns in a cheesecloth bag and add it to the soup with the salt. Simmer for another 2 hours, skimming often and adding water as necessary to keep the bones covered. Remove the bones from the pot and discard. Line a sieve with two layers of cheesecloth and place over a large bowl. Ladle in the broth. Allow to cool slightly, then refrigerate for at least 2 hours, or preferably overnight. Skim off the fat from the top of the broth and discard.

5 Cut the cooked beef across the grain into very thin slices. Place these on a plate. Cut the raw sirloin into paper-thin slices and place them on another plate.

6 Bring the beef broth back to a simmer. Season to taste. Bring a large pan of water to the boil, add 1-2 tsp of salt, if you wish, and add the noodles.

Cook the noodles for 2–4 minutes or until *al dente*.

7 Drain, and divide the noodles among 6 large soup bowls. Place a few slices each of raw and cooked beef on top of the noodles in each bowl, and ladle in a generous amount of hot broth, which will cook the raw beef. Sprinkle on half the coriander, the shallots, half the basil leaves and the spring onions. Serve with the beansprouts, chopped chillies, the remaining basil and coriander and the lime wedges on the side.

SAIGON SOUP

A hearty Vietnamese soup that is popular throughout the day, particularly in the south of the country.

SERVES 4–6

1 small chicken, about 1.25 kg jointed and skinned

3 L water

175 g pork loin

1 onion, quartered

20 ml fish sauce

5 ml vegetable oil

2 medium eggs, beaten

250 g rice noodles

1 bunch spring onions, sliced

25 g chopped fresh coriander

200 g beansprouts

salt and black pepper, to taste

1 Place the chicken, water and pork in a large, heavy-based soup pot and bring to the boil. Skim off any foam. Add the onion, reduce the heat and simmer, uncovered, for 30 minutes. Remove the white chicken meat and set aside, and simmer the broth for another 10 minutes. Take out the remaining chicken pieces and the pork from the broth and allow to cool. Line a sieve with muslin and strain the broth. Refrigerate for at least 2 hours or, preferably, overnight. Skim off the fat from the surface.

2   Meanwhile, shred the chicken and pork. Refrigerate in a covered container until ready to serve.

3   When ready to serve, bring the broth to a simmer and add the fish sauce. Season to taste.

4   Heat the oil in a small non-stick frying pan. Beat the eggs in a bowl and season. Pour the eggs into the pan and swirl, so that they spread out to make an omelette. When cooked, roll the omelette up, remove it from the pan and cut it into thin slivers.

5   Bring a large pan of water to the boil and add 1 tsp of salt and the noodles. Cook the noodles for 2–4 minutes or until *al dente*, drain and rinse with cold water.

6   Divide the noodles among 4–6 bowls. Top with the shredded chicken, pork, egg, spring onions and coriander. Ladle in a generous amount of the broth, top with beansprouts and serve.

TORTILLA SOUP

This is probably Mexico's best-known soup. The finishing touches are toasted tortilla strips and a squeeze of lime juice.

SERVES 4–6

75 ml vegetable oil

½ onion, finely chopped

2 large garlic cloves, finely chopped

450 g tomatoes, peeled

1.5 L chicken stock

8 corn tortillas, cut in strips

1 or 2 dried poblano chillies, seeded and deveined

3 tbsp chopped fresh coriander, plus additional for garnish

30 ml fresh lime juice

25 g grated Gruyère cheese or fromage frais

2 limes, cut into wedges

salt and black pepper, to taste

1   Heat 10 ml of the oil over a medium heat in a non-stick pan, and add the onion. Cook for about 5 minutes, until tender, then add the garlic. Stir together for about 30 seconds until the garlic just begins to colour, and remove from the heat. Transfer the onion and garlic to a food blender or processor and add the tomatoes. Process until smooth. Strain through a medium-mesh sieve.

2   Heat 10 ml of the remaining oil in a large pan and add the tomato purée. Cook, stirring continuously, until the purée thickens – about 8–10 minutes. Add the stock and stir well, then cover and simmer for 30 minutes over a very low heat.

3   Heat the remaining oil in a frying pan until sizzling hot, and add the tortilla strips in batches. Fry until just crisp, and drain on kitchen paper.

4   Toast the chillies in a dry frying pan over a medium heat – press them flat with a spatula until they begin to blister, then turn them over and repeat on the other side. Remove from the pan immediately and cut into small pieces. Set aside.

5   Shortly before serving, add the chilli pieces to the soup and cook for 3 minutes, until soft. Add the coriander and cook for 1 minute. Stir in the lime juice and season to taste.

6   Divide the toasted tortilla strips among 4–6 wide soup bowls. Ladle in the soup, top with a sprinkling of cheese and coriander and serve.

CLAM CHOWDER

An authentic New England chowder did not need cream because milk would have been creamier. You now need cream or half-and-half to get the right texture.

SERVES 4

1.5 kg clams

500 ml water

3–4 bacon rashers, diced

1 tbsp unsalted butter

1 medium onion, chopped, trimmings reserved

2 celery sticks, finely chopped, trimmings reserved

1 bay leaf

450 g russet potatoes, peeled and cut in 1-cm dice

375 ml milk

125 ml single cream

2–4 tbsp chopped fresh parsley

salt and black pepper, to taste

1   Scrub the clams with a small brush, then place in a bowl and cover with cold water. Add a tablespoon of salt or vinegar and leave for 30 minutes–1 hour. Drain, and wash in several rinses of clean water.

2   Combine the clams with 250 ml of the water and the trimmings from the onion and celery in a large pan. Cover and bring to the boil over a medium-high heat. Cook for about 8 minutes, until all the clams are open, shaking the pan occasionally. Remove the clams from the pan and discard any that have not opened. Strain the liquid in the pan through a sieve lined with a double thickness of cheesecloth. Remove the clams from their shells, rinse and chop coarsely.

3   Cook the bacon in a heavy saucepan over a medium heat until it is slightly crisp. Add the butter, onion, celery and bay leaf and cook for about 5 minutes, stirring, until the onions are translucent. Add the clam liquor, the remaining water and the potatoes. Bring to the boil, reduce the heat and simmer for about 10–12 minutes, until the potatoes are just tender.

4   Stir in the milk, cream or half-and-half and clams. Bring to a simmer and cook for 5 minutes. Remove from the heat and season to taste. Stir in the parsley to serve.

STARTERS AND SALADS

MARINATED HERRING SALAD

Herring salads are typical throughout the Baltic, both in Scandinavia and Northern Europe, and are an essential part of a smorgasbord. Potatoes and beetroots are an optional part of this recipe, and make for a more substantial dish.

SERVES 6–10

1 sweet onion, thinly sliced

250 ml sour cream

125 ml natural yoghurt

15 ml lemon juice

1/4 tsp sugar

2 tart eating apples, peeled, cored and thinly sliced or chopped

2 pickled gherkins, chopped

300 g marinated herring fillets, drained

2 medium potatoes, cooked and diced (optional)

1 small beetroot, cooked and diced (optional)

1 tbsp chopped fresh dill

salt and black pepper, to taste

1 Soak the onion briefly in a bowl of cold water. Drain, then toss with the sour cream, yoghurt, lemon juice and sugar. Stir in the apple and gherkins. Season to taste with salt and pepper.
2 Place half the herring in a serving dish and top with the potatoes and beetroot (if using). Cover with half the sour cream sauce. Layer the remaining herring, potatoes and beetroot over the sauce, top with the remaining sauce and cover tightly. Refrigerate for 5 hours or longer. Sprinkle with the fresh dill before serving.

TAPENADE

This creamy olive and anchovy paste is so simple to make – spread it on crusty French bread, crackers or toasted bread for a taste of southern France.

SERVES 12 AS A CANAPÉ TOPPING

2 large garlic cloves, peeled

250 g Mediterranean black olives, pitted

1 1/2 tbsp capers, drained and rinsed

4 anchovy fillets, rinsed

1 tsp fresh thyme leaves

1 tsp chopped fresh rosemary

1 tsp Dijon mustard

30 ml fresh lemon juice

30 ml olive oil

freshly ground black pepper, to taste

1 Chop the garlic in a food processor. Add the olives, capers, anchovies, thyme and rosemary, and process together until quite smooth.
2 Add the remaining ingredients, and continue to blend until you have a well-mixed paste. Alternatively, you can make the tapenade using a mortar and pestle. Transfer to a bowl and refrigerate until ready to use.

PIPÉRADE

The term 'pipérade' refers both to the pepper sauce that in the Basque region of Spain can garnish fish, meat or eggs, and also to this classic Basque egg dish.

SERVES 4

175 g prosciutto or Bayonne ham, thinly sliced

30 ml olive oil

1–2 medium onions, finely chopped

3 green peppers or 2 green peppers and 1 red pepper, seeded, cored and cut into thin strips

1 green chilli, seeded and chopped (optional)

2 garlic cloves, finely chopped

900 g tomatoes, chopped

1 tsp fresh thyme leaves

4–8 medium eggs

salt and black pepper, to taste

1 Cut 2 of the slices of ham into very thin strips and set aside.
2 Heat the oil in a large, non-stick frying pan over a medium heat and add the onions. Cook for about 5 minutes until tender, then add the peppers, chilli, garlic and 1/2 tsp salt. Cook, stirring, for about 10 minutes, until the peppers soften. Add the tomatoes, thyme and strips of ham. Stir together and cook for 5 minutes. Season with salt, reduce the heat to low and cook uncovered, stirring often, for 1 hour. The mixture should be very thick. Season to taste.
3 Towards the end of the hour, heat the grill and grill the remaining ham until it is just crisp around the edges. Remove from the heat and keep warm.
4 Beat the eggs in a bowl and add to the pepper mixture. Cook, stirring over a low heat, until they are just set but still creamy. Remove from the heat and divide among 4 plates. Top each serving with a piece of ham, and serve at once.

FRISÉE, EGG AND BACON SALAD

In Paris brasseries and Lyonnais bistros, this dish is usually served as a first course, but it also makes a good starter.

SERVES 4

2 small heads frisée

1–2 tbsp Dijon mustard

30–45 ml red-wine or sherry vinegar

125 ml groundnut oil or a combination of
groundnut and olive oil

100 g bacon, cut into 1-cm pieces

2 large slices country bread or 8 slices
baguette, cubed

4 large eggs

salt and black pepper, to taste

1 Remove the tough outer leaves
from the frisée. Separate the
remaining leaves, wash well, dry and
break them into small pieces. Place in
a large serving bowl.

2 Make the dressing. Mix together
the mustard and vinegar and whisk in
the oil. Season to taste, then set aside.

3 Heat a large frying pan over a
medium heat and add the bacon. Cook,
stirring, for 4–5 minutes. Add the bread
cubes and continue to cook for about
5–10 minutes, or until the croutons and
bacon are browned and crisp.

4 Meanwhile, poach the eggs for 4–5
minutes, according to taste.

5 Add the bacon and crouton
mixture to the leaves, pour over the
dressing and toss. Divide among 4
plates, then top each with a poached
egg to serve.

GRILLED DUCK BREAST SALAD

*This is my interpretation of the traditional
French* salade landaise, *which combines
duck with other regional salad
ingredients, such as wild mushrooms and
walnuts. I prefer to use rich breast meat
but duck livers are also often used. A
French cook would pan-fry the duck in
goose fat, but grilling is my cooking
method of choice.*

SERVES 4

1 duck breast, boned, skinned and
trimmed of fat

coarse sea salt, to sprinkle

90 ml olive oil

25 g dried ceps

2 garlic cloves, finely chopped

1 head of frisée lettuce, leaves
separated, washed and dried, or about
300 g mixed leaves such as rocket,
frisée, radicchio and chicory

50 g shelled walnuts

2 tbsp chopped fresh herbs, such as
chives, chervil or parsley

30 ml red-wine vinegar

30 ml walnut oil

chervil sprigs, to garnish

salt and black pepper, to taste

1 Sprinkle the duck breast with sea
salt and toss in a bowl with 15 ml of
the olive oil. Cover and refrigerate for
1 hour or more. Remove from the fridge
30 minutes before cooking.

2 Place the ceps in a bowl and pour
on enough boiling water to cover, leave
for 15–30 minutes until softened.
Meanwhile, place a heavy-based pan
under a grill and preheat to high.

3 Strain the mushrooms through a
muslin-lined sieve. Rinse several times
to make sure any grit is removed then
squeeze dry. If the pieces are very
large, chop coarsely.

4 Heat another tablespoon of olive oil
over a medium heat in a small frying
pan and add the soaked mushrooms
and half the garlic. Add a little salt and
cook for about 2 minutes, until the
garlic begins to colour. Remove from
the heat.

5 Combine the lettuce, walnuts,
mushrooms and chopped herbs in a
salad bowl. Mix together the vinegar,
remaining garlic, olive oil and walnut
oil, and season well.

6 Brush the duck breast with the
olive oil and juices in the bowl. Place
on the hot pan and cook for 4–5
minutes. Turn and grill for another
4–5 minutes, depending on how rare
you like it. It should be slightly pink
and juicy on the inside. Remove from
the heat and slice into thin strips.
Season with a little salt and pepper.

7 Toss the salad with the dressing.
Lay the duck strips over the top, and
garnish with sprigs of chervil to serve.

RED PEPPER RELISH

*This Balkan recipe makes a marvellous
starter spread on crusty bread.*

MAKES ABOUT 500 ML

6 red peppers

2–4 hot red chillies, to taste

2 tbsp tomato purée

60 ml water

1 tsp salt

75 ml olive oil

2 garlic cloves, puréed in a mortar and
pestle with $1/4$ tsp salt

1 Roast the peppers and chillies in
the oven or under the grill. Remove
from the heat and place in a bowl.
Cover tightly with a plate and leave for
20–30 minutes. Peel and remove the
seeds and membranes. Rinse the flesh
and transfer to a food processor.

2 Add the tomato purée to the
processor, and process until smooth.

3 Combine the pepper mixture,
water and salt in a heavy-based,
non-stick frying pan and bring to a
simmer over a medium heat. Cook,
stirring, for about 10 minutes.
Gradually stir in the oil and garlic
and continue to simmer for 1–2
minutes, until the sauce is quite thick.
Remove from the heat, cool and
refrigerate before serving.

TZATZIKI

A garlicky cucumber and yoghurt combination that is one of Greece's most popular meze *dishes. Serve with warmed pita bread alongside other Greek dishes for a delicious lunch or on its own as a simple, healthy starter.*

SERVES 4–6

1 long cucumber, peeled and grated

375 ml strained Greek yoghurt

2–3 garlic cloves, puréed

1–2 tbsp chopped mint or dill

15 ml red-wine vinegar

30 ml olive oil

salt, to taste

1 Sprinkle the grated cucumber with salt, stir well and leave to stand for 30 minutes. Rinse the cucumber and squeeze out any water.

2 Toss the cucumber with the yoghurt and the remaining ingredients. Taste and adjust the salt and garlic to your liking. Refrigerate until ready to serve.

TUNISIAN CARROT SALAD

Known as ommok houria, *this is one of the most popular salads in Tunisia – a spicy blend of cooked carrots seasoned with caraway and harissa.*

MAKES ABOUT 500 ML

450 g carrots, peeled and thinly sliced

30 ml olive oil

2 garlic cloves, finely chopped

$^1/_2$ tsp salt, to taste

1 tsp ground caraway

$^1/_4$–$^1/_2$ tsp harissa

3 tbsp chopped fresh parsley

30 ml fresh lemon juice

50 g Mediterranean black olives, such as Kalamata

2 hard-boiled eggs, cut in wedges or slices

100 g tin tuna in oil, drained (optional)

black pepper, to taste

1 Steam the carrots, or simmer them in enough lightly salted water to cover, for 5–10 minutes until tender. Drain.

2 Heat the oil over a medium heat in a large, non-stick frying pan and add the carrots, garlic, salt, caraway and harissa. Stir together, for about 3 minutes, until the carrots are nicely coated with the mixture. Add the parsley, toss together and transfer to a salad bowl. Toss with the lemon juice and season to taste. Garnish with the olives, sliced eggs and tuna fish, if desired. Serve at room temperature.

BULGAR WHEAT AND PARSLEY SALAD

Also known as tabbouleh, *this is one of the most popular salads eaten in the Middle East. Serve it in a large bowl and use Cos lettuce leaves to scoop up the salad.*

SERVES 6

120 g fine bulgar wheat

250 g fresh flat-leaf parsley, finely chopped

25 g fresh mint, finely chopped (optional)

3 ripe tomatoes, diced

4 spring onions, finely chopped

150 ml lemon juice

90 ml olive oil

small Cos lettuce leaves, for serving

salt, to taste

1 Soak the bulgar wheat in enough boiling water to cover, for 20 minutes or until tender. Drain and squeeze dry. Place in a serving bowl.

2 Add the remaining ingredients to the bowl (except the lettuce leaves) and toss well. Season with salt to taste and place the lettuce leaves around, ready to serve.

BABA GANOUJ

This aubergine dip is popular throughout the Middle East. Serve with warmed pita bread and crudités.

MAKES ABOUT 500 ML

900 g aubergines

2 large garlic cloves, puréed in a mortar and pestle with $^1/_4$ tsp salt

30–60 ml fresh lemon juice

30 ml olive oil, plus more for greasing

30 ml natural yoghurt

45–60 ml tahini

salt and black pepper, to taste

1 Preheat the oven to 220°C. Cut the aubergine in half lengthways. Score down the middle without cutting through the skin, and place cut side down on an oiled baking sheet. Bake for 25–30 minutes, or until thoroughly softened. Transfer to a colander and allow to drain for about 20 minutes, or until it becomes cool enough to handle. Alternatively, grill until charred and softened.

2 Peel the aubergine, then blend the aubergine flesh and the remaining ingredients together in a food processor, or pound in a mortar and pestle, until smooth. Season to taste.

SPRING ONION PANCAKES

One of the most widely eaten foods in Korea, these filled pancakes, or pajon, *are served at markets and rest stops, in homes and from small street stands.*

SERVES 6

FOR THE BATTER

2 eggs, beaten

200 g plain flour

1 tsp salt

15 ml vegetable oil, plus extra for frying

250 ml water

FOR THE FILLING

12 spring onions, halved lengthways and cut into 5-cm pieces

1 large carrot or red pepper, cut into 5-cm matchsticks

100 g shrimp, peeled and deveined (optional)

32 tbsp snipped fresh chives (optional)

2–4 eggs, beaten

FOR THE DIPPING SAUCE

45 ml soy sauce

7.5 ml rice wine or cider vinegar

5 ml sesame oil

1 tsp toasted sesame seeds

1 spring onion, finely chopped

1/2 tsp crushed red pepper flakes
(optional)

1 Mix together the eggs, flour, salt, vegetable oil and enough water to make a medium-thin batter. Set aside to rest for 15–20 minutes.

2 Mix together the dipping sauce ingredients.

3 Heat a large griddle or heavy-based, non-stick frying pan over a medium heat. Brush with a small amount of oil. Ladle in enough batter to make a large pancake. Wait one minute, then sprinkle some of the onions, carrot or red pepper, shrimp and chives over the batter. Ladle on some of the additional beaten egg, filling the gaps between the vegetables. Wait for the egg to set then fold the cooked bits up over the pancake. Cook for 5–7 minutes, until the pancake is browned underneath.

4 Turn the pancake over; if it breaks up, just patch it back together – you will be breaking it up to serve it anyway. Cook for another 3–5 minutes, until cooked through and browned nicely. Transfer to a plate and break, or cut up into finger-food pieces, while you make the remaining pancakes. Serve with the dipping sauce.

SPINACH WITH SESAME DRESSING

This dish is my all-time favourite Japanese starter, and is very easy to make. You could also serve it as an accompaniment.

SERVES 4

450 g spinach, thoroughly rinsed

4 tbsp sesame seeds

1 tsp fruit sugar

10 ml soy sauce

45 ml dashi, chicken stock or water

salt, to taste

1 Bring a large pan of water to the boil, add 1 tbsp of salt and the spinach. Blanch for 10–20 seconds until the leaves just wilt. Transfer to a bowl of cold water using a large slotted spoon. Drain, and gently squeeze out any water. Chop coarsely.

2 To make the dressing, heat a frying pan over a medium heat and add the sesame seeds. Stir and shake the pan constantly. As soon as the seeds turn golden, transfer them to a mortar and pestle. Grind them until just crushed.

3 Transfer to a large bowl and add the sugar, soy sauce and the dashi, stock or water to the crushed seeds and grind together to blend thoroughly. Add the spinach to the dressing and stir using a wooden spoon – be careful not to bruise the spinach leaves. Divide the dressed spinach among 4 small plates or bowls to serve.

CAESAR SALAD

This is said to have been invented by a Tijuana restaurateur by the name of Caesar Cardini. It became a favourite in California, and then in restaurants all over the United States.

SERVES 6

FOR THE DRESSING

2 garlic cloves, puréed in a mortar and
pestle with 1/4 tsp salt

2–4 anchovy fillets, rinsed and finely
chopped

15 ml fresh lemon juice

5 ml Worcestershire sauce

125 ml extra-virgin olive oil

black pepper, to taste

FOR THE SALAD

200 g croutons made with Italian bread

2 small heads of Cos lettuce, preferably
the young, tender, inner leaves, washed
and broken into small pieces

2 large eggs

50 g grated or shaved Parmesan cheese

1 Mash the garlic paste and anchovies together. Stir in the lemon juice and Worcestershire sauce, whisk in the olive oil to obtain a thick, smooth dressing and season with pepper to taste.

2 Toss together the croutons and lettuce in a serving bowl. Bring a small pan of water to the boil, turn the heat to medium and add the eggs. Boil gently for 2 minutes, then drain and rinse with cold water. Crack open the eggs and scoop onto the lettuce. Add the dressing and toss. Sprinkle on the Parmesan and serve at once.

BRAISED RED CABBAGE

This traditional German recipe is best made a day in advance, and then gently reheated, to allow all the flavours to develop. It is especially good with pork dishes or sausages.

SERVES 4

2 rashers bacon, diced

1/2 medium onion, finely chopped

1 tbsp sugar

1 large tart apple, peeled, cored and chopped

900 g red cabbage, quartered, cored and shredded crossways

60 ml red-wine vinegar

250 ml water, as needed

salt, to taste

1 Heat the bacon over a low heat in a large frying pan or casserole until it renders its fat. Add the onion and cook for about 5 minutes, until tender. Add the sugar and cook for about 5 minutes until the mixture is golden, then add the apple. Cover and cook, stirring from time to time, for 3–4 minutes.

2 Add the cabbage to the pan. Toss to coat thoroughly with the bacon fat, then stir in the vinegar and toss together. Cover the pan and cook over a low heat for 10 minutes, or until the cabbage is bright pinkish purple. Add salt to taste and about three-quarters of the water. Cover, and simmer over a low-medium heat for 1–1¼ hours, stirring occasionally. Add more water if necessary. The cabbage should be very tender. Season with salt to taste before serving.

ARTICHOKE RAGOUT

This hearty vegetable stew from the Provence region of southern France can be served hot or cold – accompany with lots of French bread to soak up the mouthwatering juices.

SERVES 6

juice of 2 lemons

6 globe artichokes or 12–18 small purple artichokes

30 ml olive oil

2 medium onions (white ones if available), chopped

1 bulb of garlic, cloves separated, crushed and peeled

2 medium red peppers

900 g tomatoes, peeled, deseeded and chopped

1 tsp fresh thyme leaves

1 bay leaf

750 ml simmering water

4 tbsp chopped fresh parsley

salt and black pepper, to taste

1 Fill a medium-sized bowl with water and add half the lemon juice. Trim the stems off the artichokes and cut off the tops with a sharp knife. Trim off the spiny tips of the outer leaves with scissors, and rub the cut parts with the remaining lemon juice. Cut the artichokes into quarters, and gently scoop out the spiny chokes. Rub the cut sides with lemon juice, and place in the bowl of water.

2 Heat the oil in a large, heavy-based, non-stick frying pan or casserole dish over a medium heat and add the onions. Cook for about 5 minutes, stirring, until tender. Add the garlic, peppers and a little salt, and

stir together for about 5 minutes, until the garlic begins to colour and the peppers begin to soften. Add the tomatoes and cook, stirring often, for about 10 minutes, until the tomatoes have broken down a little and are fragrant. Season to taste.

3 Drain the artichokes and add to the pan with the thyme, bay leaf and 500 ml of the simmering water. Bring to a simmer, cover and simmer for 30 minutes. Check the mixture, and add the remaining water if the liquid has evaporated. Continue to simmer, covered, for another 15–30 minutes, until the artichokes are tender and the leaves come away easily. Stir in the parsley, and season to taste.

GREENS WITH RAISINS AND PINE NUTS

This dish is popular throughout the Mediterranean, where greens, raisins and pine nuts are part of the gastronomic landscape. In Provence, the mixture goes into a pastry case, which is then served as a dessert.

SERVES 4

50 g raisins or sultanas

700 g greens, such as kale or spinach, thick stems removed, leaves washed thoroughly

30 ml olive oil

2 large garlic cloves, finely chopped

50 g pine nuts

salt and black pepper, to taste

1 Soak the dried fruit in warm water for 10 minutes. Drain and pat dry.

2 Bring a large saucepan of water to

the boil, add about 1 tbsp of salt and the greens. Cook for just 1 minute then drain and rinse with cold water. Gently squeeze out the water and chop coarsely.

3   Heat the oil in a large, heavy-based, non-stick frying pan over a medium heat and add the garlic and pine nuts. Cook for about 1 minute until both ingredients begin to turn golden. Stir in the greens and the raisins or sultanas. Stir together, add salt and pepper to taste and cook, stirring, for 5 minutes, until the greens are tender and the ingredients nicely mixed together. Remove from the heat. Serve hot or at room temperature. This dish benefits from sitting for a while – reheat it gently to serve.

GEORGIAN CHEESE BREAD

This is the ubiquitous fast food of Georgia, available throughout the day in cafés all over the country.

MAKES 3 LOAVES

4 tsp easy-blend dried yeast

30 ml lukewarm water

^{1}/$_2$ tsp honey

175 ml lukewarm milk

50 g unsalted butter, at room temperature

^{1}/$_4$ tsp ground coriander seeds

1^1/$_2$ tsp salt

375 g unbleached white flour, plus extra for kneading

450 g feta cheese, crumbled

450 g reduced-fat cottage cheese

3 eggs

1 tbsp butter, melted

oil or butter, for greasing

1   Dissolve the yeast in the water and add the honey and lukewarm milk. Leave to stand for 5 minutes. Add the butter and ground coriander seed. Mix together the flour and 1^1/$_2$ tsp salt, and gradually stir in. Turn onto a lightly floured board and knead for 10

minutes, until smooth and elastic. Form into a ball. Lightly oil or butter a bowl and place the dough in the bowl. Cover, and set aside for 1^1/$_2$–2 hours to rise until doubled in size.

2   Meanwhile prepare the filling. Combine the feta and cottage cheese in a food processor and blend until smooth. Add the eggs and remaining salt and blend together well.

3   Punch down the risen dough, cover and leave to rise again for about 45 minutes until doubled in size. Punch down the dough and divide it into 3 equal pieces.

4   Preheat the oven to 190°C. Roll out each piece of dough into a circle, about 30 cm in diameter, on a lightly floured board. Oil 3 x 20 cm cake tins. Place a round of dough in each tin. Place a third of the cheese mixture in the centre of each piece of dough. Fold an edge of the dough in over the filling, then turn the tin clockwise and fold another edge over the dough so that it forms a seal with the first edge. Continue folding the dough over the filling, turning the tin, until the filling is completely covered. Pinch the dough in the centre and then pull and twist into a topknot to seal. Repeat with the other tins, then set aside to rest for 10 minutes.

5   Brush each bread with melted butter, and bake in the oven for 45 minutes, or until browned. Remove from the tins and serve hot.

PIROGI

Pirogi are filled dumplings that are served throughout Russia and Poland. They can be filled with a number of ingredients – here is a recipe for a mushroom filling.

MAKES 48 DUMPLINGS

FOR THE DOUGH

2^1/$_2$ tsp dried yeast

60 ml warm water

250 ml lukewarm milk

100 g unsalted butter, diced

1 tsp salt

2 tsp sugar

2 eggs

750 g flour

1 egg, beaten

oil or butter, for greasing

MUSHROOM FILLING

25 g dried mushrooms

boiling water, to cover

50 g butter

1 large or 2 medium onions, finely chopped

2 garlic cloves, finely chopped

550 g wild or cultivated mushrooms (or a combination), trimmed, wiped clean and finely chopped

4 tbsp finely chopped fresh parsley

2 tbsp finely chopped fresh dill

2 hard-boiled eggs, finely chopped

salt and black pepper, to taste

1   To make the dough, dissolve the dried yeast in the warm water. Combine the milk and butter, and stir them into the yeast mixture. Add the salt, sugar and eggs, and mix together well. Add enough flour to make a soft but workable dough. Turn onto a floured surface and knead until smooth and elastic. Shape into a ball and place in a lightly greased bowl, rounded side down. Turn the dough over, cover and set aside to rise for about 1^1/$_2$ hours, until doubled in size.

2   To make the filling, place the dried mushrooms in a bowl and pour on the water. Leave to sit for 15–30 minutes, until softened. Drain through a cheesecloth-lined sieve. Rinse the mushrooms, squeeze dry in a cloth and chop finely.

3   Heat the butter over a medium heat in a heavy frying pan and add the onion. Cook for about 5 minutes, until tender. Add the garlic and stir together for another minute, then add the fresh and the dried mushrooms, as well as a generous amount of salt and pepper.

Cook, stirring often, until the mushrooms have softened and all the liquid in the pan has evaporated. Remove from the heat, stir in the remaining ingredients and season to taste. Allow to cool slightly.

4 Knead the dough, and divide into 48 equal-sized pieces. Cover with a cloth, and one at a time, roll each piece into a circle about 9 cm in diameter. Place a tablespoon of the filling on each piece of dough, bring the edges up and over the filling and pinch together firmly. Shape each dumpling into a half-moon by gently pinching along the middle.

5 Place the dumplings on a lightly greased baking sheet and cover with a damp cloth. Set aside to rise for about 40 minutes, until doubled in size. Meanwhile preheat the oven to 180°C. Brush each dumpling with beaten egg. Bake for 20 minutes, or until golden. Serve warm.

SPANOKOPITTA

This is just one version of the popular Greek pie made with spinach.

SERVES 6

1 kg fresh spinach, stems removed and leaves washed

30 ml olive oil, plus extra for greasing the filo pastry

3 large leeks, white part only, cleaned and thinly sliced

4 tbsp flat-leaf parsley, leaves only, chopped

2 tbsp chopped fresh rosemary

4 tbsp chopped fresh dill

1½ tsp fresh thyme leaves

3 eggs, beaten

170 g feta cheese, crumbled

¼ tsp freshly grated nutmeg

9 sheets filo pastry

1 egg white, lightly beaten

salt and black pepper, to taste

1 Wilt the spinach over a medium-high heat in a large, non-aluminium frying pan in the water left on the leaves after washing. Transfer to a colander and press out as much water as possible. When the spinach is cool enough to handle, wrap it in a cloth and squeeze out more water. Chop finely and set aside.

2 Preheat the oven to 190°C. Heat the olive oil in a frying pan over a medium heat and add the leeks. Cook for about 10 minutes, stirring often, until softened and just beginning to brown. Add the spinach and stir until it is coated with oil. Remove from the heat.

3 Add the beaten eggs, feta cheese and nutmeg to the spinach. Season well.

4 Brush a 25–30 cm pie dish with olive oil and layer in 4 sheets of filo pastry, brushing each sheet with olive oil before adding the next, placing them not quite evenly on top of each other so that the edges overlap the sides of the dish all around. Top with the spinach mixture. Fold the edges of the pastry over the spinach and brush them with olive oil. Layer the remaining pastry over the top, brush each sheet with olive oil and crimp the edges into the sides of the pan.

5 Brush the top with the beaten egg white. Pierce the top of the pie in several places with a sharp knife. Bake for 45–50 minutes, or until the top is golden brown.

CHERRY PILAF

This is a beautiful pilaf. The cherries 'bleed' into the rice, giving it a purplish hue. It goes nicely with grilled meats, poultry and fish. In Turkey it is traditionally made with sour cherries.

SERVES 6

250 g plus 2 heaped tbsp long-grain or basmati rice

25 g butter

175 g cherries, washed and pitted

1 tsp sugar

1½ tsp crushed caraway or fennel seeds

500 ml water

¾–1 tsp salt, to taste

1 Rinse the rice until the water runs clear. Drain well.

2 Melt the butter in a large, heavy-based saucepan and add the cherries and sugar. Cook for 2–3 minutes, stirring carefully. Stir in the caraway or fennel seeds and the rice, and cover with the water. Add the salt and bring to the boil. Boil for 2 minutes. Reduce the heat and simmer, uncovered, for 10–15 minutes, until almost all of the water has been absorbed.

3 Remove from the heat, cover with a clean cloth, then a tight-fitting lid and leave to steam for 20–25 minutes or until the rice is tender. Fluff with a fork. Serve with grilled or roasted chicken, fish or meat.

IRANIAN HERB OMELETTE

This green herb omelette is a symbol of fruitfulness, and a traditional New Year's dish in Iran. Eating the omelette is meant to bring prosperity and happiness.

SERVES 6

10 large eggs

¾ tsp baking powder

1 tsp flour

1 tbsp barberries (optional)

25 g chopped walnuts

50 g chopped fresh parsley

25 g fresh chives or spring onions, chopped

15 g fresh coriander, chopped

25 g fresh dill, chopped

30 ml olive oil or butter

salt and black pepper to taste

1 Beat the eggs in a bowl and stir in the remaining ingredients except for the oil or butter. Set aside for

15–30 minutes.

2 Heat the oil or butter over a medium-high heat in a heavy-based, non-stick frying pan, about 30 cm in diameter. Spoon a bit of egg into the pan and if it sizzles and cooks at once, the pan is ready. Pour in the egg and shake the pan gently to coat it. Lift up the edges of the omelette with a spatula to let the eggs run underneath during the first few minutes of cooking. Turn the heat down to low, cover and cook for 10 minutes, shaking the pan gently every once in a while. From time to time, remove the lid and loosen the bottom of the omelette with a spatula, tilting the pan so that the bottom doesn't burn. It will, however, turn a deep, golden brown. The eggs should be just about set. Meanwhile, preheat a grill to high.

3 Finish cooking the omelette under a grill for 2–3 minutes, watching very carefully to make sure the top doesn't burn (it should brown slightly, and it will puff up). Remove from the heat, shake the pan to make sure the omelette isn't sticking and set aside to cool for 5–15 minutes. Loosen the edges with a spatula. Carefully slide from the pan on to a large, round plate. Serve warm or at room temperature.

STIR-FRIED CHINESE BROCCOLI

Bok choy and spinach can be cooked using the same seasonings and method as the one used here.

SERVES 4

900 g Chinese broccoli

30 ml groundnut or vegetable oil

2 garlic cloves, finely chopped

1 tbsp grated fresh ginger

$^1/_2$ tsp coarse sea salt

$^1/_4$ tsp sugar

60 ml unsalted chicken stock, vegetable stock or water

1 tbsp Chinese sesame oil (optional)

1 Trim the ends of the broccoli stems and cut diagonally into 5-cm pieces. If the florets are very large, separate them into pieces, otherwise leave the florets and leaves intact.

2 Bring a large pan of water to the boil, add a tablespoon of salt and the broccoli. Once the water comes back to the boil, cook for just 30 seconds. Remove at once, using a slotted spoon, and plunge into a bowl of ice-cold water for 30 seconds, then drain.

3 Heat the oil over a medium-high heat in a large, heavy, non-stick frying pan or wok and add the garlic and ginger. Stir for 1 minute, until they begin to colour. Stir in the greens, salt, sugar and stock or water. Cook, stirring, for another minute, until the greens are tender but still crisp. Taste and adjust the seasoning. Remove from the heat, stir in the sesame oil if using and transfer to a warm plate.

MEE GORENG WITH PRAWNS

This is a Malaysian dish, with origins in North India, and there are many different versions served around the country.

SERVES 4–6

225 g turnip greens or mustard greens, cleaned, thick stem end discarded and the rest cut into 2.5-cm lengths, the leaves coarsely chopped

225 g egg noodles

30 ml vegetable or groundnut oil, plus 15 ml more as needed

2 eggs, lightly beaten with a little salt

15 ml soy sauce

$^1/_2$ tsp salt

1 tsp sugar

2 tbsp tomato purée

1 tsp red chilli paste or sauce

125 g tofu, cut into 5-mm slices

1 red onion, chopped

2 garlic cloves, finely chopped

2-cm piece of fresh ginger, peeled and grated or finely chopped

1 large tomato, diced

125 g medium prawns, shelled, deveined and halved lengthways

125 g beansprouts

4 tbsp chopped fresh coriander, to serve

1 lime, cut in wedges, for serving

salt, to taste

1 Bring 4 L salted water to the boil in a large pan and add the greens. Cook for 30 seconds and then remove using a slotted spoon. Immediately plunge into a bowl of cold water. Drain, and set aside.

2 Bring the water back to the boil, add the noodles and cook following the packet instructions. Drain the noodles in a colander and rinse with cold water. Shake off any excess water and set aside.

3 Heat 5 ml of the oil over a medium-high heat in a medium-sized, non-stick frying pan until a drop of egg sizzles upon contact. Add the eggs. Tilt the pan to coat it. Cook for 2–3 minutes, and as soon as the omelette is cooked, remove it from the pan. Roll up and slice thinly. Set aside.

4 In a small bowl, mix together the soy sauce, salt, sugar, tomato purée and the chilli paste or sauce. Stir the mixture to dissolve the sugar and salt, and set aside.

5 Heat a wok or large, non-stick frying pan over a medium-high heat and add the remaining oil and the tofu. Cook, stirring, until the tofu begins to brown, then add the onion, garlic and ginger. Cook, stirring constantly, for about 30 seconds or until the garlic and ginger are lightly coloured and fragrant. Add the tomato and increase the heat slightly. Stir for about 2–3 minutes, until the tomato begins to break down.

6 Add the prawns and blanched greens and cook, stirring, for 2–3 minutes, until the prawns turn pink and the greens are crisp but still tender. Add the noodles and soy sauce mixture and stir together to coat the noodles. Add the shredded egg and beansprouts, toss together quickly and remove from the heat. Sprinkle on the coriander and serve, with lime wedges on the side to squeeze over.

COOKED BLACK BEANS IN BROTH

Throughout central and southern Mexico, black beans are standard fare and are absolutely delicious. They are traditionally seasoned with a herb called epazote.

SERVES 6

450 g black beans, washed and picked over

2 L water

1 medium onion, chopped

4 garlic cloves, finely chopped

2 sprigs epazote

salt, to taste

1 Soak the beans in the water for at least 6 hours.
2 Place the beans and their soaking water in a large, heavy-based pan. Add enough water to cover by about 5 cm and bring to the boil. Skim off any foam, then add the onion, half the garlic and the epazote. Reduce the heat, cover and simmer for 1 hour.
3 Add 2 tsp of salt and the remaining garlic. Continue to simmer for another hour or until the beans are tender and the broth is thick and fragrant. Taste and adjust salt. Leave to stand overnight for the best flavour and reheat to serve.

CHILEAN BEAN AND WINTER SQUASH STEW

This hearty Chilean dish, known as porotos granados, *always includes three kinds of bean, although the types can vary.*

SERVES 6

225 g dried white beans

225 g dried pinto beans

2 L water

30 ml olive oil

1 medium onion, chopped

1 tbsp sweet paprika

3 large garlic cloves, finely chopped

1 bay leaf

700 g fresh pumpkin or winter squash, peeled and cut into cubes

225 g fresh or frozen lima beans

4 medium tomatoes, peeled, seeded and chopped

2 corn cobs, kernels removed

2 tbsp chopped fresh basil or parsley

salt and black pepper, to taste

1 Soak the dried beans in separate bowls in 3 times their volume of water for 6 hours or overnight. Drain.
2 Combine the dried beans and the water in a large pan and bring to the boil. Cover, and simmer for 45–60 minutes, or until tender. Add salt to taste and set aside.
3 Heat the oil over a medium heat in a large, heavy pan and add the onion. Cook for about 5 minutes, until the onion is just tender, and stir in the paprika. Cook, stirring, for a few minutes, and add the garlic. Stir together for about half a minute and add all but 250 ml of the cooked beans with their cooking liquid, the bay leaf, squash, lima beans and the tomatoes. Bring to the boil, season with salt, reduce the heat and cover. Simmer for about 30 minutes or until the squash and beans are tender. Add the corn kernels and simmer, uncovered, for about 5 minutes, until the corn

is tender. Stir in the basil or parsley, and season to taste.
4 Blend the reserved beans in a blender or food processor, or mash them in a mortar and pestle. Stir into the stew. Heat through and serve hot with cornbread.

RICE COOKED IN COCONUT MILK

This dish is served all over Colombia and is also popular in north-eastern Brazil, where it is called 'widow's rice'. It can be a sweet or savoury dish. Use as an accompaniment or on its own as a comforting snack or dessert.

SERVES 6

750 ml coconut milk

375 g rice

$^1/_2$–$^3/_4$ tsp salt for savoury rice; $^1/_4$ tsp salt for sweet rice

1 tbsp sugar (for sweet rice)

1 Bring the coconut milk to the boil in a medium-sized saucepan. Stir in the rice, salt and sugar, if using, cover, then reduce the heat to low and simmer for 20 minutes, or until the coconut milk has just about been absorbed by the rice.
2 Remove from the heat, place a clean cloth between the pan and the lid and leave to stand without removing the lid for 10 minutes. Fluff with a fork before serving.

FISH AND SEAFOOD

GRAVLAX

A traditional cured salmon dish from Scandinavia that is popular all over the world. It is best served with thin slices of pumpernickel bread and lemon wedges.

SERVES 6–8

225 g salmon fillets, skin on

3 tbsp coarse sea salt

3 tbsp fruit sugar

30 ml vodka or aquavit

1 tbsp coarsely crushed black peppercorns

50 g chopped fresh dill

1   Score each salmon fillet on the skin side, making several diagonal cuts about 3 mm deep. Combine the salt and sugar, and sprinkle 5 tsp over the bottom of a large baking dish.

2   Place one salmon fillet, skin-side down, in the dish. Sprinkle with half the vodka or aquavit, then sprinkle with the peppercorns. Sprinkle with 4 tsp of the salt and sugar mixture, and spread half the dill over the fillet in an even layer.

3   Rub 4 tsp of the salt and sugar mixture over the flesh side of the remaining fillet. Place this, skin-side up, on top of the first fillet. Rub the remaining mixture over the skin.

4   Cover the salmon with a sheet of greaseproof paper, then some aluminium foil. Place a flat surface, such as a chopping board, on top and weigh it down with about 2 kg – tins of food are ideal. Refrigerate for 48 hours. Check after 5–6 hours and drain off any liquid that has accumulated in the dish. Check and drain every 12 hours. Turn the salmon over and chill

for another 48 hours, turning twice during this period.

5   To serve, remove the skin and slice the fish thinly. Sprinkle with the remaining dill.

MUSSELS STEAMED IN WHITE WINE

Moules marinières, served with French fries, is one of the best meals to eat in Brussels, as well as in northern France.

SERVES 4–6

2.5 kg mussels (about 16 per person)

3 tbsp salt or vinegar

500 ml dry white wine

1 small onion or 4 shallots, finely chopped

2–3 garlic cloves, finely chopped

1 small bay leaf

4 sprigs fresh parsley

6 whole peppercorns

1 tsp fresh thyme leaves

25 g unsalted butter

3 tbsp chopped fresh parsley, to garnish

1   Inspect each mussel carefully and discard any that have opened or have cracked shells. Remove the beards. If the mussels are very sandy, scrub them with a brush. Place in a bowl large enough so the mussels can be covered with water, fill the bowl with cold water and rinse several times by pouring out the water and refilling. Drain any water from the bowl, add 3 tbsp of salt or vinegar, and fill with clean water. Leave to stand for 15 minutes. Rinse thoroughly and repeat.

2   Combine the wine, onion or shallots, garlic, bay leaf, parsley, peppercorns and thyme in a large

pan that will hold all of the mussels. Bring to the boil and cook for 2 minutes. Add the mussels and cover tightly. Cook for 5 minutes, or until the shells have opened, shaking the pan once or twice.

3   Spoon the mussels into wide soup bowls, discarding any that have not opened during cooking. Strain the broth from the pan through a fine-meshed sieve. Return the broth to a clean pan and heat gently for about 2 minutes. Add the butter to the broth, and when it has melted, spoon the broth over the mussels. Sprinkle with the parsley to serve.

CLAMS IN A CATAPLANA

A cataplana *is a cooking vessel with a hinged lid that clamps shut, which is commonly used in Portugal. Any pan with a tight-fitting lid will work.*

SERVES 4

1.25 kg very small clams

3 tbsp salt or vinegar

30 ml olive oil

1 medium onion, very thinly sliced

2–3 large garlic cloves, finely chopped

2 small dried red chillies, seeded and crumbled

50 g Spanish or Portuguese chorizo sausage, finely diced

pinch of paprika

450 g tomatoes, chopped

25 g smoked ham, Parma ham or lean bacon, finely diced

125 ml dry white wine

2 tbsp chopped fresh parsley, to serve

salt, to taste

1 Scrub the clams well and discard any that are cracked or open. Place in a large bowl and fill with water. Add the salt or vinegar and leave to stand for 1 hour. Drain and rinse well, then cover with water and leave for another 30 minutes. Drain and rinse well.

2 Heat the oil over a medium heat in a large-lidded saucepan and add the onion. Cook, stirring, for about 5 minutes, until tender, and add the garlic, chillies, sausage and paprika. Stir together for about a minute, then add the tomatoes with their juice. Cook, uncovered, for about 20 minutes, until the tomatoes have cooked down and are fragrant.

3 Stir in the smoked ham or bacon, stir well, cover and simmer for another 15–20 minutes, stirring occasionally, until the mixture is very fragrant.

4 Stir the wine into the tomato mixture and bring to a simmer. Add the clams, cover tightly and steam for about 10–20 minutes, stirring once, until the clams open up. Discard any that have not opened. Taste and add salt if necessary. Sprinkle with the parsley to serve.

TURKISH GRILLED SWORDFISH WITH DILL SAUCE

The typical marinade for grilled fish in Turkey is a mixture of onion juice, lemon or sumac juice, olive oil and bay leaves. The fish is marinated, grilled and served with a thick, delicious cool sauce.

SERVES 6

6 x 170–225 g swordfish steaks

FOR THE MARINADE

750 g onions, peeled and grated

2 tsp salt

60 ml fresh lemon or sumac juice

60 ml olive oil

8 bay leaves, crumbled

FOR THE SAUCE

250 ml thick-set yoghurt

30–60 ml fresh lemon juice

3 garlic cloves, puréed in a mortar and pestle with $\frac{1}{4}$ tsp salt

3 tbsp chopped fresh dill

salt and black pepper, to taste

1 To make the marinade, first crush the onions with the salt in a mortar and pestle, or blend to a pulp in a food processor. Leave to stand for 10–15 minutes. Sieve over a bowl to extract the juice. Measure out 125 ml of the onion juice. Mix with the other marinade ingredients, and toss with the fish. Cover and refrigerate for 1–2 hours, stirring occasionally to redistribute the marinade. If cooking the fish on the barbeque, light it now.

2 Mix together all the ingredients for the sauce. Season to taste with salt and pepper.

3 If cooking the fish under the grill, preheat it to high. Brush the fish on both sides with the marinade, and cook for 4–5 minutes on each side. Serve at once with the sauce.

CRAB CAKES

This is a quintessential American dish. Maryland residents claim it as their own, but it is popular all over coastal America.

SERVES 4

15 ml olive oil

$\frac{1}{2}$ red pepper, finely chopped

2 spring onions, trimmed and finely chopped

1 garlic clove, finely chopped

450 g crab meat

1 egg, beaten

50 g fresh breadcrumbs

60 ml mayonnaise

1 tsp mustard powder

pinch of cayenne pepper, optional

1 tsp crushed cumin seeds, optional

2 tbsp chopped fresh parsley

50 g dry breadcrumbs

25g butter

15–30 ml vegetable oil

salt and black pepper, to taste

lemon wedges, to serve

1 Heat the olive oil over a medium heat in a heavy, non-stick frying pan and add the red pepper and the spring onions. Cook, for about 5 minutes, until just about tender. Stir in the garlic and cook for 1 minute more. Remove from the heat.

2 Remove any stray bits of shell and cartilage from the crab meat. Squeeze gently to remove any excess liquid. Mix the egg, fresh breadcrumbs and mayonnaise together with the red pepper mixture, mustard, salt, pepper, cayenne and cumin seeds, if using. Add the crab meat and parsley and mix together. If the mixture seems dry and will not hold together, add a little extra mayonnaise. Season to taste.

3 Shape the mixture into 8 small or 4 large patties. Place the dry breadcrumbs on a plate and dip the cakes into them, coating both sides. Transfer the crab cakes to a plate and cover with greaseproof paper. Refrigerate for 1–2 hours.

4 Heat half the butter with half the vegetable oil over a medium-high heat in a large, heavy frying pan. When hot, add the cakes, a couple at a time, and cook for about 3–5 minutes on each side, until brown. Drain on kitchen paper. Keep warm in a low oven while you cook the remaining cakes. Serve with lemon wedges.

RED SNAPPER A LA VERACRUZANA

Snapper with a tangy tomato, olive and caper sauce is one of the best-known Mexican fish dishes. Its popularity is easy to understand as it has so many wonderful savoury flavours.

SERVES 6

6 x 175 g snapper fillets

juice of 2 limes

1.3 kg tomatoes

30 ml olive oil

8 garlic cloves; 3 left whole, 5 finely chopped

2 medium onions, chopped or thinly sliced

20 green olives, pitted; 10 chopped, 10 halved lengthways

2 tbsp capers, rinsed; 1 tbsp chopped, 1 tbsp left whole

2–3 pickled jalapeño chillies, stemmed, seeded and sliced in strips

20 ml pickling juice from the chillies

4 tbsp chopped fresh parsley

4 bay leaves

2.5-cm piece cinnamon stick

2 sprigs fresh rosemary

2 sprigs fresh marjoram or thyme

$\frac{1}{2}$ tsp dried oregano

$\frac{1}{2}$ tsp coarsely crushed black peppercorns

salt, to taste

1   Rinse the fillets, toss with the lime juice and a little salt and refrigerate for 1 hour while you prepare the sauce.
2   Plunge the tomatoes into boiling water, rinse with cold water, peel and cut in half. Set a sieve over a bowl and squeeze the seeds and juice out of the tomatoes. Chop the tomato flesh and set aside.
3   Heat the oil over a medium heat in a large, heavy-bottomed casserole dish that will also hold the fish fillets in a single layer. Add the whole garlic cloves and cook, stirring for about 5 minutes, until browned. Remove the garlic and discard. Add the onion and

cook for about 5–8 minutes, until it begins to colour. Add the chopped garlic and stir together for a minute, until the garlic smells fragrant. Stir in the tomatoes and their juice, and cook, stirring often, for 10 minutes, until they have cooked down slightly.
4   Add the chopped olives, the chopped capers, the jalapeños and their pickling juice, 2 tbsp of the chopped parsley, the bay leaves, cinnamon, rosemary, marjoram or thyme and the oregano. Add about $\frac{1}{2}$ tsp salt to taste, reduce the heat to low, cover and simmer, stirring occasionally, for 20–30 minutes. The tomatoes should cook down, but the sauce should be liquid enough to poach the fish. Remove from the heat, taste and adjust the salt.
5   Remove the fish from the fridge 15 minutes before you wish to cook it. Bring the sauce to a simmer over a medium heat and add the fish fillets. Make sure they are covered with the sauce. Cover and simmer for 4 minutes. Turn the fillets over and simmer for another 3–4 minutes (depending on the thickness of the fish), or until it flakes easily when tested with a fork.
6   Remove from the heat and serve, topping each fillet with a generous amount of sauce, and garnishing with the remaining parsley, whole capers and halved olives. Serve with rice.

CARIBBEAN CURRIED PRAWNS

Curried prawns or crab are the national dishes of Trinidad and Tobago, legacies of the Native Americans who were brought over to work the sugar plantations after emancipation. Traditionally, they are served with dumplings, but rice also makes a good accompaniment.

SERVES 4

15 ml vegetable oil

1 medium onión or 1 bunch spring onions, chopped

2 garlic cloves, finely chopped

1 tbsp grated fresh ginger

2 tbsp curry powder

375 ml coconut milk

450 g medium prawns, shelled and deveined

2 tbsp chopped fresh coriander

fresh lime wedges, for garnish

salt and black pepper, to taste

1   Heat the oil over a low-medium heat in a large, heavy, non-stick frying pan. Add the onion or spring onions and cook, stirring, for about 5 minutes, until tender. Add the garlic and ginger and continue to cook gently for another 1–2 minutes, until fragrant but not browned.
2   Stir in the curry powder and cook, stirring, for 1 minute. Add the coconut milk, season to taste and bring to the boil. Reduce the heat and simmer, stirring, for about 5 minutes, until it has thickened slightly. Stir in the prawns and cook for about 5 minutes, until they are pink and cooked through. Season to taste.
3   Sprinkle with coriander and serve garnished with the lime wedges to squeeze over.

MEAT AND POULTRY

VEAL PORKOLT

This is a delicious stew-like dish from Hungary.

SERVES 4–6

4 bacon rashers, diced

1 large onion, finely chopped

1 heaped tbsp paprika

2 garlic cloves, finely chopped

1 tsp salt

900 g lean veal, cut into 2.5-cm cubes

2 plum tomatoes, peeled and diced

1 green pepper, cored and diced

1 Heat the bacon over a low-medium heat in a heavy flameproof casserole dish and add the onion. Cook for about 10–15 minutes, stirring, until tender and light brown. Remove from the heat and mix in the paprika, garlic, salt and veal. Stir together, cover and place over a very low heat. Cook, checking every few minutes, for 10–15 minutes. If the meat begins to stick to the casserole, add a few tablespoons of water, stir together and cover.

2 Add the tomatoes and green pepper and continue to cook for 20–30 minutes, or until the veal is tender. Check every few minutes and add small amounts of water if the stew begins to stick.

3 When the meat is cooked, uncover and simmer the sauce in the casserole over a low heat for 2–3 minutes, until you have a rich, dark red-gold gravy. Serve with potatoes and seasonal vegetables.

SAUERBRATEN

This is a Rhineland sauerbraten, distinguished by its sweet and sour sauce and the presence of sultanas.

SERVES 8–10

FOR THE MARINADE

2.5 kg boned loin or shoulder of pork, rolled and tied

750 ml red wine

750 ml water

1 large onion, sliced

2 bay leaves

2 large garlic cloves, crushed

8 peppercorns

1 large carrot, sliced

salt and black pepper, to taste

FOR THE ROAST

25 g butter

4 rashers bacon, diced

2 large onions, sliced

1 bay leaf

6 cloves

1 large parsnip, cored and sliced

1 large carrot, sliced

FOR THE GRAVY

25 g butter

25 g flour

25 g sugar

30 ml lemon juice

100 g sultanas, soaked in warm water

1 Rub the pork with a little salt. Combine the wine, water, onion, bay leaves, garlic, peppercorns and carrot in a saucepan and bring to the boil. Reduce the heat and simmer for 5 minutes. Remove from the heat and allow to cool to room temperature. Place the pork in a deep, close-fitting bowl then pour the marinade over. If the meat is not thoroughly submerged in the marinade, add equal amounts of water and wine until it is. Cover tightly and refrigerate for 3–5 days, turning the meat a few times each day. Remove the meat from the marinade. Strain and reserve the marinade. Dry the meat thoroughly with kitchen paper.

2 Heat the butter over a medium-low heat in a large, heavy casserole and cook the bacon for 5 minutes. Add the meat and slowly brown for about 15–20 minutes, using the string to turn it, until golden brown on all sides. Remove the meat from the pot and add the onions. Cook for 10–15 minutes, stirring often, until the onions are golden brown.

3 Return the meat to the pot, placing it on top of the onions. Add enough marinade to reach halfway up the sides of the meat. Add the bay leaf and cloves, the parsnip and carrot, bring to the boil, cover the pot tightly and reduce the heat to very low. Simmer for 3$\frac{1}{2}$–4 hours, turning the meat two or three times. Add more marinade as necessary to keep the meat half submerged. The meat is cooked when it can be easily pierced with a fork or skewer.

4 Remove the meat to a warm plate and strain the liquid in the casserole. Skim off any excess fat and return all but 375 ml to the casserole. Melt the butter in a saucepan over a low heat and stir in the flour and sugar. Cook, stirring constantly, until the mixture turns a caramel colour. This will take at least 10–15 minutes. It's important to keep the heat low and to keep stirring so that the mixture does not burn.

5 Gradually stir in the reserved stock and whisk briskly until well amalgamated. Stir back into the casserole with the remaining marinade. Add the lemon juice and raisins. Return the meat to the pot, cover, and simmer 10 minutes. Taste and adjust the seasonings.

6 Slice the meat on a serving plate. Pour some of the gravy on to the meat and serve the rest in a sauceboat.

FLEMISH BEEF AND BEER STEW

One of the most well-known Belgian dishes, this hearty stew makes a wonderful dish for a dinner party or for everyday eating. Serve it with steamed or mashed potatoes to soak up all the delicious juices.

SERVES 4

plain flour, salt and pepper for dredging meat
900 g boneless chuck steak, cut into 2.5-cm cubes
125 g bacon, diced
25 g butter
2 large onions, thinly sliced
1 tbsp brown sugar
15 ml cider vinegar
375 ml dark beer, preferably Belgian
a bouquet garni made with a bay leaf and a few sprigs of fresh parsley and thyme
2 thick slices country bread
1 tbsp Dijon mustard
salt and black pepper, to taste

1 Combine the flour, salt and pepper and lightly dredge the meat. Set aside.
2 Heat half the bacon over a low-medium heat in a large, heavy casserole dish until it renders its fat. Add half the butter and the onions and cook for about 10–15 minutes, stirring often, until tender and light brown.

Add the sugar and stir well.
3 Meanwhile, heat the remaining bacon over a medium-high heat in a large frying pan. When it is cooked, remove from the pan and set aside. Turn the heat to medium. Add the remaining butter and brown the meat, in batches, on all sides, and transfer to the casserole with the onions. Add the vinegar to the frying pan and deglaze, scraping all the caramelized meat juices from the bottom of the pan. Pour the scrapings into the casserole. Add the beer and bouquet garni, and simmer. Reduce the heat to very low, cover and simmer gently for 2¹/₂ hours, stirring from time to time. Taste and adjust the seasoning.
4 Spread the slices of bread with mustard and cut in half. Place, mustard-side down, on the surface of the stew. Cover, and continue to simmer for another 30 minutes.

ALSATIAN TARTE FLAMBÉE

This traditional pizza from the Alsace region of France is also known as flammekeuche. It has a paper-thin crust and a creamy cheese, onion and bacon topping, and it was originally baked in a wood-fire oven, although a very hot home oven will do just fine. The trick is to roll the dough as thin as possible.

MAKES 2 x 30 CM TARTES

FOR THE DOUGH
2 tsp easy-blend dried yeast
250 ml lukewarm water
1 tsp salt
up to 450 g unbleached white flour, plus extra for dusting

FOR THE TOPPING
25 g butter
2 medium onions, sliced into very thin rounds
225 g cottage or ricotta cheese
250 ml crème fraîche, sour cream or

natural yoghurt
250 g bacon, rinded and cut into slivers
salt and black pepper, to taste

1 To make the dough, dissolve the yeast in the water in a large mixing bowl and allow it to stand for a few minutes, until the mixture is creamy. Combine the salt with half the flour and stir into the yeast mixture. Fold in the remaining flour until you can turn the dough out on to a work surface. Flour the work surface, turn out the dough and knead for 10 minutes, adding flour as necessary. The dough should be elastic and slightly sticky. Clean and oil your bowl, place the dough in it, reverse the dough and cover the bowl tightly with plastic wrap. Leave the dough to rise until it is doubled in size, about 1¹/₂–2 hours. Punch down the dough and divide it into two pieces. Shape each piece into a ball and cover with a damp cloth.
2 While the dough is rising, make the topping. Heat the butter in a large frying pan over a medium heat and add the onion. Cook, stirring, for about 5 minutes, just until tender, and remove from the heat. Blend the cheese in a food processor until smooth, scraping down the sides once or twice. Add the crème fraîche, sour cream or yoghurt and blend together. Season and stir in the onions.
3 Preheat the oven to 230°C. Flour the work surface and the top of the dough to prevent sticking, then roll one piece of the dough out into a very thin round, about 30 cm in diameter. Place on a baking sheet or pizza pan. Spread half the cheese mixture over the dough and sprinkle on half the bacon. Repeat with the remaining dough. Season each tarte liberally with pepper and bake for 20–25 minutes, until crisp. Serve immediately.

POULET BASQUAISE

This is a classic recipe from the Basque region of France. Serve it over rice.

SERVES 4–6

2 kg chicken, jointed

30 ml vegetable oil

15 ml olive oil

2 large onions, chopped

2–4 mild chillies (anaheims are ideal), cored, seeded and cut in very thin strips or 1/2 tsp hot chilli flakes

900 g red peppers, cored, seeded and thinly sliced

6 garlic cloves, thinly sliced

900 g tomatoes, peeled, seeded and chopped

100 g unsmoked ham, such as Bayonne, thickly sliced and cubed

pinch of sugar

salt and black pepper, to taste

1   Rinse the chicken pieces and pat dry with kitchen paper. Season liberally with salt and pepper. Heat the vegetable oil in a large, preferably non-stick, frying pan over a high heat and brown the chicken pieces, in batches if necessary, on each side for about 5 minutes, until the pieces turn golden brown. Remove from the pan and drain on kitchen paper. Pour away any fat in the pan.

2   Reduce the heat to medium. Add the olive oil and onions. Cook, stirring, until tender, for about 5 minutes. Add the chillies, red peppers and garlic, season with salt and cook, stirring, until the peppers begin to soften, for about 10 minutes. Add the tomatoes, ham and sugar and stir together until the tomatoes begin to bubble. Return the chicken pieces to the pan. Cook for 45–60 minutes, stirring regularly. The peppers should be very soft and the chicken quite tender and beginning to fall off the bone. Season with salt and pepper to taste and serve over a plate of rice.

PAELLA VALENCIANA

Contrary to the popular image of paella, the authentic dish from Levante in Spain does not contain a mixture of meat and seafood. Often it contains snails, and the most traditional paellas contain rabbit.

SERVES 6

125 ml dry white wine

1/2 tsp saffron threads, crumbled

1 L chicken stock

1.5 kg rabbit or chicken, jointed

60 ml olive oil

1 small onion, chopped

1 small green pepper, chopped

1 small red pepper, chopped

5 garlic cloves, finely chopped

2 large ripe tomatoes, halved crossways, seeded and grated to the skin

2 tsp sweet paprika

750 g short- or medium-grain rice

100 g fresh or thawed frozen peas

450 g assorted fresh beans, such as lima, French, butter or borlotti

2 sprigs fresh rosemary

salt, to taste

1   Stir the wine and saffron into the chicken stock and place in a saucepan over a low heat.

2   Cut the rabbit or chicken pieces into small pieces. Salt lightly. Heat 45 ml of the oil over medium–high heat in a paella pan or large non-stick frying pan and sauté the rabbit or chicken pieces for 20 minutes or until completely browned. Remove the pieces from the pan and transfer to a plate or bowl.

3   Add the remaining oil to the pan and turn the heat down to medium. Add the onion and peppers. Cook for about 5 minutes, stirring, until tender. Add the garlic, stir for a further minute until fragrant, then stir in the tomatoes, paprika and rice. Stir to coat the rice, and mix in the peas, beans and meat.

4   Bring the chicken stock to the boil and pour over the rice. Simmer over a

medium heat for 10 minutes. Taste and add more salt if necessary. Add the rosemary. Simmer for a further 15 minutes until the liquid has evaporated and the rice is cooked through.

5   Remove from the heat, cover tightly with aluminium foil and leave to cool for 10 minutes before serving.

RAGÚ

There are probably as many different recipes for ragú as there are families in Italy – this one is from Emilia-Romagna.

MAKES 1 L

100 g boneless veal shoulder

250 g boneless lean beef (skirt, chuck or blade steak)

100 g boneless pork loin or mild Italian sausage

25 g Parma ham

30 ml olive oil

50 g pancetta, finely chopped

1 medium onion, finely chopped

1 medium celery stick, with leaves, finely chopped

1 small carrot, finely chopped

175 ml dry red wine

375 ml chicken or meat stock

250 ml milk

800 g tinned plum tomatoes, with half of the juice, crushed or coarsely chopped

salt and black pepper, to taste

1   Coarsely mince together the veal, beef, pork and Parma ham in a food processor or a meat grinder. Set aside.

2   Heat the oil in a large, heavy-based frying pan over a medium-high heat. Add the pancetta, onion, celery and carrot and cook for about 5–10 minutes, stirring, until the onion just begins to colour.

3   Stir the minced meats into the frying pan and turn the heat to medium. Cook for about 15 minutes, stirring and scooping up the meats, until the meat is just cooked through and there is no pink meat left. Transfer the mixture to a sieve set over a bowl or sink and give the sieve a shake to remove any excess fat. Then transfer the mixture to a large, heavy-based pan or casserole dish.

4 Add the wine to the frying pan and reduce it by half over a low-medium heat, stirring up any glaze from the bottom of the pan into the bubbling wine. This will take about 3–5 minutes. Stir the wine into the meat mixture and then place the saucepan over a medium heat.

5 Add 125 ml of the stock to the saucepan and bring to a simmer. Cook for about 8–10 minutes over a low-medium heat, stirring often, until the stock evaporates. Add another 125 ml of the stock and repeat. Stir in the remaining stock and the milk. Turn the heat to low, partially cover and simmer for 45–60 minutes, stirring often, until the milk is no longer visible.

6 Add the tomatoes and their juice and ¹/₂ tsp of salt, and stir together. Turn the heat to very low, so that the mixture is cooking at a very gentle simmer. Cook very slowly, partially covered, for 1¹/₂–2 hours, stirring often. The sauce should be thick and meaty when it is done. Season to taste with salt and pepper before serving.

RABBIT WITH TOMATOES, SAGE AND WHITE WINE

This recipe is based on one from Ischia, an island off the coast of Campania, and is by Carlo Middione in The Food of Southern Italy.

SERVES 4–6

30 ml olive oil

1.3 kg rabbit, cut into 10 pieces

100 g pancetta, cut into small pieces

1 onion, chopped

4 garlic cloves, finely chopped

10 cm sprig fresh rosemary

3 large sage leaves

900 g tomatoes, peeled and crushed

175 ml dry white wine

175 ml boiling water

salt and black pepper, to taste

1 Heat the oil in a large, heavy-based frying pan or casserole dish over a medium-high heat and brown the rabbit pieces for about 10 minutes until golden. Remove from the pan and drain on kitchen paper. Pour off any fat remaining in the pan.

2 Add the pancetta and onion to the pan and cook for about 5 minutes, stirring, until the pancetta is browned and the onion tender. Add the garlic, stir together for about 30 seconds and add the rosemary, sage, tomatoes and seasoning. Cook for about 10 minutes, stirring often, until the tomatoes begin to cook down and thicken.

3 Return the rabbit to the pan and add the wine. Stir together and cook over a medium-high heat for 20 minutes, or until the sauce is quite thick. Stir in the boiling water, season, reduce the heat to medium, cover partially and simmer, stirring occasionally, for 10–20 minutes, until the sauce is thick and the rabbit very tender. Remove from the heat, leave to rest for at least 10 minutes, adjust the seasoning and serve.

PERSIAN STEW WITH PEACHES

The flavours in this luscious stew are typical of the Persian taste for sweet and savoury.

SERVES 4

40 g butter or 45 ml vegetable oil

2 medium onions, thinly sliced

450 g veal, beef or lamb, cut in 2.5-cm cubes

1 tsp salt

¹/₂ tsp freshly ground black pepper

¹/₂ tsp cinnamon

750 ml water

60 ml fresh lemon juice

50 g sugar

1 tbsp flour

¹/₂ tsp ground saffron dissolved in 15 ml hot water

550 g firm, not quite ripe peaches, thinly sliced

salt and black pepper, to taste

1 Heat three-quarters of the butter or oil over a medium heat in a large, heavy, flameproof casserole dish and add the onions. Cook for 3–5 minutes, stirring, until translucent, then add the meat. Cook for a further 10 minutes, until the meat and onions are browned. Add the salt, pepper, cinnamon and water. Bring to a simmer, reduce the heat to low, cover and simmer for 2–3 hours, until the meat is very tender.

2 Mix together the lemon juice, sugar, flour and saffron. Stir into the meat. Cover, and simmer for another 20 minutes.

3 Meanwhile, heat the remaining oil or butter in a large, non-stick frying pan over a medium-high heat. Add the peaches and cook, stirring, until lightly browned, for about 3 minutes. Add to the meat, cover and simmer for another 20 minutes, or until the peaches and meat are tender. Taste and adjust the seasoning to serve.

BULGAR WHEAT AND LAMB KOFTAS

This is just one of many versions of the classic and ever-popular Middle Eastern meatball. Serve as meze or as a main dish with rice.

MAKES 36–48 MEATBALLS

175 g fine bulgar wheat

1 small white onion, coarsely chopped

450 g minced lamb or beef, or a combination

1 tsp ground cinnamon

1 tsp ground cumin

1 tsp ground allspice

30 ml water

4 tbsp finely chopped fresh parsley

2 tbsp finely chopped fresh mint

oil, for greasing

salt, to taste

1   Cover the bulgar wheat with boiling water and leave to soak for 15–20 minutes, until tender. Drain and squeeze out excess water.

2   Meanwhile, process the onion with 1 tsp salt in a food processor fitted with a steel blade. Remove and set aside. Place the meat in the food processor and process until smooth. Add the onion purée and the spices, blend together, and with the machine running, add the water. Process until smooth. Add the drained, squeezed dry bulgar wheat and the herbs, and process again until smooth. Season with salt.

3   Preheat the grill to high. Moisten your hands and form the meat mixture into small balls, about 2.5 cm in diameter. Keep your hands moistened so that the mixture doesn't stick. Place the balls on a lightly oiled baking sheet and cook for about 3–5 minutes, until nicely browned. Remove from the heat. Serve warm, over rice or with a yoghurt dip.

COUSCOUS WITH CHICKEN, LEMON AND OLIVES

This Moroccan dish has the most marvellous mixture of flavours.

SERVES 4

1 medium chicken about 1.6 kg, skin removed, cut into 8 pieces

$1/2$ tsp ground ginger

$1/2$ tsp ground black peppercorns

1 tsp cracked coriander seeds

pinch of crushed saffron threads

$1/2$ tsp ground cumin

$1/2$ tsp paprika

2 large garlic cloves, finely chopped

30 ml olive oil

750 ml water

1 large or 2 medium leeks, white and light green part only, thinly sliced

a few sprigs each fresh parsley and coriander

375 g couscous

625 ml water mixed with
$1/2$ tsp salt, or chicken stock

1 preserved lemon, quartered and cut into thick slices

juice of 1–2 lemons

4 tbsp green olives, pitted and halved

4 tbsp chopped fresh parsley

4 tbsp chopped fresh coriander

salt, to taste

1   Combine the chicken, all the spices, the garlic, $1/2$ tsp of salt and 15 ml of the olive oil in a large, flameproof casserole dish. Toss together, cover and leave to stand for 30–60 minutes.

2   Add the water to the casserole, and bring to the boil over a medium-high heat. Skim off any foam that rises with a slotted spoon. When you have skimmed away all the foam, add the leeks, parsley and coriander sprigs to the casserole, reduce the heat, cover and simmer gently for 30 minutes, until the chicken is just tender.

3   While the chicken is simmering, soak the couscous in the salted water or chicken stock, stirring occasionally with a wooden spoon, for 20 minutes, until tender. Transfer to a colander and steam for 10 minutes above the chicken.

4   Add the preserved lemon and the olives to the chicken. Continue to simmer for another 10–15 minutes, until the chicken is falling off the bone. Transfer the couscous to a large bowl or serving dish and toss with the remaining olive oil. Arrange the chicken pieces and the preserved lemons and olives on top of the couscous.

5   Bring the liquid in the casserole to

the boil and reduce by half. Stir in half the lemon juice and the herbs. Taste, and adjust the seasoning, adding lemon juice or salt if required. Pour this over the chicken to serve.

LAMB AND PRUNE TAGINE

This sweetly spiced tagine is a typical example of the Moroccan love of sweet and savoury flavours in the same dish.

SERVES 6

1.3 kg shoulder of lamb, cut into 5-cm pieces

2 tbsp unsalted butter

30 ml vegetable oil

1 cinnamon stick

1 tsp ground cinnamon

generous pinch of saffron threads

1 tsp ground ginger

2 small onions, finely chopped

360 g pitted prunes

4 tbsp sugar or clear honey

2 tbsp toasted sesame seeds

salt and black pepper, to taste

1   Trim the fat from the meat. Melt half the butter with the oil over a medium heat in a large, heavy, lidded casserole. Add the cinnamon stick, half the ground cinnamon, the saffron, ginger, onions, and meat. Cook the meat gently, turning on to each side for about 5 minutes, then add enough water to barely cover the meat. Bring to the boil, season with salt, reduce the heat, cover and simmer for 1 hour.

2   Add the prunes, the remaining cinnamon and the honey or sugar to the lamb. Continue to simmer for another 30 minutes, or until the prunes have swollen and the meat is very tender. Remove the meat and prunes.

3   Increase the heat and boil the sauce until it is thick. Stir in the remaining butter, and taste and adjust the seasoning. Stir the meat and prunes back into the sauce, heat through and transfer to an attractive, deep serving dish or platter (ideally a Moroccan tagine). Scatter the sesame seeds over the top and serve with couscous.

MOGHUL-BRAISED CHICKEN

Also known as mughalai korma*, this recipe, based on one in Julie Sahni's* Classic Indian Cooking*, is typical of northern Indian cooking.*

SERVES 4

45 ml vegetable oil

2 medium onions, finely chopped

3 garlic cloves, finely chopped

1¹/₂ tbsp finely chopped fresh ginger

12 green cardamom pods, slightly crushed in a mortar and pestle

1 tsp ground cloves

4 bay leaves

2 tsp ground coriander seeds

¹/₄ tsp cayenne pepper (to taste)

375 ml natural yoghurt

750 g boneless skinless chicken breasts, cut into strips

125 ml double cream

salt, to taste

1   Heat the oil over a medium heat in a large, heavy-based, non-stick frying pan and add the onions. Cook for about 7–10 minutes, stirring, until the onions begin to brown, then stir in the garlic and ginger. Cook, stirring, for another minute, and add the cardamom, cloves and bay leaves. Cook, stirring constantly, for about 5 minutes, until the cardamom pods are puffed and the bay leaves start to colour.

2   Add the coriander and cayenne pepper, stir together for a few seconds and add 30 ml of the yoghurt. Cook, stirring, until just about dry. Add another 30 ml of yoghurt and repeat. Continue to cook in this way until all of the yoghurt is used.

3   Stir in the chicken and cook for about 5 minutes, stirring and tossing, until the meat is no longer pink. Add 175 ml boiling water and 1 tsp of salt and mix well. Reduce the heat to medium-low and simmer for about 25 minutes, stirring from time to time, until the chicken is tender and coated with a thick sauce.

4   Stir in the cream and remove from the heat. Cover, and allow the dish to rest for an hour before serving. Reheat gently, taste and add more salt if necessary.

SZECHUAN-BRAISED TOFU WITH PORK

It's hard not to like this classic, spicy Szechuan dish, even if you think you don't like tofu. This one can be very quickly thrown together – serve it with rice or noodles for a speedy meal.

SERVES 2–4

225 g firm tofu, drained

30 ml groundnut oil

2 garlic cloves, finely chopped

2 tsp grated fresh root ginger

1 tbsp finely chopped spring onion, white part only

100 g minced pork

1 tsp chilli sauce or powder

¹/₂ tsp sugar

15 ml rice wine or dry sherry

1¹/₂ tbsp soy sauce

¹/₂ tsp salt

125 ml water or chicken stock

15 ml bean sauce

¹/₄–¹/₂ tsp ground Szechuan peppercorns

1¹/₂ tsp corn flour dissolved in 15 ml water

2 tbsp sliced spring onion, green part only, to garnish

1 tbsp chopped fresh coriander, to garnish

salt and black pepper, to taste

1   Blot the tofu dry with kitchen paper and cut into 1-cm cubes. Place in a

sieve while you cook the other ingredients.

2   Heat the oil over a medium-high heat in a wok or large, heavy frying pan. When a bit of garlic sizzles upon contact, add the garlic and ginger and stir-fry for a few seconds. Add the onion and pork, and stir-fry for 2–3 minutes, until there are no traces of pink and the meat is fragrant. Add the chilli sauce or powder, the sugar, wine or sherry, soy sauce, salt, stock or water and bean sauce, and bring to the boil. Reduce the heat to low, gently stir in the tofu, cover and simmer for 15 minutes, stirring from time to time.

3   Stir in the ground peppercorns. Taste and adjust the seasoning. Add the corn flour paste and stir until thick. Transfer to a warm serving dish, sprinkle the sliced green spring onions and the coriander over the top, and serve.

PORK ADOBO

Adobo is the national dish of the Philippines. Pork is the most popular version, but the technique and tangy sauce are used with other meats and fish.

SERVES 4–6

125 ml cider vinegar

30 ml soy sauce

1 tsp salt

5 garlic cloves, finely chopped

3 bay leaves

¹/₂ tsp black pepper

1¹/₂ tbsp sugar

125 ml water

675 g pork shoulder, cut into 5-cm cubes

30 ml vegetable oil

1 onion, sliced

¹/₂ red pepper, chopped

¹/₂ green pepper, chopped

350 g tomatoes, peeled and chopped

salt and black pepper, to taste

1 Combine the vinegar, soy sauce, salt, 3 of the garlic cloves, the bay leaves, black pepper, sugar and water in a casserole dish. Mix to dissolve the sugar, then add the meat, stir together well and cover. Marinate for 1 hour, stirring occasionally.

2 Place the dish over a medium-high heat and bring to a simmer. Reduce the heat to low, cover and simmer for 1 hour, stirring often. Remove the meat from the stock using a slotted spoon. Chill the stock in the refrigerator.

3 Heat 15 ml of the oil over a medium-high heat in a large, heavy-based, non-stick frying pan and brown the meat on all sides. Remove from the pan and drain on kitchen paper. Heat the remaining tablespoon of oil over a medium heat and add the onion and peppers. Cook, stirring, for about 5–8 minutes, until tender, and stir in the remaining garlic. Stir for a further minute and add the tomatoes and salt to taste. Cook for 10–15 minutes, until the tomatoes are cooked down.

4 Skim off any fat from the reserved stock, then stir in the tomato mixture and the meat. Bring to a simmer, cover and cook, stirring and scraping the sides of the casserole from time to time, for 1–1¹/₂ hours, until the meat is very tender. Season to taste. For the best flavour, cover and refrigerate overnight. Skim or lift off any fat that has congealed on the top, and reheat gently. Serve with rice.

BARBECUED BEEF

This, the best-known Korean dish, is also known as pulgogi. *It is made with thin strips of sirloin steak that are marinated and cooked on a domed metal shield over charcoal. It can be cooked on a barbecue or a grill instead.*

SERVES 4

75 ml soy sauce

3 garlic cloves, finely chopped

2.5 cm fresh ginger, grated

30 ml dark sesame oil

2–3 tsp sugar

¹/₄ tsp freshly ground black pepper

4 spring onions, finely chopped

1 tbsp toasted sesame seeds

675 g sirloin steak, thinly sliced across the grain into strips

cooked rice, to serve

1 small head Cos lettuce, divided into leaves, to serve

kochojang (hot chilli paste) or red chilli flakes, to taste

1 Combine the soy sauce, garlic, ginger, sesame oil, 2 tsp of sugar, black pepper, spring onions and sesame seeds in a large bowl. Taste and add more sugar if desired. Add the meat and toss to coat thoroughly. Cover and refrigerate for 1–3 hours, tossing the meat occasionally.

2 Preheat a grill or prepare a barbecue for cooking. Drain the meat and discard the marinade. Cook the meat for 2–3 minutes on each side.

3 Serve the steak with rice and lettuce on the side. Alternatively make lettuce rolls: place a few teaspoons of rice on a leaf, top with the meat and *kochojang* or red chilli flakes and roll up the leaf.

CHICKEN JAMBALAYA

This classic Cajun rice dish can be made with any number of meats and seafood. There are many different versions served around the world.

SERVES 4–6

25 g butter

1 medium chicken 1.6 kg, cut into 8 pieces

700 ml chicken stock or water

1 medium onion, chopped

1 bunch spring onions, chopped

2 garlic cloves, finely chopped

1 medium green pepper, diced

2 sticks celery, diced

100 g andouille or other smoked sausage, thinly sliced

100 g smoked ham, diced

450 g tomatoes, peeled and diced (optional)

¹/₄–¹/₂ tsp cayenne pepper

300 g medium- or long-grain rice

¹/₂ tsp dried thyme

1 bay leaf

25 g chopped fresh parsley

salt and black pepper, to taste

1 Heat the butter over a medium heat in a large, lidded frying pan or casserole dish and add the chicken pieces. Brown on all sides, which will take about 10 minutes, then remove from the heat. Drain the chicken pieces on kitchen paper and set aside. Meanwhile, bring the stock or water to a simmer in a saucepan.

2 Add the onion to the frying pan or casserole and cook for about 3 minutes, stirring, until translucent. Stir in the spring onions, garlic, green pepper, celery, sausage and ham, and cook, stirring, for a further 2–3 minutes, until the vegetables have softened a bit and the mixture smells fragrant. Stir in the tomatoes and cayenne, increase the heat slightly and cook, stirring, until the tomatoes have reduced. Stir in the rice and chicken pieces, and mix well to coat the rice.

3 Stir in the simmering stock or water, the thyme, bay leaf, half the parsley and season to taste. Bring back to the boil, cover, reduce the heat to low and simmer for 30 minutes or until the chicken is cooked through, the rice tender and the liquid absorbed. If not serving straight away, place a clean cloth between the lid of the pan and the rice and recover. Garnish with the remaining parsley to serve.

GREEN ENCHILADAS WITH CHICKEN

The key to success with this classic enchilada verde, which is served all over Mexico, is the delicious green sauce. It's very flavoursome and fiery.

SERVES 4

FOR THE CHICKEN
1.25 L water
1 onion, quartered
2 garlic cloves, crushed
1 whole chicken breast, skinned and split
1/2 tsp dried thyme or oregano
salt, to taste

FOR THE SAUCE
450 g tomatillos, husked, or small green tomatoes
3–5 hot green chillies (jalapeños or serranos), stemmed (membranes and seeds removed for a milder taste)
1/2 small white onion, roughly chopped
1 large garlic clove, roughly chopped
8 sprigs fresh coriander
15 ml vegetable oil
60 ml crème fraîche or sour cream (optional)
salt, to taste

FOR THE ENCHILADAS
60 ml vegetable oil (optional)
12 corn tortillas
50 g feta cheese, crumbled
2 slices of onion, separated into rings and rinsed with cold water
sliced radishes or radish roses, to garnish

1 To cook the chicken, combine the water, onion and garlic in a large saucepan and bring to the boil over a medium heat. Add the chicken breasts. Skim off any foam that rises, then add the dried herbs. Cover partially, reduce the heat to low and simmer for 13–15 minutes, until the chicken is cooked through. Add salt to taste. Set aside the chicken to cool in the stock.

2 Remove the chicken from the stock when cool enough to handle. Bone and shred. Strain the stock through a muslin-lined sieve into a bowl. Set aside 500 ml of the chicken stock for the sauce.

3 To make the green sauce, place the tomatillos in a medium saucepan, cover with water and simmer for 10 minutes. Drain, and place in a blender or food processor. Add the chillies, onion, garlic and coriander, season with salt and purée the mixture.

4 Heat the oil in a heavy saucepan over a medium-high heat. Drizzle a little of the tomatillo mixture into the pan and if it sizzles loudly, add the rest (wait a bit if it doesn't). Cook the tomatillo purée for about 5 minutes, stirring, until it thickens and begins to stick to the pan. Add the stock, stir together and bring to a simmer. Simmer for 15–20 minutes, stirring occasionally, until the mixture is thick enough to coat the front and back of a spoon. Remove from the heat, taste and add salt if necessary. Stir in the crème fraîche or sour cream, if using.

5 Assemble the enchiladas just before serving. Heat the tortillas until they are very flexible but not falling apart. To heat them in a microwave: wrap them in a lightly moistened tea towel and heat for 30 seconds at high. To steam the tortillas: Bring 1 cm of water to the boil in the base of a steamer, wrap the tortillas in a tea towel and place above the boiling water, cover and steam for 1 minute. Leave to stand, covered, for 10 minutes. Meanwhile, preheat the oven to 180°C. Lightly oil a baking dish that will accommodate 12 rolled enchiladas.

6 Heat the green sauce to a gentle simmer. Toss the shredded chicken with 125 ml of the green sauce and keep warm in a saucepan. Spoon 250 ml of the sauce into a wide soup bowl. One by one, dip a tortilla into the sauce, flip it over in the sauce and place 2 tbsp of

the chicken across the centre. Roll up the tortilla and place in the baking dish. Fill all of the tortillas in this way. Pour the remaining sauce over the enchiladas, spread it around so that it covers the ends and cover the dish tightly with aluminium foil.

7 Warm the enchiladas for 10 minutes in the preheated oven (no longer or they will fall apart), uncover, sprinkle with the cheese, onion rings and radishes and serve at once.

JERK CHICKEN

Jamaica's most popular dishes are its fiery, barbecued meat dishes, called 'jerks'. The term refers both to the marinade and the completed dish.

SERVES 4

FOR THE JERK MARINADE
2 Scotch bonnet or habanero chillies (or more to taste), stemmed
2 bunches spring onions, coarsely chopped
4 garlic cloves, coarsely chopped
1 tbsp chopped fresh ginger
1 tsp salt
2 tsp ground allspice
1 tsp ground cinnamon
1 tsp freshly grated nutmeg
1 tsp freshly ground pepper
2 tsp fresh or dried thyme
45 ml fresh lime juice or distilled white vinegar
30 ml orange juice
30 ml vegetable oil
1 tbsp brown sugar
salt and black pepper, to taste

FOR THE MEAT
1 medium chicken about 1.6 kg, cut into 8 pieces

1 Place the chillies, spring onions, garlic, ginger, salt, spices and thyme in a food processor and process to a paste. With the machine running, add the lime juice or vinegar, orange juice and vegetable oil. Blend in the brown sugar. Taste a small amount (it will be spicy) and adjust the seasoning to taste. Blend in enough water to make a paste with a pourable consistency like ketchup.

2 Pierce the chicken in several places with a sharp knife. Rub the seasoning over the skin and under it, as well as in the incisions. Cover and marinate for 2–12 hours in the refrigerator.

3 To barbecue the chicken pieces, prepare a medium-hot charcoal or gas fire. When the coals are covered with white ash, push them to one side of the grill. Lightly oil the rack and place the chicken on it, skin-side down, on the side opposite the coals. Cover the grill and cook for 20 minutes. Turn the chicken and cook for another 30–50 minutes, until the chicken is opaque and pulls away from the bone easily.

CALLALOO

Spelled calalou *in the French Antilles and* callaloo *in the English-speaking islands, this is a Caribbean soup named after the key ingredient – a green vegetable named* callaloo.

SERVES 6

225 g bacon, rind removed and diced

2 bunches spring onions, thinly sliced

4 garlic cloves, finely chopped

1 tsp fresh thyme leaves

450 g callaloo greens or spinach, stemmed and washed

450 g okra, topped and sliced

1.5 L water

1 Scotch bonnet or habanero chilli, pierced with a knife

225 g crab meat (optional)

juice of 1–3 limes

salt and black pepper, to taste

1 Heat the bacon over a medium heat in a large saucepan until it renders its fat. Add the spring onions and garlic and cook for about 5 minutes, until tender.

2 Add the thyme and the callaloo or spinach, and cook, stirring, until the leaves wilt. Stir in the okra and water, bring to the boil and add the chilli and seasoning. Reduce the heat to low and simmer, stirring often, for 15–30 minutes, or until the okra is tender.

3 Remove the chilli and stir in the crab, if using. Continue to simmer for a further 10 minutes. Stir in the lime juice to taste, season and serve.

DESSERTS, CAKES AND BAKES

SCANDINAVIAN FRUIT SOUP

A Scandinavian classic, this sweet soup is made primarily from dried fruit. It can be served hot or chilled.

SERVES 4–6

3 tbsp quick-cooking tapioca
200 g dried apricots, halved
200 g pitted prunes, halved
100 g sultanas
150 g pitted dried cherries
2 cinnamon sticks
1.5 L apple, cranberry or pear juice
grated peel of 1 orange
2 tart apples, peeled, cored and chopped
1–2 tbsp sugar, to taste
crème fraîche or whipped cream, to serve (optional)

1 Combine the tapioca, dried fruit, cinnamon sticks and fruit juice in a large saucepan. Bring to the boil, reduce the heat to low, cover partially and simmer for 45 minutes, until the tapioca is clear and the fruit soft. Stir occasionally and add more juice if the mixture becomes too thick.
2 Add the orange peel and apples and cook for a further 10 minutes, until the apple is just tender. Taste and add sugar to sweeten to taste.
3 Allow to cool, remove the cinnamon sticks, then chill, or serve hot, topped with crème fraîche or whipped cream, if you like.

SWEDISH HONEY AND SPICE BISCUITS

These delicate biscuits are traditionally cut with 6-cm round, fluted biscuit cutters, but you could use any shapes.

MAKES ABOUT **50** BISCUITS

300 g plain flour, plus extra for dusting
$^1/_2$ tsp baking powder
$^1/_2$ tsp salt
$^1/_2$ tsp ground cinnamon
100 g unsalted butter
1 tsp ground coriander
100 g light brown sugar
75 ml mild honey, such as clover or acacia
1 egg

1 Sift together the flour, baking powder, salt and cinnamon. Cream the butter using a food processor or beat by hand. Add the ground coriander and beat well. Gradually beat in the sugar, honey and egg, and mix well.
2 Scrape the dough on to a large piece of greaseproof paper and press down or roll to a thickness of 1 cm. Wrap well and refrigerate for several hours or overnight.
3 Preheat the oven to 190°C. Divide the dough into 4 and keep in the fridge. Line several baking sheets with foil, and flour your work surface and rolling pin. Roll out one piece of dough to a thickness of 3 mm. Keep dusting the dough and your work surface with flour, and work quickly to prevent it from sticking. Cut the biscuits with your choice of cutter and place on the foil, about 2.5 cm apart. Press together the scraps, roll out and cut. Repeat until all the dough is used.

4 Bake the biscuits for 10 minutes, switching the baking sheets top to bottom and reversing them front to back halfway through to ensure even cooking. The biscuits are ready when medium-brown and almost firm to the touch. Remove from the heat and slide the foil off the baking sheets. Leave to stand for 1 minute, then transfer the biscuits to wire racks to cool. Store in an airtight container to keep crisp.

BLACK BREAD

This sticky, Russian tea bread is popular all over Central Europe. Spread with butter and serve with coffee or tea.

MAKES **2** LOAVES

FOR THE BREAD
1 tbsp easy-blend dried yeast
375 ml lukewarm water
125 ml lukewarm strong black coffee
45 ml molasses
$^1/_2$ tsp ground ginger
60 g fresh wholemeal or black breadcrumbs
500 g plain white flour
60 ml vegetable oil
375 g rye flour
2$^1/_2$ tsp salt

FOR THE GLAZE
1 egg
60 ml coffee, cooled
poppy seeds (optional)

1 Dissolve the yeast in the warm water in a large bowl or the bowl of an electric mixer and leave to stand for 5 minutes, until creamy. Stir in the coffee and molasses. Add the ginger and breadcrumbs and stir together. Stir in 280 g of the white flour gradually, using a wooden spoon or large whisk. Beat the mixture together thoroughly, scraping down the sides every now and again, or beat with an electric mixer for 2 minutes. Cover with plastic wrap and leave in a warm place for 1 hour or until bubbles start to form on the surface.

2 Fold the oil into the mixture. Combine the rye flour and salt, and fold in. Gradually add the remaining white flour, and when you can turn out the dough, scrape it out on to a floured surface and knead for 10 minutes, adding flour as needed to make a sticky dough. Shape into a ball. Clean and wipe the bowl dry, lightly oil it and place the dough in the bowl, rounded side down first, then rounded side up. Cover with plastic wrap and leave in a warm place to rise for about 1 1/2 hours, until doubled in size.

3 Punch down the dough and turn it out on to a lightly floured work surface. Moisten your hands and divide the dough in half. Shape into 2 long or round loaves.

4 Prepare the glaze by beating the egg into the coffee. Brush the loaves with the egg wash, sprinkle with poppy seeds, if using, and cover lightly with a damp cloth. Leave to rise for 40 minutes, or until nearly doubled. Meanwhile, preheat the oven to 200°C.

5 Slash the loaves across the top with a sharp knife. Bake in the centre of the oven for 45 minutes, brushing halfway through with the egg wash, until the loaves are dark blackish-brown and respond to tapping with a hollow sound. Cool on a wire rack.

SACHERTORTE

There are many versions of this Viennese chocolate cake recipe: this one is from my friend Marjorie Perloff.

SERVES 10

FOR THE SPONGE

150 g plain chocolate, broken into small pieces

150 g unsalted butter, diced

6 large eggs, at room temperature, separated

150 g icing sugar

150 g plain flour, sieved twice

1/4 tsp cream of tartar

150 g apricot jam

FOR THE ICING

100 g plain chocolate

50 g unsalted butter

45 ml water

50 g icing sugar

butter and flour, to prepare the tin

1 Preheat the oven to 180°C. Butter and flour a 25-cm round cake tin or spring-form tin.

2 Melt the chocolate and butter in a small bowl over simmering water, or in a microwave (50% power for about 2 minutes). Stir to combine the chocolate and butter, and set aside.

3 Beat together the egg yolks and 125 g of the sugar until thick and creamy. Stir in the melted chocolate and butter. Gradually stir in the flour and combine well.

4 Whisk the egg whites until they begin to foam. Add the cream of tartar and beat until stiff but not dry. Add the remaining icing sugar. Stir a quarter of the whisked egg whites into the batter, then carefully fold in the rest. Turn into the cake tin and bake for about 50 minutes, until firm. Remove from the oven and leave to cool in the tin. When cool, level the surface of the cake by pushing down the sides, then turn out on to a large plate.

5 Spread the apricot preserve in an even layer over the top of the cake.

6 To make the icing, melt the butter and chocolate in a bowl over simmering water, or in a microwave (50% power for about 2 minutes). Stir together well, then add the water. Stir in the icing sugar. Sieve, and allow to cool slightly. Ice the cake by pouring the icing over the top and spreading it all over with a palette knife.

LINZERTORTE

This rich jam-filled tart is named after the Austrian town of Linz. It is popular throughout Central Europe and is best baked a couple of days before serving.

SERVES 8–10

100 g blanched slivered almonds

150 g plain flour, sieved

125 g caster sugar

1 tsp ground cinnamon

1/4 tsp ground cloves

1/4 tsp salt

125 g unsalted butter, at room temperature

2 large egg yolks

250 g raspberry or blackberry jam

finely chopped grated peel of 1 medium lemon

finely chopped grated peel of 1 orange

whipping cream for serving, optional

1 Preheat the oven to 180°C. Place the almonds on a baking sheet and toast in the oven for 5–7 minutes until golden. Remove from the oven and set aside to cool completely. Grind in a food processor or blender.

2 Mix together the almonds, flour, sugar, spices and salt. In an electric mixer on a low speed or using a bowl and wooden spoon, work in the butter, egg yolks and grated orange and lemon peel. Work into a smooth dough, then press the dough into a round and wrap in plastic wrap. Refrigerate for at least 2 hours.

3 Remove the dough from the refrigerator and leave it to soften for at least 30 minutes. It should be soft enough to press into a tin, but not sticky. Remove a quarter of the dough and place it in the freezer. Press out the remaining dough to cover the bottom of a 25-cm loose-bottomed cake tin or spring-form tin. Spread the jam evenly over the crust and refrigerate.

4 Remove the remaining dough from the freezer. Place it between two pieces of greaseproof paper or plastic wrap and roll out to a 25-cm square. Place in the freezer for 5 minutes. Remove from the freezer and cut into 8–10 strips. If the dough is too sticky to remove from the paper or plastic wrap, place it in the freezer again for a few minutes. Arrange half the strips at equal intervals across the jam topping, and the other half at right angles over the first strips, to make a lattice topping.

5 Bake in the oven for 40 minutes, or until the lattice is golden brown. Remove from the oven and place on a wire rack. Allow to cool completely, then remove the ring of the spring-form pan or cake tin. Allow to come to room temperature before serving.

CHERRY CLAFOUTIS

This dish originally came from central France but has now become a popular dessert all over the country and beyond.

SERVES 6

750 g cherries, stems removed, pitted if desired

45 ml Kirsch

75 g fruit sugar

4 large eggs

1 vanilla pod

90 g plain flour, sieved

300 ml milk

pinch of salt

icing sugar, sieved, for dusting

butter, for greasing

1 Toss the cherries with the Kirsch and 2 tablespoons of the sugar in a bowl. Leave to stand for 30 minutes. Meanwhile, preheat the oven to 200°C. Butter a 25-cm deep-sided flan dish or baking dish.

2 Drain the liquid from the cherries and beat it together with the eggs, the seeds from the vanilla pods and the remaining sugar. Slowly beat in the flour. Add the milk and salt. Mix together well.

3 Arrange the cherries in the baking dish. Pour over the batter.

4 Bake in the preheated oven for 35–45 minutes, or until the top is browned and the clafoutis is firm. Sprinkle with the icing sugar and allow to cool on a wire rack. Serve warm or at room temperature.

APPLE AND PRUNE TART

This recipe is from south-west France and is based on one by Paula Wolfert, in her book The Cooking of South West France.

SERVES 8

250 g prunes, pitted and halved

500 ml hot orange pekoe tea

200 g fruit sugar

1.2 kg tart apples, such as Granny Smith, peeled, cored and thickly sliced

1 vanilla pod, split

2 slices of lemon peel

15 ml fresh lemon juice

30 ml Armagnac

75 g unsalted butter, melted

10 sheets filo pastry

icing sugar, to dust

1 Place the prunes in a bowl and cover with the tea. Leave to stand for an hour or more, until the prunes are soft. Drain and discard the tea.

2 Combine 165 g of the sugar with 250 ml water and bring to the boil. Boil

for 5 minutes and add the prunes. Reduce the heat and simmer for 20 minutes, stirring occasionally. Remove from the heat and allow to cool. Drain, and retain the liquid.

3 Place the apples in a saucepan and add the remaining sugar, vanilla pod, lemon peel and 75 ml of liquid from the prunes. Bring to a simmer, stir everything together, cover partially and simmer for 20 minutes over a low heat, stirring often, until the apples have softened. Remove the lemon peel and vanilla pod but scrape in the seeds. Stir in the lemon juice and Armagnac. Set aside to cool.

4 Preheat the oven to 190°C. Brush the base of a 25-cm flan tin with some of the melted butter. Layer a sheet of filo pastry in the pan. Brush it lightly with butter. Layer another sheet of pastry over the first sheet so that it covers the part of the pan left uncovered by the first sheet. Layer another 4 sheets in this way, turning the pan with each sheet and brushing each sheet with butter. The edges of the filo should fan out around the pan.

5 Drain the apples, reserving the liquid, and spread the apples over the pastry. Arrange the drained prunes over the apples. Bring the edges of the filo over the fruit to enclose it. Layer the remaining filo over the top, brushing each piece with butter and tucking the edges into the sides of the pan. Brush the top with butter, and cut a very small circle out of the middle for steam to escape.

6 Bake for 30 minutes, until brown and crisp. Remove from the oven and drizzle 60 ml of the reserved liquid into the hole in the middle. Sprinkle with icing sugar and allow to cool slightly before serving.

PECAN PIE

Pecan pie is especially popular in the American South, where pecan trees are plentiful. It is the traditional dessert for Thanksgiving dinner.

SERVES 8

FOR THE PASTRY

175 g plain flour, plus extra for dusting

1 tbsp sugar

1/4 tsp salt

100 g or 7 tbsp unsalted butter, chilled and diced

45–75 ml iced water

FOR THE FILLING

50 g unsalted butter

125 ml mild honey, such as clover, lavender or acacia

4 eggs

5 ml vanilla essence

15 ml rum

1/4 tsp freshly grated nutmeg

pinch of salt

250 g shelled pecans

whipped cream or vanilla ice cream, to serve

1 To make the pastry, mix together the flour, sugar and salt. Rub in the butter until it resembles breadcrumbs. Gradually add the water until the dough comes together (this can be done in a food processor). Roll the dough into a ball, then using a rolling pin, roll it out on a lightly floured surface and use to line a 25-cm pie dish or tin. Cover with plastic wrap and refrigerate for at least two hours.

2 Preheat the oven to 180°C. Beat together the butter and honey. Add the eggs, vanilla, rum, nutmeg and salt, and mix together.

3 Prebake the pastry for 5 minutes. Remove from the oven. Allow to cool slightly. Spread the pecans over the pastry in an even layer and pour in the butter and egg mixture. Bake for 35 minutes, until the nuts are lightly browned. The filling will puff up, then settle. Remove from the heat and allow to cool on a wire rack. Serve with whipped cream or vanilla ice cream.

BROWNIES

These popular American bakes are a cross between a cake and a biscuit, crisp on the outside and chewy within. The better the quality of chocolate you use, the better they will be.

MAKES 12 BROWNIES

50 g plain chocolate, broken into pieces

125 g unsalted butter, cut into pieces

75 g plain flour

pinch of salt

2 large eggs

250 g fruit sugar

5 ml vanilla essence

50 g shelled walnuts or pecans, coarsely chopped

125 g plain chocolate, cut into small chunks, or chocolate chips

butter, for greasing

1 Preheat the oven to 180°C. Grease a 20-cm square baking tin with a little butter.

2 Combine the bittersweet chocolate pieces and butter in a bowl set over a pan of simmering water and melt, stirring throughout. Remove from the heat just before fully melted and stir to complete the melting. Or melt in a microwave at 50% power for 2–3 minutes. Allow to cool slightly.

3 Sift the flour and salt into a bowl.

4 Beat the sugar and eggs together in another bowl until thick and creamy. Beat in the vanilla essence. Fold in the melted chocolate, then the flour mixture. Fold in the nuts and chocolate chunks or chips. Do not overwork the mixture.

5 Transfer the mixture to the prepared baking tin, and bake for 20–25 minutes, until a skewer inserted in the centre comes out with just a little mixture on it. The brownies should still be moist in the centre when cooked. Leave to cool in the tin or on a wire rack. Cut into squares to serve.

PAVLOVA

Claimed by both Australia and New Zealand, this is a delightful dessert. You can use any fresh fruits of your choice.

SERVES 8

4 egg whites

5 ml vanilla essence

5 ml lemon juice or 1/2 tsp cream of tartar

1/2 tsp salt

175 g fruit sugar

250 ml double cream, whipped

3 kiwi fruit, peeled and sliced

600 g strawberries, hulled and sliced

oil spray, for greasing

1 Preheat the oven to 120°C. Cover a baking sheet with aluminium foil and lightly spray with oil. Beat the egg whites until frothy and add the vanilla, lemon juice or cream of tartar and the salt. Beat until soft peaks form. Add the sugar gradually and continue to beat until the egg whites are stiff and glossy.

2 Spoon the meringue mixture on to the foil-covered baking sheet. Make a circle about 23 cm in diameter, with a depression in the middle about 3–4 cm thick. Bake for about 90 minutes, or until the meringue is crisp on the outside and firm to the touch. Turn off the heat and allow to cool with the oven door open.

3 Place the meringue on a serving plate. Fill the centre with the whipped cream, and top the cream with the fruit. Chill until ready to serve.

FURTHER READING

Europe

D. Allen, *Irish Traditional Cooking* (Dublin, Gill & Macmillan, 1995).

C. Andrews, *Catalan Cuisine* (New York, Atheneum, 1988).

P. Casas, *Delicioso! The Regional Cooking of Spain* (New York, Alfred A. Knopf, 1996).

P. Casas, *The Foods and Wines of Spain* (New York, Alfred A. Knopf, 1988).

A. Davidson, *North Atlantic Seafood* (London, Macmillan, 1979), p. 358, p. 385, p. 394.

J. Elkon, *A Belgian Cookbook*, (New York, Hippocrene Books, 1996).

C. Field, *Celebrating Italy* (William Morrow & Co., 1990).

J. Grigson, *English Food* (London, Penguin Books, 1977).

G. Lang, *George Lang's Cuisine of Hungary* (New York, Wings Books, 1971, 1994), p. 126.

A. Mitchell, *France: A Culinary Journey* (Sidney, Collins, Angus & Robertson, 1992).

F. Plotkin, *Italy for the Gourmet Traveler* (New York, Little, Brown and Co., 1996).

M. Sheraton, *The German Cookbook* (New York, Random House, 1965), p. 247-250.

J. Warren, *A Feast of Scotland* (London, Hodder & Stoughton, 1979).

Africa and the Middle East

S. Allison and M. Robins, *South African Cape Malay Cooking* (Bath, England, Absolute Press, 1997).

M. Aufray and M. Perret (eds.), *Cuisines d'Orient et d'ailleurs, Traditions culinaires des peuples du Monde* (Grenoble, Langues'O, Editions Glénat, 1995).

G. Basan, *Classic Turkish Cooking* (St. Martin's Press, 1997), p. 25, p. 47.

H. Batmanglij, *Food of Life, A Book of Ancient Persian and Modern Iranian Cooking and Ceremonies* (Washington, D.C., Mage Publishers, Inc., 1986), p. 23.

H. Hachten, *Best of Regional African Cooking* (New York, Hippocrene Books, 1998).

F. Hal, *Les Saveurs et les Gestes* (Paris, Editions Stock, 1995).

N. Halıcı, *Nevin Halıcı's Turkish Cookbook* (London, Dorling Kindersley, 1989).

J. B. Harris, *Iron Pots and Wooden Spoons*, Ballantine edition, 1991 (New York, Atheneum Publishers, 1989).

R. Mendy, A. Bah-Diallo, J. Bebey, K. Ben Rached, M. Rouil and D. Ben Yahmed (eds.) *Les Merveilles de la Cuisine Africaine* (Paris, Editions J. A., 1979).

C. Roden, *The Book of Jewish Food* (New York, Alfred A. Knopf, 1996).

C. Roden, *A Book of Middle Eastern Food* (Alfred A. Knopf, 1968, 1972) p. 22-23, p. 48.

P. Wolfert, *Couscous and Other Good Food from Morocco* (New York, Harper & Row Publishers, 1973).

C. A. Wright, *A Mediterranean Feast: The Story of the Birth of the Celebrated Cuisines of the Mediterranean from the Merchants of Venice to the Barbary Corsairs* (William Morrow & Co., 1999).

Asia and Australasia

K. T. Achaya, *Indian Food: A Historical Companion* (Delhi, Oxford University Press, 1994).

J. Alford and N. Duguid, *Flatbreads and Flavors* (William Morrow & Co, 1995).

E. N. Anderson, *The Food of China* (New Haven, Yale University Press, 1988).

E. Andoh, *An American Taste of Japan* (New York, William Morrow & Co., 1985).

M. Baljekar, *Mridula Baljekar's Real Balti Cookbook* (London, Ebury Press, 1996).

J. Brennan, *The Cuisines of Asia* (New York, St. Martin's Press, 1984).

J. Brennan, *Curries and Bugles: A Memoir and Cookbook of the British Raj* (New York, HarperCollins, 1990).

J. Brennan, *The Original Thai Cookbook* (New York, Perigee Books, 1981).

K. C. Chang (ed.), *Food in Chinese Culture, Anthropological and Historical Perspectives* (New Haven, Yale University Press, 1977).

P. Clark (ed.), *Best Recipes from the Weekly* (The Australian Woman's Weekly).

D. Goldstein, *The Georgian Feast* (HarperCollins, 1993).

J. Hayes and J. Gorrick, *Australia: The Beautiful Cookbook* (Sydney, Ure Smith, 1989).

W. Hutton (ed.), *The Food of Australia* (Singapore, Periplus Editions, 1996), p. 17.

C. Marks and A. Thein (cont.), *The Burmese Kitchen* (New York, M. Evans & Co., 1987).

C. Marks, *Copeland Marks' Indian & Chinese Cooking from the Himalayan Rim* (New York, Donald I. Fine Books, 1996).

M. and K. Millon, *Flavours of Korea* (London, Andre Deutsch Ltd, 1991).

B. Ngo and G. Zimmerman, *The Classic Cuisine of Vietnam* (New York, Penguin Books USA, 1986).

S. Owen, *Indonesian and Thai Cookery* (London, Judy Piatkus Publishers Ltd, 1988).

C. Selva Rajah, *Makan-Lah! The True Taste of Malaysia* (Sydney, HarperCollins, 1996).

J. Sahni, *Classic Indian Cooking* (New York, William Morrow & Co., 1980).

J. Sahni, *Classic Indian Vegetarian and Grain Cooking* (New York, William Morrow & Co., 1985).

N. Simonds, *Chinese Seasons* (Boston, Houghton Mifflin Co., 1986).

P. Sing, *The Traditional Recipes of Laos*, eds. Alan and Jennifor Davidson (Devon, Prospect Books, 1995).

Y. So, *Classic Food of China* (London, Macmillan, 1992).

Y. So, *Yan-kit's Classic Chinese Cookbook* (London, Dorling Kindersley, 1984).

C. Spencer, *The Heretic's Feast: A History of Vegetarianism* (London, Fourth Estate Ltd, 1993).

B. Tropp, *The Modern Art of Chinese Cooking* (New York, William Morrow & Co., 1982).

S. Tsuji, *Japanese Cooking: A Simple Art* (Tokyo, New York, San Francisco, Kodansha International, 1980).

C. Yeo and J. Jue, *The Cooking of Singapore* (Emeryville, Harlow & Ratnor, 1993).

The Americas

M. Adams, *Heartland* (New York, Clarkson Potter Publishers, 1991).

R. Bayless with D. G. Bayless, *Authentic Mexican* (New York, William Morrow & Co., 1987).

S. D. Coe, *America's First Cuisines* (University of Texas Press, Austin, 1994).

C. F. v. de Balsells, *Cocina Guatemalteca, Arte, Sabor y Colorido* (Guatemala City, Editorial Piedro Santa, 1982).

J. Harris, *Sky Juice and Flying Fish* (New York, Fireside, 1991).

J. Harris, *The Welcome Table: African-American Heritage Cooking* (New York, Simon & Schuster, 1995).

K. Hess, *The Carolina Rice Kitchen: The African Connection* (Colombia, South Carolina, The University of South Carolina Press, 1992).

D. Kennedy, *The Cuisines of Mexico* (New York, Harper & Row Publishers, 1972).

D. Kennedy, *Mexican Regional Cooking* (New York, Harper Pernennial, 1978, 1984, 1990).

M. Kurlansky, *Cod: A Biography of the Fish that Changed the World* (New York, Walker & Co., 1997).

J. N. Leonard and the Editors of Time-Life Books, *American Cooking: New England* (New York, Time-Life Books, 1970).

J. N. Leonard and Time-Life Books, *Latin American Cooking* (New York, Time-Life Books, 1968).

D. Madison, *The Vegetarian Table: America* (San Francisco, Chronicle Books, 1996).

C. Marks, *False Tongues and Sunday Bread, A Guatemalan and Mayan Cookbook* (New York, M. Evans & Co., 1985).

S. W. Mintz, *Tasting Food, Tasting Freedom* (Boston, Beacon Press, 1996).

S. Raichlen, *The Caribbean Pantry Cookbook* (New York, Artisan, 1995).

F. Rojas-Lombardi, *The Art of South American Cooking* (New York, HarperCollins, 1991).

R. Sokolov, *Why We Eat What We Eat* (New York, Summit Books, 1991).

J. M. Taylor, *Hoppin' John's Lowcountry Cooking* (New York, Bantam Books, 1992).

Recipes

M. K. Johnson, *The Melting pot: Balkan Food and Cookery* (Prospect Books, 1995).

G. Lang, *George Lang's Cuisine of Hungary* (New York, Wings Books, 1971, 1994), p. 126.

C. Middione, *The Food of Southern Italy* (William Morrow & Co., 1987)

J. Sahni, *Classic Indian Vegetarian and Grain Cooking* (New York, William Morrow & Co., 1985).

M. Sheraton, *The German Cookbook* (New York, Random House, 1965), p. 247-250.

INDEX

Reader's note: Countries are indexed only if they form part of an area under discussion, e.g. Scotland (as part of the British text), not where they form a main entry (where they can be found in the Contents list); or they are indexed where they influence another's cuisine, e.g. *French influences* on Scottish cuisine. Page numbers in *italics* indicate a caption to an illustration; those in **bold** indicate a boxed entry; those in ***bold italic*** indicate a boxed entry with an illustration.

Aborigines 212
Abruzzo 92–94
Achoura 129
adobo 191
Afghanistan 158
African slave influences
   Caribbean 238
   Mexico 237
   South America 241, 242, 249, **249**, 250
   USA 225, 226
Afrikaners 140
afternoon tea (break)
   Britain *15*
   Canada 231
   Malaysia 181
   Philippines 191
   Spain 81
agave *235*
Albania 105
ale
   Ireland 14
   Scandinavia **21**
   see also beer
Algeria 129, 133
All Saints' Day, Spain 78
All Souls' Day, Balkans 107
allioli 78
allspice 240
alpacas 242
Alps area in France 64
Alsace-Lorraine 56–57
amaretto **92**
anchovies **70**, 113
Andalusia 80–81
anatto 191, 233, 236
Antilles 240
appetizers, Chinese 167–168
apples *14*, 222
April 30th festival, Scandinavia 25
aquavit 20, **20**, 21
Arabs and Arab influences 118–119, 123–124
   France 69
   Indonesia 178
   Italy 90, 97
   Jews 125
   Mexico 235

North Africa 126
Arawaks 238
Argentina 247–248
Arizona 227
Armenia 153, 158
artichoke 56, 91
Aruba 240
Asian influences
   Australia 214
   Caribbean 238, 240
   China 164
   Denmark 22
   USA 229
Asturias 76
Atlantic Coast of France 61–62
aubergines 111
Auvergne 64–65
avocado leaves 237
Azerbaijan 160
Aztecs 234

B
baguettes *199*
baked beans 222
Balti cooking 151
Baltic States 32–33
bananas *197*, *238*, 245
Barbados 240
barbecues *215*, 226–227, 228, 248
barley 157
bars **93**
basil 67
Basilicata 95
Basques 72–73, 76–77, 228
bean curd 178
beans 61, 134–135, 235, *241*, 247, 250
   see also specific beans
Bedouins 118, *120*
beef
   Argentina 248
   Austria 40
   Balkans 107
   Britain 12
   Denmark 22
   Italy 89, 90
   Japan 207
   Korea 204
beer
   Africa 135
   Belgium 49
   Britain *10*
   France 55
   Germany **45**, *45*
   Netherlands 50
   Scandinavia **21**
   see also ale
beetroot 31
Belarus 312
Belgium 48–49
Belize 232
Bengal 151
berbere 138
Berbers 126, 128, 133
berries 20, 23, 230

Berry region of France 65
bessissa 129
bharat 133
birthday celebrations, Korea 205
bok choy 175
Bolivia 243
Bordeaux 62
Bosnia-Herzegovina 108
Boy's Festival, Japan 209
brandies 38, **63**, 158
brasseries **57**
Brazil 250
bread
   Africa 138
   Algeria 129
   Armenia 158
   Australia 213
   Balkans 106, 107
   Britain 13
   Central Asia **158**
   China 175
   France 54, 57, *59*, 64, 67, 70, 73
   Georgia 161, 162, 163
   Greece 100
   India **150**, 155
   Ireland 15
   Italy 90
   Italy 97
   Mexico *237*
   Middle East *118*, 120
   North Africa *131*, 133
   Portugal 83
   Scandinavia 16, 17, 21, 22–23, 24
   Singapore 193
   Spain 76
   Switzerland 46–47
   Tibet 157
   Turkey 111, 115
   Ukraine 31
   USA 222, 227
   Uzbekistan *158*
British influences 150, 240
Brittany 57–58
Brotzeit 45
Buddhism 187
Bulgaria 104, 105–106
bulls 68
buns 25
Burgundy 63–64
Burma 187
bush-tucker diet 213
butter 57, 128, 146–147
buttermilk 146

C
cabbage 30, 34
cafés
   Australia *213*
   Austria *41*
   France *57*, *70*
   Hungarian *37*
   Italy 87
   see also bars; restaurants
Cajun cuisine 225, 226

cakes and pastries
   Austria ***40***
   Belgium 48–49
   Danish ***22***
   France *55*, 70, *72*, 73
   Ireland 14
   Italy 87, 89, 94, *95*, 97
   Mexico 236
   North Africa 129
   South America *250*
   Turkey 115
Calabria 95
California 228–229
Campania 94
Canary Islands 81
Candomble religion ***249***
Cantonese cuisine 171
Cape Malay cuisine 139
Caribbean influences 226, 233, 237, 249–250
Caribs 238
carp 42, 43, 61
cassava 136, *136*, 250
casseroles 24
   see also stews
cassolita 128
Catalan 68–70
Catalonia 78
cave dwellers *113*
caviar 24
celebratory meals
   Cambodia 182
   Chinese 167
   Indonesia 178
   Japan 211
   Laos 186
   North Africa 129–131
   Singapore 193
   Vietnam 200
   see also specific celebrations, e.g. New Year
Central Africa 136–137
cereals
   Africa 134–135
   Balkans 107
   Baltic States 32
   Canada 230
   Central Asia 156
   Central Europe 35
   China 169
   France 58, 59
   Hungary 38
   India *148*
   Ireland 14
   Korea 204
   Moldova 33
   Morocco 132
   Russia 28
   Turkey 113
   Ukraine 30
   USA 227
Champagne area 55
charcuterie 59, 63–64
chat masala 147
cheese
   Australia 215

Austria 39–40
Balkans *105*, 107
Belgium 48
Britain *12*, 13
Central Asia *157*
France 57, *61*, 61, 64, 65, 70
Greece 100
India 147
Ireland 14
Italy 97
Mexico 235
Netherlands *50*, **50**
Norway 19–20
Spain 76, 78
Switzerland 46, *47*
Turkey 111
chelou **120**
cherries 90
chervil 59
chestnuts 64, 65
chicken 22, 42, 64, 185, 225
Chile 245–247
chillies
   France 72–73
   India 153
   Italy 92
   Mexico ***236***
   North Africa 126
   Peru *244*
   Thailand 195
   Turkey *112*
   USA 227
Chinese influences
   India 148, 153
   Japan 207
   Malaysia 181
   Myanmar 187
   Philippines 191
   Singapore 192, 193
   Thailand 195
   USA 229
   Vietnam 198–199
chives 59
chocolate *46*, 49, 234, 237, *245*
chopsticks *165*, *211*
Christian influences 138, 153
Christmas Day 85, 90, 25, 191
Christmas Eve 65, 90, 107
cider 76
cloudberries 16
cocido 78
coconuts 249
cod
   Caribbean 240
   France 64
   Italy 90
   Portugal 82, 83
   Scandinavia 19, 20
   Spain 77
   USA 221–222
coffee
   Africa 137, **140**
   Austria 39
   Germany 45
   Italy **93**
   Middle East **124**
   Portugal 85

Scandinavia 16, 17, 21
Colombia 249–250
confit 70
coriander 81, 237
Costa Rica 233
couscous 97, 125, *126*, 129, 131, 137
crabs 170, *229*
crayfish 24
cream 236
cream tea *15*
Creole cuisine 225, 226, 240, 241, 242, 244
crêpes *58*, 70
Croatia 109
Cuba 226, 240
Curaçao 240
curries 43, 139, 140, 189, 197

D
Danish pastries *22*
dates *126*, 128, 153–154
Deepavali 180
delicatessens *97*
dende oil 250
Denmark 16, 17, 22–23
dersa 133
dessert
    Austria 41
    Central Europe 35
    China 168
    France 65, 67
    Germany 45
    Italy 89, 97
    Morocco 132
    North Africa 129
    Scandinavia 17
    see also puddings
digestive spices 148
dill 115
dim sum 171
Djibouti 137
Dordogne 63–64
doughnuts *226*
duck 63, 169
dukkah 122
dumplings
    Africa 139
    Austria 40
    Balkans 107
    Central Europe 34
    China 168
    Germany 45
    Italy 89
    Mongolia *160*
    Russia 27
    Ukraine 31
Durga Pooja 145
durian *180*
Dutch apple cake 52

E
East Africa 137–138
Easter 28, 78, 90
eaux de vie **63**
Ecuador 245
eels 22, 61, 91

egg dishes
    China *166*
    France 73
    Iran 122
    Italy 90
    Mexico 237
    Spain 74
    Thailand *195*
Egypt 118, 123
El Salvador 232
Emilia-Romagna 90
endive 48, 55
England 10–15
epazote 237
Eritrea 137
Estonia 32–33
Ethiopa 136, 137, 138

F
fan cai **171**
far 58
fast food 220, *221, 247*
fasting days 27, 66, 101
fats
    Africa *137*
    Brazil 250
    China 166, 172
    India 151
    Middle East 123
    North Africa 128, 131–132, *133*
fava beans 123
Feast of the Redeemer 89
felafels 123, 124, *125*
figs, preserved 128
filo dough **107**
Finland 16, 17, 23–24
fish *see* seafood; shellfish
five-spice powder 168
Flag Day, Netherlands 50
fogas 38
foie gras 56, 62–63, 70
fool medames 123
Franch Comté 64
French influences
    Austria 39
    Belgium 48
    Cambodia 182
    Canada 230
    Denmark 22
    Italy 97
    Laos 184
    Luxembourg 53
    North Africa 126
    Russia 26
    Scotland 10, 12
    Southern Africa 140
    USA 226
    Vietnam 199
French Guyana 250
fritters 189, *240*, **249**
fruit
    Africa 136, 138
    Balkans 109
    Central Asia 156
    China 171
    conserve 107

drinks 163
    France 58–59
    Greece *100*
    Malaysia 181
    New Zealand 217
    North Africa 129
    Norway 20
    preserved 161
    Turkey 111–112
    USA 228–229
    Vietnam 200
fry-up *10*
Fukien 171–172
fusion cuisine 124, 175, 214–215, 228

G
Galicia 76
game
    Austria 40
    Britain 13
    Caribbean 238
    Central Europe 35
    France 56, 61
    Germany 45
    Latvia 33
    Scandinavia 21, 23
garam masala 147
garlic *34*, 61, 72
gazpacho 81
Georgia 161–163
German influences 22, 39, 53, 222–223, 227–228
Girl's Festival, Japan 209
Goa 154–155
goat 157–158
goose 63, 169
goulash **37**
grappa **92**
grolla, la 89
Guatemala 233
gullac 113
Guyana 250

H
Habsburgs 37
haddock **13**
hake 76–77
Hakka 153, 171
ham 55, 72, *74*, 170
hangi 216
Hawaii 229
hawaykji 122
hawker centres, Singapore **192**
herbs and spices
    Africa 138
    Armenia 158, 161
    Cambodia 183
    Caribbean 240
    Chile 247
    China 168, 172, 175
    France 59, 65, 67, *68*
    Georgia 162
    Germany 43
    Greece *102*
    India 147–148, 150–151, 153

Indonesia 176, 178
Mexico 235, 237
Middle East 122
Morocco 131
Myanmar **189**
North Africa 133
Portugal 82
Singapore 193
South America 250
Thailand 197
Turkey 115
Vietnam 199
herring
    Baltic States 32
    Denmark 22
    Germany 43
    Netherlands 50
    Russia 28
    Scotland *13*
    Sweden **20**, 21
Hindus 144–145
hing-shao cooking 170
honey 28, 33, 100–101, *107*
Hunan 173
Hungary 37–38
Hunzacots 158

I
Iceland 16, 17, 25
Id el fitr **132**
Igbo 137
Ile de France 58–59
Imeretian saffron 161
Incas 241–242
Indian influences
    Britain 12
    Cambodia 182
    Guyana 250
    Indonesia 178
    Malaysia 181
    Singapore 193
    Thailand 197
    Vietnam 198–199
Iran 122, 124, 161
    see also Persia
Iraq 124
Islam 156
Israel 124–125
Italian influences 37, 46, 65–66, 102 , 133

J
Jains 153
Jamaica 240
Java 178
jenever 50
jerk 240
Jewish cuisine and influences 119–120, 124–125
    Belarus 32
    Greece 101
    Turkey 110–111, *112*
    India 144
    Italy 90, 91
    Middle East 119
    North Africa 128

Central Asia 156–157
USA 222
Jura 64

K
kaeng ped 197
Karelians 23
kasha 109
Kashmir 150
kebabs *30*, 110, 112, 122, *161*, 175
khmeli-suneli 161
Khmer 182
kibbutz 125
kimchi 202, **204**
kippering *13*
kir 63
kirmizi biber 115
kiwi fruit **216**

L
lamb
    Armenia 160
    Balkans *105*
    Britain 12
    China 170
    France 57
    Iceland 25
    India 150
    Iran 12
    Italy 90, 91
    New Zealand 216
    North Africa 128
    Norway 19
    Spain 78
    Turkey 111
    Uruguay 247
Languedoc 68
Lapps 16
Latvia 32–33
Lazio 91
Le Nord area of France 55
Le Puy 64
lechón 191
lemons, preserved 128
lentils 64
lettuce *184*
Liguria 87
Limousin 65
liqueurs *63*, **92**
Lithuania 32–33
llama 241
lobster 43, 58, 140
Loire Valley 59–61
Lombardy 89
Louisiana 226
lumpfish 25
Luxembourg 50–52
Lyonnais 63–64

M
Macao 175
Macedonia 109
Madeira **82**
Madrid 78–79
Magyars 37

maize
  Africa *140*, 140
  Central America/Mexico 232, 235
  Georgia 163
  Native Americans 221
  South America 243–244
  USA 225
Malaysian influences 178, 193
Maori 216
Marche, Italy 91
Mardi Gras *87*
markets
  Balkans *107*
  France *68, 69*
  India *147*
  Mexico *233*
  North Africa **131**
  Russia *26, 27*
  Scandinavia *17, 24*
  South America *242*
  Thailand *195*
  Turkey *112*
  Turkmenistan *162*
  USA *225*
  Vietnam *200*
marriage foods, China 169
Masai 138–139
May Day, Scandinavia 25
Mayans 233, 236
Mealy Monday 15
meat
  Africa 137, 138
  Argentina 248
  Australia 213, 215, **215**
  Balkans 105–108
  Belarus 32
  Britain 12–13
  Cambodia 183
  Canada 230
  Central Europe 35
  France 66, 73
  Greece 102
  India 144–145
  Iran 122
  Italy 87
  Japan 207
  Jewish 119–120, 157
  Mexico 235
  Morocco 132
  North Africa 131
  preserved 135, *140*, 140, 157
  Russia 28
  smoked 24
  South America 242
  Turkey 111, 112
  USA 226–227, 228
  Vietnam 200
meatballs 21, 112, 113, 122
medieval processions, Belgium 49
Mediterranean cuisine and influences 39, 66, 213–214
melegueta pepper 250
menus
  French 67
  Greece 103
  India 154
  Italian 95
  Japan 208
  Kenya 137
  Middle East 125
  Peru 244
  Portugal 84
  Spanish 80
  Thailand 197
  Turkey 113

Mevlana Jalauddini Rumi 110
Mexico and influences 226, 229, 234–237
meze 104, 108
mezedes 102
mhammar 128
Miami 226
milk and milk products
  Balkans 104
  Finland 23
  Iceland 25
  India 146–147
  Russia *28*
  Tibet 157
  Turkey 112
  Ukraine *31*
millet *134*, 135, 136, 137
mint 67, 115
mint tea *132*
miso 207–208
Moghuls 150
mojos 81
molasses 222
Moldova 33
Molise 92–94
Mongolia and infuences 157–158, 161, 169–170
moon-watching festival, Japan 209
Moorish influences 74, 79, 81, 82, 95
mopani worms *139*
morels 23
Morocco 129, 131–132
muesli 47
mughal garam masala 147
mushrooms
  Belarus 32
  Belgium 49
  Finland 23
  France 59
  Poland 35
  Russia 28
  Switzerland 47
Muslims 119, 128, 144
mussaman curry paste 197
mussels *48*, 49, 55, 58, 61, 68
mustard 151
mutton *see* lamb

N
nasi kuning 178
Native Americans 221, 227, 233, 249
needlefish 250
Netherlands cuisine and influences 50, 139, 240
New England 221–222, 230
New Mexico 227
New Year 124, 168, 180, 199, 209
New York 222
Nicaragua 232
nigella 161
nomads 157
nonya cuisine 180, 181, **181**, 193
noodles
  Austria 40
  Central Europe 34–35
  China *170*, 171–172
  Germany 45
  Greece 101
  Japan 208, 209
  Malaysia 181
  Thailand 195
Normandy 57
North African influences
  French cuisine 54

North-eastern Africa 137–138
Norway 19–20
nuts, China 87, 119, 169
  see also specific nuts

O
octopus *98*
offal 171
oils *see* fats; olive oil
oja santa 237
olive oil 80, 98, *98*
olives *77, 98*
omul 33
onions 78, 235
oranges *128, 212*
ostrich eggs 136
outdoor cooking *220, 228*, 248
  see also barbecues; street food
ouzo 100
ovens *123*, 151,*172*, 227
oysters 43, 58, 61, 217

P
pachamanca festival 248
padek 184
paellas 74, 80, *81*
panarda 92–93
pancakes 14, 66, *167*
  see also crêpes; waffles
panch phoron 147
papaya *197*
paprika *34*, 35
paprikas **37**
Paraguay 247–248
Paris 58–59
Parsees 144
parsley 59, 115
pasta
  Balkans 105
  France 66
  Greece 101
  Italy 87, 90, 94
  Tunisia 133
pastis 67
pastries *see* cakes and pastries
pastry **107**
pavlova 217
peaches *225*
pears 49
pecan pie *227*
Peking cuisine 169
Pennsylvania Dutch 222–223
perch 47
Persian influences 119, 125, 150, 156
Peru 242, 243–244
pesto 87
pho **200**
picada 78
Picardy 56
pickling 102
picnics 205
Piedmont 87
pies 12–13, 27, 47, 76
pike perch 38
pineapples *178*
pizza 66, *91*, 94
plantains 136, 245
plum brandy 107
plums 49, *72*
polenta 89, 107
Polynesian influences 178, 216
poppy seeds 107
pork
  Armenia 158

Balkans 107
Belgium 49
China 168
Danish 22
France 70
Germany 43
Italy 91
Japan 209
Laos 185
Myanmar 187
Portugal 84
Spain 74, 78
Thailand 195
USA 223
porkolt **37**
porridge
  Africa 139
  Britain 15
  Latvia 32
  North Africa 129
  Scandinavia 17, 19
  Tibet 157
port *82*
Portuguese influences
  Africa 135
  China 175
  India 148–150
  Malaysia 180
  South America 241, 250
  Thailand 195
  Vietnam 199
potatoes
  Austria 40
  Belarus 32
  Colombia 249
  France 56
  Germany 42, 43
  Ireland 15
  Russia 27–28
  Scandinavia 16
  South America 245
  Tibet *156*
preserved food 128, 140, 202, 241–242
  see also specific foods
prik kaeng kio 197
Provence 65–67
puddings 13
Puerto Rica 240
Puglia 94–95
pulses *153*, 153

Q
qadra 128
quatre epices 122
Quechua 241–242, 243–244, 245
queimada 76
quinoa 244

R
Ramadan 113, **132**, 180
ras el hanout 133
rat *186*
red peppers 77, 102
red snappers *238*
reindeer 16, 21, *23*, 24
religious influences
  Central Asia 156–157, 162
  Greece 101–102
  India 144
  Italy 92
  Malaysia 180
  Middle East 119–120
  Myanmar 187
  North Africa 128
  Portugal 85
  Russian 27
  Spain 74

rempah **181**
restaurants
  Balkans 107
  Belgium *49*
  Egypt *119*
  Ethiopa 138
  Japan *208*
  Luxembourg 52
  Spain *74*
retsina 98, 100
rice
  Austria 40
  Azerbaijan 160
  Cambodia 182
  China 167
  Colombia 249
  France *65*
  Greece 102
  India 145–146, 150, 155
  Indonesia 178
  Iran **120**
  Japan 206, *206*
  Jews in Central Asia 157
  Korea 203
  Laos *185*, 185
  Malaysia 181
  Middle East 119
  Myanmar 187
  Netherlands 52
  Philippines 191
  Spain 80
  Thailand 195
  Turkey 113, *115*
  USA 225
  Vietnam 200
rijsttafels 52, **178**
Romania 106–107
Rome 91
rose petals 158
rosemary 67
rum 238
Russian influences 23, 107
Russian Orthodox Church influences 27

S
saffron 67
salads 41, 50, 70, *101*
salmon
  Britain 13
  Canada *230*
  Finland 24
  France *55*
  Ireland 15
  Norway 19
  Russia 28
  Sweden 21
salt 27, 56, 58, 72, 91, *189*
sambuca **92**
samfaina 78
Sami 16, 21, *23*
sandwich 17, 22–23, 237
Santa Marta festival 89
sardines *85*
Sardinia 97
sashimi **207**
satay 178
sauces
  Africa 134, 135, 136, 139
  Chile 247
  China 171, 172
  Germany 45
  India 151
  Laos 184, 186
  Mexico 236
  Spain 77, 81
  Thailand 195
  USA 226–227
sauerkraut 56

sausages
  France 55, 57, 64, 70
  Germany *43*
  Italy 90
  North Africa *129*
  Portugal 85
  Scandinavia 17
  Spain *74*
  Switzerland 46
  Turkey 113
scallops 58
Scottish cuisine 10–15
seafood
  Africa 138, 139
  Australia 212, 215
  Austria 40
  Balkans 105, 107
  Baltic States 32
  Belgium *48*
  Brazil *250*
  Britain 13
  Cambodia 182
  Canada 230
  Caribbean 240
  Chile 247
  Denmark 22
  dried *19*
  Finland 23–24
  France 55, 56–57, 58, 61, *61*, 65
  Georgia 13
  Greece 102
  Iceland 25
  India 145, *146*, 151, 154
  Iraq 124
  Ireland 14
  Italy 87, 89, *89*, 90, 97
  Japan 207, 209, 211
  Jewish 120
  Korea 202
  Laos 184
  Moldova *33*
  Morocco 132
  Myanmar *187*
  New Zealand 217
  Norway 19
  Peru 245
  Portugal *83*, 84
  preserved 135 , 182
  Russia 28
  smoked *13*, 43, *135*
  South Africa 140
  Spain *76*, 76–77, 78–79, 80
  Sweden 21
  Tunisia 133
  USA 221–222, 223, 228, 229
seaweed *178*, 205, 207
Second World War, effect on Britain 12
Sekels 107
Senegal 137
Serbia 107
Shanghai 170–171
Shantung 169–170
sheep *see* lamb
shellfish
  Chile 247
  France 55, 57, 58, 68
  Spain 78–79
  USA 222
  see also specific shellfish
sherry **76**
Shintoism 206
shish kebab 108
Shrove Tuesday pancakes 14
Siam 194–197
Sicily 90, 97
Sikhs 144–145
Slavs 26, 34

Slovenia 109
Smolyans 105
smorgasbord **20**
snacks *32*, **79**, *153*, *176*, 191, 233
snails 78
soda bread 15
sofrito/sofregit 78
Sologne 59–61
Somalia 137
souks **131**
soups
  Algeria 129
  Armenia 160
  Azerbaijan 160
  Balkans 105, 107
  Cambodia 183
  Canada 230
  Central Europe 35
  China 169, 171
  Egypt 123
  France 67, 73
  Germany 45
  Greece 102
  Hungary 37
  India 150
  Iran 122, *124*
  Japan 211
  Mongolia 158
  Morocco 132
  Paraguay 247
  Portugal 83, 84
  Russia 27, 28, 30
  Spain 81
  Thailand 195, 197
  Turkey **111**
  USA 223–225
  Vietnam 199, 200
South Africa 139
Southern Africa 139–140
Southern USA 223–225
soybeans 207
Spanish influences
  Caribbean 240
  Central America/Mexico 232, 234–235
  France 69, 72
  Italy 94
  North Africa 126
  Philippines 191
  South America 241, 244
  Thailand 195
  USA 227
spices *see* herbs and spices
spinach 90
splash-frying 173
spring rolls 190
squid *202*
steaming *175*
stews
  Africa 138
  Balkans 106
  Brazil *241*, 250
  Chile 247
  Hungary **37**
  Iran 122
  Japan *209*
  Laos 185
  North Africa 128
  Philippines 191
  South Africa 139
  South America 245
  Spain 74, 76, 78
  USA 222, 223
  see also sauces
stir-frying 171
stoves *see* ovens
Straits Chinese 193
strawberries *14*, 49, 58

street food/eating
  India *145*
  Indonesia *176*
  Korea *203*
  Malaysia *179*
  Mexico *233*
  Singapore **192**
  South America *247*
  USA **222**
strudels 107
sturgeon 160
Sudan 137
Sufis 110
sugar 10, 56, 82, 131, 238
Sukkot 124
sumac 115
Sumatran influence on Indonesian cuisine 178
sunflower seeds 107
supra 162
Suriname 250
sushi 207, 209
Swabia 42
Sweden 20–21
sweets/sweetmeats
  Armenia 158
  Georgia 163
  Greece 103
  India 147, 153, 155
  Italy 97
  Malaysia 181
  Middle East 124
  Morocco 132
  Thailand 197
  Turkey 111, 113
Szechwan 172

T
tabil 133
tagine 128, 131
taklia 122
tamale 232, 234, *235*, 249
tandoori food 151
tapas **79**, 81
tarragon 59
tarts 42
Tatars 26, 28
tea
  Africa **138**
  Britain 10, **12**
  China **173**
  India 148, 151, *151*
  Iran **122**
  Ireland 15
  Japan *211*, **211**
  Korea *205*
  North Africa **132**
  Turkey **115**
  Vietnam **199**
temple cuisine 204
tempura 207
Teochew 192
tequila *235*
Tet 199
Texas 226–227
Tex-Mex food 226–227
Thanksgiving 226
Thiapusam Malaysia 180
thyme 67
Tibet 157
tiffin 155
tokany **37**
tomatillo 235
tomatoes 86, *87*, 128
Topkapi Palace 110
Toulouse 70
Trentino-Alto Adige 89
trout 40, 49, 77, 158
truffles 62–63, 87, 91

tuna 97
Tunisia 133
Turkish influences 37, 43, 98, 104, 12, 158
Turkmenistan 158
turtle 240
Tuscany 90
Twelfth Night 78

U
Ukraine 30–31
Umbria 91
Uruguay 247–248

V
Valle d'Aosta 89
veal 22, 40
vegetables
  Africa 138
  Austria 41
  Balkans 107
  Belgium 48, 49
  Bulgaria 104
  China 165, 169, 171, 173, *173*
  France 55, 58–59, 65, *66*
  Georgia 162
  Greece 98
  India *154*
  Italy 91
  Japan 211
  Moldova 33
  Spain 76, 77, 79
  Ukraine 31
  see also salad vegetables
  vegetarianism 138, 144, 181, 198
Veneto 89–90
Venezuela 249–250
Venice 89, *89*
Veracruz 236–237
vinegar 61, 170, *190*
vodka **28**, 38

W
waffles 48–49, *53*
walnuts 62, 161
water buffalo 185
wedding meals 182
Welsh cuisine 10–15
West Africa 136–137
wild food *182*, 204
wine
  Armenia 158
  Australia *214*
  Balkans 107
  Chile 247
  France 61, 62, 64, 65, 67, **73**
  Georgia **160**
  Greece 98
  Hungary 38
  Italy 91
  Korea 203
  New Zealand **217**
  South Africa 139
  Spain 77
  USA **228**
wok cooking *168*, *182*, 195
Würste **43**

X
xato salad 78

Y
yak 157
yams 135
yerba mate **247**
yin and yang 165–166
yogurt 100, 111, 146

Yom Kippur 129
Yoruba 137
Yugoslavia 107–108
Yunnan 173

Z
za'atar 122
zakouski **32**
Zen Buddhism, Japan **211**
Zimbabwe 139
Zoroastrianism 144

ACKNOWLEDGMENTS

Martha Rose Shulman would like to thank the following for their assistance:

Anne Trager for help with research
Lauraine Jacobs and **Angela Kirgo** for advice on Australian and New Zealand cuisine
Diane Kochilas for advice on Greek cuisine
Clifford Wright for advice on Middle Eastern cuisine.

Carroll & Brown would also like to thank the following for their assistance in the production of the book:

Editorial Jane Bamforth, Antonia Maxwell, Dawn Titmus
Picture researcher Sandra Schneider
Indexer Michelle Clarke

Photo credits

Introduction
1 Juliet Coombe/La Belle Aurore, 2 Francine Lawrence, 4 (left) Food and Travel Magazine/Mark Luscombe-Whyte, (centre) David Murray, (right) Food and Travel Magazine/Jason Lowe, 5 (left) Juliet Coombe/La Belle Aurore, (centre) Jason Lowe, (right) Jules Selmes, 6 (first, second from top) Jules Selmes, (third from bottom) Robert Francis/Hutchison Library, (bottom) D Traverso/Robert Harding Picture Library, 7 (top) Jules Selmes, (second, third, bottom) Francine Lawrence

Europe
8 (top left) Collections/Roger Scrutin, (centre) James Davis Worldwide, (bottom) Francine Lawrence, 9 Brian and Cherry Alexander, 10 (top) Food and Travel Magazine/Mark Luscombe-Whyte, (bottom) Collections/Roger Scrutin, 11 Food and Travel Magazine/Martin Brigdale, 12 Collections/Michael St Maur Sheil, 13 Collections/Gerry Gavigan, 14 (top) Collections/VI, (bottom) Collections/Fiona Pragoff, 15 Waitrose Food Illustrated/Deidre Rooney 16 (top) Luke White/Axiom, (bottom) Knudsens Fotosenter Oslo, 17 Brian and Cherry Alexander, 18 and 19 Christine Osborne Pictures, 20 Knudsens Fotosenter Oslo, 23 Travel Ink/Andrew Land, 24 Brian and Cherry Alexander, 26 (top) Food and Travel Magazine/Angela Dukes, (bottom) Victoria Ivleva/JVZ Picture Library, 27 John Egan/Hutchison Library, 29 Brian and Cherry Alexander, 30 Robert Francis/Hutchison Library, 31 John Egan/Hutchison Library, 32 and 33 John Massey Stewart, 34 Michael St Maur Sheil/Corbis, 36 Pictures Colour Library, 37 Hungarian National Tourist Office, 38 Jason Lowe, 40 David Noble Photography, 41 Bob Krist/Corbis, 43 Eye Ubiquitous/David Cumming, 44 Pictures Colour Library, 47 (top) Travel Ink/Chris Cole, (bottom) James Davis Worldwide, 48 to 51 Pictures Colour Library, 52 Food and Travel Magazine/Angela Dukes, 53 Dave Bartruff/Corbis, 54 (top) Juliet Coombe/La Belle Aurore, (bottom) Tony Souter/Hutchison Library, 55 Jules Selmes, 56 Sopexa, 57 Jeremy Horner/Hutchison Library, 58 Travel Ink/Dorothy Burrows, 59 Susan Grossman, 60 Travel Ink/Gerry Walden, 61 Cephas/TOP/Pierre Hussenot, 62 BIVB/N Eschman, 63 Sopexa, 64 Jason Lowe, 66 Ann Usborne/

Hutchison Library, 68 Narratives /Fiona Dunlop, 69 Jules Selmes, 70 Francine Lawrence, 71 Juliet Coombe/La Belle Aurore, 72 Jason Lowe, 73 Bureau National Interprofesionnel de l'Armagnac, 74 David Murray, 75 Food and Travel Magazine/Heidi Grassley, 76 Jules Selmes, 77 PW Rippon/Hutchison Library, 78/9 Food and Travel Magazine/Heidi Grassley, 80 Food and Travel Magazine/Angela Dukes, 81 Travel Ink/Andrew Watson, 82 (bottom) Travel Ink/Simon Reddy, 83 Sue Cunningham/SCP, 84 Travel Ink/Jeremy Phillips, 85 Travel Ink/Brenda Kean, 86 (top) Food and Travel Magazine/Jason Lowe, (bottom) Juliet Coombe/La Belle Aurore, 87 Mick Rock/Cephas Picture Library, 88 The Photographers Library, 89 Juliet Coombe/La Belle Aurore, 92/93 Juliet Coombe/La Belle Aurore, 94 Cephas/Top/M Rougemont, 95 Juliet Coombe/La Belle Aurore, 96 David Noble Photography, 98 (top) M Crame/Christine Osborne Pictures, (bottom) Eye Ubiquitous/Bob Gibbons, 99 Francine Lawrence, 100 M Crame/Christine Osborne Pictures, 101 Jenny Acheson/Axiom, 102 Jenny Acheson/Axiom, 103 Narratives/Jan Baldwin, 104 Trip/F Andreescu, 105 Trip/CC, 106 Trip/P Mercea, 108 Melanie Friend/Hutchison Library, 109 Juliet Coombe/La Belle Aurore, 110 Francine Lawrence, 111 Travel Ink/Abbie Enock, 112 Francine Lawrence, 113 Jonathan Blair/Corbis, 114 Ann Jousiffe, 115 Chris Barton/Christine Osborne Pictures, 116 (top left) Sue Cunningham/SCP, (top right) J Worker/Christine Osborne Pictures, (centre) Food and Travel Magazine/Jason Lowe, (bottom) Narratives/Fiona Dunlop, 117 Ann Jousiffe

Africa and The Middle East
118 (top) Christine Osborne Pictures, (bottom) Ann Jousiffe, 119 A and P Jousiffe, 120 Christine Osborne Pictures, 121 C Constable/ Hutchison Library, 122 Christine Osborne Pictures, 123 Food and Travel Magazine/Jason Lowe, 124 Christine Osborne Pictures, 125 Christine Osborne Pictures, 126 (top) Narratives/Fiona Dunlop, (bottom) P Jousiffe, 127 Travel Ink/David Forman, 128 Travel Ink/Simon Reddy, 129 M Crame/Christine Osborne Pictures, 130 J Worker/Christine Osborne Pictures, 131 and 132 Christine Osborne Pictures, 133 Best of Morocco (e-mail: morocco@morocco-travel.com), 134 to 137 Sue Cunningham/SCP, 138 Juliet Coombe/La Belle Aurore, 139 Sue Cunningham/SCP, 140 Duncan Willetts/Camerapix, 141 Eye Ubiquitous/P Maurice

Asia and Australasia
142 (top left) Christine Osborne Pictures, (top right) Juliet Coombe/La Belle Aurore, (centre) Jason Lowe, (bottom) Jon Burbank/Hutchison Library, 143 Christine Osborne Pictures, 144 Jules Selmes, 145 Eye Ubiquitous/David Cumming, 146 Juliet Coombe/La Belle Aurore, 147 Christine Osborne Pictures, 148 Jason Lowe, 149 Jason Lowe, 151 (top) Travel Ink/David Forman, (bottom) C Spout/Christine Osborne Pictures, 152 Eye Ubiquitous/Phil Danbury, 153 Juliet Coombe/La Belle Aurore, 154 Jules Selmes, 155 Christine Osborne Pictures, 156 (top) David Murray, (bottom) Nick Dawson/Christine Osborne Pictures, 157 G Bonati/Christine Osborne Pictures, 158 to 159 Steppes East, 160 Pern/Hutchison

Library, 161 A Grachtcnencov/Hutchison Library, 162 Steppes East, 163 Eye Ubiquitous/David Cumming, 164 (top) Christine Osborne Pictures, (bottom) Wolfgang Kaehler/Corbis, 165 Juliet Coombe/La Belle Aurore, 166 (top) Eye Ubiquitous/Julia Waterlow, (bottom) Christine Osborne Pictures, 167 Eye Ubiquitous/Frank Leather, 168 J Dunn/Christine Osborne Pictures, 169 Food and Travel Magazine/Vanessa Davies, 170 (top) Eye Ubiquitous/Julia Waterlow, (bottom) Robert Francis/Hutchison Library, 172 Julia Waterlow/Eye Ubiquitous , 173 G Bonati/Christine Osborne Pictures, 174 Juliet Coombe/La Belle Aurore, 175 Juliet Coombe/La Belle Aurore, 176 Christine Osborne Pictures, 177 Christine Osborne Pictures, 178 to 180 Jules Selmes, 182 (top) Travel Ink/Charlie Marsden, (bottom) Juliet Coombe/La Belle Aurore, 183 Juliet Coombe/La Belle Aurore, 184 (top) Juliet Coombe/La Belle Aurore, (bottom) Travel Ink/Charlie Marsden, 185 to 189 Juliet Coombe/La Belle Aurore, 190 Christine Osborne Pictures, 191 James Davis Worldwide, 192 (top) Jules Selmes, (bottom) Steve Davey/La Belle Aurore, 193 Travel Ink/Charcrit Boonsom, 194 Food and Travel Magazine/Jason Lowe, 195 (top) Tourist Authority of Thailand, (bottom) Jules Selmes, 196 to 201 Jules Selmes, 202 Andrew Sole/Hutchison Library, 203 Michael Macintyre/Hutchison Library, 204 (top) Michael Macintyre/Hutchison Library, (bottom), Andrew Sole/Hutchison Library, 205 G Fuller/ Hutchison Library, 206 Angeles Marin/Christine Osborne Pictures, 207 Michael Macintyre/Hutchison Library, 208 Christine Coleman/Eye Ubiquitous, 209 Angeles Marin/Christine Osborne Pictures, 210 Frank Leather/Eye Ubiquitous, 211 Jon Burbank/Hutchison Library, 212 to 215 Christine Osborne Pictures, 216 Food and Travel Magazine/Angela Dukes, 217 Jules Selmes

The Americas
218 (top) Jason Lowe, (centre) Laurie Smith, (centre below) Francine Lawrence, (bottom) Jules Selmes, 219 Jules Selmes, 220 (left) D Traverso/Robert Harding Picture Library, 220 (right) Adam Woolfitt/Robert Harding Picture Library, 221 Gail Mooney/Corbis, 222 Nigel Francis/Robert Harding Picture Library, 223 Bob Krist/Corbis, 224 Laurie Smith, 225 Laurie Smith, 226 Robert Francis/Hutchison Library, 227 and 228 Laurie Smith, 229 (top) Laurie Smith, (bottom) Dave G Houser/Corbis, 230 (bottom) Jason Lowe, 231 Photo@ Tim Peters, 232 to 238 Francine Lawrence, 239 Andreas von Einsiedel /Elizabeth Whiting and Associates, 240 Francine Lawrence, 241 (top) Jules Selmes, (bottom) Sue Cunningham/SCP, 242 M Jelliffe/Hutchison Library, 243 and 244 Jules Selmes, 245 Evie Lawrie/Hutchison Library, 246 Jeremy Horner/Hutchison Library, 247 Jules Selmes, 248 and 249 Sue Cunningham/SCP, 250 Jeremy Horner/ Hutchison Library, 251 Travel Ink/Charlie Marsden

Front cover
(top left) Robert Francis/Hutchison Library, (centre) Juliet Coombe/La Belle Aurore, (top right) Laurie Smith, (bottom left) Jules Selmes, (centre) Susan Grossman, (bottom right) Jules Selmes